Electric Circuits

AND MACHINES

SECOND CANADIAN EDITION

Electric

Circuits

AND MACHINES

SECOND CANADIAN EDITION

Eugene C. Lister
Chief Electrical Engineer
(Retired)
Stanley Consultants, Inc.

Michael R. Golding
Chair
Electrical/Electronics Division
Fanshawe College

McGraw-Hill Ryerson Limited
TORONTO NEW YORK AUCKLAND BOGOTÁ CARACAS
LISBON LONDON MADRID MEXICO MILAN NEW DELHI
SAN JUAN SINGAPORE SYDNEY TOKYO

Electric Circuits and Machines

Second Canadian Edition

CAN©OPY

ISBN: 0-07-552603-4

1 2 3 4 5 6 7 8 9 10   BBM   5 4 3 2 1 0 9 8 7 6

Printed and bound in Canada

Care has been taken to trace ownership of copyright material contained in this text. The publisher will gladly take any information that will enable them to rectify any reference or credit in subsequent editions.

Editor-in-Chief:	Dave Ward
Developmental Editor:	Laurie Graham
Production Editor:	Edie Franks
Production Co-ordinator:	Nicla Dattolico
Interior and Cover Design:	Jack Steiner Graphic Design
Cover Photo:	Jeff Corwin/Tony Stone Images
Typesetter:	Computer Composition of Canada
Printer:	Best Book Manufacturers

Canadian Cataloguing in Publication Data

Lister, Eugene C.
   Electric circuits and machines

2nd Canadian ed.
Includes bibliographical references and index.
ISBN 0-07-552603-4

1. Electric circuits.   2. Electric machinery.
I. Golding, Michael R., 1941-   .   II. Title.

TK146.L57 1996   621.3   C95-933280-4

Contents

6 Magnetism   93

6-1 Magnets and Magnetic Materials 6-2 Magnetic Fields and Lines of Force
6-3 Magnetic Attraction and Repulsion 6-4 Nature of Magnetism 6-5 Field
Around a Current-Carrying Conductor 6-6 Field Around a Coil
6-7 Magnetomotive Force or F_m 6-8 Ohm's Law for Magnetic Circuits
6-9 Electromagnets 6-10 Saturation

7 Electromagnetic Induction   107

7-1 Induced EMF 7-2 Factors Affecting the Amount of Induced EMF
7-3 Faraday's Law of Induction 7-4 Numerical Value of Induced EMF
7-5 Direction of Induced EMF 7-6 Lenz's Law of Induction 7-7 Self-Induced
EMF: Inductance 7-8 Self-Induction in a Coil 7-9 Mutual Induction
7-10 Ignition Systems

8 Direct-Current Generators   119

8-1 Generator Construction 8-2 The Single-Coil Generator 8-3 The Simple
DC Generator 8-4 Multicoil Armatures 8-5 Methods of Field Excitation
8-6 Generator Voltage Equations 8-7 The Magnetization Curve
8-8 Commutation 8-9 Voltage Regulation 8-10 The Separately Excited
Generator 8-11 The Self-Excited Shunt Generator 8-12 The Series Generator
8-13 The Compound Generator 8-14 Efficiency 8-15 Losses and Efficiency of
a DC Machine

9 Direct-Current Motors and Controls   149

9-1 Motor Principle 9-2 Torque Development in a Motor 9-3 Measurement of
Torque 9-4 Generator Action of a Motor 9-5 Equivalent Circuit of a Motor
9-6 Power Relationships in a Motor 9-7 Interpoles 9-8 Motor Speed Control
9-9 Motor Speed Regulation 9-10 The Shunt Motor 9-11 The Series Motor
9-12 The Compound Motor 9-13 Permanent-Magnet Motors 9-14 Motor-
Starting Requirements 9-15 Controllers and Starters 9-16 Drum Controllers
9-17 Magnetic Contactors 9-18 Control of Magnetic Contactors: Motor
Protection 9-19 Magnetic Controllers for Starting DC Motors 9-20 Dynamic
Braking 9-21 Ward-Leonard System of Speed Control 9-22 Static Conversion
and Control Equipment

10 Alternating Current   185

10-1 Generation of an Alternating EMF 10-2 Alternating Current 10-3 Cycle;
Frequency 10-4 Electrical Degrees: A Measure of Time 10-5 Effective Values
of Alternating Current and EMF 10-6 Phase Relations 10-7 Phasor (Vector)
Diagrams 10-8 Addition of Phasors 10-9 Subtraction of Phasors
10-10 Properties of an Electric Circuit 10-11 Resistance in an AC Circuit
10-12 Inductance 10-13 Inductive Reactance 10-14 Capacitors
10-15 Capacitors in Series 10-16 Capacitors in Parallel 10-17 Action of a
Capacitor in an AC Circuit 10-18 Capacitive Reactance 10-19 Reactance
10-20 Impedance 10-21 Graphical Representation of Resistance, Reactance, and
Impedance in a Series Circuit

Preface

The Second Canadian Edition of *Electric Circuits and Machines* maintains the same style and readability as the First Edition. Additional, updated illustrations and photographs are used where appropriate. A greater emphasis on usage of standardized terminology and symbols is incorporated in this edition. Additional worked-out examples are provided in many chapters.

Coincident with the enhancement of various chapters throughout, new information topics are included. They are: *Thyristor Control* and *Application* related to dc and ac motors; *available short-circuit currents* and protection from the resulting *let through energy*; the principle of operation and application of *GFCIs* (ground fault circuit interrupters); principle and application of *varistors*; and *harmonics* resulting from solid-state motor control devices.

Chapter 21 has been modified to reflect current changes in some electromechanical control devices and standards relating to industry application.

Chapter 22 has undergone a major revision to address the changes in *programmable controller* technology. In the First Edition, this chapter concentrated on a specific product. The revised chapter provides the reader an overview of some of the capabilities of the programmable controller. It will then be the choice of the reader to further their knowledge in this area by either taking one of the many courses provided by the various product manufacturers, or choosing to read current literature produced for this specialized area.

In keeping with the content survey nature of this text the reader, upon completion, will receive a foundation for further education in more topic specific areas. This new edition should be well-suited to meet the needs of electrical apprentice programs, electrical courses to non-electrical technology students, survey courses in electricity taught in a *"distance learning"* mode and various introductory courses through college and secondary school continuing education centres.

The mathematics used to describe electrical theories relies on basic algebra and trigonometry. Some example problems in ac circuit analysis have also been solved using *complex quantity notation*. This additional problem-solving tool provides the instructor and student with an alternative and powerful problem-solving technique. *Appendix H* includes a brief discussion on this type of notation.

I wish to express my gratitude to Hans Duever, Rob Darling, and the electrical apprenticeship department of Fanshawe College for their cooperation and contribution to this edition. Thanks also go to John Blake of Humber College, Bob Drabiuk of N.A.I.T., Steve Finnagan of Algonquin College, and Paul Kendrick of Niagara College for reviewing this edition and making many useful comments on the manuscript's style and content. Special thanks also go to Rob Harris of Omron Canada Inc., Tim Monteith of Reliance Electric Ltd., and John Grolleman of Cooper-Bussmann for their cooperation and contribution to this edition.

I am indebted to the many readers of the First Edition who took the time to write and make comments that contributed to some of the changes made in the Second Edition. I encourage and welcome any comments, suggestions, and criticisms regarding this edition.

Michael R. Golding

Fundamental Units

While the exact nature of electricity is unknown, a great deal is known about what it can do. By the mere closing of a switch, buildings are lighted, wheels are turned, ice is made, food is cooked, distant voices are heard, and countless other tasks — ordinary and extraordinary — are performed. Although a great number of uses for electricity have been discovered and applied, the field is by no means exhausted. Electric machines and devices that have been in use for many years are being improved and are now finding wider fields of application. Extensive research is constantly bringing forth and developing new devices. Much is still to be learned about electricity.

Electricity is a convenient form of energy. It is well known that when fuels such as coal, oil, and gas are burned, energy is released. A waterfall, whether it is constructed or natural, also possesses energy. Yet, to be of value, this energy must be made available at points where it can be used conveniently. Electricity furnishes the most practicable and convenient means yet devised for doing this. The energy of burning fuel or of falling water is changed to a more convenient form — electricity — by *electric machines*. It is transmitted to distant points over *electric circuits*. It is controlled by other electric machines. At points where it is to be used, it is converted into useful work by still other electric machines and devices.

Since electricity is a form of energy, the study of electricity is the study of energy, its conversions from one form to another, and its transmission from one point to another. Electric machines are energy-conversion devices, and electric circuits are energy-transmission devices.

Although no one knows precisely what electricity is, it has been possible to develop theories about electricity through experiment and by observation of its behaviour. As a result, it is now believed that all matter is essentially electrical in nature.

In this introductory chapter, important ideas concerning electricity are presented together with a discussion of the basic units of measurement used in the study of electric circuits and machines.

1-1

The Structure of Matter

Matter has been defined as anything that occupies space and has mass. Familiar examples of matter are water, air, copper, tin, smoke, iron, and salt. Matter is made up of extremely small particles called **molecules**. A molecule is the smallest particle into which a given substance may be divided without changing its identity. For instance, water is composed of two parts hydrogen and one part oxygen. If a drop of water were divided and subdivided into smaller and smaller particles, the smallest particle into which it could be divided and still contain two parts hydrogen and one part oxygen would be called a molecule of water. If this particle were subdivided further, the resulting parts would be hydrogen and oxygen, both of which are gases and obviously do not have the physical properties of water.

Small as they are, molecules may be divided by chemical means into **atoms**. There are as many kinds of molecules as there are kinds of matter, but there are only 103 different kinds of atoms corresponding to the number of known chemical elements. As a result of the work of such Nobel prize-winning scientists as Niels Bohr and Wolfgang Pauli, much is known about the structure of the atom.

The makeup of an atom may be described in a simplified way by likening it to a miniature solar system. The core of the atom, corresponding to the sun in the solar system, is called the **nucleus**. The nucleus is formed of subatomic particles called **protons** and **neutrons**. Surrounding the nucleus and in a state of continual motion similar to the orbiting of the planets about the sun are other subatomic particles called **electrons**. Atoms of different elements contain different numbers of electrons. However, the electrons of all atoms are identical. Fig. 1-1 illustrates the Bohr model of a copper atom. Since copper is presently the most popular material used in electrical circuits, it is appropriate for this discussion. The atomic number of copper is 29 and, therefore, its atom contains 29 electrons (e). These electrons are grouped in shells and arranged

FIGURE **1-1**
Bohr model of a copper atom.

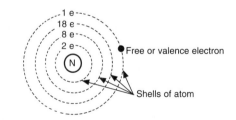

in the predictable order shown in Fig. 1-1. The remaining electron in the atom's fourth shell is called the **valence** or **free electron**. (Later we will learn the significance of this *free electron* when discussing current flow.)

It has been found that protons and electrons exert forces on one another over and above the forces of gravitational attraction between them. This force is attributed to a property of the protons and electrons known as **electric charge**. Protons exert forces of repulsion on other protons; likewise, electrons exert forces of repulsion on other electrons. However, protons and electrons attract one another. There are, therefore, two kinds of electric charge arbitrarily designated as *positive* and *negative*. The force of attraction or repulsion between two bodies (**Coulomb's Law**) can be expressed by the following equation:

$$F = \frac{kQ_1 Q_2}{r^2} \quad \text{(Newtons)} \qquad \text{[1-1]}$$

where
F = force in Newtons
k = constant of 9.0 x 10^9
Q_1 and Q_2 = the charges in coulombs on two adjacent bodies
r = distance in metres between the two charges

FIGURE **1-2**

Two negatively charged bodies located at distance r from each other will provide a force of repulsion. The quantity of this repulsive force is determined by the expression shown in Eq. (1-1).

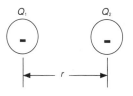

It has been found that all electrons have precisely the same negative charge and that all protons have precisely the same positive charge. Neutrons have no charge, or are electrically neutral. In the normal atom there are equal numbers of electrons and protons and, therefore, the atom is uncharged since the positive charges just balance the negative charges. Furthermore, a particular body made up of uncharged or neutral atoms is uncharged or neutral. However, nearly all atoms have some electrons which are loosely bound to their nuclei. These electrons, as we mentioned earlier, are called **free electrons** and may be dislodged by one means or another and transferred from one atom to another.

If a body is caused to lose some of its electrons or negative charges, the body is said to be positively charged (*positive ion*). Similarly, if a body is caused to gain electrons, it is said to be negatively charged (*negative ion*). For example, a dry glass rod may be charged positively if it is rubbed vigorously with a silk cloth. Some of the electrons on the glass rod are transferred to the silk cloth, leaving the rod positively charged and causing the cloth to assume a negative charge.

The forces of attraction and repulsion of electrically charged bodies form the basis for a fundamental rule of electricity; that is, *similarly charged bodies repel one another and oppositely charged bodies attract one another*. The force of attraction or repulsion depends upon the distance between the charged bodies: the greater the separation, the weaker the force. If the distance between two charged bodies is doubled, the force is decreased to one-fourth as much. Stated in mathematical terms, the force is inversely proportional to the square of the distance between the charged bodies. Refer back to Coulomb's Law [1-1].

The atoms of some materials such as copper, zinc, silver, and aluminum have many free electrons. Such materials are called **conductors**. The atoms of nonmetallic materials such as glass, slate, mica, and porcelain have electrons that are held rigidly to their nuclei; that is, they have few free electrons. These materials are called nonconductors or **insulators**. Other materials such as germanium and silicon are neither good insulators nor good conductors. These materials are called **semiconductors**. As a general rule, these three categories can be explained in the following way; a material whose atom contains:

i)   1 to 3 free electrons can be considered a conductor
ii) 4 free electrons, a semiconductor
iii) 5 to 7 free electrons, an insulator.

|1-2
Electric Current

In a conductor material, some of the free electrons are moving at random, or "migrating" from atom to atom (commonly referred to as random drift). When, in addition to this random motion, there is a drift or general movement of electrons in a *unified* direction along the conductor, this is called an **electric current**.

When a strip of zinc and a strip of copper are immersed in a solution of sulfuric acid to form a simple *electric cell*, the resulting chemical action causes the zinc strip to gain electrons from the solution, thereby causing it to become negatively charged. At the same time the copper strip has a tendency to lose some of its electrons, causing it to become positively charged. When the two plates are connected by a copper wire, which is a good conductor, the electrons on the zinc strip flow through the wire to the copper strip. This movement of the electrons from the zinc strip through the copper wire to the copper strip and back through the solution constitutes an electric current, and the entire path through which it flows is called a **circuit**. Thus, *an electric current is merely the movement of electrons or negative charges through a conductor.*

Early experimenters recognized the fact that an electric current was a movement of charges along a conductor. Since the direction of the flow of current was not known, unfortunately, it was arbitrarily chosen to be from a positively charged body to a negatively charged body (positive to negative), and this convention has been so firmly established that it is still widely in use. Thus, the conventional direction or positive direction of current flow is taken to be from positive to negative even though it is now known that the direction of electron flow, which actually constitutes an electric current, is from negative to positive. The student of electricity should be ready to learn and accept either convention, as many books and articles use both concepts.

1-3
Unit of Current: The Ampere

The smallest quantity of electricity is the electron. This particle of electricity is so small that the flow of one electron could not be detected by even the most sensitive current-detecting instrument. A **coulomb** is a much larger unit of electric charge and is used for practical measurements. One *coulomb* (C) is equal to approximately 6.24×10^{18} electrons. Since a coulomb is a quantity of electricity, then a *rate of flow* of electricity may be specified in *coulombs per second* (C/s). In practice, the term coulomb per second is seldom used; a shorter term, **ampere** (symbol A), is used instead. One ampere is equal to the movement of one coulomb of electric charge past a given point in one second.

Therefore,
$$I = \frac{Q}{t} \quad \text{(Amperes)} \qquad [1\text{-}2]$$

where I = current in amperes
Q = charge in coulombs
t = time in seconds

For example, an ordinary 100 watt (W) lamp used on a house-lighting circuit takes a current of about 0.83 A. This means that electricity is passing through the lamp at the rate of 0.83 C every second.

The flow of an electric current through a conductor is sometimes compared with the flow of water through a pipe. The quantity of electricity, measured in coulombs, is compared with the quantity of water, measured in gallons or cubic metres. The rate of flow of electricity measured in amperes is compared with the rate of flow of water measured in gallons per minute or cubic metres per second. This comparison is often helpful in learning the units of measurement of electricity.

1-4

Resistance: The Ohm

It was pointed out in Sec. 1-1 that materials which have many free electrons are called conductors, while materials having few free electrons are called insulators. Conductors are said to offer a low *resistance* or opposition to the flow of an electric current and insulators offer a high resistance to current flow. Electrical resistance, then, is defined as the opposition offered by a material to the flow of an electric current.

The practical unit of measurement of resistance is the **ohm**, which is represented by the symbol Ω (capital omega). As practical examples of resistance, an ordinary 100 W electric lamp used on a 120 V circuit has a resistance of about 144 Ω when hot. A 1000-ft. length of No. 10 American Wire Gauge (AWG) copper wire (0.1 in. in diameter) has a resistance of about 1 Ω. A round copper wire with a cross-sectional area of two square millimetres (2 mm^2) and a length of one kilometre (1 km) has a resistance of about 6.8 Ω. A 240 V, 2500 W electric heater has a resistance of about 23 Ω. Therefore, the higher the value of resistance the electric circuit offers, the smaller the amount of current that can flow per unit of electrical force.

1-5

Potential Difference and Electromotive Force: The Volt

Just as there must be a difference in water pressure to cause water to flow between two points, so must there be a difference in electric pressure to cause an electric current to flow between two points in an electric circuit. This difference in electric pressure is called **potential difference**, and it is measured in **volts**. The volt (symbol V or E) is the amount of potential difference that will cause one ampere to flow through a resistance of one ohm.

Potential differences vary from a few millionths of a volt to several million volts. The potential difference between the terminals of a common dry cell is about 1.5 V; between terminals of an automobile storage battery, about 12 V. Common potential differences applied to the terminals of electric motors are 115, 200, 230, 460, 575, and 2300 V. Potential differences between conductors on long power-transmission lines are as high as 1 000 000 V.

If two bodies have different amounts of charge, a potential difference exists between the two bodies. Potential difference is then merely a difference in electric charge. When two points having a potential difference between them are joined by a conductor, a current flows along the conductor attempting to equalize the difference in charge on the two points. When the two charges are equalized, the flow of current stops. Therefore, if a current is to be maintained between two points, the potential difference between the points must be maintained.

A device that has the ability to maintain a potential difference or a difference in charge between two points, even though a current is flowing between those points, is said to develop an **electromotive force (emf)**.

There are several ways in which an emf may be developed. The simple electric cell described in Sec. 1-2 develops an emf by *chemical* means. The electric generator in which conductors are moved through magnetic fields develops an emf by *mechanical* means. When a junction of two dissimilar metals is heated, a small emf is developed. This is the principle of the **thermocouple**. When certain substances are placed in contact with metals and the junction is illuminated, a small emf is developed. The **photoelectric cell** operates on this principle. If, when any of the above-mentioned devices is in operation, the terminals of the device are connected by a conductor, a continuous current flows through the completed circuit because the potential difference at the terminals is maintained.

Since the result of the action of an emf in a circuit is a potential difference measured in volts, emf is also expressed in volts.

Thus, a potential difference causes current to flow, and an emf maintains the potential difference. Since both are measured in volts, a common term, **voltage**, is used to indicate a measure of either. Although the terms potential difference, emf, and voltage do not mean exactly the same thing, they are often used interchangeably.

When observing a circuit, it is a common practice to show the energy source as a voltage rise to the circuit and is often labelled with the upper case letter "E", whereas the decrease in potential in an electric circuit as a result of a current flowing through a resistance is labelled "V". Remember: voltage source or rise, E; voltage drop, V.

A simple electric circuit consisting of an energy source supplying a lamp is represented in Fig. 1-3. (For a table of symbols used in circuit diagrams refer to Appendix A.) The assumed or conventional direction of current flow is out of the positive terminal of the energy source, through the lamp, and back to the negative terminal of the energy source as shown by the arrows. This convention will be used throughout.

Electric current is measured by an **ammeter**. An ammeter measures the number of coulombs per second or amperes flowing in a circuit. To measure the current flowing through the lamp of

1-6

Measurement of Current, Voltage, and Resistance

FIGURE **1-3**

A simple electric circuit consisting of an energy source, a lamp, and the connecting conductors.

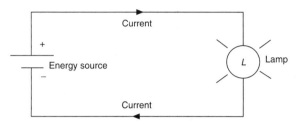

Fig. 1-3, an ammeter is connected into the circuit as shown in Fig. 1-4. Note that the ammeter is *inserted into* or made a part of the circuit.

For the purpose at hand, electricity may be considered as a fluid that cannot be compressed. If electricity is thought of in this way, it should be easy to see that in the circuit of Fig. 1-4 the same current must flow through both the ammeter and the lamp. Because an ammeter is always connected directly into the circuit, it must have a very low resistance so as not to hinder the flow of current. The ammeter is connected so that the current enters it through the positive (+) terminal and leaves it through the negative (-) terminal.

Potential difference or voltage is measured with a **voltmeter**. A voltmeter must be connected *between* or *across* the two points whose difference in potential is to be measured.

Fig. 1-5 shows the method of connecting a voltmeter to measure the voltage across the lamp. Note that the current flowing through the lamp *does not* flow through the voltmeter; the voltmeter is merely *tapped* on the circuit.

Compare the methods of connecting ammeters and voltmeters in Figs. 1-4 and 1-5. The **ammeter** is inserted *into* the circuit,

FIGURE **1-4**

The ammeter is inserted into the circuit of Fig. 1-3 to measure the electric current.

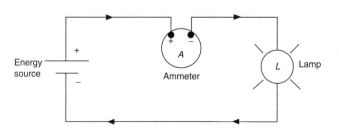

FIGURE **1-5**
The voltmeter is connected to measure the voltage applied to the lamp.

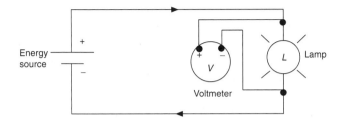

while the **voltmeter** is connected *across* the circuit. An ammeter should never be connected across a circuit, since it has such a low internal resistance that it would be ruined by the large rush of current through it. A voltmeter is not damaged by its connection across the circuit because it has a very high internal resistance.

Resistance may be measured by means of a Wheatstone bridge, an ohmmeter, or by the voltmeter-ammeter method, all of which are discussed in Chap. 19.

Most of the major countries of the world have either adopted or officially decided to use a modernized metric system of units called the International System of Units, officially abbreviated SI in all languages. In this system, all units used in the various technologies are derived from seven basic and arbitrarily defined units. These units and their symbols, which have been standardized by the General Conference on Weights and Measures (abbreviated CGPM from the official French name), are listed in Table 1-1. The units mole and candela are included in Table 1-1 for the sake of completeness and are not referred to further in this text.

In addition to the seven basic units, the CGPM has standardized many derived SI units, that is, units that have been derived from the basic units. All such units may be expressed algebraically

1-7

The International System of Units (SI)

TABLE **1-1**		Basic SI Units
Quantity	**Name**	**Symbol**
Length	metre	m
Mass	kilogram	kg
Time	second	s
Electric current	ampere	A
Temperature	kelvin	K
Luminous intensity	candela	cd
Amount of substance	mole	mol

in terms of the base SI units. As examples, the SI unit for area is the square metre (symbol m^2); the unit for volume is the cubic metre (symbol m^3); and the unit for velocity is the metre per second (symbol m/s).

The members of one group of derived SI units have been given special names. The volt and ohm are examples of such units. Other derived units with special names that will be defined and used later in this text are the Newton, watt, and joule, which are the units of force, power, and energy, respectively. Likewise, the unit of capacitance is called the farad; the unit of inductance, the henry; and the unit of frequency, the hertz.

1-8
SI Units

The following is a brief description based on the official definitions of the five basic SI units that will be referred to in this text. It will be found that in electrical technology, SI or metric units rather than Imperial units predominate and little conversion from one system to the other is required. However, important conversion factors for some of the basic units are included in the following.

The SI unit of length is the metre. One metre (m) is equal to 100 cm (centimetres), 1000 mm (millimetres), and about 39.37 inches (in.). One inch is approximately equal to 25.4 mm.

The unit of mass, the kilogram, is defined as the mass of a prototype platinum-iridium cylinder which is kept in France. One kilogram (kg) is equal to 2.205 pounds mass, or one pound mass is equal to 0.4536 kg (kilogram). Likewise, one ounce is equal to 0.02835 kg or 28.35 g (grams). (These conversions are, of course, approximations.)

The unit of time, the second, is the same in SI as in Imperial units and is approximately 1/86 400 of the mean solar day. The minute and the hour are not decimal multiples of the second and are, therefore, non-SI units, but they are so firmly established that their use is likely to continue indefinitely.

The SI temperature scale is the International Thermodynamic Temperature Scale and the SI unit is the Kelvin. On this scale, the temperature of the freezing point of water is 273.15 K and the Kelvin is defined as the fraction 1/273.15 of this temperature. A temperature change of one Kelvin is the same as a temperature change of one degree Celsius (symbol °C) which is the unit of the Celsius scale (formerly called the Centigrade scale). Wide use is made, particularly in engineering areas, of the Celsius scale because of the equality of the Kelvin and the degree Celsius. The relationship of the Kelvin, the degree Celsius, and the degree Fahrenheit is shown in Table 1-2.

The ampere is defined as that constant current which, if maintained in two parallel conductors spaced one metre apart, produces

TABLE 1-2		Comparison of Temperature Scales	
	Kelvins	Degrees Celsius	Degrees Fahrenheit
Water boils	373.15	100	212
Water freezes	273.15	0	32
Absolute zero	0	−273.15	−459.57

a specified force between the two conductors (due to their magnetic fields). The unit of current is the same in SI and Imperial units.

Two derived electrical SI units, the ohm and the volt, are so fundamental to electrical technology that their definitions are included here also with the basic SI units. The volt is defined as the difference of electric potential between two points of a conductor carrying a constant current of one ampere when the power dissipated between these points is equal to one watt. The ohm is defined as the electric resistance between two points of a conductor when a constant difference of potential of one volt, applied between these two points, produces in this conductor a current of one ampere.

So that very large or very small numbers of SI units may be avoided, decimal multiples and submultiples of the basic units are formed by the use of standard prefixes. The standard prefixes used with SI units and the symbols used to represent them are given in Table 1-3. As an example of the use of these prefixes and symbols,

1-9

Multiples and Submultiples of SI Units

TABLE 1-3	Prefixes Used With Electrical Units	
Prefix	Factor by Which the Unit is Multiplied	Symbol
tera	$1\ 000\ 000\ 000\ 000 = 10^{12}$	T
giga	$1\ 000\ 000\ 000 = 10^{9}$	G
mega	$1\ 000\ 000 = 10^{6}$	M
kilo	$1\ 000 = 10^{3}$	k
hecto	$100 = 10^{2}$	h
deka	$10 = 10^{1}$	da
deci	$0.1 = 10^{-1}$	d
centi	$0.01 = 10^{-2}$	c
milli	$0.001 = 10^{-3}$	m
micro	$0.000\ 001 = 10^{-6}$	μ
nano	$0.000\ 000\ 001 = 10^{-9}$	n
pico	$0.000\ 000\ 000\ 001 = 10^{-12}$	p
femto	$0.000\ 000\ 000\ 000\ 001 = 10^{-15}$	f
atto	$0.000\ 000\ 000\ 000\ 000\ 001 = 10^{-18}$	a

one thousand volts (1000 V) is called one kilovolt (1 kV). Likewise, one million ohms (1 000 000 Ω) is called one megaohm (MΩ) and one one-thousandth of one ampere (0.001 A) is called one milliampere (1 mA). The prefixes listed in Table 1-3 may be used with other electrical units as well as with the three basic units.

1-10
Summary of Important Ideas Concerning Electricity

Electric current is the movement of **electric charges** along a conductor.

An **electric circuit** is a path over which an **electric current** may flow.

The **ampere** is the unit of measurement of **current** and is a **rate of flow** of **one coulomb** of electricity **per second**.

Resistance is the **opposition** to the flow of an electric current.

The **ohm** is the unit of measurement of **resistance**.

Potential difference is an electrical force that causes current to flow; its unit of measurement is the **volt**.

Electromotive force, or **emf**, is required to maintain a potential difference between two points when a current flows between the two points.

An **emf** may be produced *chemically*, *mechanically*, or by means of *light* or *heat*.

Voltage is a common term used to indicate a measure of either **potential difference** or **emf**.

Current may be measured by means of a low-resistance **ammeter** that is *inserted into* the circuit.

Voltage may be measured by means of a high-resistance **voltmeter** that is tapped *across* the circuit.

Resistance may be measured by means of a **Wheatstone bridge**, an **ohmmeter**, or by the **voltmeter-ammeter method**.

The International System of Units (SI) is based on seven base units: the **metre**, the **kilogram**, the **second**, the **ampere**, the **Kelvin**, the **mole**, and the **candela**.

The **ampere** is a base SI unit, whereas the **volt** and the **ohm** are both *derived* SI units.

The basic electrical units are listed in tabular form in Table 1-4.

TABLE 1-4				Electrical Units
Quantity and Symbol		**Unit and Symbol**		**Measuring Device**
Current	*I*	ampere	A	Ammeter
Electromotive force	*E*	volt	V	Voltmeter
Potential difference	*V*	volt	V	Voltmeter
Resistance	*R*	ohm	Ω	Wheatstone bridge Ohmmeter Voltmeter-ammeter

REVIEW QUESTIONS

1 Why is electricity a convenient form of energy?
2 What is matter? Give examples.
3 What is a molecule? What is an atom?
4 The nucleus of an atom is associated with what kind of charge?
5 What are the negative charges in an atom called?
6 What is the relation between the positive and negative charges in an uncharged or neutral atom?
7 Give the rules for attraction and repulsion of electric charges.
8 What is a conductor? Give examples.
9 What is an insulator? Give examples.
10 Describe the nature of an electric current.
11 What is an electric circuit?
12 Is the assumed or conventional flow of current in the same direction as the electron flow in a circuit?
13 What is the unit of electric charge used in practical measurements? How is this unit related to the ampere?
14 What is electrical resistance? What is its unit of measurement?
15 What is potential difference? What is its unit of measurement?
16 How is a potential difference maintained between two points, even though a current is flowing between the points?
17 What is the common term used to indicate a measure of either potential difference or emf?
18 How are ammeters and voltmeters connected in an electric circuit?
19 What precaution is necessary in connecting voltmeters and ammeters?

20 As a summary, write the units of measurement of electric charge, current, voltage, and resistance.

21 What is a simpler way of expressing the term 0.000 001 A?

22 Name the seven basic SI units.

23 How many millivolts are there in 1 V?

24 How does a derived SI unit differ from a base unit?

2 Direct-Current Circuits

The basic rules governing direct-current circuits and the interrelationship of voltage, current, and resistance in those circuits are discussed in this chapter.

There are two basic ways of connecting two or more pieces of electric apparatus: they may be connected in *series* or in *parallel*.

When electric devices are connected end to end or in tandem to form a single continuous circuit, they are said to be connected in **series**. The three resistances R_1, R_2, and R_3 in Fig. 2-1 are connected in series. Note that in Fig. 2-1 there is only one path over which current may flow.

When the apparatus is connected so that there is a divided path over which current may flow — two or more alternative routes between two points in a circuit — the arrangement is called a **parallel circuit**. This combination, shown in Fig. 2-2, is also known as the multiple or shunt connection.

Other connections are combinations or variations of the two basic circuits. For example, in Fig. 2-10, the parallel combination of R_1 and R_2 is in series with R_3. In Fig. 2-11, the series combination of R_1 and R_2 is in parallel with R_3. As still more apparatus is connected into a circuit, the combinations become more complex.

2-1
Ohm's Law

Ohm's law states that the amount of steady current flowing in a circuit is directly proportional to the applied voltage and inversely proportional to the circuit's resistance. This law, experimentally determined by Georg Simon Ohm in 1826, is of the utmost importance as it forms the basis for nearly all dc circuit calculations. The law may be written briefly as

$$\text{Current} = \frac{\text{voltage}}{\text{resistance}}$$

or

$$\text{Amperes} = \frac{\text{volts}}{\text{ohms}}$$

Written mathematically, it is

$$I = \frac{V}{R} \quad \text{(Amperes)} \qquad \textbf{[2-1]}$$

where I = current, amperes
        V = voltage, volts
        R = resistance, ohms

EXAMPLE 2-1

How much current will flow through a 12-Ω electric heater when a voltage of 120 V is applied?

$$I = \frac{V}{R}$$

$$I = \frac{120}{12}$$

$$I = 10 \text{ A}$$

Eq. (2-1) may be transposed and written

$$V = IR \quad \text{(Volts)} \qquad \textbf{[2-2]}$$

That is, the voltage across a circuit is equal to the product of the current in amperes and the resistance in ohms.

EXAMPLE 2-2

What voltage is required to cause a current of 2 A to flow through a resistance of 55 Ω?

$$V = IR$$

$$V = 2 \times 55$$

$$V = 110 \text{ V}$$

Since $V = IR$, the difference in voltage between two points is often referred to as the "**IR drop**" between the two points.

The third form of Ohm's law, by again transposing Eq. (2-1), is

$$R = \frac{V}{I} \quad \text{(Ohms)} \qquad \textbf{[2-3]}$$

That is, the resistance of the circuit is equal to the voltage across the circuit divided by the current though the circuit.

EXAMPLE 2-3

What is the resistance of a lamp that draws 1.5 A from a 120-V line?

$$R = \frac{V}{I}$$

$$R = \frac{120}{1.5}$$

$$R = 80 \ \Omega$$

The three forms of Ohm's law are summarized in Table 2-1. It is important that you become familiar with all three forms of Ohm's law, since you will be using them as long as you work with electricity.

TABLE 2-1		Ohm's Law
$I = \dfrac{V}{R}$	Current $= \dfrac{\text{voltage}}{\text{resistance}}$	Amperes $= \dfrac{\text{volts}}{\text{ohms}}$
$V = IR$	Voltage $=$ current $\times$ resistance	Volts $=$ amperes $\times$ ohms
$R = \dfrac{V}{I}$	Resistance $= \dfrac{\text{voltage}}{\text{current}}$	Ohms $= \dfrac{\text{volts}}{\text{amperes}}$

2-2
Series Circuits: Current Relations

The same amount of current must flow in every part of a series circuit. This should be evident from a diagram of a series circuit. For example, in Fig. 2-1 the current that flows out of the positive terminal of the energy source must flow successively through resistances R_1, R_2, and R_3 before returning to the negative terminal of the energy source since there is only one path over which the current may flow. This is true regardless of the values of the several resistances in series. This may be easily verified experimentally by

FIGURE 2-1
The resistances R_1, R_2, and R_3 are connected in series.

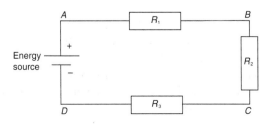

inserting an ammeter at several different points in a series circuit, such as at the points A, B, C, or D in Fig. 2-1. It will be found that the amount of current flowing at any of these points is the same.

The current is the same in all parts of a series circuit.

This rule may be stated mathematically by the expression

$$I_t = I_1 = I_2 = I_3 = \ldots \qquad \text{(Amperes)} \qquad \text{[2-4]}$$

where I_t is the total current supplied by the energy source and I_1, I_2, and I_3 are the currents in the several parts of the circuit.

This does not imply that the current of a series circuit cannot be changed by altering the circuit. A change in either the applied voltage or the resistance of the circuit will change the value of the current flowing. However, for any given value of circuit resistance and applied voltage, the same current must flow in every part of the circuit.

2-**3**
Resistance of a Series Circuit

It was shown in Sec. 2-2 that the same current flows through every part of a series circuit. Resistance is the opposition offered by a circuit to the flow of current. All parts of a series circuit have resistance, and each part of the circuit offers a part of the total resistance to the flow of current. Thus, the following rule may be stated for combining resistances in series:

The total or combined resistance of a series circuit is the sum of the resistances of the several parts.

Stated mathematically,

$$R_t = R_1 + R_2 + R_3 + \ldots \qquad \text{(Ohms)} \qquad \text{[2-5]}$$

where R_t is the total resistance and R_1, R_2, and R_3 are the resistances of the several parts of a series circuit. This is shown in Fig. 2-2.

F I G U R E **2-2**
The resistances R_1, R_2, and R_3 are connected in parallel.

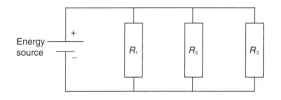

2-**4**
Series Circuits: Voltage Relations

Water pressure is required to cause water to flow through a pipe. More pressure is required to force water to flow at a given rate through a small pipe than through a large pipe since more resistance is offered to the flow in the small pipe.

Likewise, in an electric circuit an electric pressure or voltage is necessary to cause a current to flow. The greater the resistance of a circuit, the greater the voltage must be to cause a given current to flow through that circuit.

In the circuit shown in Fig. 2-3, three resistors R_1, R_2, and R_3 with resistances of 6, 18, and 12 Ω, respectively, are connected in series to a generator. Voltmeter V is connected to indicate the voltage or potential difference of 72 V maintained at the energy source terminals and applied to the entire circuit. Voltmeters V_1, V_2, and V_3 are connected across R_1, R_2, and R_3 as shown. Ammeter A is connected in series with the three resistors to indicate the total circuit current of 2 A.

Voltmeter V_1 in Fig. 2-3 indicates a voltage of 12 V. This indicates that 12 V is required to cause the current of 2 A to flow through R_1. Stated another way, there is a potential difference or a *voltage drop* of 12 V across R_1. Voltmeter V_2 indicates 36 V, or three times the voltage required across R_1. This is to be expected since R_2 has three times the resistance of R_1 and the same current of 2 A is being caused to flow through both resistors. The voltage across R_3 is only 24 V since R_3 is only twice as large as R_1. In general, it may be stated that the voltage required to cause a current to flow in a dc circuit is directly proportional to the resistance of the circuit; that is, the higher the resistance, the higher the voltage must be.

Note that in Fig. 2-3 the sum of the voltage drops across the three resistors is equal to the voltage applied to the circuit, i.e., $12 + 36 + 24 = 72$. The entire applied voltage is used in causing the current to flow through the three resistors.

FIGURE **2-3**
The sum of the voltages as indicated by voltmeters V_1, V_2, and V_3 is equal to the voltage indicated by voltmeter V.

In a series circuit, the sum of the voltages across the several parts is equal to the total voltage applied to the circuit.

Stated mathematically,

$$E = V_1 + V_2 + V_3 + \ldots \qquad \text{(Volts)} \qquad \text{[2-6]}$$

where E is voltage applied to the circuit and V_1, V_2, and V_3 are the voltage drops across the series components.

Voltage Divider Rule: *The voltage across one or more resistors can be determined in one step using the voltage divider.*

To derive this concept let's use Fig. 2-1.

a) $R_t = R_1 + R_2 + R_3$

b) $I_t = \dfrac{E}{R_t}$

c) $V_1 = I_t R_1$

From (c) above, we can substitute for I_t. Now our derived expression for V_1 is:

$$V_1 = \left(\frac{E}{R_t}\right) R_1$$

Therefore, by substitution, we can use the following expression to solve for the voltage drop across any given element in a series circuit:

$$V_x = E\left(\frac{R_x}{R_t}\right) \qquad \text{(Volts)} \qquad \text{[2-7]}$$

where V_x = the voltage drop across resistor or resistors R_x
R_x = the resistance of resistor or resistors V_x will drop across
E = the series circuit voltage source
I_t = the series circuit current

E x a m p l e   2 - 4

Let the resistors R_1, R_2, and R_3 in Fig. 2-1 have the following values respectively: 25 Ω, 40 Ω, and 15 Ω. Let V_t = 120 V. Using the voltage divider rule solve for:

a) the voltage across R_2
b) the voltage across the combination of R_1 and R_2.

SOLUTION:

a) $V_2 = E\left(\dfrac{R_2}{R_t}\right) = 120\left(\dfrac{40}{80}\right) = 60 \text{ V}$

b) $V_{(1-2)} = E\left(\dfrac{R_{(1-2)}}{R_t}\right) = 120\left(\dfrac{65}{80}\right) = 97.5 \text{ V}$

Fig. 2-5 shows three lamps L_1, L_2, and L_3 connected as three in-dependent circuits to a 120-V energy source. Obviously, a voltage of 120 V is applied to each of the three lamps since each lamp is connected directly to the same energy source. Now, if instead of making three separate circuit connections as in Fig. 2-5 the con-necting wires are replaced by one outgoing and one returning wire, the same condition exists. That is, there is still a voltage of 120 V applied to each of the three lamps. The connecting wires of Fig. 2-6 may be considered to be merely extensions of the energy source terminals so that the same voltage is supplied to each lamp. The connection shown in Fig. 2-6 is called a **parallel connection**, and the rule for voltages in a parallel circuit may be stated as follows:

The voltage across each branch of a parallel combination is the same as the voltage applied to the entire combination.

Stated mathematically,

$$E = V_1 = V_2 = V_3 = \ldots \quad \text{(Volts)} \qquad [2\text{-}8]$$

where E is the voltage across the combination and V_1, V_2, and V_3 are the voltages across the several branches.

2-5
Parallel Circuits: Voltage Relations

When one 120-Ω lamp is connected to a 120-V energy source, 1 A of current flows. When another lamp of the same size is added in parallel, 1 A flows through the second lamp and the energy source must supply a total of 2 A. Applying Ohm's law to the entire circuit with two lamps in parallel,

$$R_t = \frac{E}{I_t} = \frac{120}{2} = 60 \ \Omega$$

where R_t is the resistance of the entire circuit. Thus, the combined resistance of resistances in parallel is *less* than the resistance of ei-ther branch. This is true since as more paths are added through which current may flow the easier it is for current to flow or, in other words, the lower is the combined resistance of the circuit.

The equation for combining resistances in parallel may be de-veloped by means of **Ohm's law** and the current and voltage rules for parallel circuits. Applying Ohm's law to the entire circuit of Fig. 2-4,

$$I_t = \frac{E}{R_t} \quad \text{(Volts)}$$

where R_t is the resistance of the entire parallel combination. When Ohm's law is applied to the individual branches, the branch cur-rents are

2-6
Resistance of a Parallel Circuit

F I G U R E **2-4**

The combined resistance of a parallel circuit is less than the resistance of any one branch.

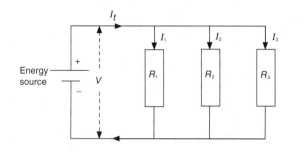

$$I_1 = \frac{V_1}{R_1} \qquad I_2 = \frac{V_2}{R_2} \qquad \text{and} \qquad I_3 = \frac{V_3}{R_3}$$

From the current rule for parallel circuits given by Eq. (2-12),

$$I_t = I_1 + I_2 + I_3$$

And by substituting the Ohm's law values of the currents in Eq. (2-12) results in

$$\frac{E}{R_t} = \frac{V_1}{R_1} + \frac{V_2}{R_2} + \frac{V_3}{R_3}$$

Then, cancelling out V from each term, (remember: $E = V_1 = V_2 = V_3$)

$$\frac{1}{R_t} = \frac{1}{R_1} + \frac{1}{R_2} + \frac{1}{R_3} \qquad\qquad \text{[2-9]}$$

Eq. (2-9) is the rule for combining resistances in parallel. It may be extended for any number of parallel branches.

E x a m p l e 2 - 5

What is the combined resistance of a circuit that has resistances of 20, 10, 40, and 80 Ω all connected in parallel?

$$\frac{1}{R_t} = \frac{1}{R_1} + \frac{1}{R_2} + \frac{1}{R_3} + \frac{1}{R_4}$$

$$\frac{1}{R_t} = \frac{1}{20} + \frac{1}{10} + \frac{1}{40} + \frac{1}{80}$$

$$\frac{1}{R_t} = \frac{4 + 8 + 2 + 1}{80} = \frac{15}{80}$$

$$15R_t = 80$$

$$R_t = \frac{80}{15}$$

$$R_t = 5.33 \ \Omega$$

Note in Example 2-5 that the combined resistance is less than the resistance of any one of the branch resistances. This is true in any parallel circuit.

The resistance of two resistances in parallel may be found by simplifying Eq. (2-9) to

$$R_t = \frac{R_1 R_2}{R_1 + R_2} \qquad \text{(Ohms)} \qquad \textbf{[2-10]}$$

That is, the combined resistance of any two resistances in parallel is equal to their product divided by their sum. This is true only for *two* resistances.

E x a m p l e   2 - 6

What is the combined resistance of a circuit composed of a 20-Ω resistor and a 30-Ω resistor connected in parallel?

$$R_t = \frac{R_1 R_2}{R_1 + R_2}$$

$$R_t = \frac{20 \times 30}{20 + 30}$$

$$R_t = \frac{600}{50}$$

$$R_t = 12 \ \Omega$$

The application of Eq. (2-9) or (2-10) to a circuit composed of two equal resistances in parallel shows that the combined resistance is one-half that of either resistance. Likewise, the combined resistance of three equal resistances in parallel is one-third of any one branch; the combined resistance of four equal resistances in parallel is one-fourth that of any one branch, and so on. In general, the combined resistance of any number of equal resistances in parallel is equal to the resistance of one branch divided by the number of branches. Stated mathematically, the combined resistance R_t of n parallel and equal resistances each of $R \ \Omega$ is

$$R_t = \frac{R}{n} \qquad \text{(Ohms)} \qquad \textbf{[2-11]}$$

E x a m p l e 2 - 7

What is the combined resistance of three 30-Ω resistors connected in parallel?

$$R_t = \frac{R}{n}$$

$$R_t = \frac{30}{3}$$

$$R_t = 10 \ \Omega$$

The relationships of current, voltage, and resistance in both series and parallel circuits are summarized in Table 2-2.

|2-**7**

Parallel Circuits: Current Relations

Since in Fig. 2-5 the energy source supplies current to each of the three independent circuits, the total current supplied must be the sum of the currents in the three circuits. Then, since Fig. 2-5 is equivalent to the parallel circuit shown in Fig. 2-6, the rule for currents in a parallel circuit may be stated as follows:

The total current supplied to a parallel circuit is the sum of the branch currents.

Mathematically,

$$I_t = I_1 + I_2 + I_3 + \ldots \qquad \text{(Amperes)} \qquad \textbf{[2-12]}$$

where I_t is the total current and I_1, I_2 and I_3 are the currents in the several branches.

Current Divider Rule: *The current through one or more resistors in parallel can be determined by using the current divider rule.* To derive this concept, let's use Fig. 2-7.

a) $I_t = I_1 + I_2$

b) $I_t = \dfrac{E}{R_t}$

c) $I_1 = \dfrac{E}{R_1}$

From part (c) above, we can substitute for E. Now our expression for I_1 is:

$$I_1 = I_t \left(\frac{R_t}{R_1} \right)$$

Therefore, by substitution, we can use the following expression to solve for the current through any given element in a parallel circuit:

$$I_x = I_t \left(\frac{R_t}{R_x} \right) \qquad \text{(Amperes)} \qquad \textbf{[2-13]}$$

FIGURE **2-5**
The three lamps are connected as three separate circuits to the same energy source.

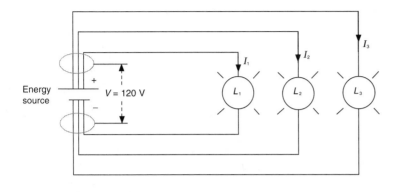

FIGURE **2-6**
The three lamp circuits of Fig. 2-5 are combined to form a parallel circuit.

FIGURE **2-7**

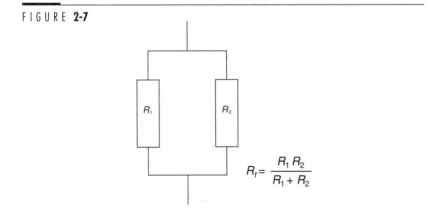

$$R_t = \frac{R_1 R_2}{R_1 + R_2}$$

where I_x = current through branch R_x
I_t = total circuit current
R_t = total circuit resistance
R_x = resistance of current branch I_x

TABLE 2-2	Summary of the Laws of Series and Parallel Circuits	
	Series Circuits	**Parallel Circuits**
Diagram		
Current	The current is the same in all parts of the circuit $$I_t = I_1 = I_2 = I_3 = \ldots$$	The total current supplied to the circuit equals the sum of the currents through the several branches $$I_t = I_1 + I_2 + I_3 + \ldots$$
Voltage	The total voltage equals the sum of the voltages across the different parts of the circuit $$E = V_1 + V_2 + V_3 + \ldots$$	The voltage across a parallel combination is the same as the voltage across each branch $$E = V_1 = V_2 = V_3 = \ldots$$
Resistance	The total resistance equals the sum of the resistances of the separate parts $$R_t = R_1 + R_2 + R_3 + R_n$$	The reciprocal of the equivalent or combined resistance equals the sum of the reciprocals of the resistances of the individual branches $$\frac{1}{R_t} = \frac{1}{R_1} + \frac{1}{R_2} + \frac{1}{R_3} + \frac{1}{R_n}$$
Voltage Divider	$$V_x = E\left(\frac{R_x}{R_t}\right)$$	
Current Divider		$$I_x = I_t\left(\frac{R_t}{R_x}\right)$$

From the above statements it can be said that the current through any parallel branch is equal to the product of the total resistance of the parallel branches and the source current divided by the resistance of the branch in which the current is being determined.

In the case of two parallel resistors as shown in Fig. 2-7,

Since
$$I_1 = I_t\left(\frac{R_t}{R_1}\right)$$

Then, by substitution: $I_1 = \dfrac{\left(\dfrac{R_1 R_2}{R_1 + R_2}\right)}{R_1} I_t$

and, therefore, $I_1 = \dfrac{I_t R_2}{R_1 + R_2}$ (Amperes)   [2-14]

Example 2-8

If the voltage across two parallel resistors in Fig. 2-7 is 50 V and resistors R_1 and R_2 respectively have a resistance of 20 Ω and 2.5 Ω, then using the current divider determine the current through

a) R_1
b) R_2

SOLUTION:

a) $I_1 = \dfrac{I_t R_2}{R_1 + R_2} = \dfrac{22.5 \times 2.5}{20 + 2.5} = 2.5$ A

b) $I_2 = \dfrac{I_t R_1}{R_1 + R_2} = \dfrac{22.5 \times 20}{20 + 2.5} = 20$ A

PROOF: $I_t = I_1 + I_2 = 2.5 + 20 = 22.5$ A

Frequently mistakes in electrical calculations are made because Ohm's law is not used properly. The law may be applied to an *entire circuit* or to *any part of a circuit*. When used for the entire circuit, values of current, voltage, and resistance must be used for the entire circuit. When used for a certain part of a circuit, values of current, voltage, and resistance must be used from only that part.

2-8
Applying Ohm's Law

Example 2-9

In the circuit represented in Fig. 2-8, find the current flowing in and the voltage across each of the two series resistances.

$$I(\text{entire circuit}) = \frac{E(\text{entire circuit})}{R(\text{entire circuit})}$$

FIGURE **2-8**
Circuit for Example 2-9. The symbol Ω is used to represent the word "ohm."

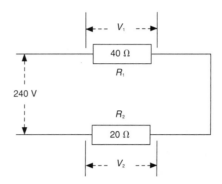

or
$$I_t = \frac{E}{R_t} = \frac{240}{(40 + 20)} = \frac{240}{60} = 4 \text{ A}$$

$$V(across\ R_1) = I(through\ R_1) \times R_1$$

or
$$V_1 = I_1 R_1 = 4 \times 40 = 160 \text{ V}$$

$$V(across\ R_2) = I(through\ R_2) \times R_2$$

or
$$V_2 = I_2 R_2 = 4 \times 20 = 80 \text{ V}$$

Example 2-10

Find the current in each branch and the line current in the parallel circuit shown in Fig. 2-9. What is the combined resistance of the two branches?

$$I(\text{branch 1}) = \frac{V(\text{branch 1})}{R(\text{branch 1})}$$

or
$$I_1 = \frac{V_1}{R_1} = \frac{120}{20} = 6 \text{ A}$$

$$I(\text{branch 2}) = \frac{V(\text{branch 2})}{R(\text{branch 2})}$$

or
$$I_2 = \frac{V_2}{R_2} = \frac{120}{30} = 4 \text{ A}$$

FIGURE **2-9**
Circuit for Example 2-10.

$$\text{Line current} = I_1 + I_2 = 6 + 4 = 10 \text{ A}$$

$$R(\text{entire circuit}) = \frac{E(\text{entire circuit})}{I(\text{entire circuit})}$$

or
$$R_t = \frac{E}{I_t} = \frac{120}{10} = 12 \text{ }\Omega$$

Notice that the combined resistance of R_1 and R_2 in parallel in Example 2-10 is less than the value of either R_1 or R_2. Resistances in parallel are discussed in Sec. 2-6.

Thus far, only simple series and simple parallel circuits as shown in Figs. 2-10 and 11 have been considered. Practical electric circuits very often consist of combinations of series and parallel resistances. Such circuits may be solved by the proper application of Ohm's law and the rules for series and parallel circuits to the various parts of the complex circuit. There is no definite procedure

|2-9

Series-Parallel Circuits

FIGURE **2-10**
The parallel combination of R_1 and R_2 is connected in series with R_3.

F I G U R E **2-11**
The series combination of R_1 and R_2 is connected in parallel with R_3.

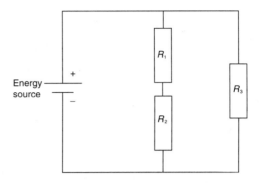

to be followed in solving complex circuits, the solution depends upon the known facts concerning the circuit and the quantities which one desires to find. One simple rule may usually be followed, however, reduce the parallel branches to an equivalent series branch and then solve the circuit as a simple series circuit.

The following examples will illustrate the solution of typical series-parallel circuits.

E x a m p l e   2 - 1 1

A resistor of 30 Ω is connected in parallel with a resistor of 60 Ω. In series with the parallel combination is a 20-Ω resistor as shown in Fig. 2-12(*a*). What is the resistance of the entire circuit?

The resistance between points B and C is

$$R_{BC} = \frac{R_2 R_3}{R_2 + R_3}$$

$$R_{BC} = \frac{30 \times 60}{30 + 60}$$

$$R_{BC} = 20 \ \Omega$$

Since R_2 and R_3 in parallel are equivalent to one 20-Ω resistance, the circuit may be reduced to the equivalent circuit shown in Fig. 2-12(*b*). The total circuit resistance is then

$$R_t = R_1 + R_{BC} = 20 + 20$$

$$R_t = 20 + 20$$

$$R_t = 40 \ \Omega$$

FIGURE **2-12**

(*a*) Series-parallel circuit for Example 2-11. (*b*) The circuit shown in (*a*) may be reduced to this equivalent circuit.

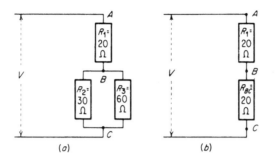

(*a*)   (*b*)

Example 2-12

Two resistors of 40 Ω and 60 Ω in parallel are connected in series with two 0.5-Ω resistors as shown in Fig. 2-13(*a*). Find the voltage across the series resistors and across the parallel resistors when 125 V is applied to the entire circuit.

The resistance between *B* and *C* is

$$R_{BC} = \frac{R_2 R_3}{R_2 + R_3}$$

$$R_{BC} = \frac{40 \times 60}{40 + 60}$$

$$R_{BC} = \frac{2400}{100}$$

$$R_{BC} = 24 \ \Omega$$

The circuit may now be represented as shown in Fig. 2-13(*b*) from which the total circuit resistance is

FIGURE **2-13**

(*a*) Circuit for Example 2-12. (*b*) This circuit is equivalent to the circuit shown in (*a*).

(*a*)   (*b*)

$$R_t = R_1 + R_{BC} + R_4$$

$$R_t = 0.5 + 24 + 0.5$$

$$R_t = 25 \ \Omega$$

Then
$$I_t = \frac{E}{R_t}$$

$$I_t = \frac{125}{25}$$

$$I_t = 5 \ A$$

The voltage across R_1 is
$$V_1 = I_t R_1$$

$$V_1 = 5 \times 0.5$$

$$V_1 = 2.4 \ V$$

and the voltage across R_4 is
$$V_4 = I_t R_4$$

$$V_4 = 5 \times 0.5$$

$$V_4 = 2.5 \ V$$

The voltage across the parallel combination is then
$$V_{BC} = 125 - (2.5 + 2.5)$$

$$V_{BC} = 120 \ V$$

$$V_{BC} = I_t R_{BC}$$

$$V_{BC} = 5 \times 24$$

$$V_{BC} = 120 \ V \qquad \text{(check)}$$

2-10
Line Drop

Thus far in dealing with electric circuits, the resistance of the connecting-line wires between the source and the load has been neglected. When connecting lines are short, the resistance is so small it can usually be neglected. However, a long line may have considerable resistance so that a certain amount of the applied voltage is used in overcoming this line resistance. This voltage is called **line drop**, and its value may be calculated by Ohm's law. Since $V = IR$, the voltage drop in the line wires is also called the IR drop in the lines. Line drop or IR drop is often expressed as a percentage of the voltage applied to the load.

While line resistance is distributed throughout the line wires, it is convenient when dealing with line resistance to consider the resistance of the circuit in two parts. One part representing the resistance of each line, the second is the resistance of the load. The combining of the line resistance and the load produces a complete series circuit. The following example will illustrate the calculation of line drop.

Example 2-13

Fig. 2-14 represents a simple lighting circuit with a source voltage of 120 V. Each lamp requires a current of 0.6 A, and each connecting wire has a resistance of 1.5 Ω. It is desired to find the line drop in volts, the voltage at the lamps, and the percentage voltage drop. Note that this problem is very similar to Example 2-12.

The line current is 0.6 × 2 or 1.2 A. Applying Ohm's law to each line wire:

$$V = IR$$

$$V = 1.2 \times 1.5$$

$$V = 1.8 \text{ V}$$

The voltage at the lamps is equal to the source voltage minus the drop in both lines, or

---

FIGURE **2-14**
Simple lighting circuit for Example 2-13 in which line resistance is taken into account.

$$V = 120 - (1.8 + 1.8)$$

$$V = 120 - 3.6$$

$$V = 116.4 \text{ V}$$

The percentage voltage drop in the lines is

$$\frac{3.6 \times 100}{116.4} = 3.09\%$$

Example 2-14

What is the voltage across each group of lamps in the lighting circuit of Fig. 2-15? Lines *AB* and *EF* have a resistance of 0.6 Ω each, and lines *BC* and *ED* have a resistance of 0.3 Ω each. Assume that each lamp takes a current of 1.5 A.

Current in lines *BC* and *DE* is 1.5 × 2 or 3 A. Current in lines AB and EF is 6 A. Line drop in AB and EF is

$$V = IR$$

$$V = 6 \times 0.6$$

$$V = 3.6 \text{ V}$$

Line drop in *BC* and *DE* is

$$V = 3 \times 0.3$$

$$V = 0.9 \text{ V}$$

Voltage across lamps at *BE* = voltage at source − line drop in
AB and *EF*

FIGURE **2-15**

Lighting circuit with lamps at two locations. See Example 2-14.

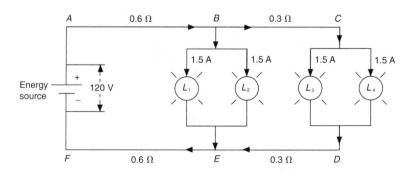

$$V_{BE} = 120 - (3.6 + 3.6)$$

$$V_{BE} = 120 - 7.2$$

$$V_{BE} = 112.8 \text{ V}$$

Voltage across lamps at CD = voltage at BE − line drop in BC and DE

$$V_{CD} = 112.8 - (0.9 + 0.9)$$

$$V_{CD} = 112.8 - 1.8$$

$$V_{CD} = 111 \text{ V}$$

2-11
Kirchhoff's Laws

Complex electric circuits may be solved with the aid of two simple rules known as Kirchhoff's laws.

Kirchhoff's Current Law. The algebraic sums of the currents at any electrical junction (node) must equal zero. Another way of stating this is to say the sum of the currents flowing away from any point in an electric circuit must equal the sum of the currents flowing toward that point.

Kirchhoff's Voltage Law. The algebraic sum of the voltages around any loop must equal zero. Another way of stating this is to say that around any path in an electric circuit, the sum of the potential drops is equal to the sum of the impressed emfs (voltage rises).

The current law should be evident since this is the principle involved in the current rule for a parallel circuit; that is, the sum of the branch currents must equal the line current. Using Fig. 2-15 as an example, the current flowing into point B is 6 A. The current in line BC is 3 A and in BE it is 3 A, or a total of 6 A flowing away from point B.

The voltage law may also be illustrated by Fig. 2-15. Considering the closed path $ABEFA$, the impressed emfs or voltage rises must equal the voltage drops, or

Rise through energy source

= drop in AB + drop in BE + drop in EF

$$120 = 3.6 + 112.8 + 3.6$$

$$120 = 120 \quad \text{(check)}$$

Likewise, in the closed path *ABCDEFA*

$$\text{Rises} = \text{drops}$$

$$120 = 3.6 + 0.9 + 111 + 0.9 + 3.6$$

$$120 = 120 \qquad \text{(check)}$$

Kirchhoff's current and voltage laws restate, in concise and usable form, principles already discussed in connection with the rules for series and parallel circuits. By means of a systematic application of these laws, the current and voltage values of the various parts of complex circuits may be found.

Example 2-15

The circuit in Fig. 2-16 illustrates the series-parallel connection of six resistors. The objective is to determine the circuits total resistance, voltage across, and the current through each resistor. The first step in the solution is to determine the total resistance of the circuit. This is accomplished by systematically breaking the circuit down into equivalent series and parallel paths. The network is processed through five steps to resolving the total resistance of the circuit.

$$R_3 + R_6 = 45 + 15 = 60 \ \Omega$$

$$60 \ \Omega \| R_5 = 60 \| 60 = 30 \ \Omega \qquad \text{(Recall from Sec. 2-6 that for resistances in parallel, } 60 \| 60 = 30 \ \Omega.\text{)}$$

$$30 \ \Omega + R_2 = 30 + 30 = 60 \ \Omega$$

$$60 \ \Omega \| R_4 = 60 \| 40 = 24 \ \Omega$$
$$24 \ \Omega + R_1 = 24 + 26 = 50 \ \Omega = R_T$$

Once the total resistance of the circuit is determined, the circuit currents and voltage drops can be determined by systematically applying Kirchhoff's voltage and current laws.

$$I_T = \frac{E}{R_T} = \frac{100}{50} = \underline{2 \text{ A}} = I_1$$

$$V_1 = I_1 R_1 = 2 \times 26 = \underline{52 \text{ V}}$$

FIGURE **2-16**

$$V_4 = E - V_1 = 100 - 52 = \underline{48 \text{ V}}$$

$$I_4 = \frac{V_4}{R_4} = \frac{48}{40} = \underline{1.2 \text{ A}}$$

$$I_2 = I_1 - I_4 = 2 - 1.2 = \underline{0.8 \text{ A}}$$

$$V_2 = I_2 R_2 = 0.8 \times 30 = \underline{24 \text{ V}}$$

$$V_5 = V_4 - V_2 = 48 - 24 = \underline{24 \text{ V}}$$

$$I_5 = \frac{V_5}{R_5} = \frac{24}{60} = \underline{0.4 \text{ A}}$$

$$I_3 = I_2 - I_5 = 0.8 - 0.4 = \underline{0.4 \text{ A} = I_6}$$

$$V_3 = I_3 R_3 = 0.4 \times 45 = \underline{18 \text{ V}}$$

$$V_6 = I_6 R_6 = 0.4 \times 15 = \underline{6 \text{ V}}$$

Proof: $E = V_1 + V_2 + V_3 + V_6$

$$100 = 52 + 24 + 18 + 6$$

$$100 = 100$$

Another simple application of Kirchhoff's laws will be illustrated in the solution of three-wire circuit problems in Sec. 2-12 which follows.

2-**12**

Three-Wire Distribution Circuits

To obtain the advantage of a higher voltage-distribution circuit and yet provide 120 V for the operation of standard incandescent lights, Edison developed the 120/240-V three-wire system of power distribution. For a fixed amount of line loss, power can be transmitted by means of the three-wire system with only *three-eighths* the line copper required for a two-wire 120-V system. (See Appendix D for an example.) The system has the further advantage of making available either 120 or 240 V for the operation of electric equipment.

The three-wire dc distribution system has been superseded generally by the three-wire ac (alternating current) system. However, since the principles of operation are essentially the same for the ac and dc systems, a description of the dc system is included here. Transformer connections used in supplying the three-wire ac system are discussed in Sec. 13-5.

Fig. 2-17 shows one method of connecting the supply for a three-wire dc system. Two 120-V dc energy sources are connected in series to supply the system, with three wires brought out, one from each outside terminal of the sources and the third, called the **neutral**, from the common connection between the sources. With

FIGURE **2-17**
Three-wire distribution circuit.

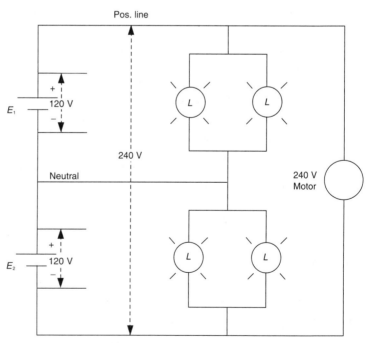

this arrangement, 120 V lamps and appliances may be connected between either outside wire and the neutral, while 240 V equipment, such as motors and electric heaters, may be connected between the two outside wires, as shown in Fig. 2-17.

When the 120 V loads are balanced on each side of the neutral as in Fig. 2-18, the neutral carries no current. If a heavier load is connected between the positive line and neutral as in Fig. 2-19, the neutral carries, toward the energy sources, the difference in current between the upper and lower lines. If the heavier load is connected between the negative line and neutral as in Fig. 2-20, the neutral carries the unbalanced current from the energy sources toward the load. That is, the current flowing in the neutral wire is always the difference between the currents in the positive and negative lines. It is desirable to keep the loads as nearly balanced as possible to keep the flow of neutral current to a minimum.

When load is connected to only one side of a three-wire system, the neutral carries the full-load current. For this reason, the neutral is usually of the same cross-sectional size as the positive and negative lines.

An accidental opening of the neutral wire when an unbalanced load is being supplied results in badly unbalanced voltages across

FIGURE **2-18**
Three-wire circuit with balanced loads. The neutral wire carries no current.

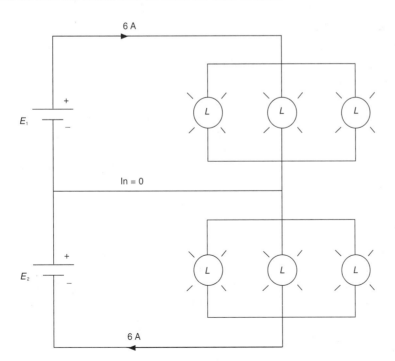

FIGURE **2-19**

Three-wire circuit with heavier load between positive line and neutral. Neutral wire carries current toward energy sources.

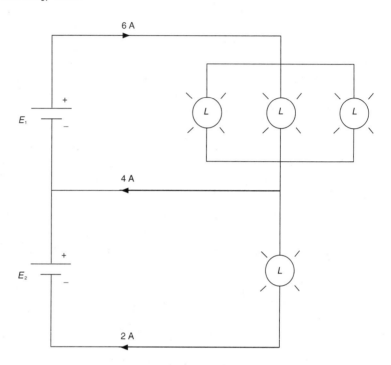

the loads. For this reason, the neutral is connected solidly from the energy sources to the load and no fuses or other overcurrent devices are installed in the neutral. For further protection against an open neutral and for protection against damage by lightning, the neutral wire is connected to earth at one or more points.

It is often necessary to find the voltage across the loads connected to a three-wire system when the line resistance and the load currents are known. The following example will illustrate this calculation for the simple case of two loads connected to the system at the same point.

Example 2-16

Two loads located 1000 ft. from a source are to be supplied from a three-wire system using three copper wires each having a resistance of 0.1 Ω. One load requires 30 A and the other 20 A. Find the voltage across each load. Source voltages are 120 V.

SOLUTION: When the loads are connected as shown in Fig. 2-20, the neutral carries 10 A toward the source. The voltage drop in each line is:

FIGURE **2-20**
Three-wire circuit with heavier load between negative line and neutral. Neutral wire carries current toward load.

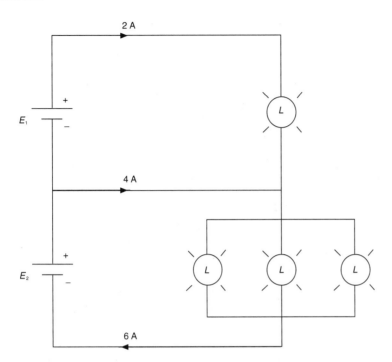

Line A	$IR = 30 \times 0.1$
	$IR = 3$ V
Neutral	$IR = 10 \times 0.1$
	$IR = 1$ V
Line B	$IR = 20 \times 0.1$
	$IR = 2$ V

Writing an equation for the upper half of the circuit in accordance with Kirchhoff's voltage law,

$$\text{Voltage rises} = \text{voltage drops}$$

$$120 = 3 + V_1 + 1$$

$$V_1 = 120 - 3 - 1$$

$$V_1 = 116 \text{ V}$$

FIGURE **2-21**
Unbalanced three-wire system for Example 2-16.

Kirchhoff's voltage equation for the entire outside loop is

$$120 + 120 = 3 + 116 + V_2 + 2$$

$$240 = 121 + V_2$$

$$V_2 = 240 - 121$$

$$V_2 = 119 \text{ V}$$

REVIEW QUESTIONS

1 What are the two basic ways in which electric apparatus may be connected?

2 What is the relation between the values of current flowing in different parts of a series circuit?

3 If the voltages across the several parts of a series circuit are known, how may the total circuit voltage be determined?

4 A voltage of 20 V is required to cause 2 A to flow through a resistance of 10 Ω. What voltage is necessary to cause the same current to flow through 40 Ω?

5 Give the rule for determining the voltage across parallel branches of a circuit when the applied voltage is known.

6 State Ohm's law in its three forms. Which form is most convenient for finding (*a*) the resistance, (*b*) the current, or (*c*) the voltage of a circuit?

7 What precautions should be observed in applying Ohm's law to a part of a circuit?

8 Give the rule for finding the combined resistance of several resistances (*a*) in a series and (*b*) in parallel.

9 Give the rule for finding the combined resistance of two resistances in parallel.

10 What is the general rule for finding the combined resistance of several equal resistances in parallel?

11 In reducing series-parallel circuits to simpler form, what is the general procedure?

12 What is meant by line drop? How is it calculated?

13 State Kirchhoff's current and voltage laws.

14 What are some advantages of the three-wire distribution system?

15 What determines the neutral current in a three-wire distribution system?

PROBLEMS

2-1 Two lamps are connected in series to a 120-V line. The voltage across one lamp is 70 V. What is the voltage across the second lamp?

2-2 Eight lamps of the same size are connected in series to a 120-V circuit. What is the voltage across each lamp?

2-3 Three lamps of equal size are connected in parallel to a lighting circuit. Each lamp draws a current of 1.5 A. What is the total line current?

2-4 Twenty lamps of equal size are connected in parallel to a 120-V lighting circuit. If the total current drawn by the 20 lamps is 15 A, what is the current through each lamp? If the lamps are reconnected in series in another circuit, so that the current through one of the lamps is 1 A, what will be the current through the other 19 lamps?

2-5 A 220 Ω lamp is connected to a 110-V circuit. What current does it take?

2-6 The field resistance of a shunt motor is 93 Ω. What will be the field current if 240 V is applied to the field terminals?

2-7 An accidental short circuit is made on a 240-V circuit by placing a 0.15 Ω resistance across the line. What will be the momentary short-circuit current?

2-8 A telephone receiver has a resistance of 1200 Ω. If a current of 0.02 A is to flow through the receiver, what voltage must be used?

2-9 What is the voltage drop across a rheostat if its resistance is 5 Ω and the current through it is 26 A?

2-10 Find the voltage across an electric furnace that has a resistance of 5 Ω and draws 43 A.

2-11 The voltage across the terminals of a motor field is 220 V and the field current is 1 A. What is the field-circuit resistance?

2-12 A relay coil draws a current of 0.03 A when connected to a 12-V battery. What is its resistance?

2-13 Find the combined resistance of a 5-Ω rheostat in series with a 56-Ω shunt field.

2-14 What is the total resistance of a string of eight Christmas-tree lights connected in series, if the resistance of each lamp is 30 Ω?

2-15 How much voltage is required to cause a current of 0.4 A to flow through a 70-Ω, a 90-Ω, and a 120-Ω lamp all connected in series?

2-16 Three lamps are connected in series across a 120-V supply and take a current of 1.25 A. If the resistance of two of the lamps is 25 Ω each, what is the resistance of the third?

2-17 How much resistance must be added in series with a 60-Ω generator field if the field current desired is 2 A and the voltage applied to the field circuit is 230 V?

2-18 A certain series street-lighting system of 60 lamps operates at a constant current of 6.6 A. How much voltage must be applied to the circuit if each lamp has a resistance of 5 Ω and the total line resistance is 10 Ω?

2-19 Four lamps of equal resistance are connected in parallel across a 120-V circuit. if the total current supplied the lamps is 3 A, what is the resistance of each lamp?

2-20 Three resistances *A*, *B*, and *C* are connected in parallel across a 120-V line. If *A* = 10 Ω, *B* = 30 Ω, and *C* = 40 Ω, calculate (*a*) the voltage across each resistance, (*b*) the current through each resistance, (*c*) the total line current, and (*d*) the combined resistance of the circuit.

2-21 The combined resistance of two resistors connected in parallel is 8 Ω. The resistance of one resistor is 14 Ω. What would be their combined resistance if they were reconnected in series?

2-22 A trolley wire is paralleled for 5 km by a heavy copper cable. The trolley-wire resistance is 0.186 Ω/km and the cable resistance is 0.062 Ω/km. When the sum of the two currents through the lines is 150 A, determine the current in each conductor.

2-23 A parallel circuit has three branches of 12, 4, and 16 Ω, respectively. If a current of 4 A flows in the branch containing 12 Ω, what current will flow in each of the others?

2-24 Three resistances of 3, 4, and 6 Ω are connected in parallel. In series with the group is an unknown resistance, R. When the circuit is connected to a 12-V battery, a current of 4 A flows. What is the resistance of R?

2-25 A resistance of 12 Ω is connected in parallel with a series circuit of a 15-Ω and a 5-Ω resistance. A 40-Ω resistance is connected in series with the combination. What is the resistance of the entire circuit?

2-26 Three resistances of 4, 8, and 10 Ω are connected so that each resistance forms the side of a triangle. Point A is the connection between the 4- and 8-Ω sides; point B, between the 8- and 10-Ω sides; point C, between the 4- and 10-Ω sides. Find the resistance between points A and B, B and C, and C and A.

2-27 Four resistors of 6 Ω each form the sides of a diamond. A fifth resistor of 10 Ω forms the long diagonal of the diamond. What is the resistance of the combination between the ends of the long diagonal? What is the resistance between one end of the long diagonal and one end of the short diagonal?

2-28 A dc motor is supplied by a dc generator. Each line connecting the two machines has a resistance of 0.15 Ω. What is the terminal voltage across the motor when the motor current is 50 A and the generator terminal voltage is 230 V?

2-29 A dc motor is located 610 m from a dc generator. The motor requires 30 A to operate a given load. The generator voltage is 220 V. Each line connecting the generator and motor is No. 0 cable which has a resistance of 0.328 Ω/km. Find the voltage at the motor.

2-30 A 240-V generator supplies 10 A to each of two motors connected in parallel. The resistance of each line wire between the generator and the first motor is 0.3 Ω, and the resistance of each line wire between the first and second motor is 0.4 Ω. What is the voltage across each motor?

2-31 Each wire of a two-wire distribution circuit has a resistance of 0.656 Ω/km. Connected to this circuit at a point 152.4 m from the generator is a motor that requires a current of 15 A and has a terminal voltage of 230 V. A second motor that requires 10 A is located on the same circuit but 228.6 m from the generator. (*a*) What is the voltage at the second motor? (*b*) What is the generator voltage?

2-32 The voltage drop across an electric heater is 225 V. If the voltage at the source is 230 V and the heater draws 15 A, what is the resistance of each connecting line wire?

2-33 If each lamp in Fig. 2-22 requires a current of 1 A, find (*a*) the current and its direction in each of the three lines, (*b*) the *IR* drop in each line, and (*c*) the voltages V_1, and V_2.

2-34 Repeat the preceding problem if one lamp in the upper bank of lamps burns out.

F I G U R E **2-22**
Three-wire circuit for Problems 2-33 and 2-34.

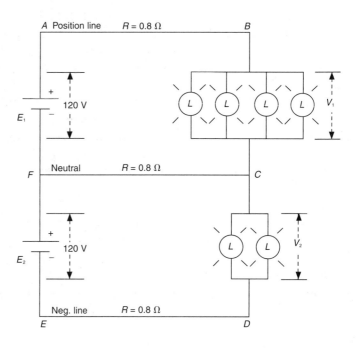

2-35 For the circuit shown in Fig. 2-23 determine (*a*) V_1, (*b*) V_2, and (*c*) V_4. Use the Voltage Divider.

2-36 For the circuit of Fig. 2-24, determine the unknown currents using the Current Divider.

FIGURE **2-23**

FIGURE **2-24**

Electric Conductors

In this chapter we discuss conductor materials, wire measurements, resistivity, and temperature coefficient of resistance — all items relating to electric conductors.

3-1
Conductor Materials

Conductor materials are those materials that have many free electrons. Such materials are said to present a low resistance to the flow of electric current or to have a high **conductance**. A good electric conductor, therefore, has a high conductance and a low resistance.

In addition to having a high conductance, a good conductor material should have a high tensile strength, relatively light weight, and a low cost. Copper and aluminum possess these qualities and are used extensively as conductors in the generation, transmission, and utilization of electric energy. Combinations of steel with copper or aluminum in the form of copper-clad steel or steel-reinforced aluminum are often used as overhead conductors where an especially high tensile strength is required.

Silver and gold are excellent conductor materials but are too expensive for extensive use. Both are used however as plating materials for electric-contact surfaces where corrosion-free, low-resistance contact must be assured.

3-2
Wire Measurements, SI Units

In metric or SI units, wire diameters are expressed in millimetres (mm) and cross-sectional areas in square millimetres (mm^2). Wire lengths are expressed in metres or kilometres (usually kilometres) and weights in kilograms per kilometre (kg/km). A table of dimensions, weights, and resistance of copper wire in SI units is included in Appendix B.

As an approximation, a 1-mm^2 copper conductor has a weight of about 9.2 kg/km and a resistance of about 17 Ω/km. Weights increase and resistances decrease in proportion to increases in cross-sectional area. Thus, a 10-mm^2 copper conductor has a weight of approximately 92 kg/km and a resistance of approximately 1.7 Ω/km. Reference should be made to Appendix B for more exact data.

3-3

Wire Measurements, Imperial System

Because the diameter of wires used as conductors of electricity may be very small, it is convenient when using the Imperial System of measurement to express wire diameters in thousandths of an inch. In order to avoid the use of decimals in expressing wire diameters, a unit of measurement known as the **mil** is in general use. *One mil is equal to one one-thousandth (0.001) of one inch.* For example, instead of saying that a wire has a diameter of 0.051 or 51/1000 in., it is said to have a diameter of 51 mils.

Example 3-1

$$1 \text{ in.} = 1 \times 1000 \text{ or } 1000 \text{ mils}$$

$$0.5 \text{ in.} = 0.5 \times 1000 \text{ or } 500 \text{ mils}$$

$$0.253 \text{ in.} = 0.253 \times 1000 \text{ or } 253 \text{ mils}$$

The cross-sectional area of round conductors is expressed in units called **circular mils** (cmil). A conductor with a diameter of 1 mil has a cross-sectional area of 1 cmil.

Since the area of a circle is proportional to the square of its diameter (*area* $= \pi d^2/4$), *the area of a circular conductor in circular mils is equal to the square of its diameter in mils.*

Example 3-2

What is the circular-mil area of a wire (*a*) 0.1 in., (*b*) 0.2 in., (*c*) 0.325 in. in diameter?

(*a*) Diameter in mils = 0.1 × 1000 or 100 mils

Area = diameter in mils squared
     = 100 × 100 or 10 000 cmil

(*b*) Diameter = 0.2 × 1000 or 200 mils

Area = 200 × 200 cmil
     = 40 000 cmil

(*c*) Diameter = 0.325 × 1000 or 325 mils

Area = 325 × 325 cmil
     = 105 625 cmil

3-4

The American Wire Gauge

In Canada it is common practice to indicate wire sizes by a gauge number. The commonly used gauge is the American Wire Gauge. American Wire Gauge (AWG) sizes range from No. 0000, (4/0) the largest size, to No. 40, the smallest size. This system is based on a constant ratio between any wire diameter and the diameter of the next smaller wire. Appendix C gives the dimensions and properties of the more commonly used AWG sizes of solid copper wire.

Several approximate rules concerning the AWG tables follow. If these simple facts are remembered, approximate values concerning many wire sizes may be calculated without referring to the tables.

1. Easily remembered **approximate** data concerning No. 10 AWG solid copper wire are

$$\text{Diameter} \approx 0.1 \text{ in. or } 100 \text{ mils}$$

$$\text{Area} \approx 10\ 000 \text{ cmil}$$

$$\text{Resistance} \approx 1\ \Omega \text{ per } 1000 \text{ ft.}$$

$$\text{Weight} \approx 32 \text{ lb. per } 1000 \text{ ft.}$$

2. An increase of three gauge sizes doubles the area and weight and halves the resistance.
3. An increase of 10 gauge sizes increases the area and weight by a factor of 10 and decreases the resistance by a factor of 10.

Example 3-3

Find the approximate resistance of No. 0 (1/0) AWG copper wire without referring to the tables.

Since No. 0 is 10 gauge sizes larger than No. 10, its resistance is $1.0/10 = 0.1\ \Omega$ per 1000 ft.

Example 3-4

Find the approximate area of No. 4 AWG copper wire without referring to the tables.

Number 4 is six gauge sizes larger than No. 10; therefore, its area is $10\ 000 \times 2 \times 2$ or $40\ 000$ cmil.

It is often necessary to convert from one system of wire measurement to another. To convert from circular mils to square millimetres, it is necessary to multiply the number of circular mils by 506.7×10^{-6} (0.000 506 7). Similarly, to convert from square millimetres to circular mils, it is necessary to multiply the number of square millimetres by 1973 (1/0.0005067).

Example 3-5

A round solid No. 0000 (4/0) AWG conductor is 0.46 in. in diameter. What is its cross-sectional area in circular mils and in square millimetres?

$$\text{Diameter} = 0.46 \text{ in. or } 460 \text{ mils}$$
$$\text{Cross-sectional area} = (460)^2 \text{ or } 211\ 600 \text{ cmil}$$

$$\text{Since cmil} \times 506.7 \times 10^{-6} = \text{mm}^2$$
$$\text{Then } 211\ 600 \times 506.7 \times 10^{-6} = 107.2 \text{ mm}^2$$

$$\text{Since mm}^2 \times 1973 = \text{cmil}$$
$$\text{Then } 107.2 \times 1973 = 211\ 600 \text{ cmil} \qquad \text{(check)}$$

The following are helpful approximate factors for converting AWG to metric or metric to AWG sizes and for visualizing relative wire sizes in the two systems:

$$1 \text{ mm}^2 \approx \text{(approx.) } 2000 \text{ cmil}$$

$$\text{No. 10 AWG} \approx \text{(approx.) } 10\ 000 \text{ cmil}$$

$$6 \text{ mm}^2 \approx \text{(approx.) } 12\ 000 \text{ cmil}$$

$$100 \text{ mm}^2 \approx \text{(approx.) No. 0000 AWG}$$

3-5
Stranded Wire

To obtain the flexibility required for easy handling, the larger sizes of wire are made in the form of a cable consisting of several small strands. Standard numbers of strands commonly used in cable are 7, 19, 37, 61, 91, and 127, since by using these numbers the strands may be laid in concentric layers about a single central wire. Wires larger than No. 0000 (4/0) AWG are nearly always stranded, and it is often desirable to use stranded wire in the smaller sizes, even as small as No. 20 AWG or 0.5 mm² SI.

The separate strands of a stranded wire are not necessarily standard wire sizes since the total cross-sectional area is equal to a standard AWG or metric size, the area of each strand being the total area divided by the number of strands.

Appendix B gives dimensions and properties of stranded metric-size copper conductors. Appendix D gives the dimensions and properties of standard AWG stranded copper conductors. Note that conductors larger than AWG No. 0000 (4/0) are listed by their circular-mil area.

As previously indicated, materials classified as conductors have many free electrons and offer a low resistance to the flow of electric current. Not all conductor materials, however, offer the same resistance to the flow of current since different materials have different numbers of free electrons. For example, copper offers a lower resistance to the flow of current than does aluminum.

Resistance depends not only on the material used for the conductor but also on the size and temperature of the conductor. In a conductor of large cross-sectional area, the number of electrons free to move is larger than in a wire of small cross-sectional area. Thus, the larger the conductor, the lower its resistance.

Resistance also depends on the length of a conductor. A conductor 10 m long has twice as much resistance as a conductor of the same material and size that is only 5 m long.

It has also been found that temperature affects the resistance of most materials. The resistance of most materials increases with an increase in temperature. For example, a tungsten lamp filament has a much lower resistance when it is cold than it has when it is white hot.

Summarizing, the resistance of a conductor depends on the material, the cross-sectional area, the length, and the temperature. Expressed as an equation, the resistance of a conductor at any given temperature is

$$R = \frac{\rho l}{A} \qquad [3-1]$$

where R = resistance in ohms
   l = length
   A = cross-sectional area
   ρ = a constant called the **resistivity** of the conductor material at a specified temperature
   (ρ, the Greek letter rho, is the standard symbol for resistivity.)

Resistivity is defined as the resistance of a conductor of unit length and unit cross section at a specified temperature. The unit of resistivity is the ohm-metre and is the resistance in ohms of a conductor one metre long having a cross-sectional area of one square metre. It is generally more convenient in calculations to use the smaller units of microhms rather than ohms and millimetres rather than metres, resulting in the unit of resistivity called the microhm-millimetre. One microhm-millimetre is equal to 10^{-9} ohm-metres. In Imperial units, resistivity is usually expressed in ohms per circular mil-foot. A circular mil-foot is a conductor having a length of one foot and a cross-sectional area of one circular mil.

3-6
Resistivity

The resistivity of annealed copper at 20°C is 10.4 Ω per circular mil-foot and 17.2 microhm-millimetres in Imperial and SI units, respectively. Likewise, aluminum has a resistivity of 17.1 Ω per circular mil-foot and 28.3 microhm-millimetres. These resistivities are at a temperature of 20°C.

Eq. (3-1) may be used to compute conductor resistance when the conductor resistivity and dimensions are known, as illustrated by the following examples.

Example 3-6

What is the resistance of a 4110-cmil copper conductor 500 ft. long, assuming a resistivity of 10.4 Ω per circular mil-foot?

$$R = \frac{\rho l}{A}$$

$$R = \frac{10.4 \times 500}{4110} \; \Omega$$

$$R = 1.26 \; \Omega$$

Example 3-7

What is the resistance of a copper conductor (resistivity 17.2 microhm-millimetres) which has a length of 1000 m and a cross-sectional area of 2.5 mm^2)?

Since there are one million square millimetres in one square metre, the conductor area, A, is

$$A = \frac{2.5}{10^6} \text{ or } 2.5 \times 10^{-6} \text{ m}^2$$

Also, since one microhm-millimetre is equal to 10^{-9} ohm-metre

$$\rho = 17.2 \times 10^{-9} \text{ ohm-metre}$$

$$R = \frac{\rho l}{A}$$

$$R = \frac{17.2 \times 10^{-9} \times 1000}{2.5 \times 10^{-6}}$$

$$R = 6.88 \; \Omega$$

We now have a method of determining the resistance of a conductor at 20°C by virtue of its material, length, and cross-sectional area. At this point we can take a further step and derive a useful Voltage Drop Formula.

Since $V = IR$, then the voltage that will drop across a resistance due to a current flowing through it is: $V_d = IR$

where V_d = voltage drop

By substitution,
$$V_d = I \frac{\rho l}{A}$$
[3-2]

The Canadian Electrical Code determines the maximum allowable voltage drop in circuit conductors in given applications. The above derived equation can now be transposed to determine the conductor size required for a given load at a given distance from the source while observing the maximum allowable voltage drop permitted.

Example 3-8

A 3.75-kW, 230-V single phase motor is located 100 m from its source. The full load motor current is 25 A. While maintaining no more than a 3 percent voltage drop in the copper supply conductors, determine:

a) the area of the supply conductors in mm^2
b) the gauge size of the supply conductors.

SOLUTION:

a) Allowable voltage drop in the supply conductors is:

$$230 \times 0.03 \text{ or } 6.9 \text{ V}$$

Total length of the supply conductors is:

$$2 \text{ cond.} \times 100 \text{ or } 200 \text{ m}$$

Therefore,

$$A = 25 \left(17.2 \times 10^{-9} \times \frac{200}{6.9} \right) \text{ m}^2$$

$$A = 12.46 \times 10^{-6} \text{ m}^2$$

$$\text{or} = 12.46 \text{ mm}^2$$

b) Comparing Tables in Appendixes C and D:
   The diameter of conductor in millimetres by interpolation is 4.56 mm. At 25.4 mm per inch, the diameter of the conductor in inches is: 4.56/25.4 or 0.18 inches, which is equal to 180 mils. By Table C, the Gauge size is number 6.

Note that if the installer of the supply conductors had simply used the motor's full load current to determine the conductor size while disregarding the distance involved, number 10 Gauge conductor would have been used with a resultant voltage drop in the supply conductors of:

$$V_d = 25 \left(17.2 \times 10^{-9} \times \frac{200}{5} \times 10^{-6} \right)$$

$$V_d = 17.2 \text{ V}$$

This increased voltage drop would decrease the effectiveness of the motor's output.

3-7
Temperature Coefficient of Resistance

Nearly all conductors of electricity show a change in resistance with a change in temperature, as was mentioned in the previous section. The resistance of a pure metal conductor increases with an increase in temperature and decreases with a decrease in temperature.

Conductor-resistance tables show resistances at a specific temperature. For example, Appendixes B, C, and D list the resistance of copper wires and cables at 20°C. A true comparison of the resistance of conductors of different sizes or materials cannot be made unless the resistances are compared at the same temperature.

It has been found by experiment that for each degree of change in temperature above or below 20°C, the resistance changes by a given percentage of what it was at 20°C. This percentage change in resistance is called the **temperature coefficient of resistance**. This coefficient for copper at 20°C is 0.003 93 and is nearly the same for other pure metals. Thus, for each degree that the temperature of a copper wire increases above 20°C, the resistance increases 0.393 of 1 percent of its value at 20°C. Likewise, for each degree the temperature falls below 20°C, the resistance decreases 0.393 of 1 percent of its value at 20°C.

The straight-line relationship between temperature and resistance holds throughout the range of temperatures normally encountered and may be expressed mathematically as follows:

$$R_2 = R[1 + a(t_2 - t)] \qquad \text{(Ohms)} \qquad \text{[3-6]}$$

where R_2 = resistance at temperature t_2
        R = resistance at 20°C
        t = 20°C
        t_2 = temperature of conductor
        a = temperature coefficient of resistance at 20°C

E x a m p l e   3 - 1 0

The resistance of a length of copper wire is 3.60 Ω at 20°C. What is its resistance at 80°C?

$$R_2 = R[1 + a(t_2 - t)]$$

$$R_2 = 3.60[1 + 0.00393(80 - 20)]$$

$$R_2 = 3.60 \times 1.236$$

$$R_2 = 4.45\ \Omega$$

3-8
Conductance

Generally a conductor or a resistive device in an electrical circuit is quantified by its characteristics that offer an opposition to the flow of current in a circuit (resistance). However, it sometimes becomes necessary to describe the conductor or resistive device in terms of its ability to conduct current rather than its ability to oppose the flow of current. This term is called **conductance** (C).

Therefore, the ability of a circuit to conduct is a ratio of the circuits quantity of current in amperes per volt applied. The unit of conductance is the **siemen** (S).

Since

$$R = \frac{E}{I} \quad \text{(ohms)}$$

then

$$C = \frac{I}{E} \quad \text{(siemens)} \qquad \text{[3-3]}$$

where C is equal to the circuit's conductance in siemens (S).

From Eq. (3-3) it becomes apparent that the unit of conductance is the reciprocal of resistance. Therefore, conductance can also be expressed in the following ways:

$$C = \frac{1}{R} \quad \text{(siemens)} \qquad \text{[3-4]}$$

and

$$C = \frac{A}{\rho l} \quad \text{(siemens)} \qquad \text{[3-5]}$$

Example 3-9

Determine the conductance in Example 3-6.

$$C = \frac{1}{R}$$

$$C = \frac{1}{1.26}$$

$$C = 0.79 \text{ S}$$

or

$$C = \frac{A}{\rho l}$$

$$C = \frac{4110}{10.4 \times 500}$$

$$C = 0.79 \text{ S}$$

REVIEW QUESTIONS

1 What are the characteristics of a good metallic electric conductor?

2 One mil is equal to what part of 1 in.?

3 What unit of measurement is used for the cross-sectional area of conductors in the metric system? In the Imperial System?

4 What is the relation between the cross-sectional area of No. 0 AWG and No. 6 AWG wire?

5 A 6-mm² conductor is slightly larger than what AWG size?

6 Define the terms resistivity and temperature coefficient of resistance.

7 Why are large conductors stranded?

8 Define the term conductance and describe its relationship to resistance in a circuit.

PROBLEMS

3-1 What are the diameters in mils of wires that have diameters of 2.0, 3/4, 0.675, 0.43, and 1/4 in.?

3-2 What is the circular-mil area of each of the wires in Prob. 3-1?

3-3 What are the nearest AWG sizes of solid wires with areas of 5000, 10 000, 40 000, and 100 000 cmil?

3-4 What is the diameter in mils of a wire that has an area of 1600 cmil? What is the nearest AWG size?

3-5 If a 150-mm^2 copper wire has a weight of approximately 1375 kg/km, what is the weight of a 300-mm^2 copper wire 1000 m long?

3-6 A conductor with a resistivity of 28.3×10^{-9} ohm-metres has a cross-sectional area of 120 mm^2 and is 1 km long. What is its resistance?

3-7 What is the cross-sectional area in square millimetres of a No. 2 AWG solid conductor?

3-8 A conductor of certain specifications can carry safely 1 A for each 300 cmil of its cross-sectional area. If the current to be carried is 20 A, what is the AWG size of the wire required?

3-9 The resistance of a copper coil is 200 Ω at 20°C. What will be the resistance of the coil when it is heated to 90°C?

3-10 The resistance of a generator field coil wound with copper wire is 130 Ω at 80°C. What is its resistance at 20°C?

3-11 Find the temperature coefficient of resistance at 20°C of a conductor that increases resistance from 20 to 24 Ω when heated from 20 to 80°C.

3-12 A copper conductor has a resistance of 400 Ω at 40°C. What will its resistance be at 60°C? (Hint: First find its resistance at 20°C.)

3-13 The resistance of a copper generator coil is 0.10 Ω at 20°C. Following operation of the generator at full load, the same coil measures 0.114 Ω. What was the temperature increase in the coil?

3-14 A 5 kW/230 V heater is to be located 50 m from its supply. While maintaining no more than a 2 percent voltage drop in transmission, determine:
   a) the circular mil area and gauge size of the conductor if copper is used.
   b) the circular mil area and gauge size of the conductor if aluminum is used.

3-15 An industrial oven contains 10 kW/230 V of electric heat. The supply conductors must run through the interior of the oven for a distance of 25 m. The oven temperature varies from 20°C to 250°C. Using copper conductors, determine the circular mil area and gauge size of the supply conductors while maintaining no more than a 3 percent voltage drop in transmission. (Hint: The specific resistance of copper at a temperature other than 20°C is no longer 17.2×10^{-9} ohm-metre.)

Energy and Power

As was stated in Chap. 1, electricity is a convenient form of energy. Therefore, the study of electricity, particularly electric power technology involves a study of energy and related subjects.

In this chapter, the concepts of weight, mass, force, work, energy, and power are introduced, together with a discussion of the units of measurement used for these quantities.

4-1
Weight and Mass

The **weight** of an object is a measure of the pull or force exerted on it by the gravitational effect of the earth. Thus, the weight of an object will vary with its position in the universe in accordance with the gravitational pull on it (note the experience of weightlessness in outer space). Although weight is actually a measure of gravitational force, the normally accepted units of measurement in commercial and everyday use are the kilogram and the pound.

The **mass** of an object is defined as the quantity of matter that it contains. Mass is usually determined by dividing the weight of an object, as determined by a weighing scale, by the **gravitational constant, g**, or

$$Mass = \frac{weight}{g}$$

The unit of mass in the SI is the **kilogram** (kg) and in the Imperial System, the **pound** (lb.). The gravitational constants at sea level on the earth are

$$SI, \quad g = 9.81 \quad (metres/sec^2)$$

$$Imperial, \quad g = 32.2 \quad (feet/sec^2)$$

4-2
Force

As systems of scientific and engineering units have evolved over the years, the concepts of force and attempts at definition have undergone many changes. However, a presently well-accepted engineering definition of the word *force* is as follows: *A force is that which changes or tends to change the state of rest or motion of a body.*

According to Newton's second law of motion, a body, when acted upon by a force, will be accelerated in direct proportion to the magnitude of the force so acting. Thus, in whatever system of units being used, a unit force acting upon a unit mass causes unit acceleration.

The SI unit of force called the **Newton** (N) is defined as the force which when applied to a mass of one kilogram (kg) gives it an acceleration of one metre per second per second. Thus, in the SI, explicitly distinct units are used for force and mass, namely, the Newton and the kilogram.

The unit of force used in engineering calculations in the Imperial System has been the **pound-force** from which the suffix force was, in practice, often dropped. This is the force which will give a mass of one pound an acceleration of one foot per second per second.

4-3
Work

Work is done when a force overcomes a resistance. In a mechanical sense, work is measured by the product of a force and the distance through which it acts. When a force of one Newton acts through a distance of one metre, one joule (J) of work is done. If a force of 20 N is required to lift a body 30 m, the work is 20 × 30 or 600 J. Thus,

$$\text{Work} = \text{force} \times \text{distance}$$

In Imperial units, the unit of work is the foot pound (ft-lb), which is defined as the work done when a force of one pound is exerted through a distance of one foot. If, for example, a force of 10 lb. is applied to move a body 6 ft., the work done is 10 × 6 or 60 ft-lb. One joule is equal to 0.737 ft-lb.

Work is not done unless resistance is overcome and movement takes place. A building foundation exerts a tremendous force in holding up the building but, since there is no motion involved or no resistance being overcome, no work is done.

4-4
Energy

Energy is the ability to do work; energy is stored work. A tank of air under pressure has energy for, when released through an air hammer, it performs work. A coiled spring has energy since it is able to run a watch for an entire day. Water stored behind a dam also has energy since it may be used to operate turbine generators to generate electricity.

Since energy is stored work, energy is expended whenever work is done. Energy may exist in many forms — mechanical, electric, chemical, heat, and light — and its form is readily changed. For example, an electric generator changes mechanical energy to electric energy; a storage battery changes chemical energy to electric energy. When coal is burned, chemical energy is changed to heat energy, and so on. In accordance with the principle of the conservation of energy, energy may be transformed but it cannot be created, nor can it be destroyed. The electric generator does not create electric energy, it merely changes mechanical energy to electric energy. Nor is the energy supplied to an electric lamp destroyed; it is merely converted to light and heat energy.

According to the definition of work, if 1000 kg of cargo is lifted to a height of 10 m, the work required is 1000 × 9.81 × 10 or 98 100 J. Nothing is said of the time required to raise the cargo, only that 98.1 kJ of work is required.

4-5

Mechanical Power

One motor driving the cargo winch may require two minutes to raise the load, while a second motor may accomplish the same result in half a minute. Work is done four times as fast by the second motor as by the first, or it is said that the second motor develops four times as much **power** as the first. Thus, *power is the rate of doing work*, or

$$Power = \frac{work}{time} \quad \text{(watt)}$$

When work is done at the rate of one joule per second, the power in SI units is one watt. In the example of the cargo winch, the power required to raise the cargo in 2 min. is

$$\frac{98\ 100}{2 \times 60} \text{ or } 817.5 \text{ W}$$

(Since 746 W = 1 hp, 817.5 W = 1.1 hp).
The horsepower required in the second case is

$$\frac{98\ 100}{30} \text{ or } 3270 \text{ W}$$

$$\frac{3270}{746} \text{ or } 4.38 \text{ hp}$$

Likewise, in SI units, when work is done at the rate of one joule per second, the power is one **watt** (W), which is the SI unit for both mechanical and electric power.

The distinctions between work, energy, and power are important. *Work is the overcoming of resistance. Energy is the ability to do work. Power is the rate of doing work or the rate at which energy is expended.*

The commonly used mechanical units of energy, work, and power are summarized in the following:

The Imperial unit of work or energy is the foot pound (ft-lb).
The SI unit of work or energy is the joule (J).

One joule = 0.737 foot pounds.

The Imperial unit of power is the horsepower (hp).
The SI unit of power is the watt (W).

One horsepower = 746 watts.

4-6
Electric Power

The unit of electric power is the *watt*. One watt is defined as being equal to work being done at the rate of one joule per second. The watt is also defined as the energy expended or the work done per second by an unvarying current of one ampere flowing under a pressure of one volt, or

$$P = IV \qquad \text{(watt)} \qquad\qquad \text{[4-1]}$$

where P = power, watts
        I = current, amperes
        V = voltage, volts

Example 4-1

What is the power used by an electric lamp that draws 2.5 A from a 120-V line?

$$P = IV$$

$$P = 2.5 \times 120$$

$$P = 300 \text{ W}$$

The fact that the watt is a unit of power or a unit of a rate of doing work cannot be emphasized too strongly. It will be remembered that current in amperes is a rate of flow of electricity or is equal to the number of coulombs per second. The power formula may then be written

$$\text{Power in watts} = \frac{\text{coulombs}}{\text{second}} \times \textit{volts}$$

In other words, *the watt is a measure of how fast a quantity of electricity is being moved through a difference in potential.*

Since by Ohm's law $V = IR$, this value of V may be substituted in Eq. (4-1) to obtain another useful power formula:

$$P = IV$$

$$P = I \times IR$$

or $$P = I^2R \qquad\qquad \text{[4-2]}$$

Example 4-2

What is the power used in a 60-Ω generator field rheostat when the field current is 2 A?

$$P = I^2R$$

$$P = 2^2 \times 60$$

$$P = 240 \text{ W}$$

A third power formula may be derived from the fact that $I = \dfrac{V}{R}$ by Ohm's law. Substituting in Eq. (4-1),

$$P = IV$$

$$P = \frac{V}{R} V$$

or
$$P = \frac{V^2}{R} \qquad [4\text{-}3]$$

Example 4-3

What is the power used by a 15-Ω electric heater when a voltage of 120 V is applied?

$$P = \frac{V^2}{R}$$

$$P = \frac{120^2}{15}$$

$$P = \frac{14\ 400}{15}$$

$$P = 960 \text{ W}$$

As illustrated in the above examples, Eq. (4-1) is used to find the power in a circuit when the current and voltage are known, Eq. (4-2) when the current and resistance are known, and Eq. (4-3) when the voltage and resistance are known.

Since the watt is a small unit, a larger unit — the **kilowatt** (kW) — is often used instead. *One kilowatt is equal to one thousand watts.*

Calculations concerning electric machinery often involve both the electric unit of power (watt) and the mechanical unit (horsepower). *One horsepower is equal to 746 W.* Therefore, to change power in watts to power in horsepower, it is necessary to divide the number of watts by 746.

> ### E x a m p l e 4 - 4
>
> The input to a motor is 20 kW. What is the horsepower input?
>
> $$20 \text{ kW} = 20 \times 1000 \text{ W} = 20\ 000 \text{ W}$$
>
> $$\text{Horsepower} = \frac{\text{watts}}{746} = \frac{20\ 000}{746} = 26.8 \text{ hp}$$

For most purposes, the relation between the horsepower and the kilowatt may be taken as

$$1 \text{ hp} = 0.75 \text{ kW} \qquad \text{(approximately)}$$

|4-**7**
Electric Work and Energy

Power is a measure of how fast work is being done or of how fast energy is being expended, that is,

$$\text{Power} = \frac{\text{work or energy}}{\text{time}}$$

Thus, the energy used by an electric device is the rate at which the energy is being used (the power) multiplied by the time during which the device is in use. When power is measured in watts and time in hours, then

$$\text{Power} \times \text{time} = \text{energy}$$

or $$\text{Watts} \times \text{hours} = \text{watt hours}$$

the **watt hour** (Wh) being the energy expended when one watt is used for one hour.

The watt hour is a relatively small unit, so the **kilowatt hour** is used much more extensively in commercial measurements. One kilowatt hour is equal to one thousand watt hours.

> ### E x a m p l e 4 - 5
>
> How much energy is used by a 1500-W heater in 8 h?
>
> $$\text{Energy} = \text{power} \times \text{time}$$
>
> $$= 1500 \times 8$$
>
> $$= 12\ 000 \text{ Wh}$$
>
> $$= \frac{12\ 000}{1000} \text{ or } 12 \text{ kWh}$$

If power is measured in watts and time in seconds, then

$$\text{Power} \times \text{time} = \text{energy}$$

and $$\text{Watts} \times \text{seconds} = \text{watt seconds}$$

The watt second is called a **joule**, which is the SI unit for electric as well as mechanical energy. Since there are 3600 seconds in an hour and 1000 W in a kilowatt, one kilowatt hour is equal to 3 600 000 J or 3.6 MJ.

Example 4-6

How much energy in joules, megajoules, and kilowatt hours is used by a 100-W lamp in 12 h?

$$\text{Energy in joules} = \text{watts} \times \text{seconds}$$

$$= 100 \times 12 \times 3600$$

$$= 4\ 320\ 000 \text{ J}$$

$$= 4.32 \text{ MJ}$$

$$\text{Energy in kilowatt hours} = \frac{\text{watts} \times \text{hours}}{1000}$$

$$= \frac{100 \times 12}{1000}$$

$$= 1.2 \text{ kWh}$$

$$1.2 \text{ kWh} \times 3.6 = 4.32 \text{ MJ} \qquad \text{(check)}$$

Power is the rate of expending energy just as speed is a rate of motion. If the average speed of an automobile is known for a given time, the distance travelled is the average speed multiplied by the time travelled. Likewise, if the average power required by an electric motor for a given time is known, the energy used by the motor is the average power multiplied by the time the motor is used. The reader should make sure that the difference between power and energy is understood. Power is the *rate* of expending energy or of doing work, just as speed is a *rate* of motion.

The commonly used electrical units of energy, work, and power are summarized in the following:

The Imperial unit of work or energy = watt hour (Wh).
The SI unit of work or energy = joule (J).

$$1 \text{ Wh} = 3600 \text{ J}$$

$$1 \text{ kWh} = 3.6 \text{ MJ}$$

The Imperial unit of power = watt (W).
The SI unit of power = watt (W).

4-**8**

Measurement of Electric Power and Energy

It should be noted that the SI units for work, energy, and power are the same whether the process is mechanical or electrical.

The power being used by a lamp, motor, or other device in a dc circuit may be determined by measuring both the current and the voltage and calculating the power by means of the formula $P = IV$. Power may also be measured directly by means of a **watt meter**. The watt meter, which is described in Chap. 19, is an instrument with both a current and a voltage or potential element. The current element is connected in series and the potential element in parallel with the circuit in which the power is being measured, as shown in Fig. 4-1. The power in watts, being a product of current and voltage, is indicated directly on the scale of the watt meter.

Electric energy is measured by means of the **watt hour meter**. This is the familiar type of meter used in the home to determine the monthly electric bill. The connections of the watt hour meter are the same as those of the watt meter, a current element being connected in series and a potential element being connected in parallel with the circuit. However, the watt hour meter has a rotating element, the speed of which at any time is proportional to the power being used at that time. The total number of revolutions over a period of time is then proportional to the energy used in

F I G U R E **4-1**
Connection of a wattmeter to measure the power supplied to the load.

FIGURE **4-2**

Typical dial arrangement of a kWh meter. See Fig. 19-13 for pictorial view.

that time. The rotating element drives a gear train that records on a row of dials the number of kilowatt hours used. The amount of energy, in kilowatt hours, used during a certain period is then the dial reading at the beginning of the period subtracted from the dial reading at the end of the period. See Fig. 4-2.

The user of electricity then pays for the amount of energy or *kilowatt hours* used and not the power in kilowatts. Power is the measure of how fast energy is being used at any given time as evidenced by the speed of the rotating element of the watt hour meter at that time. The energy used, however, over a certain period of time is determined by the total number of revolutions made by the watt hour meter in that time.

E x a m p l e 4 - 7

For the dial positions of Fig. 4-2, determine the energy cost if the previous reading was 6420 kWh, and the average cost is $0.03 per kWh.

SOLUTION:

(new reading − previous reading)

9521 − 6420 = 3101 kWh used

3101 kWh × $0.03/kWh = $93.03

E x a m p l e 4 - 8

What is the total cost when the following appliances are in use?

a) 4 − 60 W lamps for 6 h
b) 1 − 1250 W toaster for 10 min.
c) 1 − 1200 W kettle for 20 min.
d) 1 − 5500 W clothes dryer for 1.5 h
e) 1 − 600 W washing machine for 0.75 h

Average cost is $0.03 per kWh.

SOLUTION:

$$\text{Energy in Wh} = (4 \times 60 \times 6) + \left(1250 \times \frac{1}{6}\right)$$

$$+ \left(1200 \times \frac{1}{3}\right) + (5500 \times 1.5)$$

$$+ (600 \times 0.75)$$

$$= 10\ 750$$

$$10\ 750\ \text{Wh}/1000 = 10.75\ \text{kWh}$$

$$\text{Cost} = 10.75\ \text{kWh} \times \$0.03/\text{kWh} = \$0.3225 \text{ or } 32.25\text{¢}$$

4-9
Line Loss

Whenever a current flows through a resistance, the resistance becomes heated, or it is said that electric energy is transformed into heat energy. The rate at which the electric energy is transformed into heat is called power, and the common way of finding this power is by the formula $P = I^2R$. In other words, the rate at which energy is expended in a resistance is proportional to the square of the current.

Because the conductors of a transmission or distribution circuit have resistance, the conductors become heated whenever a current flows through them. Since this heat is lost to the surrounding air, it is called a **line loss**. This loss of power is proportional to the square of the current flowing, and for this reason it is desirable to transmit power with as low a current value as possible to keep the line losses from being excessive. Power supplied to a load is the product of current and voltage. The current required to transmit a given amount of power may be made small by using higher voltages. The higher the voltage, the lower the current for a given amount of power. The advantages obtained by increasing the voltage used to transmit a given amount of power will be illustrated by the following example.

Example 4-9

A 12-kW load is supplied from a line that has a resistance of 0.1 Ω in each conductor. Find the line loss in watts when the load is supplied at (*a*) 120 V and (*b*) 240 V.

$$(a) \qquad I = \frac{P}{V}$$

$$I = \frac{12\ 000}{120}$$

$$I = 100\ \text{A}$$

Line loss (both lines) $P = I^2 R$

$$P = 100^2 \times 0.2$$

$$P = 2000\ \text{W}$$

(b) $$I = \frac{P}{V}$$

$$I = \frac{12\ 000}{240}$$

$$I = 50\ \text{A}$$

Line loss (both lines) $P = I^2 R$

$$P = 50^2 \times 0.2$$

$$P = 500\ \text{W}$$

Note in the above example that the same power may be transmitted at 240 V with one-fourth the line loss as at 120 V. Or the power could be transmitted at the same loss with conductors one-fourth as large at 240 V as at 120 V.

Example 4-10

If a 1200 watt/240 volt electric baseboard heater is operated at 120 V, determine the amount of power in the form of heat the heater will provide.

$$P' = \left(\frac{V}{V'}\right)^2 P$$

$$P' = \left(\frac{120}{240}\right)^2 1200$$

$$P' = 300\ \text{W}$$

where P' = power at V'
 P = power at V

$$P = \frac{V^2}{R} \quad \therefore R = \frac{V^2}{P}$$

$$R = \frac{240^2}{1200}$$

or $$R = 48$$

$$P' = \frac{V'^2}{R}$$

$$P' = \frac{120^2}{48}$$

$$P' = 300 \text{ W}$$

Example 4-10 illustrates that any power-rated device must be at a specified voltage. When the voltage is varied from rated value, the power dissipated by the device will vary as per the square of the voltage change.

4-10

Efficiency and Losses

Efficiency can be described as a ratio of output power to input power. This expression is usually in the form of a percent.

$$\% \eta = \frac{P_o}{P_i} \times 100 \qquad\qquad \text{[4-4]}$$

where η (eta) is the symbol used for efficiency
      P_o = output power
      P_i = input power

Therefore,

$$\text{Efficiency} = \frac{\text{Power output}}{\text{Power input}}$$

Example 4-11

An electric motor delivers 5 hp to its connected load when connected to a 230 V source while drawing 25 A. Determine the efficiency of the motor.

SOLUTION:

$$\% \eta = \frac{P_o}{P_i} \times 100$$

$$\%\eta = \frac{5 \times 746}{230 \times 25} \times 100$$

$$\eta = 64.9\%$$

Equipment or machine losses are defined as the difference between the power delivered to the machine and the power output of that machine.

$$\text{Losses} = \text{Power input} - \text{Power output}$$

These losses can occur in several forms. Types of losses will be described in further chapters where specific electric equipment is discussed.

Example 4-12

A generator has an efficiency of 85 percent. Its output voltage is 115 V while delivering 30 A. Determine the input power delivered to drive the generator.

SOLUTION:

$$\eta = \frac{P_o}{P_i}$$

Therefore,

$$P_i = \frac{P_o}{\eta}$$

$$P_i = \frac{115 \times 30}{0.85}$$

$$P_i = 4059 \text{ W}$$

FIGURE **4-3**
Efficiency of systems in cascade.

FIGURE **4-4**
Block diagram format of Fig. 4-3.

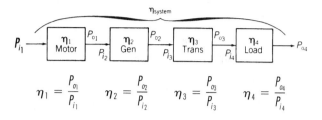

$$\eta_1 = \frac{P_{o_1}}{P_{i_1}} \qquad \eta_2 = \frac{P_{o_2}}{P_{i_2}} \qquad \eta_3 = \frac{P_{o_3}}{P_{i_3}} \qquad \eta_4 = \frac{P_{o_4}}{P_{i_4}}$$

The total efficiency of the system can be determined by forming the product of these four efficiencies:

$$\eta_1 \times \eta_2 \times \eta_3 \times \eta_4 = \frac{P_{o_1}}{P_{i_1}}$$

$$\eta_2 = \frac{P_{o_2}}{P_{i_2}} \qquad \eta_3 = \frac{P_{o_3}}{P_{i_3}} \qquad \eta_4 = \frac{P_{o_4}}{P_{i_4}}$$

Since $P_{o_1} = P_{i_2}$ and
          $P_{o_2} = P_{i_3}$ and
          $P_{o_3} = P_{i_4}$ then

these quantities can be cancelled in the above expression, leaving P_{o_4}/P_{i_1}, which is an expression of the efficiency of the entire system.

Therefore, $\eta_{Total} = \eta_1 \times \eta_2 \times \eta_3 \times \eta_4 \times \eta_n$ [4-5]

Example 4-13

Determine the overall efficiency of the system in Fig. 4-4 if:

$$\eta_1 = 80\%$$

$$\eta_2 = 65\%$$

$$\eta_3 = 90\%$$

$$\eta_4 = 96\%$$

SOLUTION:

$$\eta_T = 0.8 \times 0.065 \times 0.9 \times 0.096$$

$$\eta_T = 0.449 \text{ or } 44.9\%$$

REVIEW QUESTIONS

1 Define the term weight. What are the Imperial and SI units of measurement in everyday commercial use?

2 What is meant by the term mass? How is it determined for any object? What are the units?

3 Give a generally accepted definition of force.

4 What is the SI unit of force? How is it defined?

5 Define work. What are the Imperial and SI units? What is the numerical relationship between the two units?

6 What is energy? Give some examples of different kinds of energy.

7 How is power defined? What are the Imperial and SI units of mechanical power?

8 What is the unit of electric power?

9 Give the power formula in three forms.

10 One kilowatt is equal to how many watts?

11 One horsepower is equal to how many watts?

12 One horsepower is equal to approximately how many kilowatts?

13 How many horsepower are there in one kilowatt?

14 What is another name for the watt second?

15 One kilowatt hour is equal to how many megajoules?

PROBLEMS

4-1 The work done in moving a body through a distance of 40 m is 800 J. What is the value of the force?

4-2 A crane lifts a 3629 kg cargo to a height of 6 m. What is the work done by the crane?

4-3 If the crane in the preceding problem raises the cargo in 30 seconds, what is the average power in (a) in watts; (b) in horsepower?

4-4 A force of 60 Newtons is applied to a body to move it through a distance of 20 m in 8 seconds. What is the value of the power?

4-5 An electric heater has a resistance of 57 Ω. (a) Find the power in kilowatts when the heater is drawing a current of 3.8 A. (b) What is the energy used by the heater in 4 hours in kilowatt hours and in megajoules?

4-6 A 120-V lamp draws 0.8 A. What power does it dissipate?

4-7 The energy used by an electric heater in 24 hours is 1728 MJ. What was the energy used in kilowatt hours? If the heater operated continuously for the 24 hours, what was the average power used?

4-8 A current of 8 A flows through a resistance of 20 Ω. How much power is consumed (*a*) in watts; (*b*) in kilowatts?

4-9 A motor takes 11.2 kW when it is connected to 220-V mains. What current does the motor take?

4-10 The output of a motor is 1.2 kW. What is the horsepower output?

4-11 A dc motor is connected across 10 V supply and draws 50 A. What is the horsepower input to the motor?

4-12 A dc shunt motor draws 60 A at 550 V. (*a*) Find the power consumed in kilowatts. (*b*) If the energy cost is $0.05 per kilowatt hour, find the cost of operating this motor for 10 hours.

4-13 An electric heater uses 20 kWh in 8 hours. If the voltage at the heater is 240 V, what is the resistance of the heater?

4-14 Find the current taken by 40, 60, and 100-W lamps when connected to a 120 V power supply. Determine the time (in hours) needed for each of these lamps to consume 1 kWh.

4-15 The load voltage of a 12-kW load is 400 V. The resistance of each line wire connecting the load to the source is 0.1 Ω. (*a*) What is the voltage at the source? (*b*) What is the power dissipated as heat by the lines? (*c*) How much energy is used by the load in 24 hours? (*d*) How much energy is lost in the lines in 24 hours?

4-16 A motor draws 28 A when connected to a 230-V line. Determine the output hp if the efficiency is 60 percent.

4-17 If the efficiency of η_2 in Example 4-12 is increased to 78 percent, determine the new system efficiency.

Primary and Secondary Batteries

Devices in which chemical energy is changed to electric energy are called **electric cells**. When several cells are connected electrically (usually in series), they form a **battery**.

The essentials of any cell are two *dissimilar* metals or conductors that are immersed in a conducting liquid.

Cells or batteries may be classified into two general types: **primary** and **secondary**. In the primary cell it is necessary to renew the active materials from time to time or to discard the cell when electric energy can no longer be obtained from it. In the secondary, or storage, cell the active materials may be restored by passing a current through the cell in a direction opposite to that of discharge.

In this chapter, the principles of operation and the characteristics of the several types of both primary and secondary cells are discussed.

5-1
Primary Cells

When two dissimilar conductors are placed in a conducting solution that will act chemically on one of the conductors, an electromotive force is developed between the two conductors. The conductors are called **plates** or **electrodes**, and the solution is called the **electrolyte**. When the electrodes are connected by a conductor, a current will flow from one electrode to the other through the conductor with the circuit being completed through the electrolyte. The electrode from which the current leaves the cell is called the **positive electrode**, and the other is called the **negative electrode**.

The emf developed in any cell depends on the materials used for electrodes and electrolyte. For example, if electrodes of zinc and lead are placed in a solution of sulfuric acid, the emf developed is about 0.5 V; zinc and mercuric oxide in potassium hydroxide, about 1.35 V; and zinc and manganese dioxide in potassium hydroxide, about 1.5 V. The size and spacing of the electrodes do not affect the emf developed but do affect other characteristics of the cell.

Numerous combinations of materials have been used in the past for electrodes and electrolytes of primary cells. Early primary cells had spillable electrolytes and, therefore, were not readily portable.

Because of its portability and compact size, the dry cell is now by far the most widely used primary cell.

The performance of primary cells depends upon conditions of service such as temperature, rapidity of discharge, and on whether discharge is continuous or intermittent. Primary cells, therefore, are often rated for a specific use. A cell may be rated, for example, for photo-flash use, flashlight use, transistor radio use, or heavy-duty industrial use. Likewise, cells are designed for special uses such as in watches, hearing aids, cameras, or other electronic equipment.

5-2
Dry Cells

Four widely used types of dry cells are the carbon-zinc (Leclanche and zinc chloride types), the alkaline, the mercuric oxide, and the silver oxide cells. Actually, these cells are not dry but have an electrolyte which is combined with an absorbent inactive material. The cells are, however, sealed into waterproof containers so that they may be easily transported or operated in any position.

The most widely used and probably the most familiar type of dry cell is the general purpose Leclanche type, commonly referred to as the carbon-zinc cell. The basic design of this cell has remained largely unchanged for over half a century. The construction of a typical cell of this type is shown in Fig. 5-1.

F I G U R E **5-1**
Cutaway view of a general purpose carbon-zinc cell.
(Eveready Batteries.)

CUTAWAY OF A CYLINDRICAL GENERAL PURPOSE LECLANCHE CELL

The waterproof zinc can enclosure of the Leclanche cell also serves as the negative electrode. Inside the zinc can is an absorbent or gelatinous substance that is saturated with the electrolyte, which is zinc chloride and ammonium chloride. The positive electrode is a mixture of manganese dioxide and powdered carbon surrounding a carbon rod which serves as a current collector. The mixture serves as a depolarizing agent which prevents the formation of hydrogen bubbles on the carbon rod during discharge of the cell.

The open-circuit emf of a new Leclanche dry cell is about 1.5 V. The capacity of the cell is dependent upon the size of the cell and the rate at which energy is withdrawn. The lower the rate, the more efficiently the cell is able to convert the available chemical energy into electric energy. For this reason, the best application of this cell is for use in intermittent-, light-, or medium-drain service, such as in flashlights or portable radios.

The zinc chloride type of carbon-zinc cell is designated by some manufacturers as their heavy-duty cell. The essential difference between the Leclanche and the zinc chloride cells is that all or most of the ammonium chloride is omitted from the electrolyte in the latter. This results in better performance of the zinc chloride cell for medium- to high-drain duty. Both the Leclanche and zinc chloride cells are recommended for intermittent rather than continuous service.

The alkaline-manganese dioxide cell, commonly referred to as the alkaline cell, was developed to fill the need for a higher continuous-rate energy source than was available in the carbon-zinc cells. Alkaline cell applications include use in portable radios, cassette recorders and players, battery-powered toys, electronic flashes, and similar heavy-drain applications.

The alkaline cell employs a powdered zinc negative electrode, a positive electrode of manganese dioxide, and an electrolyte of potassium hydroxide. It has an open-circuit voltage of 1.5 V, a low internal resistance, and it may be used to replace the carbon-zinc cell where heavier drain and longer life are required. The alkaline cell may contain 50 to 100 percent more total energy than a Leclanche carbon-zinc cell of the same size.

Mercuric oxide and silver oxide cells have similar low-rate, continuous-drain applications. They are often designed to match specific uses rather than for general use. Typical applications are in hearing aids, watches, photoelectric exposure devices, and measuring instruments. Both are fabricated in a flat or "button" configuration. The mercuric oxide cell is also manufactured in a cylindrical cell structure.

Electrochemically, the mercuric oxide and silver oxide cells both use zinc negative electrodes and an electrolyte of either potassium hydroxide or sodium hydroxide. The positive electrode of the silver oxide cell is silver oxide mixed with a small amount of manganese dioxide, resulting in an open-circuit voltage of 1.6 V.

The mercuric oxide cell with a 100 percent mercuric oxide positive electrode has an open-circuit voltage of 1.35 V. With a mixed mercuric oxide and manganese oxide positive electrode, the open-circuit voltage is 1.4 V or more with a slightly different discharge characteristic.

5-3
Internal Resistance of a Cell

The entire resistance encountered by a current as it flows through a cell from the negative terminal to the positive terminal is called the internal resistance of the cell. As in any other conductor of electricity, the resistance of a cell depends on the materials, the cross-sectional area, the length of the current path, and the temperature. Thus, the area and spacing of the electrodes both affect the internal resistance of a cell even though the emf developed is independent of these factors.

The current delivered by a cell depends not only on the emf of the cell and the load resistance, but on the internal resistance of the cell as well. By Ohm's law, the current delivered by a cell is

$$I = \frac{E}{R_i + R_L} \qquad\qquad [5\text{-}1]$$

where I = current, amperes
E = emf, volts
R_i = internal resistance of cell, ohms
R_L = load resistance, ohms

On open circuit, the terminal voltage of a cell is equal to the emf developed. However, when a cell delivers current, some of the emf developed must be used in overcoming the resistance of the

FIGURE **5-2**
Equivalent circuit of a cell or battery.

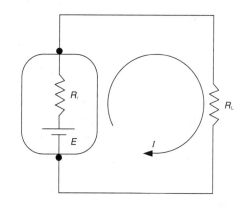

cell itself so that the terminal voltage is lower than the emf. The greater the current delivered, the greater the voltage drop, or IR drop, in the cell and the lower the terminal voltage becomes. The terminal voltage in any case is

$$V_t = E - IR_t \qquad\qquad [5\text{-}2]$$

where V_t = terminal voltage, volts
E = emf, volts
I = current, amperes
R_i = internal resistance, ohms

By transposing Eq. (5-2), we have the following expression for internal resistance:

$$R_i = \frac{E - V_t}{I} \qquad\qquad [5\text{-}3]$$

The relation given in Eq. (5-3) suggests a method of measuring internal resistance. First the open-circuit voltage of the cell is measured to get the value of E. A high-resistance voltmeter should be used so that the current drawn by the voltmeter is negligible. Then, with the cell delivering a current I, the terminal voltage V_t is measured. The internal resistance R_i may then by obtained by means of Eq. (5-3).

The following example will illustrate the effect of different values of internal resistance on the amount of current that a cell is able to deliver to a particular load.

Example 5-1

A coil that has a resistance of 0.05 Ω is connected to a cell that develops an emf of 1.5 V. Find the current flowing if the internal resistance of the cell is (a) 0.1 Ω and (b) 0.01 Ω.

(a) $I = \dfrac{E}{R_i + R_L}$ (b) $I = \dfrac{E}{R_i + R_L}$

$I = \dfrac{1.5}{0.1 + 0.05}$ $I = \dfrac{1.5}{0.01 + 0.05}$

$I = 10$ A $I = 25$ A

5-4
Secondary, or Storage, Cells

A cell in which the physical state and chemical condition of the electrodes and electrolyte may be restored by charging is called a secondary, or storage, cell. Charging such a cell consists of passing current through the cell in a direction opposite to the direction of current flow on discharge. There are several types of storage cells in use, the more common ones being the **lead-acid** and the **nickel-cadmium-alkaline** cells.

As in the primary cell, the emf of a secondary cell depends on the materials used for electrodes and the electrolyte. The average terminal voltage of a lead-acid cell is approximately 2.0 V, while that of the nickel-cadmium-alkaline cell is approximately 1.2 V.

The capacity of a cell, for a given plate thickness, depends on the total plate area — the greater the plate area, the greater the capacity.

5-5
Theory of the Lead-Acid Cell

The positive plate of a lead-acid storage cell is lead peroxide, PbO_2, and the negative plate is pure sponge lead, Pb. Dilute sulfuric acid, H_2SO_4, is used as the electrolyte. When the cell supplies current to a load or is discharging, the chemical action that takes place forms lead sulfate, $PbSO_4$, on both plates with water being formed in the electrolyte. After a certain amount of energy has been withdrawn from the cell, both plates having been transformed into the same material, the cell is no longer able to develop an emf.

To charge the cell, a current is caused to flow through the cell in the opposite direction; this reverses the chemical process and again forms a lead peroxide positive plate and a pure lead negative plate, at the same time restoring the electrolyte to its original condition. The chemical reaction may be represented as follows:

Positive plate	Negative plate	Electrolyte	Positive plate	Negative plate	Electrolyte
PbO_2	+ Pb	+ $2H_2SO_4$	$\rightleftharpoons$ $PbSO_4$	+ $PbSO_4$	+ $2H_2O$

$$\text{Cell charged} \qquad\qquad\qquad \text{Cell discharged}$$

This equation represents the discharging action when read from left to right and the charging action when read from right to left.

5-6
Relative Density of Lead-Acid Cells

The ratio of the weight of a volume of any liquid to the weight of the same volume of water is called the relative (specific) density of the liquid. For example, the relative density of sulfuric acid is 1.840, which means that sulfuric acid is 1.840 times as heavy as water.

The electrolyte of a lead-acid battery is a solution of sulfuric acid in water. In a battery used for stationary work, in which a large volume of electrolyte may be used, the relative density in the fully charged state is about 1.210 to 1.225. In a portable battery, such as those used in automobile and airplane service, and where space and weight are limited, a smaller volume of electrolyte is used. The relative density of the electrolyte in portable batteries is 1.265 to 1.300 when fully charged.

The climate or temperature at which batteries are to be operated is also a factor that is taken into account in determining the relative density to be used. Batteries used in extremely cold climates require electrolytes of higher relative density to prevent freezing. Batteries used in torrid climates require electrolytes of lower relative density to prevent their overheating while in operation.

The amount of decrease in relative density from the fully charged state to the discharged state varies with the volume of the electrolyte. For large volumes of electrolyte, the drop may be as small as 0.030 and for small volumes, as in automobile batteries, it may be as large as 0.145.

The relative density of a cell electrolyte varies with temperature with an increase in temperature of 1°C (3°F) amounting to a drop of about 0.254 mm (0.001 in.) in relative density, or vice versa.

If the relative density of a cell electrolyte is known for the fully charged and discharged conditions, relative density readings may be used as an indication of the state of charge of a battery. Temperature corrections should be used if widely varying temperatures are encountered.

For measuring relative density, an instrument called a **hydrometer** is used. In the syringe-type hydrometer, a part of the electrolyte is drawn from the cell into the syringe. A weighted bulb floats in the electrolyte inside the syringe, the depth at which it floats being a measure of the relative density of the electrolyte being tested. The lower the bulb floats, the lower the relative density. The stem on the bulb is marked for different values of relative density so that the reading on the stem at the surface of the liquid is the density reading of the electrolyte in the syringe.

5-7
Construction of Lead-Acid Batteries

In the pasted-plate battery, used in both stationary and motive power applications, the plates are formed by applying a special lead oxide paste to lead frames or grids. Grids are alloyed with either antimony or calcium to harden the lead and to facilitate the casting of the grids. After charging, the lead oxides become the active material of the plate. The grids serve to hold the active material in place and to distribute the current evenly over the surface of the plate.

Another type of lead-acid cell, known as the tubular-plate cell, is often used in stationary applications. The positive-plate active material in this type of cell is retained in a series of porous plastic or glass fibre tubes supported on a lead grid. The tubular construction is used only on the positive plate for this cell. The positive tubular and the negative pasted plates of a typical tubular-plate cell are shown in Fig. 5-3.

FIGURE **5-3**
Positive (left) and negative (right) plates with separators used in the tubular-plate cell construction.
(Exide Corporation.)

Plates of lead-acid cells are formed into positive and negative groups so that they may be nested together. The number of negative plates is always one more than the number of positive plates so that both sides of each positive plate will be acted upon chemically. This is necessary since the active material on the positive plate expands and contracts as the battery is charged and discharged, and this expansion and contraction must be kept the same on both sides of the plate to prevent buckling.

Separators of wood, rubber, or glass mat similar to those shown in Fig. 5-3 are placed between the positive and negative plates to prevent the plates from coming into contact with each other. Separators are grooved vertically on one side and are smooth on the other. The grooved side is placed against the positive plate to permit free circulation of the electrolyte around the positive plate where the greater chemical action takes place.

The well-known automobile storage battery consists of three or six cells (6- or 12-V nominal rating) connected in series and assembled into one case. The case is made of lightweight acid-proof material such as polypropylene and is divided into separate compartments to accommodate each of the cells. Intercell connections are made with lead-alloy links, and the battery terminals are brought out through sealed openings on the side or top of the case.

Lead-acid cells intended for stationary use are usually contained in glass or plastic jars with hard-rubber covers. For the common application of stationary batteries as the source of control power in power plants or in emergency lighting systems, 60 cells are mounted on steel or wood racks and connected in series to form a nominal 125-V battery. The battery is maintained at full charge by "floating" it continuously on a battery charger at 129 V. A typical 60-cell installation is shown in Fig. 5-4.

The capacity of a battery depends upon the number, the design, and the dimensions of the plates and the quantity of the electrolyte. The amount of energy that any given fully charged battery can deliver also depends upon several variables such as the discharge rate, the temperature, and the relative density of the electrolyte.

Because of the many variables involved, there are several methods of rating battery capacity. Generally, the capacity of any battery may be expressed in **ampere-hours** (Ah), which is simply the product of the discharge in amperes and the duration of the discharge in hours. However, since batteries are often adapted to a particular kind of service, the rating may be based on the requirements for that service.

Stationary batteries for comparatively low-rate discharge service, such as those used in telephone exchanges or as control power supplies in power plants, are rated in ampere-hours at an 8-h rate. This is an ampere-hour rating based on a continuous discharge rate for 8 h under specified conditions, to a final voltage of 1.75 V per cell. Thus, a battery capable of an 8-h discharge rate of 25 A would have an 8-h capacity of 8 × 25 or 200 Ah.

5-**8**

Lead-Acid Battery Ratings

F I G U R E **5-4**

Typical installation of a 60-cell tubular-plate type lead-acid battery.

(Exide Corporation.)

Batteries used in automobiles are given two ratings to express the battery power characteristics. One rating is called the **cold cranking performance rating**. This rating is defined as the number of amperes that a battery can deliver at $-17.8°C$ (0°F) for 30 s and maintain a voltage of 1.2 V per cell or higher. The second rating, called the **reserve capacity performance rating**, is a measure of the ability of a battery to supply an automobile electric load in the event of a failure of the charging system. This rating is defined as the number of minutes a battery at 26.7°C (80°F) can be discharged at 25 A and maintain a voltage of 1.75 V per cell or higher. As an example, a six-cell, 12-V passenger automobile battery might have cranking performance rating of 450 A and a reserve capacity performance rating of 138 min.

5-9
Operation and Maintenance of Lead-Acid Batteries

In the normal operation of a conventional lead-acid storage battery, a certain amount of water is lost from the electrolyte by evaporation and because of gassing. Gassing takes place during charging when the water in the electrolyte is decomposed to hydrogen and oxygen, each of which are given off in the form of gas. The level of the electrolyte should never be allowed to fall below the tops of the plates, and it should be kept at the proper level by adding pure distilled water at regular intervals. Acid is not added to a battery unless the electrolyte has been spilled.

Lead-acid batteries should not be discharged further after a terminal voltage of about 1.75 V per cell is reached and the relative density has dropped its normal amount. Further discharge produces an excess of lead sulfate on the plates.

A lead-acid battery should not be left in the discharged condition for any length of time since the lead sulfate on the plates crystallizes so that proper reforming of the plates becomes difficult if not impossible. If a battery is to be stored for any length of time, water should be added to the proper level, after which the battery should be fully charged. At intervals of 4 to 6 weeks the battery should be given a freshening charge to keep it in the fully charged state.

Batteries may be charged at almost any rate provided the cell temperature does not exceed 43°C (110°F) and that excessive gassing does not take place. Usual practice is to charge at a tapered rate, that is, at a high rate at first but at a gradually reduced rate as the battery becomes nearly charged. Charging should continue until all cells are gassing freely and until the relative density of the electrolyte and the terminal voltage of the battery are constant for a period of 1 h. Although violent gassing or gassing for long periods should be avoided, a small amount of gassing for a short time at the end of a charge is desirable to ensure that no lead sulfate remains on the plates.

As indicated in Sec. 5-9, a lead-acid battery produces both hydrogen and oxygen during the recharging process. This results in the loss of water in the battery electrolyte, particularly in an automobile battery which may often be subjected to overcharging. This has led to the development of the so-called maintenance-free battery for automotive use.

The maintenance-free battery has a modified design which limits the amount of gassing and thereby eliminates the need for adding water periodically. Grids of this battery are alloyed with calcium rather than antimony. Impurities in grids, electrolyte, lead, and other parts of the battery are reduced to a minimum. Also, more space is provided for the electrolyte. As a result of these design modifications, gassing is virtually eliminated.

Since there is no need to add water in the maintenance-free battery, no vent caps are provided. Thus the relative density of the battery cannot be measured by conventional means to indicate the state of charge. The state of charge must be determined from voltage readings taken during a load test prescribed by the battery manufacturer. Some batteries have a built-in hydrometer to give some measure of the battery state of charge.

In addition to the elimination of the need for the periodic addition of water, the maintenance-free battery has reduced terminal corrosion and long shelf life and, because of its low internal resistance, it has a good cold cranking performance rating. A typical heavy-duty, maintenance-free 12-V automotive battery with a built-in hydrometer is shown in Fig. 5-5. This battery has a cold cranking performance rating of 475 A and is recommended for use with large diesel or gasoline engines.

5-10
Maintenance-Free Automotive Batteries

The nickel-cadmium-alkaline battery, usually referred to as the nickel-cadmium battery, has been used in Europe since about 1910 but did not find extensive acceptance in North America until after about 1945. Experience indicates that the nickel-cadmium battery is extremely reliable and has a long life expectancy.

In the nickel-cadmium cell, the principal active material in the positive plate is nickel hydroxide; in the negative plate it is cadmium hydroxide. The electrolyte is potassium hydroxide. During charge or discharge there is practically no change in the relative density of the electrolyte. The sole function of the electrolyte is to act as a conductor for the transfer of hydroxyl ions (electrically charged particles) from one plate to the other depending on whether the cell is being charged or discharged.

5-11
The Nickel-Cadmium Battery

FIGURE **5-5**
Maintenance-free automotive battery.
(Delco-Remy Division, General Motors Corporation.)

Nickel-cadmium cells may be the vented type or the sealed type. Under certain charging conditions the vented type of cell will liberate gases, which are vented to the atmosphere through a valve in the top of the cell. In the sealed type, the design of the cell is such that the evolution of hydrogen gas is completely suppressed at the negative plate, and the oxygen which is evolved at the positive plate combines chemically with the cadmium of the negative plate.

The average discharge voltage per cell of the nickel-cadmium battery is 1.2 V. However, the voltage per cell may be as high as 1.40 to 1.44 V when the cell is being maintained in the fully charged state by a trickle charger. Ten cells make up a nominal 12-V battery which is normally trickle-charged at about 14.0 V.

The nickel-cadmium battery is characterized by its low maintenance cost, long life, and reliability under severe operating conditions. The battery can be left idle for long periods of time in any state of charge without deteriorating. It will not freeze even in the completely discharged condition. Sealed cells and batteries have a life expectancy in excess of 300 to 500 cycles of charge and discharge under normal operating conditions. Vented-cell life expectancy in cyclical operation is claimed to be more than 2000 cycles.

Two different basic constructions are used in the nickel-cadmium cell: the pocket-plate and the sintered-plate constructions.

The term **pocket-plate cell** is derived from the manner in which the cell plates are constructed. In this type of cell, pockets are used to hold the active materials. As constructed by one manufacturer, the pockets are made with finely perforated nickel-plated steel strips formed into channels. A perforated steel cover strip is crimped into place to form a permanent envelope to hold the active materials. Pockets are interlocked, cut to length, and inserted into a steel frame. Alternate positive and negative plates, with insulation between, form plate groups which are assembled into translucent plastic containers. A number of cells may be enclosed in one container to form a battery of the required nominal voltage, or the battery may be formed by interconnecting a number of individual cells mounted on a rack. A cutaway view of a single pocket-plate cell is shown in Fig. 5-6, and an assembly of cells forming a 24-V battery is shown in Fig. 5-7.

Pocket-plate batteries, because of their rugged construction and ability to withstand temperature extremes, are often used for train-car lighting and diesel engine cranking service. Other applications include use as emergency power supplies and as control power batteries in power stations.

5-12
The Pocket-Plate, Nickel-Cadmium Cell

F I G U R E **5-6**
Cutaway view of a pocket-plate, nickel-cadmium cell.
(Cooper Power Systems.)

F I G U R E **5-7**
A typical 24-V assembly of pocket-plate, nickel-cadmium cells.
(Cooper Power Systems.)

5-13

The Sintered-Plate, Nickel-Cadmium Cell

Sintered-plate cells may be either vented or scaled and are made in several physical configurations. The most widely used is the sealed cylindrical type, which is sometimes used as a direct replacement for primary cells in such devices as portable tape recorders, radios, or calculators. These cells are available in capacities ranging from about 1 to 7 Ah.

Plates of the sintered-plate cell are made from a nickel powder applied to a nickel-plated steel base and heated to a very high temperature. The resulting plate is a highly porous structure whose pores are impregnated with the active material, forming a plate with a large surface area.

The plates in cylindrical sintered-plate cells are wound to form a compact coil and are isolated from each other by a porous separator, usually nylon. The separator is saturated with the potassium hydroxide electrolyte. A nickel-plated steel shell serves as the negative terminal, and the cell cover, which is insulated from the shell, serves as the positive terminal. Several sizes of cylindrical sealed nickel-cadmium cells are shown in Fig. 5-8.

In addition to the widely used cylindrical configuration, sealed sintered-plate cells are available in rectangular and oval shapes having greater capacities than the cylindrical types.

Applications of sealed nickel-cadmium cells, in addition to replacements for primary cells, include their use as power supplies for cordless devices, as alternate battery power sources, and as emergency stand-by power sources.

5-14

Applications of Storage Batteries

A very important use of storage batteries is in the providing of stand-by power for various electrical systems. In some electrical systems, storage batteries are connected in parallel with the generator and the load. When the generator is in operation, the battery draws enough current to keep it fully charged. When the generator is shut down, the battery supplies the load. Batteries are also an essential part of uninterruptable power supplies as described in Chap. 20.

Railway car lighting systems are supplied from axle-driven generators when the train is in motion, with batteries supplying the system when the train runs at slow speeds or is stopped.

Automobile electrical systems are similar to the above-mentioned system in that the generator, battery, and load are connected in parallel, and the battery supplies power for starting and lighting when the generator is not in operation.

In ac generating plants, storage batteries are used to energize control apparatus and, during emergency shutdowns of the generators, are used to supply emergency lights. Hospitals and other

FIGURE **5-8**
Sealed nickel-cadmium batteries with charger.

(General Electric Company.)

places where a continuous source of power is absolutely essential often use batteries as an emergency supply.

Applications in which storage batteries supply the primary or normal current are in industrial-truck or mine-locomotive propulsion, portable lighting equipment, portable radios, and other applications in which continuous connection to a generator is impractical.

PROBLEMS

1 What is the function of an electric cell?
2 What are the essential parts of an electric cell?
3 Upon what does the emf of a cell depend?
4 How do primary and secondary cells differ?
5 Upon what factor does the internal resistance of a cell depend?
6 Why does the terminal voltage of a cell drop with increases in current output?
7 How can internal resistance be determined?
8 Name four types of dry cells.

9 Describe the construction of the Leclanche dry cell.

10 What materials are used for electrodes in the mercuric oxide cell?

11 Name two types of storage cells.

12 Describe briefly the chemical action that takes place in the lead-acid cell.

13 What is meant by the term relative density? Why is it valuable to know the relative density of the electrolyte of a lead-acid cell? How is it measured?

14 How are lead-acid batteries rated as to capacity?

15 Describe briefly the construction of the lead-acid battery.

16 Why is it necessary to add water to the electrolyte of a lead-acid cell?

17 Why should lead-acid cells not be discharged below certain levels? Should a lead-acid battery be left standing in the discharged condition? Why?

18 What two things limit the charging rate of a lead-acid cell?

19 What are the active materials in the nickel-cadmium cell?

20 What are the two types of construction used in the nickel-cadmium cell?

21 Give some of the more important characteristics of the nickel-cadmium battery.

22 Give several general applications of storage batteries.

Magnetism

Magnetism is involved in the operation of a great number of electric devices, such as generators, motors, measuring instruments, and transformers. For this reason, a knowledge of the underlying principles of magnetism is essential before the operation of electric machinery may be understood. This chapter and the following one, therefore, are intended to provide background information for the later discussions of electric machinery.

6-1

Magnets and Magnetic Materials

It has been known for centuries that certain materials have the ability of attracting iron and steel. A body possessing this property is called a **magnet**. Magnets are found in a natural state in the form of the mineral called magnetite. However, natural magnets have little practical value and commercial magnets are made artificially from iron and steel or alloy materials.

Magnets may be classified as being **permanent** or **temporary**, depending on their ability to retain magnetism. Hardened steel and certain alloys of nickel and cobalt, when magnetized, retain their magnetism indefinitely and are called **permanent magnets**. However, when a piece of soft iron is magnetized, it retains but a small part of its magnetism after the magnetizing force is removed.

The amount of magnetism retained by a magnet after the magnetizing force is removed is called **residual magnetism**. The fact that temporary magnets are able to retain even a small amount of magnetism plays an important part in the operation of generators, as will be shown in Chap. 8.

Permanent magnets are used extensively in electric instruments and in meters, telephone receivers, and magnetos. In electric generators and motors where it is desirable to control the amount of magnetism present in the magnet, soft-iron temporary magnets are used.

Materials that are attracted or repelled by a magnet are called **magnetic materials**. Iron and steel are by far the most common magnetic materials. Nickel and cobalt and some of their alloys are also magnetic, the alloys being used in high-grade, permanent magnets.

When a material is easy to magnetize, it is said to have a high *permeability*. Soft iron, being relatively easy to magnetize, has a high permeability. Steel is hard to magnetize and, therefore, has a much lower permeability than soft iron.

A straight bar of steel when magnetized is called a **bar magnet**. When a bar magnet is dipped into iron filings, it is found that the filings are attracted in great numbers at the ends of the bar while very few are attracted to the centre of the magnet. The areas at the end of the magnet where the attractive force is the greatest are called the **poles** of the magnet.

6-2
Magnetic Fields and Lines of Force

It has been stated that magnets have an attractive force for certain materials. With the aid of a compass, which is merely a freely suspended magnetized steel needle, the direction of the magnetic force may be determined at various points near a magnet. As shown in Fig. 6-1, the marked end of the compass needle always points away from one pole and toward the other. At the centre of the magnet the needle points in a direction parallel to the magnet. The pole toward which the needle points is called the **south pole** of the magnet, and the other pole is called the **north pole**.

Another way of determining the polarity of a magnet is to suspend or pivot it at its centre. The magnet will then come to rest in a north-south direction. The end of the magnet pointing north is called the **north pole** of the magnet, while the end pointing south is called the **south pole**.

When the directions to which the compass needle points as it is moved slowly from the north to the south pole of the magnet are plotted as in Fig. 6-1, the resulting figure shows that the magnetic force has definite direction at all points and acts along a curved line from north to south. Such a line is called a **line of force**, or a **flux line**. While lines of force are really imaginary lines surrounding a magnet, they are helpful in forming a picture of the nature of magnetism.

The space around a magnet or the space in which magnetic forces act is called a **magnetic field** and may be considered to be

---

FIGURE **6-1**
Direction of the magnetic force around a bar magnet as indicated by a compass needle.

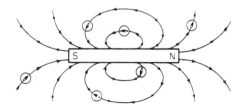

made up of many lines of force. The compass needle shows that the lines of force emerge from the north pole of a magnet, pass through the surrounding medium, and reenter via the south pole. Inside the magnet, each line of force passes from the south pole to the north pole, thus forming a complete closed loop or magnetic circuit independently; that is, the lines do not cut across or merge into other magnetic lines.

An excellent graphical demonstration of the magnetic field pattern around a magnet may be made by placing a sheet of cardboard over a magnet and sifting fine iron filings over the cardboard. The filings, being magnetic bodies, arrange themselves in definite paths or lines between the poles. The pattern formed shows the shape of the field to be about as shown in Fig. 6-2.

To show that the magnetic field exists on all sides of the magnet, the magnet may be turned on edge. A pattern similar to that of Fig. 6-2 again results. The magnetic field exists in the entire space surrounding a magnet.

The magnetic field surrounding a magnet is called the **magnetic flux**, and the unit of magnetic flux is the **weber** (wb). Its symbol is Φ (phi), where $1wb = 1 \times 10^8$ lines of magnetic force. The intensity of the magnetic flux or the flux per unit area is called the **flux density**. The unit of flux density is the **tesla** (T) and is equal to a density of one weber per square metre.

$$B = \frac{\phi}{A} \quad \text{(Tesla)} \qquad\qquad \text{[6-1]}$$

where $B = wb/m^2$,   (webers per square metre or Teslas)
            $\Phi = wb$,   (weber)
            $A = m^2$ (square metres)
Therefore, $1T = 1\ wb/m^2$

FIGURE **6-2**
Field around a bar magnet.

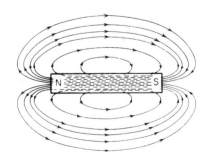

Example 6-1

The field flux from a 10-cm square magnet is 400 x 10⁻⁴ wb. Determine the flux density.

SOLUTION:

$$B = \frac{\phi}{A}$$

$$B = \frac{400 \times 10^{-4}}{(10 \times 10^{-2})^2}$$

$$B = 4 \text{ T}$$

The path in which magnetic flux is established is called a **magnetic circuit**. The magnetic circuit of a bar magnet consists of the path of the magnetic flux through the magnet and the surrounding space. The opposition offered to the establishment of magnetic flux in a magnetic circuit is called the **reluctance** of the circuit. Air has a much higher reluctance than does iron or steel. For this reason, magnetic circuits such as are used in generators and motors are designed with very small air gaps, the greater part of the path followed by the flux being iron.

6-3

Magnetic Attraction and Repulsion

When two magnets are suspended freely with their north poles toward each other, the two magnets push each other apart. The same happens when two south poles are placed near each other. However, when a north pole of one magnet and a south pole of the other are placed near each other, the two magnets attract each other.

The rule of magnetic attraction and repulsion is, then, that *like magnetic poles repel* and *unlike magnetic poles attract* one another.

Upon this rule is based a more accurate picture of a magnetic line of force. If a small north pole were free to move in the field about a magnet, it would be repelled by the north pole of the magnet and attracted by the south pole. The path that this small north pole would follow in moving from north to south is called a line of force, or line of flux. When the paths of flux lines are in parallel and in the same direction they tend to repel each other. Conversely, when the flux lines are parallel and in opposite directions, they tend to attract each other. The understanding of this fact is important when studying the principles of torque development in electric motors.

If a bar magnet is broken into two parts, each part is in itself a complete magnet with both a north and a south pole. If each part is again broken, the resulting parts are magnets. If the process is continued, it is found that the smaller and smaller particles retain their magnetism. If it were physically possible to break a magnet into so many pieces that each piece was a molecule, it would be logical to assume that each of these molecules would be a magnet.

Weber's theory of the nature of magnetism is based on the assumption that each of the molecules of a magnet is a tiny magnet referred to as a magnetic domain. According to this theory, an unmagnetized bar of iron or steel is composed of these tiny molecular magnets and is haphazardly arranged so that the magnetism of each of the molecules is neutralized by an adjacent molecule. See Fig. 6-4(a). However, when a magnetizing force is applied to the iron or steel, the molecules become arranged in a definite pattern with their north and south poles pointing in opposite directions. The magnetism of each of the molecules acting in the same direction establishes the north and south poles of the magnet. See Fig. 6-4(b).

After a magnetizing force is removed from a piece of hardened steel, the molecules of the steel retain their positions indefinitely, while the molecules of a soft-iron bar tend to return to their original position.

In 1819, Oersted found that a definite relation existed between electricity and magnetism. This discovery and later experiments by Henry and Faraday laid the foundation for the development of modern electric machinery.

When a compass is brought into the vicinity of a current-carrying conductor, the needle sets itself at right angles to the conductor, thereby indicating the presence of a magnetic field. If a conductor is passed through a hole in a sheet of cardboard as

6-4
Nature of Magnetism

6-5
Field Around a Current-Carrying Conductor

FIGURE 6-3
Experiment for exploring the field around a conductor.

FIGURE **6-4(a)**
Magnetic domains arranged in a haphazard formation producing no resultant magnetic field in or about the material.

FIGURE **6-4(b)**
Magnetic domains arranged in uniformity, thereby producing a resultant magnetic field in and about the material.

shown in Fig. 6-3 and a current is passed through the conductor, the shape and direction of the field may be determined by setting the compass at various points on the cardboard and noting its deflection. This experiment shows that the magnetic field exists in concentric circles around the conductor. When the current is flowing downward as shown in Fig. 6-3, the field direction is clockwise. However, if the supply polarity is reversed so that current flows upward, the field is found to be counterclockwise. A simple rule, called the right-hand rule for a conductor, for relating the directions of current and field has been established.

Imagine the conductor being grasped in the right hand with the thumb pointing in the direction of the current flow. The fingers then point in the direction of the field around the conductor.

The symbol ⊙ is used in diagrams to denote a cross-sectional view of a conductor carrying current toward the reader, while the symbol ⊕ is used to indicate current flowing away from the reader. These symbols may be thought of as views of an arrow pointing in the direction of current flow; in the former the arrow is approaching, and in the latter the arrow is going away from the reader. Fig. 6-5 illustrates the use of these symbols.

6-6
Field Around a Coil

The magnetism associated with a current-carrying conductor can be intensified by forming the conductor into a **coil** or **solenoid**.

It may be shown how the field is established around a coil by first considering two parallel conductors carrying current in the same direction as in Fig. 6-6. Lines of force pass around each conductor in the same direction, resulting in a field that entirely sur-

FIGURE 6-5

FIGURE **6-5**
Representation of the field around a conductor carrying current (*a*) toward the reader and (*b*) away from the reader.

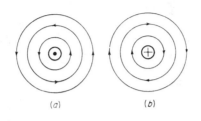

(*a*)   (*b*)

FIGURE **6-6**
Field around two parallel conductors.

rounds the two conductors. Likewise, the field established by a belt of several conductors, all carrying current in the same direction, completely envelops the conductors as shown in Fig. 6-7(*a*). When the current is reversed, the direction of the field is reversed, as in Fig. 6-7(*b*).

FIGURE **6-7**
Field around several conductors all carrying current (*a*) away from the reader and (*b*) toward the reader.

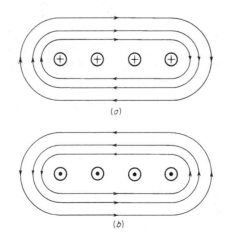

(*a*)

(*b*)

FIGURE **6-8**

(*a*) Coil wound on a hollow tube. (*b*) Cross-sectional view showing the field produced by the coil.

(*a*)   (*b*)

Fig. 6-8(*a*) represents a coil formed by wrapping a conductor on a hollow fibre or cardboard tube. Note that when current flows through the coil in the direction shown, current is flowing away from the observer in the upper part of each turn (at points 1, 2, 3, 4, and 5) and toward the observer in the lower part of each turn (at points 6, 7, 8, and 9). This is further illustrated in the cross-sectional view of the coil in Fig. 6-8(*b*). As indicated by the right-hand rule for a conductor, the field around conductors 1, 2, 3, 4, and 5 is in a clockwise direction and in a counterclockwise direction around conductors 6, 7, 8, and 9. Thus the field established by the coil is similar to that of a bar magnet, with flux emerging from one end of the coil and entering the other. The end of the coil from which the flux emerges is called the north pole of the coil.

The polarity of any coil may be found by means of the right-hand rule for a coil, which may be stated as follows:

Imagine the coil being grasped in the right hand with the fingers pointing in the direction of the current in the coil; the thumb then points toward the north pole of the coil.

6-7

Magnetomotive Force or F_m

A measure of the ability of a coil to produce flux is called **magnetomotive force** (abbreviated F_m). Magnetomotive force corresponds to emf in an electric circuit and may be considered to be a magnetic pressure, just as emf is considered an electric pressure. The mmf of a coil varies directly with the current flowing in the coil and the number of turns on the coil. The product of the current in amperes and the number of turns is called the **ampere-turns** of the coil. The ampere-turn is taken as a practical unit of F_m.

$$F_m = IN \qquad \text{(ampere-turns)} \qquad \text{[6-2]}$$

where F_m = IN (ampere turns)
$\qquad N$ = number of turns,
$\qquad I$ = current in amperes

Example 6-2

A coil consisting of 550 turns of copper wire has a current of 12 amperes flowing through the circuit. Determine the magnetomotive force produced by this coil.

SOLUTION:

$$F_m = IN$$

$$F_m = 12 \times 550$$

$$F_m = 6600 \text{ AT}$$

Ohm's law for the electrical circuit is $I = E/R$. The magnetic circuit equivalent to this is

$$\phi = \frac{F_m}{R_m} \qquad \text{(webers)} \qquad [6\text{-}3]$$

where Φ and F_m have been previously defined, and R_m represents the reluctance of the magnetic circuit.

We will not do any magnetic circuit calculations in this book. However, it is important to remember that to get a given amount of magnetic flux in a given magnetic circuit the ampere turns of magnetizing force must be the same no matter how it is accomplished. In a given magnetic circuit we get the same flux with 3 A flowing in 450 turns as we get with 10 A flowing through 135 turns. A coil of 100 turns carrying 10 A and a second coil of 70 turns carrying 5 A (if connected so that their mmf's add together) also produce the same flux as would an 8 A coil with 250 turns and a second coil having 10 A and 65 turns connected so that their mmf's oppose each other.

A coil with a given amount of mmf is able to produce a much greater amount of flux when an iron core is inserted into the coil, since the permeability of iron is so much greater than that of air. Very powerful magnets called **electromagnets** may be made by placing a coil around an iron core.

The strength of an electromagnet depends on the number of ampere-turns of the exciting coil and on the permeability of the core. Soft iron is the material usually used for the core of an electromagnet because of its high permeability. The strength of an electromagnet with a given number of turns on the exciting coil may be varied by varying the amount of current through the coil. This is the method of varying the amount of flux and, hence, the amount of generated emf in a generator.

6-8
Ohm's Law for Magnetic Circuits

6-9
Electromagnets

Electromagnets have a multitude of applications in electric machinery. One important application, as mentioned above, is in the generator. The magnetic circuit of a two-pole dc generator is shown in Fig. 6-9. A strong magnetic field is produced by the two field coils that are wound around the iron pole cores. As the armature is turned through the magnetic field, emf is generated in the armature conductors.

FIGURE **6-9**
Magnetic circuit of a two-pole generator.

The **relay** shown in Fig. 6-10 illustrates an important application of electromagnetism. A relay is a switch that is operated by an electromagnet. The relay electromagnet consists of a coil and a stationary iron core. The relay contacts are mounted on a hinged iron bar called the **armature**. When the electromagnet is energized by a current passing through the coil, the armature is attracted to the electromagnet core, thereby closing the relay contacts. When the coil is deenergized, the contacts are opened by a spring.

A very small amount of current is required to energize a relay electromagnet and close the relay contacts. Relay contacts can be designed to carry large currents. For example, the relay shown in Fig. 6-10(a) requires only 0.24 A for operation while the contacts are rated to carry 25 A. Relays, therefore, are used when it is desired to control a device with a high current rating, such as an electric heater or similar device, from a remote point. It is not necessary to run the main supply lines for the device to the point of control. The remote-control wires need to be large enough to carry only the relay coil current. An electrical diagram of the relay in Fig. 6-10(a) is shown in Fig. 6-10(b) connected to a control switch that will energize the relay's holding coil (HC) which, in turn, will operate the contacts to switch the heater.

FIGURE **6-10a**
Typical three-pole relay.

FIGURE **6-10b**
The electrical diagram of the relay operating an electrical heater remotely controlled by a single-pole switch (sw).

Another application of electromagnetism is in the solenoid-operated brake. The brake shown in Fig. 6-11 is called a spring-set, electrically released brake. As the name indicates, this brake is set by the coil spring on the top of the brake and is released electrically by energizing the solenoid on the left-hand side of the mechanism. Brakes of this type are used as holding brakes on cranes, hoists, conveyors, machine tools, or similar machines. They may also be used as stopping brakes when they are applied within their heat-dissipating ability.

FIGURE **6-11**
Solenoid-operated brake.
(General Electric Company.)

Other typical applications of electromagnets are in lifting magnets for moving scrap iron, solenoid-operated valves, magnetic clutches, and magnetic separators used for removing tramp iron from coal before coal is fed into pulverizers.

6-10
Saturation

In a coil with air as the core, the flux produced is directly proportional to the ampere-turns of the coil. This is approximately true for an iron-cored coil up to a certain stage of magnetization of the core. Above this point, increases in ampere-turns produce smaller and smaller increases in flux in the core; then the core is said to be **saturated**.

The saturation of iron may be explained by Weber's theory of magnetism. As the ampere-turns of an exciting coil are increased from zero, molecules are moved into their magnetized position relatively easily since there are many haphazardly arranged molecules in the unmagnetized iron. When the larger share of these molecules is arranged in a definite order, the iron is said to be saturated. Further increases in ampere-turns produce smaller increases in magnetism of the iron since fewer molecules are left to bring into the magnetized position.

The effect of the saturation of iron on the operation of generators will be dealt with in Chap. 8.

R E V I E W Q U E S T I O N S

1 What is a magnet? Into what two classifications may magnets be divided?
2 What is the magnetism called that is retained by a magnet after its magnetizing force is removed?
3 What distinguishes magnetic materials from nonmagnetic materials?
4 How can the north and south poles of a magnet be identified?
5 What is a magnetic line of force? What is a magnetic field?
6 What is the unit of magnetic flux?
7 How many flux lines are represented by 1 wb?
8 What is meant by the term **flux density**? What is the SI unit of flux density?
9 Give the rule of magnetic attraction and repulsion.
10 Describe, briefly, Weber's theory of magnetism.
11 How may it be shown that there is a magnetic field around a current-carrying conductor? Give the rule that relates the current direction and the field direction.
12 What determines the polarity of a coil? State the rule for finding the polarity of a coil.

13 Define magnetomotive force. What is the practical unit?
14 In an electric circuit an emf causes a current to flow through a resistance in accordance with Ohm's law. What are the corresponding quantities in a magnetic circuit?
15 Upon what does the strength of an air-cored coil depend? An iron-cored coil? How is the strength of an electromagnet varied?
16 Give some applications of electromagnets.
17 When is a bar of iron said to be magnetically saturated?

Electromagnetic Induction

It can be shown experimentally that an electromotive force can be produced in a conductor by moving the conductor through a magnetic field. The discovery of this principle was announced by Faraday in 1831. It has been called the most important in the history of electricity since it has led to the development of the electric generator, the transformer, the telephone, and numerous other electric devices.

7-1
Induced EMF

If the ends of a conductor are connected to a low-reading voltmeter and the conductor is moved into the field of a magnet as shown in Fig. 7-1, a momentary reading will be noted on the voltmeter. As the conductor is withdrawn from the field, the meter will deflect momentarily in the opposite direction. If the conductor is held stationary and the magnet moved so that the field cuts the conductor, the same results are obtained. The voltage developed across the terminals of the voltmeter when the conductor is moved through the magnetic field (or when the field is moved across the conductor) is known as an **induced electromotive force**. The current caused to flow in the conductor by the induced emf is sometimes called an **induced current**. The phenomenon whereby an emf is induced in a conductor when the conductor cuts or is cut by a magnetic field is called **electromagnetic induction**.

The principle of inducing an emf in a conductor by moving the conductor through a magnetic field is used in the dc generator (Chap. 8). Stationary electromagnets establish the magnetic field through which conductors are moved, causing an emf to be induced in them. In summary, the conditions required to induce an emf are a conductor, a magnetic field, and relative motion between the two.

In ac generators, because of insulation and mechanical design problems, the conductors are stationary while the electromagnets are revolved (see Chap. 14). The principle is the same in both ac and dc generators, however, in that lines of force are being cut by a conductor in either case.

An emf is induced in the conductor *AB* when it is moved through the magnetic field.

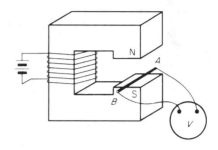

7-**2**

Factors Affecting the Amount of Induced EMF

When the conductor of Fig. 7-1 is replaced by a coil of several turns as in Fig. 7-2 and the experiment is repeated, it will be found that the voltmeter deflection is greater than when the single conductor was used, other conditions being the same. Each turn of the coil now has an emf induced in it and, since the turns are in series, the total emf of the coil is the sum of the emfs of each of the turns. If a coil of still more turns is used, correspondingly greater emfs will be induced, the amount of emf increasing directly with the number of turns on the coil.

When the speed at which a given coil is moved into the field is increased, the emf induced is increased, the emf being directly proportional to the speed at which the lines of force are cut.

The strength of the field is also a factor since, at a given speed, more lines of force are cut per second in a strong field than in a weak field. Other factors involved in inducing an emf are the angle at which the field is cut and the length of the section of conductor that is being moved through the field.

F I G U R E **7-2**
Electromotive force is induced in each turn of the coil as it is moved through the magnetic field.

All the above-mentioned factors that are involved in the induction of an emf concern the *rate* at which the magnetic field is being cut by a conductor or the rate at which the number of lines of force through a coil is changing. In general:

Whenever the number of lines of force threading through a coil is changed, an emf is induced in that coil. The amount of emf induced is proportional to the rate at which the number of lines of force through the coil is changing.

This is known as Faraday's law of induction.

7-3
Faraday's Law of Induction

The quantity of induced emf in a single conductor is a function of the density of the magnetic field, the length of the conductor in the magnetic, the angle at which the conductor cuts the field's flux, and the velocity of the conductor's motion through the field. The summary of these factors can be explained in Eq. (7-1).

7-4
Numerical Value of Induced EMF

$$E_{induced} = Blv \times \sin\theta \qquad [7\text{-}1]$$

where E = the quantity of induced emf in the conductor in the magnetic field (in volts)

B = the flux density of the magnetic field (in Teslas)

l = the length of the conductor in the magnetic field (in metres)

v = the velocity of the conductor's motion in the magnetic field (in metres/second)

$\sin\theta$ = sine of the angle between the conductor's motion and a line perpendicular to the lines of flux. (resultant component of flux being cut by conductor at right angle to the magnetic field)

Example 7-1

A conductor 10 cm in length is moving at 90° to the field flux produced by a pair of magnets that has a magnetic field 15×10^{-2} Teslas. The velocity of the conductor is 100 m/s. Determine the induced voltage in the conductor.

SOLUTION:

$$E_{induced} = Blv \times \sin\theta$$

$$E = (15 \times 10^{-2})(10 \times 10^{-2})(100)(1)$$

$$E = 1.5 \text{ V}$$

If the conductor in Example 7-1 cut the field flux at an angle of less than 90°, the resultant voltage would have been less than 1.5 volts due to fewer lines being cut at that velocity.

It has been shown that when flux is changing through a coil an emf is induced. When the flux through a one-turn coil is changing at the rate of one weber per second, one volt is induced in the coil. If the coil happens to be cutting lines of flux at varying angles, the ability to determine the average induced emf is also important.

Therefore,
$$E_{av.} = N \frac{d\phi}{dt} \quad \text{(volts)} \qquad [7\text{-}2]$$

where $E_{av.}$ = average induced voltage
   N = number of turns on coil
   $\dfrac{d\phi}{dt}$ = rate of change in flux (in webers) cut per second

Example 7-2

Determine the quantity of induced emf when the flux changes from 0.02 wb to 0.04 wb in 1 ms. The coil contains 5 turns.

SOLUTION:

$$E = N \frac{d\phi}{dt}$$

$$E = 5 \frac{0.04 - 0.02}{0.001}$$

$$E = 5 \frac{0.02}{0.001}$$

$$E = 100 \text{ V}$$

7-5

Direction of Induced EMF

As the conductor in Fig. 7-1 is moved into the magnetic field from right to left, the voltmeter indicates that an emf is induced from A to B. When the conductor is withdrawn from the field, the direction of the emf is reversed or is induced from B to A. If the polarity of the electromagnet is reversed, emf is induced from B to A as the conductor is moved into the field and from A to B when the conductor is withdrawn. The relation between the directions of motion, field, and induced emf is given by **Fleming's right-hand rule:**

Extend the thumb, forefinger, and middle finger of the right hand at right angles to one another as in Fig. 7-3. Point the forefinger in the

FIGURE **7-3**
Fleming's right-hand rule for determining the direction of an induced emf.

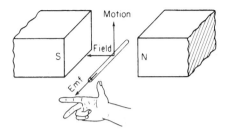

direction of the magnetic field and the thumb in the direction of motion of the conductor. The middle finger then points in the direction of motion of the induced emf.

Fleming's right-hand rule is established for a *stationary field* and a *moving conductor*. However, it may also be applied in the case of a moving field and a stationary conductor if the *relative* motion of the conductor is considered. If the conductor *AB* were stationary in Fig. 7-1 and the field moved toward the right, emf would be induced from *A* to *B* just as if the conductor were moved to the left into a stationary field. That is, the motion of the conductor relative to the field is to the left in either case. Therefore, it must be kept in mind when using Fleming's right-hand rule that the thumb must point in the direction of relative motion of the conductor.

According to Faraday's law, whenever the flux threading through or linking with a closed circuit is changed, an emf is induced which causes a current to flow in the circuit. The direction of the induced current has a definite relation to the variation of the field that produces it. This relation is formalized by **Lenz's law of induction**, which may be stated as follows:

An induced emf will cause a current to flow in a closed circuit in such a direction that its magnetic effect will oppose the change that produces it.

This rule follows directly from the law of the conservation of energy; that is, to cause an induced current to flow requires the expenditure of energy. In the case of a generator, for example, when the induced current is caused to flow through a load connected to the generator, electric energy is expended. The field produced by the current is always in a direction so that it reacts with the main generator field, to oppose the turning action of the prime mover driving the generator. Thus, the greater the electric energy supplied to the load, the greater is the reaction and in turn the greater

7-6

Lenz's Law of Induction

is the mechanical energy required from the prime mover. Energy must be supplied to the generator at least at the same rate that it is being taken from the generator.

7-7
Self-Induced EMF: Inductance

When a conductor is carrying a current, there is a magnetic field around the conductor. When the current ceases to flow, the field ceases to exist. When the current changes in intensity, the field likewise changes in intensity. It has been shown that when the amount of flux threading through, or linking with, a circuit is changed, an emf is induced in that circuit. When this is due to a change of current in a circuit itself, the induced emf is called the **emf of self-induction**.

Since, according to Lenz's law, any induced emf acts to oppose the change that produces it, a self-induced emf is always in such a direction as to oppose the *change* of current in the circuit in which it is induced. When a coil or other electric circuit has the property of opposing any change of current in the circuit, it is said to possess *self-inductance* or simply *inductance*.

The unit of inductance is the **henry**. *A circuit has an inductance of one henry if an emf of one volt is induced in the circuit when the current changes at the rate of one ampere per second.*

7-8
Self-Induction in a Coil

A circuit consisting of a straight wire contains a certain amount of inductance because a change of current in the wire produces a change in the flux enveloping or linking the circuit. However, a circuit containing a coil has a much higher value of inductance because a change in current in such a circuit produces much more of a change in the flux linking the circuit.

Fig. 7-4 represents a vertical cross section of a coil. When the switch S is closed, current will flow from the battery into the coil at A. As the current increases in value, the magnetic lines expand from the centre of each turn of the coil and cut across adja-

---

FIGURE **7-4**

As the current increases in the coil, the expanding flux lines from each turn of the coil move across adjacent turns, inducing an emf in them.

cent turns. For example, the lines set up by the current in turn *A* expand and cut across turn *B*, which is the equivalent of moving *B* into the field of *A*. Fleming's right-hand rule shows the resulting induced emf to be toward the reader at *B* or *against* the flow of current. Other turns of the coil react in the same way. The increase of current in the coil is thus opposed.

When the switch is opened, the collapsing field of the coil cuts across the coil in a direction opposite to that of the increasing flux. This induces an emf in the reverse direction or in the *same* direction as the current flow, tending to maintain the current flow or, at least, to oppose its decrease.

Thus, a circuit that has inductance opposes any *change* in current through the circuit. In the coil of Fig. 7-4, the self-induced emf opposes the increase in current as the switch is closed and opposes the decrease in current as the switch is opened. When a current is unchanging in value, the inductance of the circuit has no effects on its flow. A steady current is opposed only by the resistance of the circuit.

When a highly inductive circuit (such as a generator field circuit) is opened, the self-induced emf may be high enough to damage the insulation of the coil or to endanger the life of the person opening the switch. For this reason, a discharge resistor is often connected across the coil at the same instant that the switch blade is opened. The induced emf then causes a current to flow through the resistor and permits the field to collapse gradually, thus limiting the value of the self-induced emf.

7-9
Mutual Induction

In Sec. 7-1 it was shown how an emf may be induced by moving either a conductor or the magnets that produce the field, as in the case of electric generators. Electromotive forces may also be induced by devices in which neither the conductor nor the magnets move but in which the magnetic field is made to vary in strength or direction.

If two coils are placed adjacent to one another as in Fig. 7-5, a part of the flux produced by coil *A* passes through or links with coil *B*. If the field strength of coil *A* is increased or decreased, there is a corresponding increase or decrease in the field strength inside coil *B*. Since, according to Faraday's law, an emf is induced whenever the flux is changing through a coil, each change of field strength through coil *B* causes an emf to be induced in that coil. Electromotive force is induced in one direction in coil *B* as the field expands and in the other direction as the field collapses, the direction in each case being that indicated by Fleming's right-hand rule or by Lenz's law.

FIGURE **7-5**
A change in the amount of current flowing in coil *A* induces an emf in coil *B*.

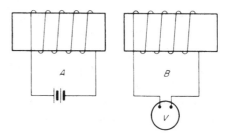

Coil *A*, the coil that is connected to the supply and that produces the original flux, is called the **primary coil**. Coil *B* is called the **secondary coil**. If the two coils are wound on the same iron core, the flux established by the primary coil is not only greater, but a larger part of it is made to cut or link with the secondary coil as it expands or collapses. An emf induced in a secondary coil by a change of current in the primary coil is said to be induced by **mutual induction**.

The field established by the primary coil and which links with the secondary coil may be made to vary by one of three methods: *by varying the intensity of the primary current, by periodically reversing the primary current, or by interrupting or "making and breaking" the primary current.*

An example of the use of a varying primary current to induce an emf in a secondary circuit is in the telephone. A battery, the telephone transmitter, and the primary of an induction coil are connected in series as shown in Fig. 7-6. The sound waves of the speaker's voice cause the transmitter diaphragm to vibrate, which in turn varies the resistance of the transmitter. The primary current thus increases and decreases in value with the variations of the transmitter resistance, thereby causing a variation in the amount

FIGURE **7-6**
Telephone-transmitter circuit, simplified diagram.

of flux linking the secondary coil of the induction coil. The varying emf so induced in the secondary circuit causes a varying current to flow over the line and through a distant receiver.

The transformer is a mutual-induction device used for changing the value of alternating voltages. It consists of two windings, a primary and a secondary, wound on the same iron core. When an alternating voltage is applied to the primary winding, an alternating current (or a current that flows back and forth) flows in the primary winding. The flux produced in the core increases, decreases, and reverses with the primary current. This induces an alternating emf in the secondary winding which is directly proportional to the number of turns on the secondary winding. Transformers are discussed in detail in Chap. 13.

7-10
Ignition Systems

The method of interrupting the primary-coil current to induce an emf in the secondary coil is used in internal-combustion-engine ignition systems. Fig. 7-7 shows a simplified circuit diagram of an automobile engine ignition system.

The ignition coil consists of a primary coil of a few turns of relatively heavy wire wound on an iron core and a secondary coil of many turns of fine wire wound directly around, but insulated from, the primary coil and the core. Primary current is supplied from a 12-V storage battery.

In automobile ignition systems used prior to about 1975, contacts called breaker points are connected in series with the primary coil and the battery and are alternately opened and closed by a mechanically driven cam. When the points are closed, current from the battery flows through the primary coil, establishing a flux that links both primary and secondary coils. At the proper instant the cam "breaks" the points, opening the primary circuit. At the same time the distributor arm connects the secondary coil to the proper spark plug. As the field collapses around the secondary coil, the

FIGURE **7-7**
Simplified diagram of an engine ignition system.

high voltage induced is applied across the spark-plug gap, causing an arc between the spark-plug points, which ignites the mixture in the combustion chamber. The sequence of events is then repeated when the distributor arm advances to fire the next spark plug as the cam again breaks the points.

In the newer electronic-type ignition systems, the ignition coil is used to perform the same function as in the older breaker-point system. In the electronic system, however, the alternate opening and closing of the primary-coil circuit is performed by a solid-state switching transistor instead of by breaker points. The transistor is controlled by an electronic control module which, in turn, receives its signals from a magnetic signal generator on the distributor shaft. The electronic-type system can provide higher secondary voltages and more precise control of the spark-plug firing. This results in improved combustion in the engine with reduced pollution emissions.

REVIEW QUESTIONS

1 What is an induced emf?
2 What factors affect the amount of emf induced in a coil?
3 State the general rule that covers all the variable factors involved in inducing an emf.
4 Numerically, what rate of change of flux is necessary to induce 1 V?
5 State Fleming's right-hand rule. How may it be applied to a moving field and a stationary conductor?
6 State Lenz's law of induction. Upon what fundamental law is it based?
7 What is an emf of self-induction? Under what conditions of current flow is this emf induced? What is its direction in relation to any change in current?
8 In an inductive circuit, does the inductance have any effect on the flow of a steady current? Why?
9 Why is a coil said to have a higher value of inductance than a straight wire?
10 What is the unit of inductance?
11 What is the purpose of a discharge resistor used in conjunction with opening a highly inductive circuit?
12 Show how a change of current may be made to induce an emf in an adjacent circuit. Using the relation given by Lenz's law, determine the direction of the flux established by an induced secondary-coil current in relation to an increasing primary flux.

13 Give three ways in which flux that mutually links two circuits may be varied. Which of these methods is used in (*a*) the telephone, (*b*) the transformer, (*c*) the ignition system?

14 What would be the effect of connecting a transformer to a dc supply?

15 Describe briefly the action of the telephone-transmitter circuit.

16 Why is the secondary coil of an ignition coil wound with many turns of wire?

Direct-Current Generators

A dc machine may be used either to convert mechanical energy to electric energy or to convert electric energy to mechanical energy. When a dc machine is driven mechanically by a prime mover such as a steam turbine, hydraulic turbine, or diesel engine and delivers electric energy to electric lights or machines, it is called a **generator**. If electric energy is supplied to the machine and its output is used to drive mechanical devices such as conveyors or machine tools, it is called a **motor**. Generators are rated as to the *kilowatts* they can deliver without overheating at a rated voltage and speed. Motors are rated as to the *horsepower* (Imperial) or *kilowatts* (SI) they can deliver without overheating at their rated voltage and speed.

F I G U R E **8-1**
Direct Current Motor-Generator Set.
(Courtesy of Reliance Electric.)

This chapter deals with dc machines used as generators, although much of what is said concerning generators is equally applicable to motors. Motors are discussed in Chap. 9.

8-1

Generator Construction

Flux produced by the field windings of a generator is established in the field yoke, pole cores, air gap, and armature core, all of which form what is known as the **magnetic circuit** of a generator. The magnetic circuit of a four-pole generator is shown in Fig. 8-2. The **field yoke**, or frame, being made of cast steel or rolled steel, serves as a mechanical support for the pole cores as well as serving as part of the magnetic circuit. **End bells**, which support the brush assembly and which in all but the very large machines also support the armature bearings, are also attached to the yoke.

Generator **pole cores** are made of sheet-steel laminations that are insulated from each other and riveted together, the core then being bolted to the field yoke. The pole face, which is the surface of the core next to the air gap, is made larger than the main body of the core. This is to reduce the reluctance of the air gap and to provide a means of support for the field coils.

An assembled **armature core** and commutator, without the armature windings, are shown in Fig. 8-3. The core is made of

---

F I G U R E **8-2**
The parts of the magnetic circuit of a four-pole generator.

FIGURE **8-3**
Armature core with assembled commutator in the foreground.
(Courtesy of Reliance Electric.)

sheet-steel laminations that are keyed to the shaft or are keyed to a spider which, in turn, is keyed to the shaft. The outer surface of the core is slotted to provide a means of securing the armature coils.

The **air gap** is the space between the armature surface and the pole face and varies in length with the size of the machine but is of the order of 1.5 to 6.5 mm.

The **electric circuits** of a dc generator are made up of the armature winding, commutator, brushes, and field windings. Except on small armatures, armature windings consist of coils that are wound to their correct shape and size on a form, after which they are completely insulated. After the formed coils are slipped into their proper places in the armature slots, they are securely wedged into place and the coil ends are connected to the proper commutator segments. On small armatures, the windings are not form-wound but are wound by hand or by machine directly into the slots of the armature core.

The **commutator** consists of a number of copper segments that are assembled into a cylinder which is secured to, but insulated from, the shaft as shown in Fig. 8-3. The segments are well-insulated from each other, mica being the insulating material commonly used. To these commutator segments are soldered the ends of the armature coils.

Brushes that rest on the face of the commutator form the sliding electrical connection between the armature coils and the external circuit. Brushes are made of carbon of varying degrees of hardness and, in some cases, are made of a mixture of carbon and copper. The brushes are held in place under spring pressure by brush holders, the electric connection between the brush and brush holder being made by a flexible copper conductor called a **pigtail**.

The **field coils** are placed around the pole cores as shown in Fig. 8-2. The coils of each of the poles are connected in series to form the field circuit. Field circuits may be designed to be connected either in series or in parallel with the armature circuit. Parallel- or shunt-field coils have many turns of wire of small cross section and a relatively high resistance, while series-field coils have few turns of wire of large cross section and relatively low resistance. In order to obtain special operating characteristics, some generators (compound generators) are equipped with both shunt- and series-field coils placed on the same pole cores, as indicated in Fig. 8-2.

Most generators are equipped with small poles called **interpoles** or **commutating poles**, which are placed midway between the main poles, as shown in Fig. 8-2. Flux is established in these poles only when current flows in the armature circuit, the purpose of the flux being to improve commutation, as explained in Sec. 8-8.

A dismantled small generator is shown in Fig. 8-4. Note that the brush assembly and the bearings are supported by the end bells. A completed larger generator designed for direct connection to an engine is shown in Fig. 8-5.

F I G U R E **8-4**
Generator dismantled to show the various parts.
(Robbins & Myers, Inc.)

FIGURE **8-5**
DC generator for direct engine drive.
(Kato Engineering.)

Fig. 8-6 represents a simple two-pole single-coil generator with the armature core and commutator omitted for the sake of simplicity. The single armature coil can be rotated about its axis O-O in the uniform magnetic field produced by the two poles. As the coil is rotated through the field by some mechanical means not shown, the number of lines of force through the coil changes continually. In Chap. 7 it was shown that when the number of lines of force through a coil is changed, an emf is induced in that coil. The amount of emf induced depends on the rate at which the flux is changing through the coil, and its direction is determined by Fleming's right-hand rule. In a single-coil generator with a constant field strength, the amount of emf induced at any instant then depends upon how fast the coil is cutting across the field at that instant. An emf produced by the movement of a coil through a magnetic field, as in a generator, is called a **generated emf**.

8-**2**

The Single-Coil Generator

FIGURE **8-6**
Two-pole single-coil generator with the armature coil in the neutral plane.

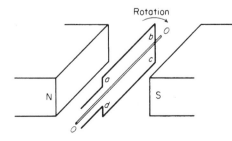

F I G U R E **8-7**
Armature coil in the 90° position.

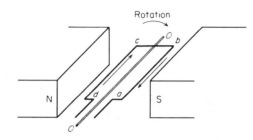

When the coil is in the vertical position shown in Fig. 8-6, the coil edges are moving parallel to the lines of force so that the flux enclosed by the coil is not changing. Thus, no emf is generated when the coil is in this position. When the coil is in this position, it is said to be in the **neutral plane**.

As the coil is turned in a clockwise direction at a constant speed, the coil edges begin to cut across the field, slowly at first but at a gradually increasing rate. Thus, the amount of emf generated gradually increases as the coil moves around to the position shown in Fig. 8-7, which is 90° from the position shown in Fig. 8-6. As determined by Fleming's right-hand rule, the direction of the emf generated as the coil moves through the 90° position is from *b* to *a* and from *d* to *c*. In the 90° position, the coil edges are moving at right angles to the field and, therefore, are cutting across the field at a maximum rate; consequently, the emf generated at this point is at a maximum value.

As the coil is turned on past the 90° position, the rate at which the conductors cut across the field gradually decreases, causing the amount of generated emf to decrease gradually. When the coil

F I G U R E **8-8**
Armature coil in the 180° position.

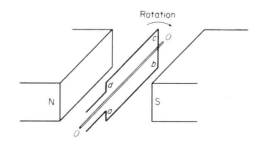

FIGURE **8-9**
Armature coil in the 270° position.

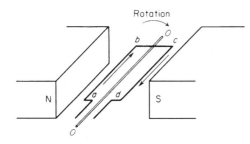

reaches the position shown in Fig. 8-8, the coil is again in the neutral plane and the generated emf is again zero.

When the coil is moved in a clockwise direction from the 180° position in Fig. 8-8, the coil sides again begin to cut the field. However, the direction of the generated emf is now from *a* to *b* and from *c* to *d*. The amount of emf gradually increases until a maximum value is induced again at the 270° position shown in Fig. 8-9.

A comparison of Figs. 8-7 and 8-9 shows the directions of the generated emfs in the two coil sides to be reversed but, in each case, the emf in the side *ab* adds to that generated in the side *cd*.

As the coil is moved from the 270° position, the generated emf gradually decreases until the coil again reaches the neutral plane where the emf is zero. The cycle then repeats for each revolution of the armature.

Thus when a coil is rotated in a two-pole magnetic field, an emf is generated in one direction during the first half and in the opposite direction during the second half of each revolution. Such an emf is called an **alternating emf**. If the value of the generated emf is plotted for a number of the positions the coil passes through in one revolution, a curve similar to that shown in Fig. 8-10 results. This is referred to as one **alternating current cycle**.

If the number of poles in Fig. 8-13 was increased to four, the number of ac alternations shown in Fig. 8-10 would double for each mechanical revolution of the coil. In fact, as pairs of poles are added to a dc generator, the alternations of the induced emf increases in proportion.

The single-coil generator may be connected to an external circuit by connecting the coil terminals to two continuous and insulated rings, called **slip rings** or **collector rings**. These rings are mounted on the generator shaft and rotate with the coil and the

FIGURE **8-10**

Curve showing the variation of generated emf in a coil rotated in a uniform magnetic field.

Coil positions in degrees

shaft so that two stationary brushes, one bearing on each ring, connect the coil to the external circuit as shown in Fig. 8-11. When the coil is rotated, the generated alternating emf causes a current to flow first in one direction and then the other through the coil and external circuit. Such a current is called an **alternating current**.

8-3

The Simple DC Generator

It has been shown that the emf generated in a rotating armature coil is alternating. When this coil is connected to an external circuit by means of slip rings, an alternating current flows through the external circuit. Therefore, slip rings cannot be used if direct current, which always flows in the same direction, is desired.

However, the alternating current in the armature coil may be converted into direct current for the external circuit by using a single split ring as shown in Figs. 8-12, 8-13, and 8-14. The two sections or segments that are insulated from each other and from the shaft form a simple **commutator**. Each end of the armature

FIGURE **8-11**

Slip rings and brushes are used to connect the coil to an external circuit.

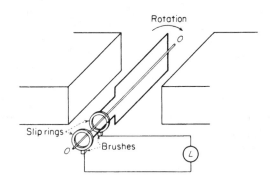

FIGURE **8-12**
Single-coil generator with a commutator.

coil is connected to a segment. The action of the commutator is
to reverse the armature coil connections to the external circuit at
the same instant that the current reverses in the armature coil. This
action is described more fully in the following paragraphs.

When the armature coil is being turned in the clockwise direction, as in Fig. 8-12, emf is generated in the coil sides from *b* to *a*
and from *d* to *c* as the arrows indicate. The circuit is completed by
the lamp that is connected across the two brushes. The generated
emf causes current to flow out through segment *e*, the upper brush,
through the lamp, into the lower brush and segment *f*, and around
the armature coil as indicated by the arrows. When the coil is
turned 90° into the neutral plane as shown in Fig. 8-13, the generated emf and, hence, the current drop to zero. At this point the
brushes make contact with both segments. As the coil is moved on
past the neutral plane through another 90° to the position shown

FIGURE **8-13**
Coil in the neutral plane.

F I G U R E **8-14**
Coil rotated 180° from the position shown in Fig. 8-12.

in Fig. 8-14, emf is generated from *a* to *b* and from *c* to *d*. However, the upper brush now makes contact with segment *f* and the lower brush with segment *e*. A comparison of Figs. 8-12 and 8-14 shows that, while the current has reversed in the armature coil, it flows out of the upper brush, through the lamp, and into the lower brush in each case. The emf and current drop to zero when the coil is moved another 90° into the neutral plane where the connections to the lamp are again reversed.

Although the current through the lamp is always in the same direction, it is not a steady current, since the emf, generated in the armature coil and applied to the brushes, varies from zero to a maximum and back to zero twice each revolution. The variation in brush voltage is shown graphically in Fig. 8-15.

A pulsating direct current such as is produced by a single-coil generator is not suitable for most commercial uses. However, by using a large number of coils and commutator segments, with the coils evenly distributed around the surface of the armature, the brush voltage may be made practically constant. Fig. 8-16 illus-

F I G U R E **8-15**
Variation in brush voltage of a single-coil generator with a commutator.

FIGURE **8-16**
Approximate dc voltage waveform of multi-coil armature.

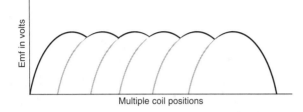

trates the approximate waveform of a multi-coil armature. The su-
perimposed voltages occurring only a few degrees apart will produce only a small ripple on top of the resultant wave as shown in
this figure in heavier line.

The voltage generated by a single-turn armature coil is small.
For this reason, the coils used in commercial generators consist of
several turns in series, thereby increasing the amount of generated
emf in direct proportion to the number of turns in the coil.

The method of connecting several armature coils to form a continuous or closed armature winding may be illustrated by the ring
winding represented in Fig. 8-17(*a*). A ring winding is formed by
winding the armature conductors around an iron ring or hollow
iron cylinder as shown in the diagram. This is an early form of
armature winding which has been replaced by the more efficient,
drum type of winding. However, the principle of the two windings
is fundamentally the same, and the action of the ring winding is
much more clearly represented by a diagram than that of the drum
winding. Hence, the ring winding is used here as an illustration.

|8-4

**Multicoil
Armatures**

FIGURE **8-17**
(*a*) Two-pole ring-armature winding. (*b*) Equivalent circuit of the ring winding.

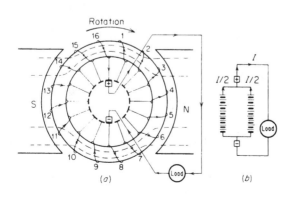

Fig. 8-17(*a*) represents a two-pole ring winding with 16 coils of one turn each. By starting at the bottom brush and tracing through the winding to the upper brush, it may be seen that there are two separate paths through the winding. Coils 8 to 1 form one path, and coils 9 to 16 form the other. When the armature is turned in a clockwise direction, emf is generated away from the reader in the conductors under the face of the north pole and toward the reader in the conductors under the face of the south pole, causing currents to flow in the directions indicated by the arrows. The emf generated in each path is additive; that is, the emf generated in the path 8 to 1 is the sum of the emfs generated in each of the eight coils. Likewise, the emf in the path 9 to 16 is the sum of the emfs generated in coils 9 to 16. However, since the two paths are connected in parallel, the voltage between the two brushes is equal to the emf generated in either of the two parallel paths. For example, if the average emf generated in each of the 16 coils is 5 V, then the average emf generated in each path is 40 V and the brush voltage is 40 V.

Since the two paths through the armature winding are in parallel, any current supplied to the load divides equally between the two paths. For example, if the load current is 30 A, then 15 A is supplied by each of the two halves of the armature winding.

The armature winding of Fig. 8-17(*a*) may be represented by the equivalent circuit of Fig. 8-17(*b*), in which each of the 16 coils is represented by a battery cell. The emf generated in each path is the sum of the emfs generated in the eight coils in that path, and the brush voltage is equal to the voltage of either path.

Since current is assumed to flow from the positive terminal of a source through a circuit and back into the negative terminal, the upper brush in Fig. 8-17 is called the positive brush and the lower brush the negative brush.

The drum-type armature winding used in modern dc machines has the advantages of being easier to build and repair and of being more efficient than the ring winding. It is formed by placing the armature conductors, usually in the form of coils, in slots on the surface of a drum-shaped or cylindrical iron core. An armature core designed for drum winding is shown in Fig. 8-3 and a completed drum-wound armature is shown in Fig. 8-4.

In general, there are two types of drum-armature windings: the **lap** and the **wave** windings. Each type of winding may be further classified as being a **simplex** (single) or a **multiplex** (double or triple) winding. Both lap and wave windings are closed-circuit windings; that is, they close upon themselves to form a closed electric circuit, just as does the ring winding shown in Fig. 8-17. Both windings are formed by interconnecting a number of separately insulated winding elements or coils, which have been laid in place in the armature core slots.

The general kinds of dc generators take their names from the kinds of field excitation used. When a generator is excited from a storage battery or from a separate dc source, it is called a **separately excited generator**. If the field of a self-excited generator is connected in parallel with the armature circuit, it is called a **shunt generator**. When the field is in series with the armature, the generator is called a **series generator**. If both shunt and series fields are used, the generator is called a **compound generator**. Compound generators may be connected *short-shunt* with the shunt field in parallel with the armature only or *long-shunt* with the shunt field in parallel with both the armature and series field. The circuit diagrams of the various types of generators are shown in Fig. 8-18. Field rheostats, as shown in this figure, are adjustable resistances placed in the field circuits to provide a means of varying the field flux and, thereby, the amount of emf generated by the generator.

8-5
Methods of Field Excitation

The average generated emf, E, of a generator may be calculated from the formula

$$E = \frac{pZ\phi n}{60b} \quad \text{(volts)} \quad [8\text{-}1]$$

where p = number of poles
Z = total number of conductors on armature (sometimes called **inductors**)
Φ = flux per pole, webers
n = the speed of the armature, revolutions per minute
b = number of parallel paths through armature, depending on type of armature winding

8-6
Generator Voltage Equations

For any given generator, all the factors in Eq. (8-1) are fixed values except the flux per pole, Φ, and the speed n. Therefore, Eq. (8-1) may be simplified to the form

$$E = K\phi n \quad \text{(volts)} \quad [8\text{-}2]$$

where K is equal numerically to all the fixed values or constants for a given generator.

$$\left(K = \frac{pZ}{60b}\right)$$

Eq. (8-2) is merely a restatement of Faraday's law of induction: the value of an induced emf in any circuit is proportional to the

FIGURE **8-18**
Circuit diagrams of dc generators: (*a*) separately excited, (*b*) shunt, (*c*) series, (*d*) short-shunt compound, and (*e*) long-shunt compound generators.

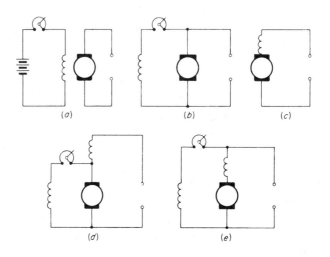

rate at which flux is being cut by the circuit. Thus, if the flux per pole of a generator is doubled with the speed remaining constant, the generated emf will be doubled; or if the speed is doubled, the flux remaining constant, the generated emf will be doubled.

In practice, generators are usually operated at nearly constant speed, with the generated emf being adjusted to the desired value by adjusting the field flux. The field flux, being established by the field current, is controlled by the field rheostat.

Example 8-1

When a generator is being driven at 1200 r/min, the generated emf is 125 V. What will be the generated emf (*a*) if the field flux is decreased by 10 percent with the speed remaining unchanged, and (*b*) if the speed is reduced to 1100 r/min, the field flux remaining unchanged?

SOLUTION:

(*a*) With a 10% reduction in the field, the resultant field strength will then be 90% (0.90) of its original value. Therefore:

$$E_2 = 125 \times 0.90$$

$$E_2 = 112.5 \text{ V}$$

$$(b) \qquad \frac{E_1}{E_2} = \frac{n_1}{n_2} \quad \text{or} \quad \frac{125}{E_2} = \frac{1200}{1100}$$

$$E_2 = \frac{1100 \times 125}{1200}$$

$$E_2 = 114.6 \text{ V}$$

The terminal voltage V_t differs from the generated emf of a generator by the voltage drop in the armature series circuit. The armature-circuit resistance consists of the resistance of the armature windings, the series field and commutating pole windings if used, and the brushes — in other words, the entire resistance between the positive and negative terminals of the generator. At no load, the terminal voltage is equal to the generated emf since there is no IR drop in the armature circuit. However, load current flowing through the armature circuit produces an IR drop which, of course, increases as the load current increases.

A convenient way of representing the relationship between the generated emf, the IR drop in the armature circuit, and the terminal voltage is shown in the equivalent armature circuit of Fig. 8-20. The generated emf, E, is represented as a storage battery with zero internal resistance and the entire armature-circuit resistance by the resistor, R_a, in series with the battery.

From this circuit, then,

$$V_t = E - I_a R_a \qquad \text{(volts)} \qquad \text{[8-3]}$$

where I_a is the armature current. Substituting the value of E from Eq. (8-2) in Eq. (8-3) results in the equation

$$V_t = K\phi n - I_a R_a \qquad \text{(volts)} \qquad \text{[8-4]}$$

FIGURE **8-19**
Equivalent circuit of a generator armature.

This equation is called the **fundamental generator equation** because it contains all the factors that govern the value of the terminal voltage. Note that there are three factors that may affect the generator terminal voltage: (1) Φ, the flux per pole; (2) n, the speed in r/min; and (3) $I_a R_a$, the voltage drop in the armature circuit.

8-7
The Magnetization Curve

According to the molecular theory of magnetism (Chap. 6), the molecules of an unmagnetized piece of iron are not arranged in any definite order. When the iron is magnetized by passing current through a coil placed around the iron, the molecules become arranged in a definite order. To arrange the greater part of the molecules in a definite order or to magnetize the iron up to a certain point requires relatively few ampere-turns of applied F_m. In this stage of magnetization, the amount of flux established in the iron increases almost directly with increases in the ampere-turns applied. However, above this point, which is called the **saturation point**, it becomes increasingly difficult to magnetize the iron further, since the unmagnetized molecules become fewer and fewer. Above the saturation point, when much larger increases in ampere-turns are required for corresponding increases in flux in the iron, the iron is said to be *saturated*. The fact that the iron has become saturated does not mean that a further increase in magnetism is impossible; the increases in magnetism merely require very much larger increases in applied ampere-turns than before the iron became saturated.

It was shown in Sec. 8-6 that the generated emf is proportional to both the flux per pole and the speed of the generator. If the speed is held constant, the generated emf then depends directly on the flux per pole. Since the flux is produced by the ampere-turns of the field coils, and since the number of turns on field coils is constant, the flux must depend on the amount of field current flowing. However, the flux is not directly proportional to the field current at all times, owing to the fact that the magnetic circuit of the generator becomes saturated. The variation of the generated emf with the field current for a given generator driven at a constant speed and at no load may be shown by a curve called the **magnetization curve**. This curve is sometimes called the generator-saturation curve or the no-load characteristic.

The magnetization curve of a shunt generator is shown in Fig. 8-20. With zero field current, that is, with the field circuit open, the generated emf is equal to about 2 V. This is because of the weak flux produced by the residual magnetism in the poles. As the field current is increased, the generated emf increases in a nearly straight line up to about 102 V when the field current is 0.8 A. At this point, the magnetic circuit of the generator approaches satu-

FIGURE **8-20**
Generator magnetization curve.

ration. Beyond this point, larger increases in field current are necessary to produce proportionate increases in generated emf. For example, before the field becomes saturated, an increase of field current from 0.4 to 0.6 A increases the generated emf from 60 to 84 V. However, after the field becomes saturated, an increase of field current from 1.2 to 1.4 A raises the generated emf from 125 to 132 V. An increase of 0.2 A in field current in the first case causes an increase of 24 V, but the same increase in field current in the second case causes an increase in generated emf of only 7 V.

The process of reversing the direction of the current in an armature coil as the commutator segments to which the coil is connected pass under a brush is called **commutation**. During the short time that the commutator segments to which a coil is connected are passing under the brush, the current must be completely reversed so that an arc is not formed as the commutator segments move from under the brush. Sparking at the brushes causes the commutator to pit which, in turn, increases the brush-contact resistance and also causes the brushes and commutator to wear excessively. Sparking at the brushes, then, must be avoided.

Since an armature coil is partially surrounded by iron, it has a considerable amount of inductance. It was shown in Chap. 7 that in an inductive circuit each change in current is opposed by an emf of self-induction. The emf of self-induction in an armature coil, then, opposes the reversal of the coil current while the coil is short-circuited by the brush and maintains a current flow around the short-circuited coil, thereby producing a spark as the commutator segments leave the brush.

8-8

Commutation

Since the emf of self-induction in an armature coil is due to a property of the coil, namely, its inductance, it cannot be prevented. However, it can be neutralized by causing an emf to be induced in the coil *opposite* in polarity to the self-induced emf. This is accomplished by the use of **interpoles**.

Interpoles, or commutating poles (see Fig. 8-2), are small poles placed between the main poles of a generator and connected so as to have the same polarity as the following main pole in the direction of rotation. Thus, an armature coil undergoing commutation is caused to cut flux which is in the same direction as that of the following main pole, thereby generating emf in a direction opposite to that of the self-induced emf in the coil.

Since the amount of emf of self-induction present in an armature coil varies with the amount of armature current flowing, the amount of commutating flux necessary also varies. To make the commutating flux produced by the interpoles proportional to the armature current, interpole windings are connected in series with the armature circuit. Fig. 8-21 shows a simple armature circuit. The dashed line above the centre armature coil indicates the direction of the induced emf in that coil by the interpole. The circular arrow in this coil undergoing commutation represents the direction of the self-induced emf in that coil. It is apparent the direction of the interpole-induced emf and the coil's self-induced emf are in opposite directions. If the F_m of the interpole is equal to the F_m of self-induction, they will cancel each other resulting in sparkless commutation.

8-9
Voltage Regulation

As load is added to a generator, the terminal voltage will change unless some provision is made to keep it constant. A curve that shows the value of the terminal voltage for different values of load current is called the **load-voltage characteristic** or the **regulation curve**. The values of voltage for various load currents may be cal-

FIGURE **8-21**
The function of the interpole.

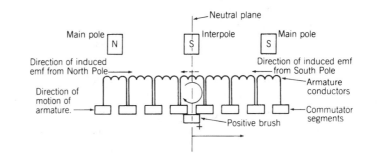

culated or may be obtained from an actual test. Readings of current and voltage obtained from a test are taken at a constant speed and with the field excitation adjusted so that rated voltage is obtained at full load.

Voltage regulation is defined as the difference between the no-load and full-load terminal voltage of a generator and is expressed as a percentage of the full-load value, the full-load voltage being the rated or normal voltage of the generator. Thus,

$$\text{Percent regulation} = \frac{\text{no-load voltage} - \text{full-load voltage}}{\text{full-load voltage}} \times 100$$

$$\%V_r = \frac{V_{NL} - V_{FL}}{V_{FL}} \times 100 \qquad \text{[8-5]}$$

It is important to know how the terminal voltage of a generator varies with different amounts of load in order to determine the suitability of the generator for a specific use. For example, a generator to be used to supply a lighting circuit should have a very low percentage regulation; that is, its terminal voltage should be very nearly the same at full load as it is at no load. It is not unusual for the percent regulation of some types of generators to have a negative regulation. This will be discussed later in this chapter.

8-10
The Separately Excited Generator

The separately excited generator is supplied field excitation from an independent dc source such as a storage battery or separate dc generator. The connection diagram is shown in Fig. 8-17a. A field rheostat is connected in series with the field to provide a means of varying the field excitation.

Fig. 8-22 shows the regulation curve of a typical separately excited generator. It will be noted that as the load current increases, the terminal voltage decreases. There are two important reasons for this decrease in terminal voltage:

FIGURE 8-22
Regulation curve of a separately excited generator.

1. The amount of effective field flux is reduced and the generated emf E thereby decreased by the demagnetizing effect of the armature current. Armature currents establish an mmf that distorts and weakens the main field flux, especially in non-interpole machines. This effect of armature current on the field flux of a generator is called **armature reaction**.
2. There is a voltage drop due to the armature-circuit resistance. These two factors affecting the terminal voltage are indicated in Fig. 8-22.

The separately excited generator has a decided advantage over the self-excited generator in that it will operate in a stable condition with any field excitation. Thus, a wide range of output voltages may be obtained. The main disadvantage of a separately excited generator lies in the inconvenience and expense of providing the separate excitation source. For this reason the use of this type of generator is largely confined to experimental and testing laboratories where such a source is available and a wide variation of output voltage is desirable.

8-11
The Self-Excited Shunt Generator

A self-excited generator depends on the residual magnetism of its field poles for its operation (see Sec. 6-1). Ordinarily there is some residual magnetism in the field poles if the poles have at a previous time been magnetized. If, then, a shunt generator is brought up to speed, the armature conductors will cut the small amount of flux present and a small amount of emf will be generated. As the shunt field is connected directly across the brushes as in Fig. 8-18(*b*), a current will flow in this winding. If the field resistance is sufficiently low and if the current is in such a direction that it increases the field strength, a higher emf is generated which, in turn, causes more current to flow through the field windings. This again increases the field flux and generated emf. At first it would appear that this building-up process would go on indefinitely, but a limit is reached owing to the saturation of the magnetic circuit. As the generator magnetic circuit approaches saturation, smaller and smaller increases in generated emf produce smaller and smaller increases in field current until the building-up process stops. At this point of equilibrium, the field current produces just enough flux to generate the emf that causes the field current to flow. After the voltage has been built up, it may be adjusted to the desired value by an adjustment of the field rheostat.

The regulation curve of a typical shunt generator is shown in Fig. 8-23. This curve shows the performance of a shunt generator to be similar to that of the separately excited generator, except that the voltage of the shunt generator falls off more rapidly with the

FIGURE **8-23**
Regulation curve of a shunt generator.

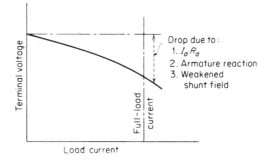

Drop due to:
1. $I_a R_a$
2. Armature reaction
3. Weakened
   shunt field

(y-axis: Terminal voltage; x-axis: Load current; Full-load current)

addition of load. As in the separately excited generator, armature reaction and *IR* drop in the armature circuit cause the terminal voltage to decrease. Since the field excitation is obtained from the generator itself, the decrease in terminal voltage, because of the above-mentioned effects, also decreases the voltage applied to the field circuit. This causes a decrease in field current and field flux which, in turn, causes a further decrease in the terminal voltage. These three important components of voltage drop are indicated in Fig. 8-23.

The shunt generator may be used for supplying excitation to ac generators or in other applications where the distance from the generator to its load is short. It is also used for charging storage batteries.

8-12
The Series Generator

The series generator is a self-excited generator with armature, field windings, and load all connected in series. Thus, the field current and field flux are proportional to the load current. When the generator is running without load, there is a small emf generated owing to the residual magnetism. As an external load is applied and current begins to flow in the field windings, the terminal voltage of the generator is increased. The terminal voltage continues to increase until the magnetic circuit becomes saturated. A series generator regulation curve is shown Fig. 8-24.

The series generator has very few practical applications. An understanding of the action of the series field is desirable, however, in the study of the compound generator.

8-13
The Compound Generator

It was pointed out in Sec. 8-11 that the terminal voltage of a shunt generator drops considerably with the addition of load. Many applications, such as lighting circuits, require a practically constant source of voltage; for such applications the shunt generator is unsuitable, especially if the amount of load is variable.

F I G U R E **8-24**
Regulation curve of a series generator.

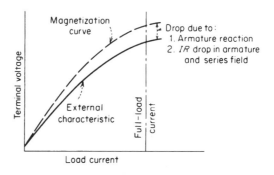

The decrease in terminal voltage of a shunt generator is due mainly to armature reaction and IR drop in the armature circuit. Both of these factors are proportional to the armature current. A generator may be made to supply automatically a constant terminal voltage by the use of a series-field winding placed on the same poles as the shunt-field winding. The series field, which carries full armature current, supplies an emf to compensate for the decrease in terminal voltage due to armature reaction and armature-circuit IR drop. A generator with both a series- and a shunt-field winding is called a **compound generator**. When the series field is so connected that its ampere-turns act in the same direction as those of the shunt field, the generator is said to be a **cumulative-compound generator**.

The cumulative-compound generator combines the characteristics of the shunt and the series generators. At no load, the shunt winding provides all the field flux, since there is no current in the series-field winding. As load is increased on the generator, the series field adds an increasing amount of field flux to that of the shunt field. The terminal voltage of the loaded generator will depend on the relative strength of the two fields. If the full-load terminal voltage is equal to the no-load terminal voltage, the generator is said to be **flat-compounded**. If the series ampere-turns at full load are more than enough to compensate for armature reaction and armature-circuit IR drop, the terminal voltage is higher than at no load and the generator is said to be **overcompounded**. Similarly, a generator is said to be **undercompounded** when the full-load terminal voltage is less than the no-load terminal voltage. Voltage regulation curves for over-, under-, and flat-compounded generators are shown in Fig. 8-25.

If, however, the series field is accidentally connected in such a way as to produce a magnetic field in a direction opposite to the

FIGURE **8-25**
Regulation curves of compound generators with varying degrees of compounding.

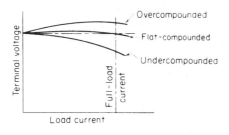

shunt field, then the generator is said to be differentially compound. The results of this type of connection will cause the terminal voltage of the generator under load to drop drastically. This connection has no practical application.

The compound generator is used more extensively than other types of generators because it may be designed to have a wide variety of characteristics. Overcompounded generators are used when they are located some distance from the loads that they supply. The increase in generator terminal voltage compensates for the voltage drop in the load feeder circuits.

When the shunt field of a compound generator is connected in parallel with the armature only, the connection is called a **short-shunt connection**. If the shunt field is connected in parallel with the circuit containing the armature and the series field, the connection is called a **long-shunt connection**. These connections are shown in Figs. 8-18(*d*) and 8-18(*e*). The operating characteristics are practically the same with either connection.

8-14
Efficiency

The efficiency of any machine is the ratio of the useful power output to the total power input. A part of the energy delivered to a generator or a motor is converted into heat and, therefore, is wasted. Thus, the useful output is never as large as the total input. There are always unavoidable losses even in the most perfectly constructed machines. Efficiency is usually expressed as a percentage. Thus, the ratio of output to input expressed as a decimal must be multiplied by 100 to change it to a percentage. Of course, output and input must be expressed in the same units. Thus, the definition of efficiency stated as a formula is

$$\% \eta = \frac{P_{\text{output}}}{P_{\text{input}}} \times 100 \qquad \text{[4-4]}$$

Suppose it is desired to find the efficiency of a generator whose input is 14.92 kW (20 hp) and whose terminal voltage is 240 V when it is supplying 50 A to a load. The output of the generator is

$$P = V_t I$$

$$P = 240 \times 50$$

$$P = 12\ 000\ \text{W}$$

The input to the generator in watts is

$$\text{Input} = \text{hp} \times (\text{watts per hp})$$

$$\text{Input} = 20 \times 746$$

$$= 14\ 920\ \text{W}$$

The percentage efficiency is

$$\frac{P_{\text{output}}}{P_{\text{input}}} \times 100$$

$$= \frac{12\ 000}{14\ 920} \times 100$$

$$= 80.4\%$$

8-15

Losses and Efficiency of a DC Machine

The losses of generators and motors consist of the copper losses in the electric circuits of the machine and the mechanical losses due to the rotation of the machine. The important losses may be outlined as follows:

I. Copper (winding) losses
   A. Armature I^2R losses
   B. Field losses
      1. Shunt field I^2R

F I G U R E **8-26**
Generator input/output power flow diagram.

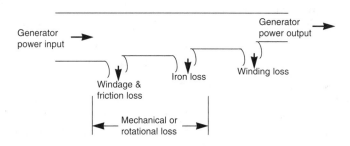

      2. Series field I^2R

      3. Interpole/compensating field I^2R

II. Mechanical or rotational losses

   A. Iron losses

      1. Eddy-current loss

      2. Hysteresis loss

   B. Friction losses

      1. Bearing friction

      2. Brush friction

      3. Windage or air friction loss

The copper losses are present because power is used whenever a current is made to flow through a resistance. When an armature current I_a flows through the armature-winding resistance R_a, the power used is $I_a^2R_a$. Likewise, the power used in overcoming the resistances of the series field winding and the interpole winding is expressed as $I_a^2R_s$ and $I_a^2R_i$, where R_s and R_i are series-field and interpole-field resistances, respectively.

The shunt-field loss is equal to V_tI_f where V_t is the terminal voltage of the machine and I_f is the shunt-field current. This includes the shunt-field rheostat loss.

As the armature rotates in a magnetic field, the iron parts of the armature cut lines of force as do the armature conductors. Since iron is a conductor of electricity, the emf induced in the iron parts causes currents to flow through these iron parts. These circulating currents are called **eddy currents**, and their flow causes the iron through which they flow to become heated. This heat is dissipated into the air and represents energy wasted.

To increase the resistance of the paths followed by eddy currents, armature cores are made of laminated steel sheets, stacked and secured in a position perpendicular to the shaft and parallel to the direction of the magnetic field. A thin layer of insulation is placed between the laminations. This insulation may be a type of insulating varnish or merely the oxide that is allowed to form on the surfaces of each lamination. The eddy currents, therefore, are confined to the individual laminations, and their heating effect is greatly reduced. Laminating the armature core does not increase its reluctance, for the laminations are parallel to the magnetic field.

When a magnetic material is magnetized, first in one direction and then the other, an energy loss takes place owing to the molecular friction in the material. That is, the molecules of the material resist being turned first in one direction and then the other. Thus, energy is expended in the material in overcoming this resistance. This loss is in the form of heat and is called **hysteresis loss**.

Hysteresis loss is present in a rotating armature core, for the magnetism of the core is continually being reversed as the armature moves through the stationary magnetic field.

Other rotational losses are bearing friction, the friction of the brushes riding on the commutator, and air friction or windage.

Since it is wasteful and sometimes difficult to measure directly the input and output of dc machines, especially in the larger sizes, their efficiencies are often calculated by first determining their losses and then working out their efficiency.

R E V I E W   Q U E S T I O N S

1 What is (*a*) a generator, (*b*) a motor?
2 Name the parts of the magnetic circuit of a generator.
3 Name the parts that make up the electric circuits of a generator.
4 What are the neutral planes of a generator?
5 Explain why an alternating emf is generated in a coil that is rotated in a magnetic field.
6 If it is desired to bring alternating current out of a generator, what kind of a "take-off" system is used?
7 Describe the action of a commutator.
8 In a single-coil dc generator is the brush voltage constant? Why?
9 Why is more than one coil used on a generator armature?
10 Give three methods of providing field excitation for a dc generator.
11 What is the purpose of the field rheostat?
12 Name the factors that determine the amount of emf generated. Which are variable?
13 When a generator supplies load, the terminal voltage is not the same as the generated emf. Why?
14 Draw an equivalent circuit of a generator armature.
15 What is the fundamental generator equation?
16 The magnetization curve shows the relation between what two things?
17 Explain why the generator magnetization curve is not a straight line.
18 Why is a commutating flux necessary? How may it be obtained?
19 What is an interpole? What is its purpose? How is its winding connected?
20 The regulation curve shows the relation between what two factors?
21 Give the formula for finding the voltage regulation of a generator.

22 Give two reasons for the drop in terminal voltage of a separately excited generator as load is increased.

23 Explain the "building-up" process of a self-excited shunt generator.

24 A certain generator may be connected for either separate or self-excitation. Which of the two connections should be used to obtain the better voltage regulation?

25 Why is a small emf generated in a series generator at no load? What happens to the generated emf as load is added?

26 What is a compound generator? What is a cumulative-compound generator?

27 When is a generator said to be (a) flat-compounded, (b) overcompounded?

28 When might it be desirable to use an overcompounded generator?

29 Define efficiency. How is it usually expressed?

30 Name three classes of dc machine losses.

31 How are eddy-current losses reduced in dc machines?

PROBLEMS

8-1 How many amperes will a 50-kW 240-V dc generator deliver at full load?

8-2 What is the full-load kilowatt output of a dc generator if the full-load line current is 30 A and the terminal voltage is 115 V?

8-3 A shunt generator generates 100 V when its speed is 900 r/min. What emf does it generate if the speed is increased to 1200 r/min and the field flux remains unchanged?

8-4 A generator produces an emf of 520 V, has 2000 armature conductors or inductors, a flux per pole of 0.013 wb, a speed of 1200 r/min, and the armature winding has four paths. Find the number of poles.

8-5 If the generated emf of a generator is 125 V and the *IR* drop in the armature circuit is 5 V, what is the terminal voltage?

8-6 A self-excited shunt generator delivers 20 A to a load. Its field current is 1.5 A. What is the armature current?

8-7 A 240-V shunt generator has a field-circuit resistance of 150 Ω. What is the field current when the generator operates at rated voltage?

8-8 A shunt-field winding of a 240-V generator has a resistance of 60 Ω. How much field-rheostat resistance must be added to limit the field current to 3 A when the generator is operating at rated voltage?

8-9 A 120-V shunt generator has a field-circuit resistance of 90 Ω. What is the armature current when the generator supplies 25 A to a load?

8-10 A shunt generator is rated 200 kW at 240 V. (*a*) What is the full-load current? (*b*) If the field-circuit resistance is 100 Ω, what is the field current? (*c*) What is the full-load armature current?

8-11 The terminal voltage of a shunt generator is 115 V when the generated emf is 119 V and the armature current is 20 A. What is the armature-circuit resistance?

8-12 The terminal voltage of a 75-kW shunt generator is 600 V at rated load. The resistance of the shunt-field circuit is 150 Ω, and the armature-circuit resistance is 0.1 Ω. Find the generated emf.

8-13 In a 50-kW 250-V shunt generator, 258 V are generated in the armature when the generator delivers rated load at rated voltage. The shunt-field current is 4 A. Find the resistance of the armature.

8-14 A load that has a resistance of 8 Ω is connected to a separately excited generator that has an armature-circuit resistance of 0.5 Ω. (*a*) What is the armature current when the generated emf is 130 V? (*b*) What is the generator terminal voltage?

8-15 A shunt generator has a full-load terminal voltage of 120 V. When the load is removed, the voltage increases to 150 V. What is the percentage voltage regulation?

8-16 A shunt generator has a field resistance of 50 Ω. When the terminal voltage of the generator is 120 V, the field current is 2 A. How much resistance is cut in on the shunt-field rheostat?

8-17 The no-load terminal voltage of a separately excited generator is 130 V. When the generator is supplying 50 A to a load, the speed and field excitation remaining unchanged, the terminal voltage is 115 V. If the armature-circuit resistance is 0.25 Ω, how much of the 15-V drop is due to the effect of armature reaction?

8-18 A shunt generator has an armature-circuit resistance of 0.4 Ω, a field-circuit resistance of 60 Ω, and a terminal voltage of 120 V when it is supplying a load current of 30 A. (*a*) Find the field current. (*b*) Find the armature current. (*c*) Find the copper losses at the above load. (*d*) If the rotational losses are 350 W, what is the efficiency at the above load?

8-19 Find the efficiency at full load of a 50-kW generator when the input is 80 hp.

8-20 The losses of a 20-kW generator at full load are 4500 W. (*a*) What is the efficiency at full load? (*b*) At no load?

8-21 A shunt generator requires 53-hp input from its prime mover when it delivers 150 A at 240 V. Find the efficiency of the generator.

8-22 The full-load losses of a 20-kW 230-V shunt generator are as follows:

Field I^2R loss	180 W
Armature I^2R loss	1200 W
Windage and friction losses	550 W
Iron loss	500 W

Find the efficiency at full load.

8-23 A shunt generator supplies a load with 106 A at 125 V. The shunt-field resistance is 31.2 Ω and the armature resistance is 0.11 Ω. Find (*a*) the shunt-field copper loss and (*b*) the armature copper loss.

8-24 From the following data concerning a shunt generator, calculate the efficiency at full load:

Rated kilowatt output	10 kW
Rated voltage	230 V
Armature-circuit resistance	0.4 Ω
Field-circuit resistance	192 Ω
Rotational losses at full load	750 W

8-25 A short-shunt-connected compound generator delivers 216 A to a load at 250 V. Its shunt-field resistance is 26.8 Ω, its shunt-field rheostat resistance is 6.2 Ω, its series-field resistance is 0.042 Ω, and its armature resistance is 0.096 Ω. Find the copper losses in (*a*) the shunt-field winding, (*b*) the shunt-field rheostat, (*c*) the series field, and (*d*) the armature winding.

8-26 A compound generator, short-shunt-connected, has a terminal voltage of 230 V when the line current is 50 A. The series-field resistance is 0.04 Ω. Find (a) the voltage drop across the series field, (*b*) the voltage across the armature, (*c*) the armature current if the shunt-field current is 2 A, and (*d*) the efficiency if the losses are 1950 W.

Direct-Current Motors and Controls

A motor is a machine that converts electric energy into mechanical energy. The dc motor is very similar to a dc generator in construction. In fact, a machine that runs well as a generator will operate satisfactorily as a motor.

One common constructional difference between motors and generators should be noted, however. Since motors often are operated in locations in which they may be exposed to mechanical damage, dust, moisture, or corrosive fumes, they are normally more completely enclosed than are generators.

FIGURE **9-1**
DC motor and control panel.
(Courtesy of Reliance Electric.)

Two general classifications for dc motor enclosures have been established by motor manufacturers: **open motors** and **totally enclosed motors**. Open motors have ventilating openings which permit the passage of external cooling air over and around the motor windings. Although external air is admitted into the open motor, the ventilating openings are constructed to restrict the entrance of liquids or solid objects. Such open motors are classified according to their construction as being dripproof, splashproof, weatherprotected, or guarded. For example, the motor shown in Fig. 9-2 is classified by its manufacturer as being a dripproof, fully guarded motor. It is considered to be dripproof because liquids or solids falling from above cannot interfere with the operation of the motor. It is called a guarded motor because openings in the motor are arranged so that accidental contact cannot be made with live or rotating parts.

F I G U R E **9-2**
Cutaway view of a dc motor.
(General Electric Company.)

Totally enclosed motors, as the name indicates, are completely enclosed so that no ventilating air can enter the motor. The heat developed by the motor must be entirely dissipated by radiation from the motor enclosure.

Although the mechanical construction of dc motors and generators is similar, their functions are different. The function of a generator is to *generate a voltage* when conductors are moved through a field, while the function of a motor is to develop a *turning effort* or a *torque*.

In this chapter, the motor principle and the characteristics of the several types of dc motors are discussed. A brief introduction to motor control circuits and equipment is also included.

9-1

Motor Principle

Every conductor carrying current has a magnetic field around it, the direction of which can be established by the right-hand rule. The strength of the field depends on the amount of current flowing in the conductor.

If a wire carrying current away from the reader is placed in a uniform magnetic field, the combined fields will be similar to that shown in Fig. 9-3. Above the conductor, the field due to the conductor is from left to right, or in the same direction as the main field. Below the conductor, the magnetic lines from the conductor and the main field magnetic lines are in opposite directions. The result is to strengthen the field or increase the flux density above the conductor and to weaken the field or decrease the flux density below the conductor.

It is convenient to think of magnetic lines as elastic bands under tension that are always trying to shorten themselves. Thus, the

FIGURE **9-3**
Effect of placing a current-carrying conductor in a magnetic field.

lines of force above the conductor exert a downward force on the conductor. Likewise, if the current in the conductor is reversed, the increased number of magnetic lines below the conductor will exert an upward force on the conductor.

While the above explanation of how a force is developed on a conductor is convenient, it is somewhat artificial. However, it is based on a fundamental principle of physics which may be proved experimentally and which may be stated as follows:

A conductor carrying current in a magnetic field tends to move at right angles to the field.

If the single conductor illustrated in Fig. 9-3 now forms a single coil as in Fig. 9-4, the direction of the current flowing in the single coil also produces a magnetic field about each conductor and distorts the main field. The distortion of the main field will result in a force on each coil side in an aiding direction resulting in the coil rotating in a counterclockwise direction. The right-hand rule for generators as described in Fig. 7-3 can now be modified for a motor by changing from the right hand to the left-hand rule. With the forefinger pointing in the direction of the **field flux** and the middle finger in the direction of the **applied emf** in the conductor, the thumb will now point in the resultant direction of that conductor. From this, the direction of rotation can be predicted.

FIGURE **9-4**
Fleming's left-hand rule for motors.

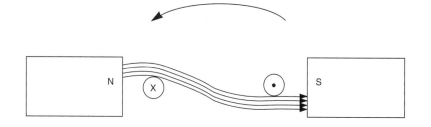

9-2

Torque Development in a Motor

Torque is defined as the action of a force on a body that tends to cause that body to rotate. Thus, the measure of the tendency of a motor armature to rotate is called the torque of the motor. Torque is, therefore, a force acting upon a radius.

$$T = Fr \qquad\qquad [9\text{-}1]$$

Torque can be in units of newton-metres (SI) or pound-feet (Imp.).

Motor-armature windings are wound in the same manner as are generator windings. When a voltage is applied to the brushes of a motor, current flows into the positive brush, through the commutator and armature windings, and out the negative brush. Armature conductors are wound so that all conductors under the south field poles carry current in one direction, while all the conductors under the north field poles carry current in the opposite direction. Fig. 9-5 shows the distribution of armature currents in a four-pole motor for a given polarity of applied terminal voltage.

When voltage is applied to a motor, such as is shown in Fig. 9-5, current flows through the field winding, establishing the magnetic field. Current also flows through the armature winding from the positive brushes to the negative brushes. Since each armature conductor under the four-pole faces is carrying current in a magnetic field, each of these conductors has a force exerted on it, tending to move it at right angles to that field, Fig. 9-4.

An application of the left-hand rule to the armature conductors under the north pole *D* in Fig. 9-5 shows the magnetic field to be strengthened under the conductors, resulting in an upward force on the conductors. Similarly, force is exerted to the right on the conductors under south pole *E*, downward on the conductors under north pole *F*, and to the left on the conductors under south pole *G*. Thus, there is a force developed on all the active armature conductors tending to turn the armature in a clockwise direction.

FIGURE **9-5**
Armature-current directions in a four-pole motor for clockwise rotation.

The force in newtons multiplied by the radius of the armature in metres is equal to the torque in *newton-metres* (N·m). If the armature is free to turn, that is, if the connected load is not too great, the armature will begin to rotate in a clockwise direction.

As the armature rotates and the conductors move from under a pole into the neutral plane, the current is reversed in them by the action of the commutator. For example, in Fig. 9-5, as the conductor at *A* moves from under the north pole and approaches the neutral plane, the current is outward. At the neutral plane the current is reversed so that as it moves under the south pole as at *B* it carries current inward. Thus, the conductors under a given pole carry current in the same direction at all times.

It should be evident from Fig. 9-5 that if the armature current were reversed by reversing the armature leads but leaving the field polarity the same, torque would be developed in a counterclockwise direction. Likewise, if the field polarity were reversed leaving the armature current as shown, torque would be developed in a counterclockwise direction. However, if both armature-current direction and field polarity were changed, torque would be developed in a clockwise direction. *The direction of rotation of a dc motor may be reversed by reversing either the field or the armature connections. If both are reversed, the direction of rotation remains unchanged.*

The force developed on each conductor of a motor armature is due to the combined action of the main field and the field around the conductor. It follows, then, that the force developed is directly proportional to the strength of the main field flux and to the strength of the field around each conductor. The field around each armature conductor depends on the amount of armature current flowing in that conductor. Therefore, the torque developed by a motor may be shown to be

$$T = K'\Phi I_a \qquad [9\text{-}2]$$

where

T = torque
K' = a constant depending on physical dimensions of motor
Φ = flux per pole
I_a = armature current

This important equation is of use in analyzing a motor's performance under various operating conditions.

9-3
Measurement of Torque

The torque developed by a motor may be measured by means of a **prony brake** attached to the motor pulley as shown in Fig. 9-6. Any desired load may be placed on the motor by adjusting the pressure of the brake shoes. The energy output of the motor is dissipated as heat, which is produced as the pulley turns in the

FIGURE **9-6**
Prony brake for measuring the torque developed by a motor.

brake shoes. For any given load, the torque output of the motor is the length of the brake arm *r* multiplied by the force *F* as registered on the spring scales.

The length of the brake arm *r* is measured in metres and the force *F* in newtons. If the spring scale is calibrated in kilograms, its reading must be multiplied by the gravitational constant 9.81 to obtain the force in newtons.

Example 9-1

A prony brake arm is 0.75 m long. The spring scale is calibrated in kilograms and, for a particular adjustment of pressure on the motor pulley, it reads 4.0 kg. What torque is the motor developing?

Force = (mass in kg) × (gravitational constant of 9.81)

F = mg

Therefore, the force on the spring scale = 4.0 × 9.81
or 39.24 newtons

$$T = Fr = 0.75 \times 39.24 \text{ N·m}$$

$$= 29.43 \text{ N·m}$$

The turning or twisting effort that a motor develops at the instant of starting is called its **starting torque,** It may be measured with a prony brake by clamping the brake arm securely so that the pulley cannot turn. With the motor connected to the supply lines and the armature remaining stationary, the force is measured with the scale. The starting torque is then equal to the force multiplied by the brake-arm length. Torque also can be measured using an **electro-dynamometer,** not shown here.

As the armature of a generator is rotated by a prime mover, a torque is developed in the generator opposing the action of the prime mover. This countertorque may be considered to be a motor action in a generator. Likewise, a generator action is developed in every motor. Whenever a conductor cuts lines of force, an emf is induced in that conductor. The driving force is immaterial; if a conductor is moved through a magnetic field, an emf will be induced in that conductor. The direction of that emf is in accordance with Fleming's right-hand rule for generator action.

The conductor of Fig. 9-7 represents one of many current-carrying conductors of a motor armature. For the field polarity shown, the current in the conductor is such that by motor action it will be moved downward. As the conductor is moved downward, it cuts lines of force and an emf is induced in it. The direction of this emf by Fleming's right-hand rule for a generated emf is found to be toward the reader. Since this emf is in a direction opposite to the flow of current in the conductor, it is called a **counter electromotive force**.

The counter emf of a motor is generated by the action of armature conductors cutting lines of force, therefore, its value will depend on the field strength and the armature speed. The value of the counter emf E that is generated in a motor is given by the relation

$$E = K\Phi n \qquad \text{[9-3]}$$

where K is a constant depending on the physical properties of the motor. It will be remembered that Eq. (9-3) was used as Eq. (8-2) to determine the generated emf of a generator.

The effective voltage acting in the armature circuit of a motor is the applied or terminal voltage minus the counter emf. The armature current by Ohm's law is

9-4

Generator Action of a Motor

FIGURE **9-7**
Counter emf is induced in a direction opposite to the flow of armature current.

$$I_a = \frac{V_t - E}{R_a} \qquad\qquad [9\text{-}4]$$

where I_a = armature current
        V_t = motor terminal voltage
        E = counter emf
        R_a = armature-circuit resistance

Multiplying both sides of Eq. (9-4) by R_a, and transposing, results in

$$V_t = E + I_a R_a \qquad\qquad [9\text{-}5]$$

which is the fundamental motor equation. Note that this is the same as the generator equation with the sign of the $I_a R_a$ term changed. The counter emf of a motor is always less than its terminal voltage.

Example 9-2

Find the counter emf of a motor when the terminal voltage is 240 V and the armature current is 60 A. The armature resistance is 0.08 Ω.

$$V_t = E + I_a R_a$$

or

$$E = V_t - I_a R_a$$

$$E = 240 - (60 \times 0.08)$$

$$E = 240 - 4.8$$

$$E = 235.2 \text{ V}$$

9-5

Equivalent Circuit of a Motor

It is convenient when dealing with dc motors to represent the armature as an equivalent circuit. As in the generator, the armature circuit is equivalent to a source of emf in series with a resistance as shown in Fig. 9-8. However, in the motor, current flows from the line into the armature against the generated emf. It is evident from Fig. 9-8 that the terminal voltage must be balanced by both the *IR* drop in the armature circuit and the counter emf at all times. This is apparent also from Eq. (9-5).

A comparison of the equivalent circuit of a generator (Fig. 8-19) and the equivalent circuit of a motor (Fig. 9-8) shows that the only difference is the direction of flow of armature current. In the generator, the generated emf is larger than the terminal voltage, resulting in a flow of current *from* the generator. In the motor,

FIGURE **9-8**
Equivalent circuit of a motor armature.

the generated emf is smaller than the terminal voltage, resulting in a flow of current *into* the motor. This again brings out the fact that the dc machine is a reversible machine. When it is supplied with mechanical energy, it delivers electric energy; when it is supplied with electric energy, it delivers mechanical energy.

If each term of the fundamental motor equation is multiplied by I_a, the resulting equation is

$$V_t I_a = E I_a + I_a^2 R_a$$

The term $V_t I_a$ is the power supplied to the armature of the motor. The power lost as heat in the armature circuit is represented by the term $I_a^2 R_a$. Thus, the term $E I_a$ must represent the power developed by the armature. This power is not all available at the pulley since some of this developed power must be used to overcome the mechanical or rotational losses of the motor.

9-6
Power Relationships in a Motor

Example 9-3

What is the power developed by the motor in the preceding example (*a*) in watts and (*b*) in horsepower?

(*a*)   Developed power $= E I_a$ watts

$$= 235.2 \times 60 \text{ W}$$

$$= 14\ 112 \text{ W}$$

(*b*)   Horsepower $= \dfrac{\text{watts}}{746}$

$$\dfrac{14\ 112}{746} = 18.92 \text{ hp}$$

The power output of a motor is

$$\text{Power output in watts} = \frac{2\pi nT}{60} \text{ or } \frac{nT}{9.55} \qquad [9\text{-}6]$$

where n = speed of motor, r/min
$\quad\quad\quad T$ = torque at motor pulley, newton-metres

Thus, the power output of a motor may be readily obtained by measuring its useful torque with a prony brake and measuring its speed with a tachometer. The power output may then be calculated by means of Eq. (9-6).

Example 9-4

The measured speed of a motor is 1100 r/min. The net force registered on the scale used with a prony brake is 5 kg. If the brake arm measures 0.8 m, what is the power output of the motor?

$$F = mg$$

$$\text{Force} = 5 \times 9.81$$

$$= 49.1 \text{ N}$$

$$T = Fr = 49.1 \times 0.8$$

$$= 39.24 \text{ N·m}$$

$$\text{Power output in watts} = \frac{nT}{9.55} = \frac{1100 \times 39.24}{9.55}$$

$$= 4520 \text{ W or } 4.52 \text{ kW}$$

9-7
Interpoles

Interpoles perform the same function in a motor as they do in a generator; that is, they provide a commutating flux that generates the emf necessary to neutralize the emf of self-induction in the armature coils undergoing commutation. Since the motor field flux is distorted in a direction opposite the field distortion in a generator, it follows that motor interpoles must be of a polarity opposite that of generator interpoles; that is, *motor interpoles must have a polarity opposite that of the following main pole in the direction of armature rotation.* It should be noted that for given external connections, a dc machine that has correct interpole polarity when operated as a generator will have the correct interpole polarity when operated as a motor, since a reversal of armature current changes the polarity of the interpoles.

The factors that may affect motor speed become evident when Eq. (9-3) for counter emf is combined with the fundamental motor equation, Eq. (9-5). This results in

$$V_t = K\Phi n + I_a R_a$$

or
$$n = \frac{V_t - I_a R_a}{K\Phi}$$ [9-7]

Eq. (9-7) is called the motor speed equation. From this equation it can be seen that motor speed n is dependent upon four variables, namely, the field flux Φ, the armature-circuit resistance R_a, the terminal voltage V_t, and the armature current I_a.

Speed control of a motor can be effected by the manipulation of three of the variables in Eq. (9-7) by manual or automatic means. The armature current I_a is determined by the amount of load being supplied by the motor armature and, hence, cannot be used for motor speed control. Thus, the three basic speed-control methods are

1. Control of field flux Φ
2. Control of armature-circuit resistance R_a
3. Control of terminal voltage V_t

Field Flux Control

Field current and, in turn, field flux in a shunt or compound motor is readily varied by means of a field rheostat connected in series with the shunt field. Increasing resistance in the field circuit causes a decrease in field flux and, therefore, an increase in speed. Likewise, a decrease in field-circuit resistance causes a decrease in speed.

Armature-Circuit Resistance Control

Motor armature-circuit resistance may be changed by introducing a variable resistance in series with the armature. As the series resistance is increased, the voltage across the motor armature is reduced and motor speed decreases. Likewise, motor speed is increased when the series resistance is decreased. This is the method of speed control normally used for series motors.

Terminal Voltage Control

Motor speed can be controlled by varying the voltage applied to the armature circuit. Prior to the advent of relatively inexpensive solid-state components, the provision of a variable or multivoltage supply of dc voltage was very costly. This method of speed control, therefore, was largely limited to the Ward-Leonard system or variations thereof for the control of very large motors. (The Ward-Leonard system of speed control is discussed in Sec. 9-21. Adjustable-speed motor drives employing solid-state components are discussed in Sec. 9-22.)

9-9
Motor Speed Regulation

Speed regulation of a motor is a term which describes the variation of motor speed as load on the motor is changed. If a motor is able to maintain a nearly constant speed for varying loads, the motor is said to have good or low speed regulation. The speed regulation of a given motor is dependent upon that motor's inherent characteristics and is usually expressed as a percent as in the following:

$$\text{Percent regulation} = \frac{\text{no-load speed}}{\text{full-load speed}} \times 100 \qquad [9\text{-}8]$$

Example 9-5

The no-load speed of a dc shunt motor is 1200 r/min. When the motor carries its rated load, the speed drops to 1120 r/min. What is the speed regulation as a percent?

$$\text{Percent regulation} = \frac{\text{NL speed} - \text{FL speed}}{\text{FL speed}} \times 100$$

$$= \frac{1200 - 1120}{1120} \times 100$$

$$= 7.14\%$$

9-10
The Shunt Motor

This is the most common type of dc motor. It is connected in the same way as the shunt generator, that is, with the shunt field directly across the terminals in parallel with the armature circuit. A field rheostat is usually connected in series with the field.

A shunt motor has good speed regulation and is classed as a constant-speed motor even though its speed does decrease slightly with an increase in load.

As load is added to a shunt motor, the motor immediately tends to slow down. The counter emf immediately decreases since it is dependent on the speed and the practically constant field flux. The decrease in the counter emf permits the flow of an increased armature current, thus providing more torque for the increased load. The increased armature current causes a larger $I_a R_a$ drop, which means that the counter emf does not return to its former value but remains at some lower value. This is shown to be true by the fundamental motor equation introduced in Sec. 9-4

$$V_t = E + I_a R_a \qquad [9\text{-}5]$$

Since V_t is constant, the sum of the counter emf and the I_aR_a drop must remain constant. If I_aR_a becomes larger owing to an increase in load, E must decrease, thus causing a corresponding decrease in speed.

The basic speed of a shunt motor is the full-load full-field speed. Usual speed adjustment is made by inserting resistance in the field circuit with a field rheostat, thereby weakening the field flux. This method of speed control provides a smooth and efficient means of varying the motor speed from basic speed to a maximum speed which is set by both electrical and mechanical limitations of the motor. *Care must be taken never to open the field circuit of a shunt motor that is running unloaded.* The loss of the field flux causes the motor speed to increase to dangerously high values.

It should be noted that a very small change in field flux will bring about a very large change in armature current. This consequent increase in armature current will increase the torque output of the motor and also the speed. Example 9-6 will illustrate this.

The speed of a shunt motor may also be changed by means of an adjustable resistance in the armature circuit, but this method is less efficient than the shunt-field control. The method is also objectionable because it causes the motor to have a very poor speed regulation.

The field flux of a shunt motor is very nearly constant. Since the torque of a motor is equal to $K'\Phi I_a$, the torque is directly proportional to the armature current. Figure 9-9 shows both the torque-load and the speed-load characteristics of a typical shunt motor. Note that the torque increases in a very linear line with an increase in armature current, while the speed drops slightly as armature current is increased.

Starters used with dc motors are usually designed to limit the armature starting current to 125 to 200 percent of full-load

FIGURE **9-9**
Speed-load and torque-load curves of a shunt motor.

current. Since the torque of a shunt motor is proportional to the armature current, the starting torque will be 125 to 200 percent of full-load torque, depending on the value of the starting resistance. For example, if the starting current of a given shunt motor is 150 percent of full-load current, then the starting torque is 150 percent of full-load value (note Fig. 9-9).

Since the speed of a shunt motor may be fixed at any value between a maximum and minimum value, it is often used for driving such loads as machine tools. The operator may select any speed within the rating of the motor by adjusting either the field rheostat or the armature voltage control. But at any one setting the motor speed remains practically constant for all loads.

Example 9-6

The voltage input to a shunt motor is 120 V. The present load connected to the motor is drawing an armature current of 10 A. The resistance of the armature circuit is 0.4 Ω.

Determine the percent increase in torque output of the motor if the field flux is reduced by 10 percent.

E_1, the counter emf under the original load condition, is

$$E_1 = V_t - I_a R_a$$

$$E_1 = 120 - 10 \times 0.4$$

$$E_1 = 116 \text{ V}$$

A 10 percent decrease in field flux will bring about an immediate 10 percent decrease in cemf. ($E = K\Phi n$) Therefore,

$$E_2 = 116 \times 0.9$$

$$E_2 = 104.4 \text{ V}$$

The new armature current as a result of this decrease in cemf is, therefore,

$$I_a = \frac{V_t - E_2}{R_a}$$

$$= \frac{120 - 104.4}{0.4}$$

$$= 39 \text{ A}$$

The percentage increase in armature current is $(39/10) \times 100$ or 390 percent.

Since torque ($T = K\Phi I_a$) with a 390 percent increase in armature current and a 10 percent decrease in field flux, the motor's immediate response will be an increase in torque of 351 percent.

In the series motor, the field is connected in series with the armature. As the series field must carry full armature current, it is wound with a few turns of comparatively large wire. Any change in load causes a change in armature current and also a change in field flux. Therefore, as the load changes, the speed changes.

It was shown that the speed of a shunt motor is inversely proportional to the field flux. This is true also in a series motor. The armature-circuit *IR* drop also varies with the load, but its effect is very small compared with the effect of the field flux. Therefore, the speed of a series motor depends almost entirely on the flux; the stronger the field flux, the lower the speed. Likewise, a decrease in load current and, therefore, in field current and field flux causes an increase in speed. Thus, the speed varies from a very high speed at light load to a low speed at full load.

A series motor does not have a definite no-load speed. As load is removed from the motor, the field flux decreases. If all the load is removed, the flux drops to practically zero and the motor speed may become dangerously high. For this reason, *the load should never be removed completely from a series motor*. A series motor is used only where load is directly connected to the shaft or geared to the shaft. Very small series motors usually have enough friction and other losses to keep the no-load speed down to a safe limit. The speed-load curve of a typical series motor is shown in Fig. 9-10.

In a shunt motor the torque is practically proportional to the armature current since the field flux is almost constant. In the series motor the field flux varies with the armature current, and for small loads the field flux is almost directly proportional to the armature

FIGURE **9-10**
Speed-load and torque-load curves of a series motor.

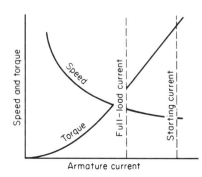

current. Since torque is equal to $K'\Phi I_a$, this means that for small loads the torque is proportional to I_a^2. However, as the armature current approaches full-load value, the saturation of the magnetic circuit and armature reaction both prevent the torque from increasing as rapidly as the square of the current. This causes the torque-load curve to straighten out for the heavier loads as shown in Fig. 9-10.

It has been pointed out that the series motor develops a large torque for large armature currents and also operates at low speed for large armature currents. Therefore, it is a suitable motor for starting heavy loads. It is often used for driving cranes and winches where heavy loads must be moved slowly but where the lighter loads may be moved with greater speed. Another common application of the series motor is in electric-railway service.

9-**12**

The Compound Motor

The cumulative-compound motor combines the operating characteristics of the shunt and series motors. It has a definite no-load speed and may be safely operated at no load. As load is added, the increased amount of field flux *in the series field* causes the speed to decrease more than does the speed of a shunt motor. Thus, the speed regulation of a cumulative-compound motor is poorer than that of a shunt motor.

The torque of the cumulative-compound motor is greater than that of the shunt motor for a given armature current owing to the series field flux. The torque-load and speed-load curves are shown in Fig. 9-11.

Cumulative-compound motors are used where a fairly constant speed is required with irregular loads or suddenly applied heavy loads. Such loads as presses, shears, and reciprocating machines are often driven by compound motors.

F I G U R E **9-11**
Speed-load and torque-load curves of a cumulative-compound motor.

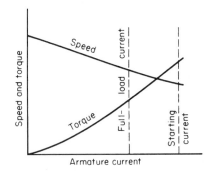

Fig. 9-12 shows a comparison of the characteristics of series, shunt, and cumulative-compound motors with the same full-load horsepower output and the same light-load speed. A representative value of starting current is shown, being 150 percent of full-load current.

The speed regulation of the shunt motor is much better than that of the series or compound motor. Thus, the shunt motor is suitable for constant-speed applications. The compound and series motors are used where good speed regulation is not essential or where a varying speed may be desirable.

The exceptionally high starting torque of the series motor makes it an ideal motor for starting heavy loads at a reduced speed. It will be noted from Fig. 9-12 that the series motor develops much more torque than the compound or shunt motors for a given armature current, at all but the lighter loads.

Thus, the different types of dc motors have widely varying characteristics. The nature of the load, of course, determines the type of motor to be used in each case.

Caution must be taken when connecting the shunt and series fields of a cumulative compound motor. If the series field is accidentally connected differentially (series field opposing the shunt field), the results could be quite dangerous and damaging to motor and connected load alike. Initially, under no-load the differentially connected compound motor will operate similarly to a shunt motor, since the series field effect will be very small. As the connected load increases, the armature current and series field current will also increase. Since the series field flux is opposing the shunt field, the net field will be weakened. This will result in an increase in armature speed. As the connected load continues to increase, the speed of the armature will rise. At some point the series field could

FIGURE **9-12**
Comparative speed-load and torque-load curves for series, shunt, and compound motors.

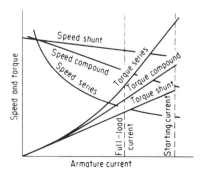

be equal to the shunt field in strength. if this occurs, the net field flux of the motor will be zero. At this point a very large armature current will flow, determined only by the motor's terminal voltage and the resistance of the armature circuit. This very high armature current will change the polarity of the field poles since, at this point, the reversed series field F_m will be greater than the shunt field F_m. The reversed polarity of the motor's field will result in a rotation change of the armature (left-hand rule for motors). The motor's reversal of rotation, as you can imagine, could have very damaging effects on the motor and connected load.

9-13
Permanent-Magnet Motors

Permanent magnets rather than electromagnets are used to provide the magnetic field flux in permanent-magnet motors. The armature and commutator assemblies of these motors are similar to those of wound-field motors. Since no electric power is required for supplying the field in the permanent-magnet motor, the attendant field copper losses are eliminated. More importantly, the size and weight of the permanent-magnet motor is reduced substantially below that of the wound-field counterpart with a similar power rating. The development of higher-performance magnets is expected to reduce still further the size and weight of these motors. Permanent-magnet motors are most often used in the smaller sizes, usually fractional horsepower motors.

Operationally, permanent-magnet motors are characterized by their high starting torque, their relatively high torque at low speeds, and their high efficiency. Typical applications include their use in line-printer drives, in precision positioning systems, and as reel motors in tape transports.

9-14
Motor-Starting Requirements

Two requirements must be met in starting dc motors, especially if they are to be started under load:

1. Both the motor and the supply lines must be protected from the flow of excessive current during the starting period.
2. The motor-starting torque should be made as large as possible, to bring the motor up to full speed in a minimum period of time.

At starting, when a motor armature is stationary, no counter emf is being generated. This means that the only thing to limit the amount of current being drawn from the supply is the armature-circuit resistance which, in most motors, is very low — being of the order of 1 Ω or less. To meet the first starting requirement, an external resistance is placed in series with the motor-armature circuit during the starting period. To show why this is necessary, consider a 10-hp motor with an armature resistance of 0.5 Ω. If this motor were connected directly to a 230-V supply line, the resulting starting current would be

$$I = \frac{V}{R}$$

$$I = \frac{230}{0.5}$$

$$I = 460 \text{ A}$$

which is roughly 12 times normal full-load armature current for a motor of this size. This large inrush of current would in all probability damage the brushes, commutator, or windings. Starting resistances are usually designed to limit the starting current of a motor to 125 to 200 percent of the full-load current.

The amount of starting resistance required to limit the armature starting current to the desired values is

$$R_s = \frac{V_t}{I_s} - R_a \qquad [9\text{-}9]$$

where R_s = starting resistance, ohms
V_t = motor terminal voltage, volts
I_s = desired armature starting current, amperes
R_a = armature-circuit resistance, ohms

Example 9-7

If the full-load armature current of the above motor is 40 A and it is desired to limit the starting current to 150 percent of this value, find the starting resistance that must be added in series with the armature.

$$R_s = \frac{V_t}{I_s} - R_a$$

$$R_s = \frac{230}{40 \times 1.5} - 0.5$$

$$R_s = \frac{230}{60} - 0.5$$

$$R_s = 3.33 \ \Omega$$

Starting resistors are variable resistances, with the value of the resistance in the circuit at any time being manually or automatically controlled. The maximum value of the resistance is inserted in the armature circuit when the motor is first connected to the supply. As the motor speed increases, the counter emf increases, thereby decreasing the armature current. The starting resistance may then be cut out by successive steps until the motor has reached its full speed.

The second motor-starting requirement is met by providing a maximum value of field flux and by allowing a maximum safe value of armature current to flow during the starting period. In shunt and compound motors, a maximum field flux is obtained by cutting out the shunt-field rheostat, thereby applying full line voltage to the shunt field. In the series motor, the field flux is at a maximum by virtue of the heavy starting current flowing through the field winding. With a maximum field flux and a maximum allowable armature current, the starting torque (equal to $K'\Phi I_a$) developed is at a maximum value, thereby bringing the motor to full speed in a short time.

9-15
Controllers and Starters

A controller is a device for regulating the operation of the apparatus to which it is connected. A dc motor controller performs several basic functions such as starting, stopping, reversing, controlling speed, and providing some measure of protection for the motor that it governs.

A starter is a controller whose main function is to start and accelerate a motor.

9-16
Drum Controllers

The drum controller is a manually operated controller often used for starting and controlling the operation of dc motors. A drum controller consists essentially of a cylinder insulated from a central shaft on which is mounted a series of copper segments. As the cylinder is rotated by a handle, which is keyed to the shaft, the various contact segments come in contact with contact fingers. The contact fingers are held in place by adjusting screws and by springs strong enough to ensure a good electric connection with the contact segments. By designing the controller with different sequences for the making and breaking of the contacts as the drum is rotated, a great variety of switching operations may be performed.

The drum controller is no longer widely used as a control apparatus for direct current motors. Even though many still exist, they are largely replaced by automatic control equipment.

Automatic starting, stopping, and reversing of dc motors are commonly accomplished by means of magnetically operated switches called **magnetic contactors**. Controllers using magnetic contactors to control the operation of the motor to which they are connected are called **magnetic controllers**.

Magnetic controllers may be actuated by means of a push button which is often located at some point remote from the motor and controller. Controllers are also made entirely automatic by actuating them by various automatic devices. If, for example, a motor drives an air compressor that supplies air to a storage tank, the starting and stopping "signals" to the motor may be given by a pressure switch connected to the tank. When the pressure falls below a certain value, the motor is started; it is stopped again when the pressure has risen to the desired value.

The basic part of all magnetic controllers is the magnetic contactor. An operating coil is placed on an iron core so that when current flows through the coil, the iron core becomes magnetized. This attracts a movable iron armature that carries one or more insulated electric contacts. As the armature is moved toward the core, the moving contacts are moved against stationary contacts. The contacts are connected in series with the controlled device, such as a motor-armature circuit, thereby completing the circuit when the operating coil is energized. When the circuit of the operating coil is open, the iron core becomes demagnetized and the armature is released, being returned to its open position by means of a spring or by gravity. Since the contacts of a magnetic contactor may be designed to carry heavy currents, a means is provided whereby large amounts of current can be controlled by means of the relatively feeble current needed for energizing the operating coil.

To aid in extinguishing the arc formed when heavy currents are interrupted by electric contacts, **magnetic blowouts** are used. A magnetic blowout is an electromagnet constructed so that its field is set up across the arc. When the contacts open, the arc is moved at right angles to the field in the same way as a current-carrying conductor is acted upon. The field and contacts are so arranged that the arc is drawn away from the contacts, breaking it in a short time. To make the field strength proportional to the current being interrupted, the blowout coil is connected in series with the circuit being opened. A single-pole magnetic contactor equipped with a magnetic blowout coil is shown in Fig. 9-13.

Magnetic contactors are used when it is desired to control a motor or other device from a remote point. It is not necessary to run the main supply lines to the point of control. Only small control wires need be used.

9-**17**
Magnetic Contactors

FIGURE **9-13**
Sectional view of a one-pole magnetic contactor equipped with magnetic blowout coil.
(Square D Company.)

If a switch is to be opened and closed frequently, magnetic control is also desirable. An operator is easily able to operate a push button to actuate a contactor several times a minute, whereas the operation of heavy manual controls might cause undue equipment and personnel fatigue.

Undervoltage release, undervoltage protection, and overload protection are easily provided by the use of magnetic contactors as is described in the following sections.

9-**18**
Control of Magnetic Contactors: Motor Protection

Fig. 9-14 shows a wiring diagram and a schematic control diagram of a two-wire control circuit using a magnetic contactor for connecting a motor to the line. It will be noted that the wiring diagram identifies the electric devices, terminals, and interconnecting wiring. The control schematic shows by means of graphic symbols the

FIGURE **9-14**

Undervoltage release provided by two-wire control of the magnetic contactor. (*a*) Wiring diagram. (*b*) Schematic control diagram.

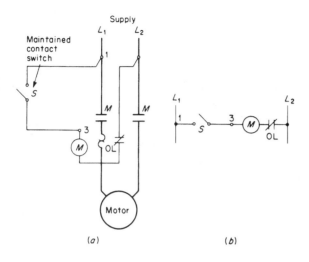

(*a*)   (*b*)

electrical connections and functions of the control circuits. The schematic diagram facilitates tracing the circuit and its functions without regard to the physical location of the component parts. Commonly used graphic symbols are shown in Appendix A.

When the switch S in Fig. 9-14 is closed, the operating-coil circuit is completed from point 1 on L_1 through the switch, coil M, and the normally closed overload relay contacts to L_2. This closes the main contacts M connecting the motor to the supply. The method for cutting out the starting resistance is not shown as this will be considered in Sec. 9-19. When the switch S is opened, contactor coil M is de-energized, the main contacts M open, and the motor is disconnected from the line.

If, while the motor in Fig. 9-14 is in operation, the supply voltage falls below a certain value or fails completely, the contactor disconnects the motor from the line. When the supply voltage is restored, the contactor M is reenergized and the motor restarts. This type of control is said to provide the motor with **undervoltage release**. This is desirable where it is necessary that the motor be restarted automatically after a voltage failure.

The switch S in Fig. 9-14 may be replaced by any of the number of automatic devices such as a thermostat, float switch, photoelectric cell, or limit switch.

A three-wire push-button control circuit for a contactor is shown in Fig. 9-15. The START button is a momentary contact switch that is held normally open by a spring. The STOP button is

FIGURE **9-15**
Three-wire push-button control providing undervoltage protection for the motor. (*a*) Wiring diagram.
(*b*) Schematic control diagram.

(*a*)   (*b*)

held normally closed by a spring. When an operator depresses the
START button, the operating-coil circuit is completed from point
1 on L_1, through the STOP button, the START button, the coil, and
the normally closed overload relay contacts to L_2. This energizes
contactor M, closing the main contacts M which connect the motor
to the supply. At the same time, contactor M auxiliary or interlock
contacts M-1 are closed.

When contacts M-1 close, a new circuit is established from
point 1 through the STOP button to point 2, through contacts
M-1 to point 3, through coil M and the overload relay to L_2. Since
the operating-coil circuit is now maintained by the M-1 contacts,
the operator may release the START button and the motor will
continue to run. When the STOP button is depressed, the coil is
de-energized, thereby opening both the main and auxiliary contacts
and stopping the motor.

If the supply voltage drops below a certain value, or fails while
the motor is running, the main contacts and the auxiliary contacts
are both opened. Upon return of the supply voltage, the contactor
cannot close until the START button is again closed. Because a
contactor that is controlled by a three-wire control circuit maintains the interruption of the circuit even after the line voltage is
restored, it is said to provide **undervoltage protection** for the
motor. This protection is used when it is desired to prevent the
unexpected starting of a motor.

Overload protection for motors is used to protect the motor
from excessive heating due to motor overloads. **Thermal-overload**

relays are commonly used for motor-overload protection. There are two principal types of thermal-overload relays. Both types are operated from the heat generated in a heating element through which the motor current passes. In one type the heat bends a bi-metallic strip, and in the other the heat melts a film of solder. Both act to open the motor control circuit.

A bimetallic strip is made of two different metals whose surfaces have been welded together. One of the metals expands rapidly when heated, while the other is not affected greatly by the heat. When heat is applied, the strip is caused to deflect or curl up due to the different expansion of the two metals. When the motor current reaches a predetermined value, the heat generated deflects the strip far enough to trip a latch that opens the motor-control circuit. When the strip cools sufficiently, the relay may be reset and the motor restarted.

In the solder-film type of overload relay, the heat generated at a given overload current melts the film, which releases a latch arrangement and opens the motor control circuit. When the solder has cooled enough to hold the latch, the relay may be reset.

In either type of thermal relay, the time required to operate is determined by the amount of current flowing in the heater. Thus, the relay operates slowly for light overloads but disconnects the motor in a short time for dangerously heavy overloads. Relays in which the time of operation is inversely proportional to the amount of current flowing are called **inverse-time relays**.

Overload relay heating elements and contacts are connected in the motor main and control circuits respectively, as shown in Figs. 9-14 and 9-15.

9-19
Magnetic Controllers for Starting DC Motors

It was shown in Sec. 9-14 that a resistance must be connected in series with a dc motor-armature circuit during the starting period. If magnetic control is to be used for starting a motor, some method must be used for automatically inserting this resistance at starting and removing it when the motor reaches normal speed. A device that is often used to accomplish this is the **time-limit acceleration starter**. This starter cuts out the starting resistor in steps with contactors that operate successively at definite time intervals as the motor accelerates.

A time-limit acceleration starter is shown in Fig. 9-16. Fig. 9-17 shows a schematic wiring diagram for this type of starter in which the starting resistors are bypassed in two steps as the motor accelerates.

The time-limit acceleration starter shown in Fig. 9-17 is controlled with a three-wire push-button control circuit. Depressing the START button energizes the main contactor M, the contacts of which connect the motor shunt-field and armature circuits to the

F I G U R E **9-16**
Time-limit acceleration starter.
(Square D Company.)

supply lines and start acceleration timer $1AR$. The two acceleration timers are wired in series with the acceleration contactor coils and appear on the diagram as normally open time-closing contacts. Immediately following the closing of main contactor M, resistors R_1 and R_2 are both connected in series with the armature circuit since the contacts of both acceleration contactors $1A$ and $2A$ are open. After a time delay during which the motor begins to accelerate, timer $1AR$ closes its contact to energize contactor $1A$, which bypasses resistor R_1 and also starts timer $2AR$. As the motor continues to accelerate, timer $2AR$ closes its contact to energize contactor $2A$, which bypasses resistor R_2. This applies full line voltage to the armature circuit, and the motor accelerates to its normal speed.

Time-limit acceleration starters used with motors of 10 hp and larger are usually designed to have three, four, or five acceleration points rather than the two points shown for the starter in Fig. 9-17. These starters may also be designed to provide for dynamic braking and reversing service.

9-**20**

Dynamic Braking

Often it is desirable to have a means of stopping a motor quickly. One method of bringing a motor to a quick stop is **dynamic braking**. If a running motor is disconnected from its supply lines and a resistance load (often the starting resistance) is placed across the armature terminals, the motor then acts as a generator, sending a current through the resistance. This causes the energy stored by

FIGURE **9-17**
Schematic diagram of a time-limit acceleration starter.
(Square D Company.)

the rotating armature to be expended quickly in the form of heat in the parallel resistance, which brings the motor to a standstill quickly. The amount of braking effort available depends on the motor speed, the motor field strength, and the value of the resistance. This type of braking is used extensively in connection with the control of elevators and hoists and in other applications in which motors must be started, stopped, and reversed frequently.

Some applications of dc motors require a wide and finely graduated range of speed control. The Ward-Leonard, or adjustable-voltage, system provides such control and involves a separate generator that drives an adjustable-speed motor. By varying the field excitation of the generator, the voltage applied to the motor may be varied over a wide range, resulting in a wide speed range on the motor.

A simplified diagram of the system is shown in Fig. 9-18. The driving motor is usually a constant-speed ac motor. Directly

9-**21**
Ward-Leonard System of Speed Control

FIGURE **9-18**
Simplified diagram of the Ward-Leonard system of speed control.

connected to the prime mover is the separately excited dc main generator G that drives the main motor M. To supply the field excitation of both G and M, a small self-excited dc generator or exciter E is also connected directly to the driving motor. Some systems use a static power supply for the field excitation in place of a rotating exciter.

To start the motor M, the field excitation of G is raised so that the voltage V_t is gradually increased across M, which causes the motor to accelerate. No starting resistance is needed since the voltage V_t is raised from a very low value, allowing the counter emf of the motor to increase with the applied voltage. The motor speed may be set at any speed between zero and its maximum speed by adjusting the field excitation of the generator G to the desired value. Since the field flux of motor M is constant, it has the speed-load characteristics of a shunt motor and the speed regulation is good at a given armature voltage.

If, while the motor M is operating, the voltage V_t is suddenly decreased to a value below the counter emf of the motor, the armature current is reversed with the motor acting as a generator, driving G as a motor. Dynamic braking is thus established, which brings the motor to a quick stop. The motor M may be reversed by dropping V_t to zero and reversing the generator field current. As the voltage V_t is increased with the opposite polarity, the motor accelerates in the opposite direction.

An important requirement in many industrial motor control applications is the maintenance of a constant speed of a drive motor or the maintenance of a variable speed which is a function of some operating quantity. For example, the speed of the individual sections of a paper making machine must be maintained within an accuracy of a fraction of one percent. Special control systems, called **closed-cycle feedback control systems**, have been developed for use with the conventional Ward-Leonard system to obtain extremely accurate speed control.

Some common applications of the Ward-Leonard system are in steel mills for reversing rolling mills, excavator drives, elevators for tall buildings, gun turrets, and special hoist motors.

The first cost of the Ward-Leonard system is high, and it is relatively inefficient since several energy transformations are involved. However, the speed control provided is very effective; that is, the response to changes in speed is fast, a wide range of speeds is available, and reversing and dynamic braking are provided. In applications where these factors are important, the advantages gained in using the Ward-Leonard system justify the increased cost and low efficiency.

Following the advent and development of semiconductor electronic components, static ac-to-dc conversion systems became economically feasible. These systems, using **silicon controlled rectifiers** (SCR) or **thyristors** together with other solid-state components, provide a relatively low-cost method for supplying and controlling dc motors from commercial ac supply systems. These systems are finding wide application not only in the control of general-purpose dc motor drives, but also in highly automated steel mill drives where formerly the Ward-Leonard system, or modifications thereof, was used.

Thyristor power supply and control units offer higher efficiency, lower installation and maintenance costs, greater flexibility, and faster response than motor-generator sets of the same rating.

Static ac-to-dc conversion equipment has found widespread use for supplying and controlling dc motors from ac supplies.

A dc rectifier drive system is an adjustable-speed drive consisting of a rectifier, control equipment, and a dc motor, all of which is suitable for operating directly from a standard commercial ac supply system. Such drive systems may be very simple ones such as those used with small single-phase motors, or they may be complex industrial drive systems with ratings up to 100 hp, or even higher.

The basic elements of a dc rectifier drive for a shunt-wound dc motor are shown in Fig. 9-19. This is the configuration of a general-purpose drive suitable for powering conveyors, elevators, and machine tools, or for other loads requiring a continuously variable, closely regulated speed. As indicated by the diagram, the SCR unit converts the incoming ac supply voltage to an adjustable dc voltage. The contactor F connects the motor armature to the dc supply voltage.

9-**22**
Static Conversion and Control Equipment

FIGURE **9-19**
Simplified schematic diagram of a dc adjustable-speed drive.

The operator's control station contains a START-STOP button to control contactor F and a potentiometer used to set the speed level of the motor. During operation of the motor, the feedback voltage is compared with the reference voltage established by the setpoint on the potentiometer. The difference in these two voltages is used to regulate the triggering of the SCR unit which, in turn, regulates the output voltage of the conversion unit and hence the speed of the motor. DC excitation for the motor field is supplied by a diode rectifier in the SCR conversion unit. A typical drive of this type may have a speed control range of 30 to 1 and a speed regulation of 2 percent. A more precise degree of speed regulation may be obtained when the feedback signal is obtained from a tachometer generator driven from the dc motor shaft. Speed regulation with this arrangement may be held to within 0.1 percent on some drives.

Many of the larger, more sophisticated dc adjustable-speed drives for industrial use provide for motor reversing, dynamic braking, and regeneration. Regeneration is the ability of a motor to return power to the ac source when the motor load becomes overhauling and the load attempts to drive the motor. A basic regenerative dc drive allows operation of the drive motor in any of four modes: forward motoring, forward regeneration, reverse motoring, and reverse regeneration. Other features often supplied with larger dc drives include special protective features such as motor field loss protection and protection against ac line disturbances. Special test and diagnostic equipment is also sometimes furnished as a part of the drive. A typical dc SCR drive unit which provides many of these features is shown in Fig. 9-20.

F I G U R E **9-20**
DC motor drive unit.
(Courtesy of Reliance Electric.)

TABLE **9-1**   **Summary of DC Generator and Motor Characteristics**

Characteristic	Generator	Motor
Purpose	To generate an emf	To develop a torque
Capacity rating	Kilowatts	Horsepower (Imperial)
		Kilowatts (SI)
Opposing action	Countertorque	Counter emf
Fundamental equation	$V_t = E - I_a R_a$	$V_t = E + I_a R_a$
Variation in field excitation		
results in	Change in voltage	Change in speed
Interpoles	Same polarity as following main pole	Opposite polarity from following main pole
Effect of increase in load:		
Shunt machine	Voltage decreases	Small decrease in speed
Series machine	Voltage increases	Large decrease in speed
Cumulative-compound machine	Voltage may remain constant, increase, or decrease, depending on compounding	Large or small decrease in speed depending on compounding

Characteristic	Generators and Motors
Generated emf	$E = K\Phi n$
Methods of field excitation	Separately excited, shunt, series, compound
Losses	Winding, iron, friction and windage
Efficiency	Percent efficiency = output/input × 100

REVIEW **Q**UESTIONS

1. What is the function of a motor?
2 Upon what fundamental principle does motor operation depend?
3 Define torque. What is the unit?
4 Describe how torque is developed in a motor.
5 How may the direction of rotation of a dc motor be reversed?
6 What two things determine the amount of force developed on an armature conductor?
7 Give the torque equation of a motor.
8 If the mechanical output of a motor is increased, what must happen to the electrical input?
9 Explain how the torque of a motor may be measured.
10 What is starting torque?
11 When a motor is in operation, why is the armature current not equal to the line voltage divided by the armature resistance? Give the correct equation for armature current.

12 What is the fundamental motor equation? How does it differ from the generator equation?

13 Given a prony brake and a tachometer, explain how the output of a motor may be measured. What other instruments would be needed to obtain data for finding the efficiency of a motor?

14 What is the unit of torque in Imperial units? In SI units?

15 When the torque and speed are known, what is the formula for computing motor output?

16 What is the purpose of interpoles?

17 If the resistance of a motor shunt-field rheostat is increased, what happens to the speed of the motor?

18 What is a common method of controlling the speed of a shunt motor?

19 Define speed regulation.

20 Explain how a motor automatically adjusts its input to take care of changes in mechanical load.

21 What happens to the speed of a shunt motor as load is increased?

22 How is the basic speed of a shunt motor defined?

23 Is it possible to lower the speed below the basic speed by varying the shunt-field-rheostat resistance?

24 Why is it dangerous to open the field of a shunt motor running at no load?

25 If the torque of a shunt motor is doubled, what happens to the armature current, assuming a constant field flux?

26 Why is the speed regulation of a series motor poorer than that of a shunt motor?

27 Why should a series motor never be operated without load?

28 Describe the fundamental differences between the possible racing conditions that exist between the series motor and the shunt motor.

29 Why does a series motor have a higher starting torque than a shunt motor of similar capacity?

30 What are some common applications of (*a*) shunt motors, (*b*) series motors?

31 How does the speed regulation of a compound motor compare with that of (*a*) a series motor, (*b*) a shunt motor?

32 How does the starting torque of a compound motor compare with that of (*a*) a series motor, (*b*) a shunt motor?

33 What caution should be taken when connecting a compound motor? Why?

34 Give some applications of compound motors.

35 What two requirements must be met in starting dc motors?

36 What is the purpose of the starting resistance used with dc motors?

37 Give some of the functions of a controller.

38 Name three methods by which speed of a dc motor may be controlled.

39 Explain what is meant by undervoltage protection of a motor.

40 Where is the drum controller used?

41 What is a magnetic blowout? How does it operate?

42 What are some advantages of using magnetic contactors to control the operation of electric motors?

43 What is meant by undervoltage release? In what application would it be desirable?

44 What kind of protection is provided for a motor by the three-wire push-button control of a magnetic contactor?

45 How is overload protection commonly provided for a motor?

46 How is time delay obtained for operation of the accelerating contacts in a time-limit acceleration starter?

47 Describe what is meant by dynamic braking.

48 What are some advantages of the Ward-Leonard system of speed control? What are some disadvantages?

PROBLEMS

9-1 A 120-V shunt motor develops a torque of 30 N·m when the armature current is 12 A. Assuming a constant value of field flux, what torque will the motor develop when the armature current is 20 A?

9-2 When developing a torque of 25 N·m, a 120-V shunt motor draws a current of 10 A from the source. The field current is 1.5 A. What current will the motor draw from the line when it is developing a torque of 80 N·m, assuming that the field flux does not change in value?

9-3 A prony brake attached to a motor pulley has a brake-arm length of 0.5 m. If, when the motor runs at 1150 r/min, the scale indicates a net force of 3.5 kg, what is the kilowatt output?

9-4 A prony brake is to be built to measure the torque output of a 10-hp motor that operates at a speed of 1200 r/min. If the scale available has a maximum capacity of 7 kg, what is the length of the shortest brake arm that could be used to measure any torque output of the motor up to 125 percent of its rated value?

9-5 A shunt motor on a 240-V line has an armature current of 75 A. If the field-circuit resistance is 100 Ω, find the field current, the line current, and the kilowatt input to the motor.

9-6 A shunt motor draw 6 kW from a 240-V line. If the field resistance is 96 Ω, find the line current, the field current, and the armature current of the motor.

9-7 A shunt motor connected to a 120-V line runs at a speed of 1200 r/min when the armature current is 20 A. The armature resistance is 0.1 Ω. Assuming constant field flux, what is the speed when the armature current is 50 A? (*Hint*: Speed is directly proportional to counter emf.)

9-8 Find the armature current of a shunt motor when the terminal voltage is 112 V, the counter emf is 107 V, and the armature-circuit resistance is 0.3 Ω.

9-9 The armature resistance of a 240-V shunt motor is 0.16 Ω. At no load, the line current is 6.4 A at rated voltage. The field current is 2.2 A, and the speed is 1280 r/min. Find the motor speed when the line current increases to 75 A, the field current remaining the same. Assume that armature reaction does not affect the field flux.

9-10 The counter emf of a shunt motor is 227 V, the field resistance is 160 Ω, and the field current is 1.5 A. The line current is 36.5 A. (*a*) Find the armature resistance. (*b*) If the line current during starting must be limited to 60 A, how much starter resistance must be added in series with the armature?

9-11 A shunt motor draws a current of 38 A from a 120-V source. The field-circuit resistance is 50 Ω, and the armature-circuit resistance is 0.25 Ω. Find (*a*) the field current, (*b*) the armature current, (*c*) the counter emf, and (*d*) the counter emf at starting (armature at a standstill).

9-12 Find the horsepower developed by the motor in the preceding problem. If the mechanical and iron losses total 550 W, what is the horsepower output?

9-13 What is the kilowatt output of a motor that is running at 1200 r/min and is supplying a torque of 24 N·m to the load?

9-14 What horsepower is developed by a motor when the armature current is 20 A, the applied voltage is 115 V, and the counter emf is 110 V?

9-15 A 10-hp motor has a shunt-field resistance of 115 Ω and a field current of 2 A. What is the applied voltage?

9-16 A certain shunt motor is connected to a 240-V line. The armature-circuit resistance is 0.05 Ω. When the armature current is 60 A, what is the counter emf?

9-17 A motor has a no-load speed of 900 r/min and a full-load speed of 850 r/min. What is the speed regulation?

9-18 The armature resistance of a shunt motor is 0.048 Ω. When the motor is connected across 120 V, it develops a counter emf of 113 V. Find (*a*) the *IR* drop in the armature circuit, (*b*) the armature current, (*c*) the armature current if the armature were stationary, and (*d*) the counter emf when the armature current is 160 A.

9-19 The efficiency, at rated load, of a 100-hp 600-V shunt motor is 85 percent. The field resistance is 190 Ω, and the armature resistance is 0.22 Ω. The full-load speed is 1200 r/min. Find (*a*) the rated line current, (*b*) the armature current at full load, (*c*) the counter emf at full load, and (*d*) the field current.

9-20 The power input to a shunt motor is 5600 W for a given load on the motor. The terminal voltage is 220 V, the $I_a R_a$ drop is 6.4 V, and the armature resistance is 0.27 Ω. Find (*a*) the counter emf, (*b*) the power taken by the field, and (*c*) the field current.

9-21 At full load a 15-hp motor draws 54.8 A from a 240-V line. (*a*) What is the motor efficiency? (*b*) What is the motor efficiency at no load?

9-22 At rated load the rotational losses (iron losses plus mechanical losses) of a 240-V shunt motor are 865 W. The field resistance is 92 Ω and the armature-circuit resistance is 0.12 Ω. The rated motor current is 140 A. Find (*a*) the field copper losses, (*b*) the armature copper losses, (*c*) the rated horsepower output, and (*d*) the efficiency.

9-23 A long-shunt compound motor requires an armature current of 12 A to carry a certain load. The armature resistance is 0.05 Ω, and the series-field resistance is 0.15 Ω. The motor is connected to a 115-V source. Find (*a*) the counter emf and (*b*) the developed horsepower.

9-24 A 10-hp compound motor connected short-shunt is supplied by a 115-V source. The full-load current is 90 A. The shunt-field resistance is 90 Ω, the armature resistance is 0.08 Ω, and the series-field resistance is 0.04 Ω. Find (*a*) the shunt-field current, (*b*) the armature current, (*c*) the counter emf, (*d*) the efficiency at full load, (*e*) the full-load copper losses, and (*f*) the rotational losses (iron losses plus mechanical losses).

Alternating Current

Over 90 percent of the electric energy used in most countries is generated and distributed as alternating-current energy. Perhaps the greatest single reason for this widespread use of alternating current is the fact that an alternating voltage may be easily raised or lowered in value. Because of this, ac energy may be generated and distributed efficiently at a relatively high voltage and then reduced to a lower usable voltage at the load.

Direct-current voltages are not easily changed in value; hence, dc energy is usually generated at the voltage at which it is to be used or more often, ac energy is distributed to the load where it is converted to dc energy by means of rectifiers.

In addition to the fact that alternating voltages are easily changed in values, there are other reasons for the use of alternating currents. Alternating-current generators require no commutators with their accompanying troubles and maintenance. This means that commutation need not limit the size and speed of ac generators as it does dc generators. In general, ac motors and controls are simpler, lighter in weight, and more reliable than dc equipment of similar rating. The more extensive commercial development of ac equipment is still another reason for its use.

Although alternating current is used predominantly, there are some types of work for which direct current must be used or where it has a definite advantage. In mills and factories and in electric-railway service, where efficient speed control of motors is important, direct current has a definite advantage. Direct current is also commonly used for high-intensity light sources in searchlights and projectors, for charging storage batteries, for field excitation of ac generators and synchronous motors, and for many electrochemical processes.

In this chapter, the basic ideas concerning alternating-current systems are presented. Single-phase and three-phase circuit principles are included in Chaps. 11 and 12.

10-**1**

Generation of an Alternating EMF

It was explained in connection with dc generators (Chap. 8) that when a coil is rotated in a uniform magnetic field an emf is generated in that coil. This emf reverses its direction at regular intervals and is continually varying in strength. Such an emf is called an **alternating emf**. The value of the emf at any given time is called the **instantaneous value of emf**, and the symbol is e.

The manner in which an alternating emf may be generated is illustrated in Fig. 10-1, which represents a cross-sectional view of a two-pole generator with the armature rotating in a counterclockwise direction through a uniform magnetic field. For convenience, positions 30° apart are marked off on the armature surface. These are the positions through which a given armature conductor passes as the armature makes a complete revolution. Position 0 will be used as a starting point. At position 1 the conductor will have moved 30°, at position 2 it will have moved 60°, etc.

A graph showing the instantaneous values of emf generated in a conductor as the armature rotates also is shown in Fig. 10-1. Twelve equally spaced points are marked off on the horizontal line XX' to correspond to the conductor positions on the armature. The vertical lines at each point (e_1, e_2, e_3, etc.) represent the amount of emf generated at each conductor position as the armature rotates.

The amount of emf generated when the conductor moves through position 0 is zero since this position lies in the neutral plane of the generator and no lines of force are being cut. As the conductor moves through points 1 and 2, it cuts across the field and generates an emf whose direction is away from the reader. Lines e_1 and e_2 represent the values of the emf generated at points 1 and 2, respectively. At position 3, or 90°, the conductor moves at right angles to the field and generates a **maximum value of emf** (symbol E_m) which is represented by the line e_3.

F I G U R E **10-1**

Curve showing the variation of generated emf in a conductor as it is rotated through a uniform magnetic field.

As the conductor moves from position 3 around to position 6, the direction of the emf remains unchanged but its value is diminishing as shown by e_4 and e_5 on the graph. At position 6, or 180°, the emf is again zero. As soon as the conductor passes point 6, it begins to cut across the field in the opposite direction, reversing the direction of the generated emf. The values of emf generated in this direction are represented below the horizontal line on the graph.

At position 9, or 270°, the conductor is again cutting the field at a maximum rate and the emf, e_9 or $-E_m$, is at a maximum. From position 9 to position 0 the emf gradually decreases until it again becomes zero at 360° — the starting point. The cycle of events then repeats as the armature completes each successive revolution.

The curve plotted from the values of the emf generated at the various points represents the variation of the generated emf in a conductor for a complete revolution in a two-pole generator. It is customary to speak of the values of emf above the horizontal line as being in the positive direction and those below the line as being in the negative direction. Most modern generators generate values of emf whose positive values are exactly like the negative values, and when these values are plotted, as in Fig. 10-1, the curve is of the same shape as a curve showing the values of the sine of the various angles of rotation. Therefore, the curve is called a **sine wave**. A discussion of trigonometric functions is given in Appendix F.

To determine the instantaneous value of induced emf, e, when the maximum value E_m is known, the sine of the angle of degree of rotation must be taken.

$$e = E_m \sin\theta \qquad\qquad \text{[10-1]}$$

where e = the instantaneous induced emf
E_m = the maximum induced emf
θ = the angle of rotation in degrees

Example 10-1

With reference to Fig. 10-1, determine the instantaneous induced emf at positions 0, 2, 3, and 7 if the maximum induced emf is 100 V.

At angle 0° $e = 100 \times \sin 0° \quad = 100 \times 0 = 0$ V

60° $e = 100 \times \sin 60° \ = 100 \times 0.866 = 86.6$ V

90° $e = 100 \times \sin 90° \ = 100 \times 1 = 100$ V

210° $e = 100 \times \sin 210° = 100 \times -0.5 = -50$ V

All ac circuit problems discussed in this text are based on the assumption that the emfs and currents are sine waves.

10-2

Alternating Current

When an alternating emf is applied to a circuit, an alternating current is caused to flow. In general, if a sine-wave emf is applied, the resulting current varies as does a sine wave (transient state ignored). An alternating current may be defined as a current that flows back and forth through a circuit at regular intervals. An alternating current varies in intensity as does an alternating emf. The value at any given time is called the instantaneous value (symbol i), and the greatest value reached by the current is called its maximum value (symbol I_m).

The quantity of instantaneous current, i, flowing in an ac circuit can be determined in the same manner as the induced emf e. If the quantities shown in Fig. 10-1 were substituted with i and I_m and these same quantities substituted into Eq. (10-1), we would now have an expression for i when I_m and angle θ is known.

$$i = I_m \sin\theta \qquad \text{[10-2]}$$

10-3

Cycle; Frequency

When the value of an alternating emf or current rises from zero to a maximum, falls to zero, increases to a maximum in the reverse direction, and falls back to zero again, the complete set of values passed through is called a **cycle** (see Fig. 10-1). The number of complete cycles passed through in one second is called the **frequency**. The SI unit for frequency is the **hertz** (symbol Hz). The hertz supersedes **cycles per second** as a unit of frequency, although the latter is still used.

The common power frequency in North America is 60 Hz, but in Europe and in most of Asia and Africa it is 50 Hz. Many early electric power systems had rated frequencies of 25 Hz, but most of these systems have been converted to 50- or 60-Hz systems.

10-4

Electrical Degrees: A Measure of Time

In any generator, a conductor must be moved past a north and a south pole to have one complete cycle generated in it. Therefore, the space through which a conductor must be moved to generate one cycle depends on the number of poles on the generator. In the two-pole generator, a conductor must make one complete revolution, or pass through 360° in space. In a four-pole generator, a conductor needs to be moved through only ½ revolution, or 180°, to generate one cycle. It is evident, then, that if the number of space degrees passed through by a conductor were used in plotting the emf wave generated, the number of degrees per cycle would vary with the number of poles on the generator.

Eq. (10-3) formulates this concept.

$$\theta = \frac{\phi P}{2} \qquad \text{[10-3]}$$

where θ = number of electrical degrees
    Φ = number of mechanical degrees
    P = number of poles

Example 10-2

An armature of a generator rotates through 360 mechanical degrees at a speed of 1800 r/min. Determine the frequency of the induced emf if the generator has:

a) 2 poles   b) 4 poles   c) 6 poles   d) 36 poles

At an armature speed of 1800 r/min, the speed in revolutions per second is 1800/60 = 30 r/s. The time required for the armature to make one revolution is 1/30 = 0.0333 s. Since one cycle is equal to 360 electrical degrees and one hertz is equal to one cycle per second, then:

a) $\theta = 360° \times 2/2 = 360°$

$$360/360 = 1 \text{ cycle per rev.} \times 30 \; r/s$$
$$= 30 \text{ Hz.}$$

b) $\theta = 360° \times 4/2 = 720°$

$$720/360 = 2 \text{ cycles per rev.} \times 30 \; r/s$$
$$= 60 \text{ Hz.}$$

c) $\theta = 360° \times 6/2 = 1080°$

$$1080/360 = 3 \text{ cycles per rev.} \times 30 \; r/s$$
$$= 90 \text{ Hz.}$$

d) $\theta = 360° \times 36/2 = 6480°$

$$6480/360 = 18 \text{ cycles per rev.} \times 30 \; r/s$$
$$= 540 \text{ Hz.}$$

Since the time required to generate one cycle is constant for a given frequency regardless of the number of poles on the generator, emf waves are plotted with time as the horizontal axis. Time in seconds may be used, but it is more convenient to divide the time required to generate one cycle into 360 divisions called **electrical degrees**. The relation of time in seconds and time in electrical degrees for a frequency of 60 Hz is shown in Fig. 10-2. The complete cycle is generated in 1/60 s or in the time required to move an armature conductor past one pair of poles. For this frequency, 360 electrical degrees is equivalent to 1/60 s. One-half cycle is generated in 1/120 s or 180 electrical degrees, 1/4 cycle in 1/240 s or 90°, and 1/8 cycle in 1/480 s or 45°. It must be kept in mind

FIGURE **10-2**
Relation between time in seconds and time in electrical degrees for a frequency of 60 Hz.

|10-**5**

Effective Values of Alternating Current and EMF

that electrical degrees used in this sense represent **time**. This concept will be found useful in specifying phase relationships.

As the value of an alternating current is continually fluctuating between a maximum in one direction and a maximum in the other direction, some effective value of an alternating current must be established. A natural question arises at this point. How can an alternating current deliver any power when it is continually changing its direction of flow? The answer to this is that the amount of power used by a dc circuit is $P = I^2R$ regardless of the direction of the current flow through the resistance. This is easily verified experimentally by connecting a resistance to a battery through a reversing switch and measuring the power used with the current first in one direction and then in the other. It will be found that the power is the same in either case. Alternating current is merely a current that reverses its direction of flow periodically. It follows then that power is used during both halves of the cycle when an alternating current flows through a resistance.

The rate at which heat is produced in a resistance forms a convenient basis for establishing an effective value of alternating current. *An alternating current is said to have an effective value of one ampere when it will produce heat in a given resistance at the same rate as does one ampere of direct current.*

The symbol for effective alternating current is I. The rate at which heat is produced in a dc circuit is equal to I^2R. Likewise, the rate at which heat is being produced by an alternating current at any instant is I^2R. Therefore, the heating effect of an alternating current over a period of time depends on the average of the squares of the instantaneous values of current over that period of time. For this reason the effective value of a sine-wave current is often called the **root-mean-square**, or **rms**, value. It is the square root of the mean or average square of the instantaneous values. By squaring a number of instantaneous values, averaging these squared values, and extracting the square root of this average, the effective value of any sine-wave current may be found. By this method or by mathematical means, it may be shown that the *effective value* (I) *of any sine-wave current is always* 0.707 *times the maximum value* (I_m).

Since alternating currents are caused to flow by alternating emfs, the ratio between effective and maximum values of emfs is the same as for currents. The effective, or rms, value (E) of a sine-wave emf is 0.707 times the maximum value (E_m).

When an alternating current or voltage is specified, it is always the effective value that is meant unless there is a definite statement to the contrary. In practical work, effective values are of more importance than instantaneous or maximum values and the common types of measuring instruments are calibrated to read effective values of current and voltage.

Alternating currents are caused to flow by alternating voltages of the same frequency. When the current and voltage pass through their zero values and increase to their maximum values in the same direction at the same time, the current is said to be **in phase** with the voltage. However, in some types of circuits (to be discussed in later sections) the current and voltage zero and maximum values *do not occur* at the same time. When this happens, the current is said to be **out of phase** with the voltage.

There are three possible phase relations between a current and a voltage in a circuit:

1. The current and voltage may be in phase as shown in Fig. 10-3(*a*).
2. The voltage may pass through its zero value and increase to a maximum at some time earlier than the current as in Fig. 10-4(*a*). In this case the current is said to **lag** the voltage.
3. The voltage may pass through its zero value and maximum value at some time later than the current as in Fig. 10-5(*a*). In this case the current is said to **lead** the voltage.

The amount of time that a current leads or lags the voltage varies in different circuits from the **inphase** condition to a lead or lag of ¼ cycle, or 90°. Since time may be measured in electrical degrees (Sec. 10-4), this difference in time, or **phase difference**, of a current and voltage is commonly expressed in electrical degrees and is called the **phase angle**. The usual symbol for the phase angle is the Greek letter theta (θ).

Just as the current and voltage of a circuit may have a phase difference, two or more voltages or currents in the same circuit may be out of phase. This difference in phase must be taken into

10-6
Phase Relations

FIGURE **10-3**
Current and voltage are in phase.

(a)

(b)

FIGURE **10-4**
Current lags the voltage by 30°.

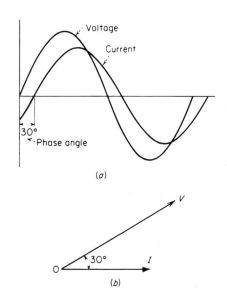

(a)

(b)

FIGURE **10-5**
Current leads the voltage by 30°.

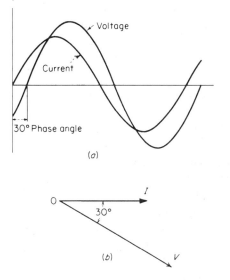

(a)

(b)

account when such voltages or currents are added or subtracted. Methods of combining currents and voltages that are out of phase will be discussed in Secs. 10-8 and 10-9.

It has been shown in previous sections how alternating currents and voltages and their phase relations may be represented by means of sine waves. This method of representation is quite cumbersome; a simplified method is universally employed in ac circuit analysis in which currents and voltages are represented by straight lines having definite direction and length. Such lines are called **phasors** (formerly called vectors), and diagrams in which these lines are used to represent sine-wave currents, voltages, and their phase relations are called **phasor diagrams**. Phasor diagrams may be drawn to represent either maximum or effective values of sine-wave quantities. Because effective values are of much more importance, however, phasor diagrams are nearly always drawn to represent effective values.

When drawing phasor diagrams, certain conventions should be adopted to ensure consistent and accurate results. Some of the more common conventions or usual practices in regard to phasor diagrams are listed.

1. It is common practice to consider the counterclockwise direction as being the positive direction of rotation of phasors. That

10-**7**

Phasor (Vector) Diagrams

is, phasors rotated in a counterclockwise direction from a given phasor are said to lead the given phasor, while phasors rotated in a clockwise direction are said to lag the given phasor.

2. For series circuits in which the current is common to all parts of the circuit, the current phasor is usually drawn on a horizontal line and used as a reference line for other phasors in the same diagram.

3. Since, in a parallel circuit, a common voltage is applied to all branches of the circuit, the voltage phasor is drawn on the horizontal reference line and other phasors are referred to the common voltage phasor.

4. It is not necessary to use the same scale for current and voltage phasors; in fact, it is often desirable to draw the current phasor to a larger scale than the voltage phasor when the values of current being represented are small. However, if several current phasors are to be used in the same diagram, they should all be drawn to the same scale. Likewise, all voltage phasors in the same diagram should be drawn to the same scale.

5. To distinguish between current and voltage phasors, the current phasors may be drawn with closed arrowheads and the voltage phasors with open arrowheads.

To illustrate the methods used in drawing phasor diagrams, the sine-wave currents and voltage of Figs. 10-3(*a*), 10-4(*a*), and 10-5(*a*) are represented by phasor diagrams in Figs. 10-3(*b*), 10-4(*b*), and 10-5(*b*), respectively.

Fig. 10-3 represents a case in which the current and voltages are in phase; that is, the phase angle is 0°. The phasor diagram showing this relation is drawn in Fig. 10-3(*b*). The phasor representing the effective current is drawn to some convenient scale on a horizontal line, starting at the point *O*. Likewise, the phasor representing the effective voltage is drawn starting at the same point *O* and extending in the same direction as the current phasor. The fact that the two phasors lie along the same line indicates that the current and voltage being represented are in phase.

In Fig. 10-4 the current is shown lagging the voltage by 30°. The current phasor is drawn as before on the horizontal reference line. However, to represent the fact that the current lags the voltage by 30°, the voltage phasor is drawn 30° ahead of (or in the counterclockwise direction from) the current phasor as in Fig. 10-4(*b*).

Fig. 10-5 represents a circuit in which the current leads the voltage by 30°. The current phasor is drawn on the horizontal reference line as before but with the voltage phasor 30° behind (or in the clockwise direction from the current phasor) as in Fig. 10-5(*b*).

Thus, phasor diagrams, when drawn to scale, provide a simple means of representing both the phase relations and the magnitudes of the currents and voltages involved in a given circuit.

A phasor has both direction and magnitude. Therefore, the addition of quantities that are represented as phasors, such as alternating currents and voltages, must take into account both the direction and magnitude of those quantities.

The phasor sum of two phasors may be found by constructing a triangle, the two phasors forming two sides of the triangle and their sum forming the third side. To construct such a triangle, the first phasor is drawn to scale starting at some point *O*. For convenience, this phasor is usually drawn as a horizontal line to the right of the origin *O*. The second phasor is then drawn to scale from the arrow end of the first phasor. If the second phasor is defined as leading the first phasor by θ degrees, the second phasor is drawn 0 degrees in a counterclockwise direction from the first phasor. If it lags the first phasor, it is drawn at the designated angle in a clockwise direction from the horizontal. The phasor sum is then the line drawn from the origin to the arrow end of the second phasor.

Several examples follow that illustrate the addition of two phasors. Several special conditions are illustrated that are often encountered. However, it should be noted that the procedure in constructing each of the diagrams is the same. The two original phasors are placed without changing their direction so as to form two sides of a triangle. The third side of the triangle is then the phasor sum of the two original phasors.

Addition of Inphase Phasors

The phasor sum of two inphase phasors is their direct or arithmetic sum.

Example 10-3

Find the phasor sum of a current of 3 A and a current of 4 A, the two currents being in phase.

$$\text{Phasor sum} = 3\text{ A} + 4\text{ A} = 7\text{ A}$$

Addition of Phasors Out of Phase by 180°

The phasor sum of two phasors 180° out of phase is their numerical difference, the direction of the result being the same as the larger phasor.

10-**8**

Addition of Phasors

Example 10-4

A voltage V_1 of 125 V leads a voltage V_2 of 100 V by 180°. Find their phasor sum.

$$\text{Phasor sum} = 125 \text{ V} - 100 \text{ V} = 25 \text{ V}$$

or $$= 125 \text{ V} + (-100 \text{ V}) = 25 \text{ V}$$

The direction of the resultant phasor is the same as the direction of V_1.

Addition of Phasors Out of Phase by 90°

The phasor sum C of two phasors A and B that are out of phase 90° is

$$C = \sqrt{A^2 + B^2}$$

or, in Rectangular Notation (see Appendix H),

$$C = A + jB$$

All example problems in this chapter show both **polar** and **rectangular** methods of determining the solution. It should be noted, however, that a thorough study of Appendix H should be made to properly understand the solutions using the **rectangular** method.

Example 10-5

A current I_2 of 8 A leads a current I_1 of 6 A by 90° as shown in Fig. 10-6(*a*). Find their phasor sum.

GRAPHICAL SOLUTION: Lay off I_1 to scale along the horizontal to the right of the origin as in Fig. 10-6(*b*). Starting at the arrow end of I_1, lay off to scale I_2, 90° ahead of or in a counterclockwise direction from I_1. The phasor sum is the length of the line OB. The resultant phasor I_R leads I_1 by the angle θ.

FIGURE **10-6**
Addition of two phasors out of phase by 90°. See Example 10-5.

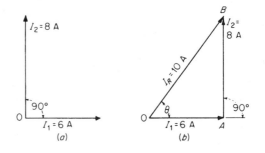

MATHEMATICAL SOLUTION: Since the triangle OAB is a right triangle,

$$I_R = \sqrt{(I_1{}^2) + (I_2{}^2)} = \sqrt{6^2 + 8^2} = 10 \text{ A}$$

and $\quad \tan \theta = \dfrac{8}{6} = 1.33$

From tables or by calculator, $\theta = 53.13°$. (For trigonometric functions and a table of values, see Appendixes F and G.)

or $\quad I_R = I_1 + jI_2 = 6 + j8 = 10 \; \underline{/53.13°} \text{ A}$

Addition of Phasors Out of Phase by Any Angle

Example 10-6

Add two voltages of 100 V each that are out of phase by 30°.

GRAPHICAL SOLUTION: The two phasors drawn from the same origin are shown in Fig. 10-7(a). Lay off to scale one phasor on the horizontal to the right of the origin as in Fig. 10-7(b). Starting at the arrow end of the first phasor, scale off the second phasor 30° in a counterclockwise direction from the horizontal. Draw a line from the origin O to the end of the second phasor. The length of this line is the phasor sum, to scale, of the two phasors. Measure angle θ.

MATHEMATICAL SOLUTION: In Fig. 10-7(b), draw a perpendicular from C to the horizontal. The phasor sum OC is then the hypotenuse of the right triangle OBC.

Side $CB = 100 \sin 30° = 100 \times 0.5 = 50$

Line $AB = 100 \cos 30° = 100 \times 0.866 = 86.6$

Side $OB = OA + AB = 100 + 86.6 = 186.6$

FIGURE **10-7**
Addition of two phasors out of phase by 30°. See Example 10-6.

(a)   (b)

$$\text{Side } OC = \sqrt{(OB^2) + (CB)^2}$$

$$= \sqrt{(186.6)^2 + (50)^2}$$

$$= 193.2 \text{ V}$$

$$\tan \theta = \frac{50}{186.6} \text{ or } 0.268$$

$$\theta = 15°$$

or $100 \underline{/0°}$ V to rectangular notation $= 100.0 + j0$

$+ 100 \underline{/30°}$ V to rectangular notation $= \underline{86.6 + j50}$

$$186.6 + j50$$

$$= 193.2 \underline{/15°} \text{ V}$$

Example 10-7

A voltage of 120 V leads a voltage of 240 V by 120° as shown in Fig. 10-8(*a*). What is their phasor sum?

FIGURE **10-8**
Addition of two phasors out of phase by 120°. See Example 10-7.

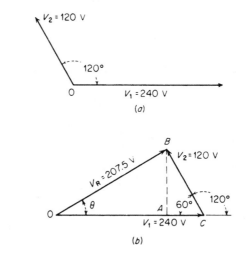

(*a*)

(*b*)

GRAPHICAL SOLUTION: The graphical construction is shown in Fig.10-8(*b*). The phasor sum is line *OB* at the angle θ from the horizontal.

MATHEMATICAL SOLUTION: In Fig. 10-8(*b*), draw the perpendicular line *BA*. The phasor sum *OB* is then the hypotenuse of right triangle *OAB*.

$$\text{Side } AB = 120 \sin 60° = 120 \times 0.866 = 103.9$$

$$\text{Line } AC = 120 \cos 60° = 120 \times 0.5 = 60$$

$$\text{Side } OA = OC - AC = 240 - 60 = 180$$

$$\text{Side } OB = \sqrt{(OA)^2 + (AB)^2}$$

$$= \sqrt{(180)^2 + (103.9)^2}$$

$$= 207.5$$

$$\tan \theta = \frac{103.9}{180} \text{ or } 0.577$$

$$\theta = 30°$$

or $\qquad$ 240 $\underline{/0°}$ V to rectangular notation $= 240.0 + j0$

$+$ 120 $\underline{/120°}$ V to rectangular notation $= -60.0 + j103.9$

$$180.0 + j103.9$$

$$= 207.5 \; \underline{/30°} \text{ V}$$

If three phasors are to be added, the sum of two of the phasors may be found by the methods outlined above, then their sum may be added to the third phasor. This method may be extended to any number of phasors.

A phasor *B* may be subtracted from a phasor *A* by reversing the phasor *B* (rotating it by 180°) and adding it to the phasor *A*. This can best be explained by an example.

| 10-**9**

Subtraction of Phasors

F I G U R E **10-9**
Subtraction of two phasors out of phase by 30°. See Example 10-8.

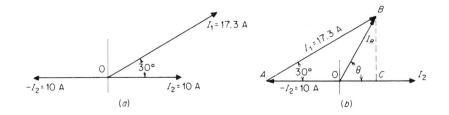

E x a m p l e   1 0 - 8

Subtract a current of 10 A from a current of 17.3 A when the 17.3-A current leads the 10-A current by 30° as in Fig. 10-9(a).

GRAPHICAL SOLUTION: Draw I_t, I_2, and $-I_2$ as shown in Fig. 10-9(b). The phasor-difference current is the line OB, which leads I_2 by the angle θ.

MATHEMATICAL SOLUTION: In Fig. 10-9(b), draw a perpendicular from B to the horizontal. The line OB is then the hypotenuse of the right triangle OBC.

$$\text{Side } BC = 17.3 \sin 30° = 17.3 \times 0.5 = 8.66$$

$$\text{Side } AC = 17.3 \cos 30° = 17.3 \times 0.866 = 15$$

$$\text{Side } OC = 15 - 10 = 5$$

$$\text{Side } OB = \sqrt{(8.66)^2 + (5)^2}$$
$$= 10$$

$$\tan \theta = \frac{86.6}{5} \text{ or } 1.73$$

$$\theta = 60°$$

or $17.3 \underline{/30°}$ A to rectangular notation $= 14.98 + j8.65$

$-\ 10.0 \underline{/0°}$ A to rectangular notation $= \underline{10.0 \quad + j0}$

$$4.98 + j8.65$$

$$= 10 \underline{/60°} \text{ A}$$

The value of a direct current flowing in a circuit for a given constant value of impressed voltage is determined wholly by the **resistance** of the circuit. The value of an alternating current flowing in a circuit depends not only on the resistance of the circuit, but on the **inductance** and **capacitance** of the circuit as well. Resistance offers the same kind of opposition to the flow of an alternating current as it does to direct current and, for most practical purposes, the ac resistance and dc resistance of a circuit are considered to be the same.

This statement, however, is not true when the frequency of the supply increases to very high values, such as in radio frequencies. Inductance and capacitance affect only a *change* in current or voltage. Since alternating currents and voltages are continually changing in magnitude and direction, both inductance and capacitance affect the flow of an alternating current. The nature of the circuit properties and the effects of each in ac circuits are discussed in the following sections.

When a dc potential is applied to a resistance, the value of the current that flows, according to Ohm's law, is proportional to the voltage: the greater the voltage, the greater the current. The same is true when an alternating voltage is applied to a resistance. As the voltage is increased, the current is increased; as the voltage is decreased, the current is decreased. The maximum value of current and voltage occur at the same time, and their zero values occur at the same time. Thus, the current and the voltage are in phase and the *phase angle is zero in a purely resistive circuit.*

When a circuit contains resistance only, the effective current flowing in that circuit is equal to the effective applied voltage divided by the resistance of the circuit, or

$$I_R = \frac{V_R}{R} \qquad \text{[10-4]}$$

E x a m p l e   1 0 - 9

What is the effective current flowing through a resistance of 30 Ω when a 120-V 60-Hz voltage is applied as in Fig. 10-10(*a*)?

$$I_R = \frac{V_R}{R} = \frac{120}{30} = 4 \text{ A}$$

The phasor diagram is shown in Fig. 10-10(*b*).

Inductance is a circuit property just as is resistance. Any circuit that is capable of producing flux has inductance, as was pointed out in Chap. 7. Any change in the value of current flowing in such a circuit also causes a change in the flux linking the circuit, thereby causing an emf to be induced. Since the emf is induced in the

10-**10**

Properties of an Electric Circuit

10-**11**

Resistance in an AC Circuit

10-**12**

Inductance

F I G U R E **10-10**
Circuit and phasor diagram for Example 10-9.

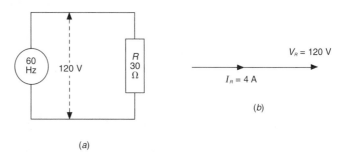

(a)

(b)

circuit owing to a change of current in the circuit itself and since any induced emf opposes the change that produces it, it is called the **counter emf of self-induction**. Thus, an opposition to any *change* in the current flowing is present in a circuit containing inductance.

The unit of inductance is the **henry**, and the symbol is L. As was stated in Sec. 7-7, a circuit has an inductance of one henry (H) if, when the current is changing at the rate of one ampere per second, the average counter emf induced is one volt.

An inductive circuit is usually in the form of a coil, very often wound around a magnetic core. Motor, generator, and transformer windings are examples of circuits that have inductance. However, a long, straight wire also has a certain amount of inductance, and calculations of transmission-line performance must take into account the inductance of the line.

10-**13**

Inductive Reactance

In an inductive dc circuit, the inductance affects the current flow only when the current is changing in value. Upon closing a dc circuit, the inductance opposes the increase in current; upon opening the circuit, it opposes the decrease in current. However, the flow of a steady direct current is opposed only by the resistance of the circuit.

In an inductive ac circuit, the current is changing continuously and therefore is continuously inducing an emf of self-induction. Because this induced emf opposes the continuous change in the current flowing, its effect is measured in ohms. This opposition of the inductance to the flow of an alternating current is called **inductive reactance** and is represented by the symbol X_L. The current flowing through a circuit that contains only inductive reactance is

$$I_L = \frac{V_L}{X_L} \qquad\qquad \text{[10-5]}$$

where I_L = inductive current, amperes
        X_L = inductive reactance, ohms
        V_L = effective voltage across the reactance, volts

Either absolute or complex notation may be used for Eq. (10-5).

The value of inductive reactance in any circuit depends on the inductance of the circuit and on the rate at which the current through the circuit is changing. The rate of change of current depends on the frequency of the applied voltage. Inductive reactance in ohms may be calculated from the formula

$$X_L = 2\pi f L \qquad\qquad \text{[10-6]}$$

where π = 3.14
        f = frequency, hertz
        L = inductance, henries

When rectangular notation is used, prefix X_L with $+j$. In polar form, suffix with $\underline{/90°}$.

The amount of any induced emf in a circuit depends on how fast the flux that links the circuit is changing. In the case of self-induction, a counter emf is inducted in a circuit because of a change of current and flux in the circuit itself. This counter emf, according to Lenz's law, opposes any change in current, and its value at any time depends on the rate at which the current and flux are changing at the time. In an inductive circuit in which the resistance is negligible in comparison to the inductive reactance, the voltage applied to the circuit must at all times be equal and opposite to the emf of self-induction.

Fig. 10-11 shows the variation of the induced counter emf with the variation of a sine-wave current. At points a, c, and e the current is not changing in value, and the self-induced emf is zero. Between

FIGURE **10-11**
(a) Variation of current, self-induced emf, and applied voltage in an inductive circuit. (b) Phasor diagram showing the relation between the applied voltage and the current.

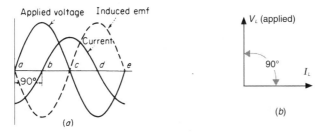

the points *a* and *c* the current is increasing in value from its negative maximum to its positive maximum. Therefore, during this time, the induced emf is negative in value, opposing the increase in current. Between the points *c* and *e*, the current is decreasing from positive maximum to negative maximum so that the induced emf is positive and is attempting to oppose the decrease in current. The current changes at its greatest rate at the points *b* and *d*, causing the induced emf to reach its maximum values at these points. The value of the self-induced emf then varies as a sine curve and lags the current by 90° as shown in Fig. 10-11. Since the applied voltage must be equal and opposite to the self-induced emf at all times, it is evident from Fig. 10-11 *that the current lags the applied voltage by 90° in a purely inductive circuit.* If, as is usually the case, resistance is present in the circuit, the angle of lag will be less than 90°, depending on the relative values of resistance and inductive reactance in the circuit.

Example 10-10

A 0.2-H choke coil with negligible resistance is connected to a 120-V 60-Hz supply as in Fig. 10-12(*a*). Find (*a*) the inductive reactance of the coil, and (*b*) the current flowing; (*c*) draw the phasor diagram showing the phase relations between the current and the applied voltage.

(*a*) $X_L = 2\pi f L = 2 \times 3.14 \times 60 \times 0.2 = 75.4\ \Omega$

(*b*) $$I_L = \frac{V_L}{X_L} = \frac{120}{75.4} = 1.59\ \text{A}$$

(*c*) The phasor diagram showing the current lagging the voltage by 90° is shown in Fig. 10-12(*b*).

10-14
Capacitors

Any two conductors that are separated by an insulating material form a simple **capacitor** (formerly called a **condenser**). The conductors are called the **plates** of the capacitor and the insulating material is called the **dielectric**. A common type of capacitor used in power and communication circuits is the parallel-plate capacitor. Such capacitors are constructed by interleaving sheets of tin or

---

F I G U R E **10-12**
Circuit and phasor diagram for Example 10-0.

aluminum foil with sheets of waxed or paraffined paper. Alternate plates are connected to each of two terminals so that each terminal and group of plates to which it is attached is insulated electrically from the group of plates connected to the other terminal. Thus, each group of plates forms a large conductor surface that is separated from another large conductor surface by the dielectric.

Capacitors are used extensively in telephone and radio circuits. Power supply companies are using them in increasing numbers on distribution systems to correct for some of the effects of inductive loads. Capacitors play an important part in the operation of various other kinds of electric apparatus, such as automobile ignition systems, single-phase motors, and control relays.

Fig. 10-13 shows a capacitor AB connected in series with two galvanometers (sensitive current-detecting instruments) C and D, with the switch S arranged either to connect the capacitor to the battery or to short-circuit the terminals of the capacitor. Immediately after the switch is closed to the left, connecting the capacitor to the battery, galvanometer C indicates a momentary current flow toward plate A and galvanometer D indicates a current flow away from plate B. A movement of electric charge or electrons takes place in the circuit until the potential difference between plates A and B becomes the same as the battery potential difference. This causes plate A to become positively charged and plate B to become negatively charged. Hence, a capacitor in this condition is said to be charged. If the switch is opened, the capacitor retains its charge indefinitely (if there is no leakage between the plates), since plate B is left with an excess of electrons and plate A has a deficiency of electrons.

If the switch S is closed to the right while the capacitor is still charged, the galvanometers indicate a flow of current out of plate A and into plate B. This flow of current is momentary, being only long enough to neutralize the charged atoms on each plate. The capacitor is then said to be *discharged*.

The amount of charge that a capacitor receives for each volt of applied potential is called the **capacitance** of the capacitor. The

FIGURE **10-13**
The capacitor AB is charged when the switch S is closed to the left and discharged when the switch is closed to the right.

unit of capacitance is the **farad** (F), and the symbol is C. A capacitor has a capacitance of one *farad* when an applied potential of one volt causes the capacitor to take a charge of one **coulomb**. The farad is much too large a unit for practical use, and therefore the **microfarad** (μF) is more commonly used. One farad is equal to one million microfarads. Eq. (10-7) is an expression that relates the capacitance of a capacitor with respect to the quantity of charge in coulombs per volt.

$$C = \frac{Q}{V} \qquad\qquad \text{[10-7]}$$

where C is in farads
        Q is in coulombs
        V is in volts

The capacitance of a capacitor is directly proportional to the area of the plates and inversely proportional to their separation. It has been found by experiment that the material used for the dielectric also affects the capacitance. For example, when glass is substituted for air as a dielectric, the capacitance increases approximately eight times. Likewise, capacitors using mica, paraffin, transformer oil, paper, and various other insulating materials for dielectrics have a higher capacitance than do similar air capacitors. These materials are said to have a higher **dielectric constant** than air. Eq. (10-8) is a mathematical expression describing the relationship between the quantities described.

$$C = \frac{\varepsilon A}{d} \qquad\qquad \text{[10-8]}$$

where C = capacitance, farads
        ε = the permittivity of the dielectric medium, farads/metre
        A = the cross-sectional area of the capacitor's plates, square metres
        d = the distance of separation of the plates, metres

One ampere is defined as the rate of flow of an electric charge of one coulomb per second. If the voltage applied to a one-farad capacitor is increased at the rate of one volt every second, the increase in charge on the capacitor will be one coulomb every second. Since one coulomb of electricity or electric charge is moved every second, the average current flowing into the capacitor must be one ampere. Likewise, if the potential being applied to a one-farad capacitor is being decreased by one volt every second, the average current flowing out of the capacitor will be one ampere. Thus, a current flows in a circuit containing a capacitor while the applied voltage of that circuit is changing, even though there is a complete break in the circuit. *The amount of current flowing depends on the capacitance of the circuit and the rate at which the applied voltage is changing.* If either the capacitance of a circuit or the rate at which the applied voltage is changing (the frequency) is increased, the amount of current flowing is also increased.

It may be shown mathematically that the combined capacitance C of several capacitors C_1, C_2, C_3, ... in series may be found by the relationship

10-**15**

Capacitors in Series

$$\frac{1}{C} = \frac{1}{C_1} + \frac{1}{C_2} + \frac{1}{C_3} + \cdots \qquad [10\text{-}9]$$

The reciprocal of the combined capacitance of several capacitors in series is equal to the sum of the reciprocals of the capacitances of the separate capacitors. Connecting several capacitors in series is essentially equivalent to increasing the distance between the plates of one capacitor without changing its plate area or its dielectric. As illustrated in Eq. (10-9), the net capacitance decreases as more capacitors are added in series.

Example 10-11

Three capacitors, connected in series, have capacitances $3\,\mu\text{F}$, $5\,\mu\text{F}$, and $10\,\mu\text{F}$. Determine the total capacitance of the group.

$$\frac{1}{C} = \frac{1}{3\,\mu\text{F}} + \frac{1}{5\,\mu\text{F}} + \frac{1}{10\,\mu\text{F}}$$

$$\frac{1}{C} = \frac{19}{30}$$

$$C = \frac{30}{19}$$

$$C = 1.58\ \mu\text{F}$$

When capacitors are connected in parallel, the effect is the same as increasing the number of plates, and the capacitance of the circuit is increased. In a parallel circuit the combined capacitance of several capacitors C_1, C_2, C_3, ... is

10-**16**

Capacitors in Parallel

$$C = C_1 + C_2 + C_3 + \cdots \qquad [10\text{-}10]$$

When capacitors are connected in parallel, their total capacitance equals the sum of the capacitances of the separate capacitors.

Example 10-12

The three capacitors in Example 10-11 are reconnected in parallel. The total capacitance is:

$$C = C_1 + C_2 + C_3$$

$$C = 3\mu F + 5\mu F + 10\mu F$$

$$C = 18\mu F$$

10-17

Action of a Capacitor in an AC Circuit

In a dc circuit containing a capacitor, there is only a momentary flow of current immediately after the voltage is applied. As soon as the voltage across the capacitor reaches its steady-state value, the current flow ceases. However, when a capacitor is connected to an ac supply in series with an ac ammeter, the ammeter indicates a flow of current as long as the supply is connected. The circuit appears to be complete and not one that has a complete break in it. The reason for this is that the current alternately flows into and out of the capacitor as the capacitor is charged, discharged, charged in the opposite direction, and discharged again.

The variation of an alternating voltage applied to a capacitor, the charge on the capacitor, and the current flowing are represented in Fig. 10-14. Since the current flowing in a circuit containing capacitance depends on the rate at which the voltage changes, the current flow is greatest at points *a*, *c*, and *e*; it is at these points the voltage is changing at its maximum rate. Between the points *a* and *b*, while the voltage and charge on the capacitor are both increasing, the current flow is into the capacitor but decreasing in value. At point *b* the capacitor is fully charged and the current is zero. From *b* to *c* the voltage and charge both decrease as the capacitor discharges, its current flowing in a direction opposite to the voltage. From *c* to *d* the capacitor begins to charge

FIGURE **10-14**
Variation of voltage, charge, and current in a capacitor.

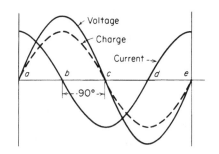

in the opposite direction and the voltage and current are again in the same direction. The capacitor is fully charged at *d* where the current flow is again zero. From *d* to *e* the capacitor discharges, the flow of current being opposite to the voltage. The cycle then repeats. An inspection of Fig. 10-14 shows the current to be *leading* the applied voltage by 90°. This is true in any purely capacitive circuit and is in contrast to a purely inductive circuit in which the current *lags* the voltage by 90°. Therefore, the effect of capacitance in a circuit is exactly opposite to the effect of inductance.

Capacitive reactance is the opposition offered by a capacitor or by any capacitive circuit to the flow of current. It was shown in Sec. 10-14 that the current flowing in a capacitive circuit is directly proportional to the capacitance and to the rate at which the applied voltage is changing. The rate at which the voltage changes is determined by the frequency of the supply. Therefore, if either the frequency or the capacitance of a given circuit is increased, the current flow increases. This is equivalent to saying that if either the frequency or capacitance is increased, the opposition to the current flow is *decreased*. Therefore, capacitive reactance, which is the opposition to current flow, is *inversely* proportional to frequency and capacitance. Capacitive reactance, X_c, is measured in ohms, as are resistance and inductive reactance, and may be calculated by the formula

10-**18**

Capacitive Reactance

$$X_c = \frac{1}{2 \pi f C} \qquad \text{[10-11]}$$

where f = frequency, hertz
π = 3.14
C = capacitance, farads

In rectangular notation, prefix X_c with $-j$. In polar form, suffix with $\underline{/90°}$.

If, as is usually the case, the capacitance is expressed in microfarads ($C_{\mu F}$), then

$$X_c = \frac{10^6}{2 \pi f C_{\mu F}} \qquad \text{[10-12]}$$

The current flowing in a circuit containing only capacitive reactance is

$$I_C = \frac{V_C}{X_C} \qquad \text{[10-13]}$$

where I_c = capacitive current, amperes
V_c = effective voltage across the capacitive reactance, volts
X_C = capacitive reactance, ohms

Example 10-13

An 8-μF capacitor is connected to a 240-V 60-Hz circuit (Fig. 10-15). (a) Find the capacitive reactance, (b) find the current flowing, and (c) draw the phasor diagram.

(a) $$X_C = \frac{10^6}{2\pi f C_{\mu F}} = \frac{10^6}{2 \times 3.14 \times 60 \times 8} = 331.7 \ \Omega$$

(b) $$I_C = \frac{V_C}{X_C} = \frac{240}{331.7} = 0.723 \ A$$

(c) The phasor diagram showing the current leading the voltage by 90° is drawn in Fig. 10-15(b).

10-19
Reactance

Inductive reactance causes the current to *lag* behind the applied voltage, while capacitive reactance causes the current to *lead* the voltage. Therefore, when inductive reactance and capacitive reactance are connected in series, their effects neutralize each other and their combined effect is then their difference. The combined effect of inductive reactance and capacitive reactance is called **reactance** and is found by subtracting the capacitive reactance from the inductive reactance, or, as an equation,

$$X = X_L - X_C \qquad \textbf{[10-14]}$$

where X = reactance, ohms
X_L = inductive reactance, ohms
X_C = capacitive reactance, ohms

In rectangular notation, $X = j(|X_L| - |X_C|)$.

10-20
Impedance

Impedance is the total opposition offered by a circuit to the flow of current. It is the combined effect of the **resistance** and the **reactance** of a circuit. The symbol for impedance is Z, and it is measured in ohms. The impedance of an ac circuit is equal to the effective applied voltage divided by the effective current that flows, or

---

FIGURE **10-15**
Circuit and phasor diagram for Example 10-13.

(a)

(b)

$$Z = \frac{E}{I_T} \qquad\qquad \text{[10-15]}$$

also $\qquad E = I_T Z \qquad$ and $\qquad I_T = \frac{E}{Z}$

Eq. (10-15) is valid for either absolute or complex quantities.

In a circuit containing resistance only, the IR drop is in phase with the current. In a circuit containing inductive reactance only, the IX_L drop leads the current by 90°, which is, of course, equivalent to saying that the current lags the IX_L drop by 90°. Likewise, in a capacitive circuit, the IX_C drop lags the current by 90°. In a circuit containing both resistance and reactance, the total voltage drop, or the IZ drop, is equal to the sum of IR and IX drops. Since the IR and IX drops are out of phase by 90°, this phase difference must be taken into account when they are added. As was shown in Sec. 10-8, the sum of two phasor quantities such as IR and IX that are out of phase by 90° is $\sqrt{(IR)^2 + (IX)^2}$. Thus,

$$IZ = \sqrt{(IR)^2 + (IX)^2}$$

and dividing each term by I results in

$$Z = \sqrt{R^2 + X^2} \qquad\qquad \text{[10-16]}$$

or $\qquad Z = R \pm jX \qquad$ (Rectangular Notation)

Because of their different effects, then, resistance and reactance cannot be added arithmetically but must be combined according to the relationship given in Eq. (10-13).

Since reactance has been defined as $X_L - X_C$, the complete expression for the impedance of a series circuit is

$$Z = \sqrt{R^2 + (X_L - X_C)^2} \qquad\qquad \text{[10-17]}$$

When a circuit contains a negligible amount of X_C compared with its R and X_L, the above expression reduces to

$$Z = \sqrt{R^2 + (X_L - 0)^2} = \sqrt{R^2 + X_L^2}$$

Likewise, when a circuit contains a negligible amount of X_L, the impedance becomes

$$Z = \sqrt{R^2 + (0 - X_C)^2} = \sqrt{R^2 + (-X_C)^2}$$

The minus sign has no effect on the magnitude of Z, since a minus number squared is equal to a positive number.

FIGURE **10-16**

Construction of the impedance triangle for Example 10-14.

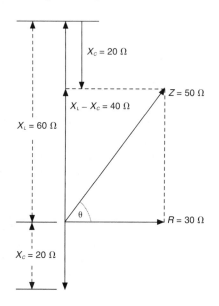

Example 10-14

A resistance of 30 Ω is connected in series with an inductive reactance of 60 Ω and a capacitive reactance of 20 Ω. What is the impedance of the circuit?

$$Z = \sqrt{R^2 + (X_L - X_C)^2}$$

$$= \sqrt{(30)^2 + (60 - 20)^2}$$

$$= \sqrt{900 + 1600} = \sqrt{2500} = 50 \ \Omega$$

or $Z = R + j(X_L - X_C)$

$$= 30 + j(60 - 20) = 30 + j40 = 50 \ \underline{/53.1°} \ \Omega$$

10-**21**

Graphical Representation of Resistance, Reactance, and Impedance in a Series Circuit

The relations expressed by the formula

$$Z = \sqrt{R^2 + X^2} \qquad \text{[10-16]}$$

may be represented by a right triangle, where Z is the hypotenuse and R and X form the other two sides of the triangle, since the hypotenuse of a right triangle is equal to the square root of the sum of the squares of the other two sides (see Appendix F). The value of the resistance is drawn to a convenient scale on the horizontal to form the base line. In a circuit containing only resistance and inductive reactance, the value of the reactance is laid off on a vertical line above the resistance line as in Fig. 10-17. If the circuit contains capacitive reactance, the reactance line is laid off below the horizontal line as in Fig. 10-18. If the circuit contains both X_L and X_C, the reactance is laid off on the vertical above or below the horizontal, depending on whether X_L or X_C is the larger. Such a triangle is called an **impedance triangle** and, when it is carefully drawn to scale, it affords an excellent check on the mathematical calculations of impedance.

FIGURE **10-17**
Impedance triangle: resistance and inductive reactance in series.

FIGURE **10-18**
Impedance triangle: resistance and capacitive reactance in series.

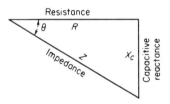

R E V I E W Q U E S T I O N S

1 Give four advantages of alternating current over direct current.
2 List some applications in which direct current is preferred to alternating current.
3 Describe briefly the generation of an alternating emf. In general, what two factors will determine the amount of emf generated in a conductor?
4 What is meant by an instantaneous value of emf? What is the symbol? What is the unit?
5 What is meant by a maximum value of emf? What is the symbol? What is the unit?

6 When a conductor is revolved in a uniform magnetic field and the instantaneous values of emf are plotted against degrees of rotation, what is the resulting curve called?

7 Define an alternating current.

8 What is the symbol for (*a*) an instantaneous value of current, (*b*) a maximum value?

9 What is a cycle? What is frequency? What is the unit of frequency?

10 How many electrical degrees correspond (*a*) to one cycle, (*b*) to one-half cycle, (*c*) to two cycles? In a 60-Hz generator, what fraction of a second does it take to generate one cycle?

11 How many cycles are generated in a coil that makes one revolution in a 24-pole generator?

12 Define an effective ac ampere.

13 What is the ratio of the effective to the maximum values of a sine-wave current?

14 What is the effective value of current sometimes called?

15 What is the symbol for effective current?

16 Do common ac ammeters and voltmeters read instantaneous, maximum, or effective values?

17 What is meant when it is said that a current and voltage are in phase?

18 What are three possible phase relations between a current and a voltage?

19 What is the phase angle of a circuit?

20 What is a phasor? What is a phasor diagram?

21 Two phasors are drawn starting at a common point. Phasor 1 extends to the right from the point along the horizontal, and phasor 2 is drawn upward from the point at right angles to phasor 1. Does phasor 1 lead or lag phasor 2 by 90°?

22 Draw a phasor diagram of a current of 10 A lagging a voltage of 125 V by 45°.

23 What are the three circuit properties?

24 What is the phase relation of the current and voltage in a circuit containing resistance only?

25 Why does inductance affect the flow of an alternating current and not the flow of a steady direct current?

26 What is the unit of inductance? What is the symbol?

27 What is inductive reactance? What is the unit? What is the symbol?

28 What is the phase relation between (*a*) the applied voltage and the emf of self-induction, (*b*) the applied voltage and the current in a circuit containing inductance only?

29 Describe a parallel-plate capacitor.

30 What is capacitance? What is the unit? What is the symbol?

31 Upon what three things does the capacitance of a capacitor depend?

32 Why does a circuit containing a capacitor appear to be complete when an alternating emf is applied?

33 What is the phase relation between the applied voltage and the current flowing in a circuit containing capacitance only?

34 What is the unit of capacitive reactance? What is the symbol?

35 What is the effect on the capacitive reactance if the capacitance of a circuit is doubled, the frequency remaining constant?

36 To what is the reactance of a circuit equal?

37 Impedance is the combined effect of what two things in a circuit?

38 Show how an inductive reactance of 16 Ω and a resistance of 12 Ω may be combined graphically to form an impedance of 20 Ω.

39 Draw to scale an impedance triangle of a circuit in which the resistance is 3 Ω, the inductive reactance is 5 Ω, and the capacitive reactance is 2 Ω.

P R O B L E M S

10-1 Determine the instantaneous voltage on a sine curve at 25° when the maximum voltage is 250 V.

10-2 Determine the maximum voltage when the instantaneous voltage is 70 V at angle 15°.

10-3 The maximum current is 10 A. What is the instantaneous current at 80°?

10-4 An alternating current has a maximum value of 50 A. Find the effective value of the current.

10-5 Find the maximum value of an alternating current whose effective value is 100 A.

10-6 Find the maximum value of an alternating voltage whose effective value is 240 V.

10-7 Standard ac ammeters and voltmeters read effective values of current and voltage. If the maximum value of current in a circuit is 7 A, find the reading of an ammeter that is placed in the circuit.

10-8 A voltmeter reads 480 V. Find the maximum value of the voltage wave. What is the effective value of the wave?

10-9 A current of 20 A lags a current of 40 A by 90°. Find the phasor sum of the two currents.

10-10 What is the phasor sum of two currents of 10 A each that are out of phase by 60°?

10-11 Two voltages of 120 V each are in phase. What is their phasor sum?

10-12 Two voltages of 120 V each are out of phase by 120°. What is their phasor sum?

10-13 Three voltages of 240 V are displaced symmetrically in time phase by 120°. What is their phasor sum?

10-14 Subtract a current of 10 A from a current of 14.14 A when the 14.14-A current leads the 10-A current by 45°.

10-15 A coil has an inductance of 0.2 H. Find its inductive reactance on a line frequency of 60, 120, and 600 Hz.

10-16 A coil has an inductive reactance of 40 Ω at a frequency of 60 Hz. Find the inductance of the coil.

10-17 A coil has an inductance of 0.05 H. The inductive reactance is 100 Ω. Find the line frequency.

10-18 A certain coil has an inductance of 0.30 H. What is its reactance at 60 Hz and at 25 Hz?

10-19 The coil in the preceding problem is connected across 115 V. What current will flow when the frequency is (*a*) 60 Hz, (*b*) 25 Hz? Neglect the resistance of the coil.

10-20 A capacitor has a capacitance of 40 μF. What is its capacitive reactance at 60 Hz and at 120 Hz?

10-21 Determine the capacity of a capacitor if its capacitive reactance on a 60-Hz system is 80 Ω.

10-22 What is the capacitive reactance of a 0.5-μF capacitor at 60 Hz and at 600 kHz (600 000 Hz)?

10-23 What current will flow when a 10-μF capacitor is connected to a 240-V 60-Hz supply?

10-24 A series ac circuit has a capacitive reactance of 40 Ω and a resistance of 20 Ω. Compute the impedance.

10-25 A series circuit has negligible resistance. Its X_C is 100 Ω and its X_L is 40 Ω. Compute the impedance.

10-26 Find the impedance of a series circuit if it has 30 Ω resistance and 20 Ω capacitive reactance.

10-27 What is the impedance of a coil that has a resistance of 8 Ω and an inductive reactance of 20 Ω?

10-28 Find the impedance of a circuit that consists of the coil of Prob. 10-27 in series with a capacitor that has a capacitive reactance of 32 Ω.

10-29 A coil has a resistance of 3 Ω and an X_L of 30 Ω. Find the impedance of the circuit if a capacitor having an X_C of 30 Ω is connected in series with the coil.

10-30 A coil having a resistance of 2 Ω and an inductance of 0.25 H is connected to a 12-V storage battery. What steady-state current will flow through the coil?

10-31 Three capacitors of 4, 8, and 16 μF, respectively, are connected so that each capacitor forms the side of a triangle. Point A is the connection between the 4- and 8-μF sides; point B between the 8- and 16-μF sides; point C between the 4- and 16-μF sides. Find the capacitance between points A and B, B and C, and C and A.

Single-Phase Circuits

Power in a dc circuit is equal to the product of the current and voltage. The power in an ac circuit at any instant is equal to the product of the values of current and voltage at that instant. When an alternating current and voltage are in phase, the average power over a complete cycle is equal to the product of the effective current and voltage. However, when reactance is present in the circuit, the current and voltage are out of phase so that at times during each cycle the current is negative while the voltage is positive. This results in a value of power in the circuit which is less than the product of I and E.

11-1
Power and Power Factor

The product of the effective values of current and voltage in an ac circuit is expressed in **voltamperes** (VA) or in **kilovoltamperes** (kVA) — often referred to as **Apparent Power** since 1 kVA is equal to 1000 VA. The useful or **actual power** is measured in watts and is the value obtained when the voltamperes of the circuit are multiplied by a factor called the **power factor**. Thus, power in a single-phase ac circuit is

$$P \text{ (in watts)} = EI \times \text{power factor} \qquad \textbf{[11-1]}$$

$$P \text{ (in kilowatts)} = \frac{EI}{1000} \times \text{power factor} \qquad \textbf{[11-2]}$$

By rearranging Eq. (11-1)

$$\text{power factor} = \frac{P}{EI} \qquad \textbf{[11-3]}$$

Thus, *power factor* may be defined as *the ratio of the actual power in watts to the voltamperes of an ac circuit.*

The value of the power factor depends on how much the current and voltage are out of phase. When the current and voltage are in phase, power is equal to $I \times E$ or, in other words, the power factor is unity. When current and voltage are out of phase by 90°, as in a purely capacitive or inductive circuit, the power factor is zero, thus resulting in a zero value of actual power. In circuits containing both resistance and reactance, the value of the power factor is some value between 1 and zero, its value depending on the relative values of resistance and reactance in the circuit.

Power factor may be expressed either as a decimal or as a percentage. For example, a power factor of 0.8 may be expressed as 80 percent and a power factor of 1.0 as 100 percent. Some typical average power factors are incandescent lights, 95 to 100 percent; large induction motors carrying rated load, 85 to 90 percent; fractional-horsepower induction motors, 60 to 75 percent, all with the current lagging the voltage.

The current flowing in an ac circuit may be considered as being made up of two components: a component in phase with the voltage and a component out of phase with the voltage by 90° as shown in Fig. 11-1. The in-phase component is called the **active** component since this value when multiplied by the voltage gives the useful or actual power of the circuit. The out-of-phase component is called the **reactive** component, or the wattless component, since it contributes nothing to the actual power of the circuit. The product of the reactive component of the current and the voltage is called **reactive power** or **reactive voltamperes** and is measured in **vars**, a word coined from the first letters of the words "voltamperes reactive." A larger unit of reactive power is the **kilovar**, one kilovar being equal to 1000 vars.

Fig. 11-1 shows that the greater the phase angle θ, the greater is the value of the reactive component and the smaller the value of the active component of a given value of total current.

In Fig. 11-1, the cosine of the phase angle θ is the ratio of the active current to the total current, or

$$\cos\theta = \frac{\text{active } I}{I}$$

or   active $I = I \cos\theta$

Then, since the actual power is the voltage multiplied by the active component of current,

---

F I G U R E **11-1**
Two components of current in an ac circuit.

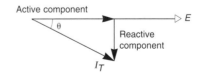

$$P = V_R \times \text{active } I_R$$

or
$$P = EI_T \cos \theta \qquad \text{[11-4]}$$

Since power has already been shown to be EI multiplied by a power factor, it follows that the *power factor of an ac circuit is equal to the cosine of the phase angle*.

The values of the cosines of angles from $0°$ to $90°$ are given in Appendix G. Note that the values range from 1.000 for an angle of $0°$ to 0.000 for an angle of $90°$.

The relation between the power in watts, the voltamperes, and the reactive voltamperes, or vars, may be represented by a triangle as shown in Fig. 11-2, the angle θ being the phase angle of the circuit being represented. The base of the triangle represents the actual power, the altitude the reactive voltamperes, and the hypotenuse the voltamperes. Since the voltamperes are equal to EI, the actual power is $EI \cos \theta$, and the reactive voltamperes are $EI \sin \theta$. Also the following relation is true:

$$\text{Voltamperes} = \sqrt{(\text{power})^2 + (\text{reactive VA})^2}$$

From the definition of the effective ac ampere (Chap. 10), power is also equal to the effective current squared multiplied by the resistance of the circuit, or

$$P = I_R^2 R \qquad \text{[11-5]}$$

This is true in any single-phase ac circuit regardless of the phase relation between the current and the voltage.

Figs. 11-3, 4, and 5 illustrate, using an oscillogram, the relationship that exists between voltage, current, and power. In Fig. 11-3(*a*) the current and voltage are in phase. Note the **power** waveform "*P*" is positive going regardless of the negative voltage and

---

FIGURE **11-2**
Relation between power, voltamperes, and reactive voltamperes.

P—Actual power (watts)

θ $EI_T \cos \theta$

PX—Reactive voltamperes (vars)

PA—Voltamperes (VA)

$EI_T \sin \theta$

(EI_T)

FIGURE **11-3**

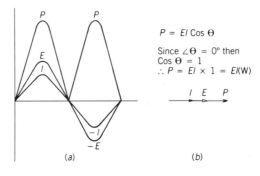

$P = EI \cos \Theta$

Since $\angle \Theta = 0°$ then
$\cos \Theta = 1$
$\therefore P = EI \times 1 = EI(\text{W})$

(a)   (b)

current. This is a result of the product of the negative voltage and current producing a positive resultant, **power**.

In Fig. 11-4(*a*) the phase relationship between voltage and current is 90°. Fig. 11-4(*b*) illustrates this in a phasor diagram. However, the resultant **power** in this condition is zero due to the sums of the positive and negative elements of power shown on the waveform. This would be true whether the current is leading or lagging the voltage by 90°.

In Fig. 11-5(*a*) the phase relationship between voltage and current is 45°. Fig. 11-5(*b*) illustrates this in a phasor diagram. Note, however, the positive *power* waveform is much larger in magnitude and in duration than the negative *power* waveform. The resultant of this is indicated in Fig. 11-5(*b*). The negative element of *power* illustrated in Figs. 11-4(*a*) and 11-5(*a*) is out of phase with the positive element of *power* by 90°.

This negative element of *power* is properly referred to as **reactive power** (vars), and the positive element of *power* is referred

FIGURE **11-4**

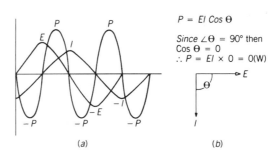

$P = EI \cos \Theta$

Since $\angle \Theta = 90°$ then
$\cos \Theta = 0$
$\therefore P = EI \times 0 = 0(\text{W})$

(a)   (b)

FIGURE **11-5**

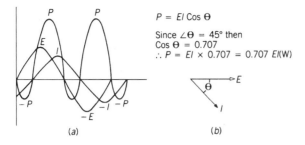

$P = EI \cos \Theta$

Since $\angle\Theta = 45°$ then
$\cos \Theta = 0.707$
$\therefore P = EI \times 0.707 = 0.707\ EI(\mathrm{W})$

(a)   (b)

to as **true power** (watts). The power triangle in Fig. 11-2 shows their relationships to one another. The phasor sum of *true power* (watts) and *reactive power* (vars) is **apparent power** (VA). This description is made valid by the fact of simply measuring the voltage across a device and the current flowing through it and taking the product of these two values with complete disregard to the phase angle between current and voltage.

Current and voltage relations in ac circuits containing resistance only, inductance only, and capacitance only were considered in the preceding chapter. In practice most circuits are combinations of two or, often, all three of these basic types of circuits. For example, transformer, generator, and motor windings all contain resistance and inductance. Even though the resistance and inductance are distributed throughout the windings, it is convenient when studying such circuits to consider the circuit as being made up of a pure resistance in series with a pure inductance.

Two rules similar to those of dc series circuits apply to the current and voltage relations of an ac series circuit:

1. In an ac series circuit, the current has the same value in all parts of the circuit.
2. The voltage applied to an ac series circuit is equal to the *phasor* sum of the voltages across the several parts of the circuit.

Fig. 11-6(*a*) represents a circuit with resistance and inductance in series. The phasor diagram is drawn in Fig. 11-6(*b*). The current phasor is used as a reference, since the current is the same in all parts of a series circuit. Since the voltage across a resistance is in phase with the current through the resistance, the phasor $V_R = IR$ is drawn along the current phasor. However, the voltage across an inductance leads the current through the circuit by 90°. Therefore, $V_L = IX_L$ is drawn 90° ahead of the current phasor I. The applied voltage E is equal to the phasor sum of V_R and V_L. The phasor

11-2

Current and Voltage Relations in Series Circuits

11-3

Resistance and Inductance in Series

FIGURE **11-6**
(*a*) Circuit with resistance and inductance in series. (*b*) Phasor diagram.

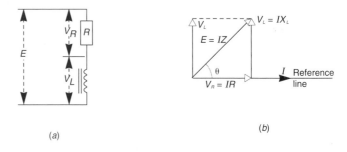

(*a*)

(*b*)

addition may be performed by moving the phasor V_L to the arrow end of V_R and completing the triangle, the hypotenuse of the triangle representing E or IZ. The angle θ, or the angle between the applied voltage E and the current I, is the phase angle of the circuit.

Power in the circuit of Fig. 11-6(*a*) may be calculated from the formula

$$P = EI \times \text{power factor}$$

Since the power factor is the cosine of the phase angle, the power factor from Fig. 11-6(*b*) is

$$\text{Power factor} = \cos \theta = \frac{V_R}{E} = \frac{IR}{IZ} = \frac{R}{Z} \qquad \textbf{[11-6]}$$

Hence, the power factor of a series circuit is equal to the ratio of the resistance to the impedance of the circuit.

The following example will illustrate the method of calculating the current, power factor, and power of a simple *RL* (resistance-inductance) series circuit.

Example 11-1

The circuit represented in Fig. 11-7 has a resistance of 6 Ω in series with an inductance of 0.0212 H. The circuit is connected to a 120-V 60-Hz supply. Find (*a*) the circuit impedance, (*b*) the

FIGURE **11-7**
Circuit and phasor diagram for Example 11-1.

(*a*)

(*b*)

current flowing, (c) the voltage across the resistance, (d) the voltage across the inductance, (e) the power factor, and (f) the power.

(a) $X_L = 2\pi f L$

$$= 2 \times 3.14 \times 60 \times 0.0212 = 8 \; \Omega$$
$$Z = \sqrt{R^2 + X^2} = \sqrt{6^2 + 8^2} = 10 \; \Omega$$

(b) $I = \dfrac{E}{Z} = \dfrac{120}{10} = 12 \text{ A}$

(c) $V_R = IR = 12 \times 6 = 72 \text{ V}$

(d) $V_L = IX_L = 12 \times 8 = 96 \text{ V}$

$$E = \sqrt{V_R^2 + V_L^2} = \sqrt{72^2 + 96^2} = 120 \text{ V} \qquad \text{(check)}$$

(e) Power factor $= \cos \theta = \dfrac{R}{Z} = \dfrac{6}{10} = 0.6 \text{ or } 60\%$

(f) $P = EI \cos \theta = 120 \times 12 \times 0.6 = 864 \text{ W}$
also $P = I^2R = (12)^2 \times 6 = 864 \text{ W} \qquad \text{(check)}$

Note that E is not equal to the arithmetic sum of V_R and V_L (72 + 96 = 168).

The phasor diagram is drawn in Fig. 11-7(b).

11-4
Resistance and Capacitance in Series

A capacitance and resistance in series are shown in Fig. 11-8. The current, being common to both branches, is used as a reference in the phasor diagram. The phasor representing the voltage across the resistance V_R is drawn in phase with the current. However, the current through a capacitance leads the voltage across the capacitance by 90°. Thus, the phasor V_C is drawn 90° behind the current. Again the applied voltage E is equal to the phasor sum of the voltages across each part of the circuit. The phasor addition by the triangle method is shown in Fig. 11-8(b).

The power factor is equal to the cosine of the phase angle, or R/Z. The power taken by the circuit is equal to $EI \cos \theta$, or I^2R.

FIGURE **11-8**
(a) Circuit with resistance and capacitance in series. (b) Phasor diagram.

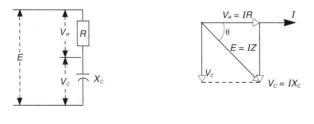

(a)   (b)

Example 11-2 illustrates the method of calculating RC (resistance-capacitance) series circuits.

E x a m p l e   1 1 - 2

A resistance of 80 Ω in series with a 50-μF capacitor is connected to a 120-V 60-Hz source. Find (*a*) the circuit impedance, (*b*) the current flowing, (*c*) the voltage across the resistance, (*d*) the voltage across the capacitor, (*e*) the power factor, and (*f*) the power. The circuit diagram and phasor diagram are shown in Figs. 11-9(*a*) and (*b*).

(*a*) $X_C = \dfrac{1}{2\pi fC} = \dfrac{10^6}{2\pi fC_{\mu F}}$

$= \dfrac{10^6}{2 \times 3.14 \times 60 \times 50} = 53.1\ \Omega$

$Z = \sqrt{R^2 + X^2} = \sqrt{80^2 + 53.1^2} = 96\ \Omega$

(*b*) $I_T = \dfrac{E}{Z} = 1.25\ \text{A}$

(*c*) $V_R = IR = 1.25 \times 80 = 100\ \text{V}$

(*d*) $V_C = IX_C = 1.25 \times 53.1 = 66.4\ \text{V}$

$E = \sqrt{V_R^2 + V_C^2} = \sqrt{100^2 + 66.4^2} = 120\ \text{V}$ (check)

(*e*) Power factor $= \cos\theta = \dfrac{R}{Z} = \dfrac{80}{96} = 0.833$

(*f*) $P = EI\cos\theta = 120 \times 1.25 \times 0.833 = 125\ \text{W}$
also $P = I^2R = (1.25)^2 \times 80 = 125\ \text{W}$ (check)

F I G U R E **11-9**
Circuit and phasor diagram for Example 11-2.

(*a*)   (*b*)

This type of circuit may be solved by the same methods as those used in Secs. 11-3 and 11-4. The current phasor is used as a reference in series circuits in general because it is common to all elements of the circuit. The voltage drop across the resistance of the circuit ($V_R = IR$) is in phase with the current, and its phasor is drawn along the current phasor. The phasors representing the voltage drop across the inductance ($V_L = IX_L$) and the voltage drop across the capacitance ($V_C = IX_C$) are drawn 90° ahead of and 90° behind the current phasor, respectively. The phasor sum of the voltages V_R, V_L and V_C is equal to the impressed voltage E. The power factor and power are also found by the same methods used in the simpler series circuits. An example will illustrate.

11-5
Resistance, Inductance, and Capacitance in Series

Example 11-3

Fig. 11-10(a) shows a circuit diagram of a circuit containing a resistance of 20 Ω, an inductance of 0.10 H, and a 100-μF capacitor, all connected in series. The applied voltage is 240 V at 60 Hz. It is desired to find (a) the circuit impedance, (b) the current flow, (c) the voltage across each part, (d) the power factor, (e) the voltamperes, and (f) the power.

(a) $$X_L = 2\pi fL = 2 \times 3.14 \times 60 \times 0.10 = 37.7 \ \Omega$$

$$X_C = \frac{10^6}{2\pi fC_{\mu F}} = \frac{10^6}{2 \times 3.14 \times 60 \times 100} = 26.5 \ \Omega$$

$$X = X_L - X_C = 37.7 - 26.5 = 11.2 \ \Omega$$

$$Z = \sqrt{R^2 + X^2} = \sqrt{20^2 + 11.2^2} = 22.9 \ \Omega$$

FIGURE **11-10**
Circuit and phasor diagram for Example 11-3.

(a)   (b)

(b) $I = \dfrac{E}{Z} = \dfrac{240}{22.9} = 10.48$ A

(c) $V_R = IR = 10.48 \times 20 = 209.6$ V

$V_L = IX_L = 10.48 \times 37.7 = 395$ V

$V_C = IX_C = 10.48 \times 26.5 = 278$ V

The phasor diagram is drawn in Fig. 11-10(b) showing the position of the three voltages relative to the current. As a check on the work, the three voltages may be added as phasors by first adding V_L and V_C and then adding the result to V_R. Since V_L and V_C are exactly opposed, their resultant is $V_L - V_C$ as shown. This resultant is added to V_R by the triangle method as shown.

Mathematically,

$$E = \sqrt{V_R^2 + (V_L - V_C)^2}$$

$$= \sqrt{(209.6)^2 + (395 - 278)^2} = 240 \text{ V} \qquad \text{(check)}$$

(d) Power factor $= \cos \theta = \dfrac{R}{Z} = \dfrac{20}{22.9} = 0.873$

The current lags the voltage since X_L is greater than X_C.

(e) Voltamperes $= EI = 240 \times 10.48 = 2515$ VA

(f) $P = EI \cos \theta = 2515 \times 0.873 = 2195$ W

or $P = I^2R = (10.48)^2 \times 20 = 2195$ W   (check)

11-6
Impedance in Series

When several electric devices are connected in series, the total impedance of the circuit is the phasor sum of the impedances of the separate parts. This total impedance may be found by adding arithmetically all the resistances, all the inductive reactances, and all the capacitive reactances and then combining these totals, using the relationship

$$Z = \sqrt{R^2 + (X_L - X_C)^2}$$

Example 11-4

Find the total impedance of two coils and a capacitor in series. Coil 1 has a resistance of 15 Ω and an inductive reactance of 35 Ω. Coil 2 has a resistance of 20 Ω and an inductive reactance of 45 Ω. The capacitor has a capacitive reactance of 60 Ω and has negligible resistance.

The total resistance of the circuit is the sum of the resistances of all the parts, or

$$R = 15 + 20 = 35 \ \Omega$$

The total inductive reactance is

$$X_L = 35 + 35 = 80 \ \Omega$$

The net reactance of the circuit is

$$X_L - X_C = 80 - 60 = 20 \ \Omega \qquad \text{(inductive)}$$

The combined impedance is

$$Z = \sqrt{R^2 + X^2} = \sqrt{35^2 + 20^2} = 40.3 \ \Omega$$

A series circuit in which the inductive and capacitive reactances are equal is said to be **resonant**. In such a circuit, the net reactance is zero and the impedance is equal to the resistance.

As an example, consider a circuit consisting of a 10-Ω resistance, a 30-Ω inductive reactance, and a 30-Ω capacitive reactance all connected in series to a 120-V 60-Hz supply. Since $X_L = X_C$, the reactance of the circuit is zero and the impedance is equal to the resistance, i.e., 10 Ω. The power factor of the circuit is unity since power factor is equal to R/Z. The current in the circuit is V/Z or 12 A. The voltage drop V across the resistance is IR or 120 V. Likewise, the voltage drop V across each reactance is IX or 360 V. However, the voltage across the inductive reactance is 180° out of phase with the voltage across the capacitive reactance, and while the effective value of each of these voltages may be relatively large, their phasor sum is zero.

If the frequency of the supply voltage for the circuit just described were lower than 60 Hz, the X_L of the circuit would be less than 30 Ω, the X_C would be greater than 30 Ω, and the total impedance would be greater than 10 Ω. Likewise, the impedance of the circuit would be greater than 10 Ω at frequencies greater than 60 Hz. In other words, a given series circuit is resonant at only one frequency and, at the resonant frequency, the impedance is at a minimum. Since at resonance $X_L = X_C$, then

$$2\pi f L = \frac{1}{2\pi f C}$$

Solving this equation for f results in the following value of frequency at resonance:

$$f = \frac{1}{2\pi\sqrt{LC}} \qquad \text{[11-7]}$$

11-7
Series Resonance

F I G U R E **11-11**

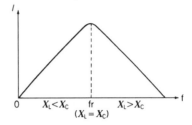

Fig. 11-11 illustrates the Resonance Concept in a series circuit using frequency and current for the X- and Y-axes, respectively.

Note the current is greatest at resonant frequency since the circuit impedance is only that of the circuit's resistance.

Resonance is usually to be avoided in power circuits because of the possibility of excessive voltages existing across parts of the circuit. However, in communications circuits, advantage is taken of the phenomenon in the tuning of circuits to obtain selectivity or the ability to respond strongly to a given frequency and discriminate against others.

11-8
Parallel Circuits

Practically all lighting and power circuits are constant-voltage circuits with the loads connected in parallel. As in parallel dc circuits, the voltage is the same across each branch of a parallel ac circuit. The total line current supplied to the circuit is equal to the *phasor* sum of the branch currents. The total current supplied to a parallel circuit may be found by finding the current taken by each branch and adding these currents, taking into account their phase relations, or by finding an equivalent impedance and dividing the applied voltage by the equivalent impedance.

The aid offered by a phasor diagram in the solution of parallel-circuit problems will be found to be indispensable. Some examples will illustrate the principles involved in parallel-circuit calculations.

Example 11-5

(Resistance and inductance in parallel.) A 0.06-H inductance coil with negligible resistance is connected in parallel with a 30-Ω resistance as in Fig. 11-12. When a voltage of 120 V at 60 Hz is applied, find (*a*) the current, (*b*) the power factor, and (*c*) the power taken by the circuit.

FIGURE **11-12**
Circuit and phasor diagram for Example 11-5.

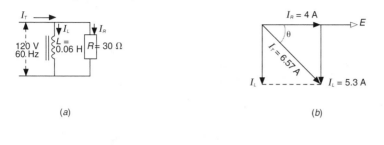

(a) $X_L = 2\pi fL = 2 \times 3.14 \times 60 \times 0.06 = 22.62 \ \Omega$

$$I_L = \frac{V_L}{X_L} = \frac{120}{22.62} = 5.3 \text{ A}$$

$$I_R = \frac{V_R}{R} = \frac{120}{30} = 4 \text{ A}$$

The phasor diagram is drawn in Fig. 11-12(*b*). In a parallel circuit the voltage phasor is used as a reference, since the voltage is the same for all branches of the circuit. Hence, the voltage phasor is laid off along the horizontal line. The current I_R is in phase with the voltage, and the current I_L lags the voltage by 90° as shown in the phasor diagram. The total current I is the phasor sum of I_R and I_L, the phasor addition being made as shown. Mathematically,

$$I = \sqrt{I_R^2 + I_L^2} = \sqrt{4^2 + 5.3^2} = 6.57 \text{ A}$$

(*b*) The total current I lags behind the applied voltage by the angle. The power factor of the circuit is

$$\text{Power factor} = \cos \theta = \frac{I_R}{I} = \frac{4}{6.57} = 0.609$$

(*c*) $P = EI \cos \theta = 120 \times 6.57 \times 0.609 = 480 \text{ W}$

Example 11-6

(Resistance, inductance, and capacitance in parallel.) A resistance of 80 Ω, an inductance of 0.15 H, and a capacitance of 25 μF are connected in parallel, and a voltage of 240 V at 60 Hz is applied. Find (*a*) the current, (*b*) the power factor, (*c*) the power, and (*d*) the equivalent or combined impedance of the combination.

The circuit and phasor diagrams are shown in Fig. 11-13. Note that the voltage phasor is used as a reference and that the

F I G U R E **11-13**
Circuit and phasor diagram for Example 11-6.

(a)

(b)

current taken by the inductance lags the voltage by 90° and that taken by the capacitance leads the voltage by 90°.

(a) $I_R = \dfrac{V_R}{R} = \dfrac{240}{80} = 3 \text{ A}$

$X_L = 2\pi f L = 2 \times 3.14 \times 60 \times 0.15 = 56.55 \ \Omega$

$I_L = \dfrac{V_L}{X_L} = \dfrac{240}{56.55} = 4.24 \text{ A}$

$X_C = \dfrac{10^6}{2\pi f C_{\mu F}} = \dfrac{10^6}{2 \times 3.14 \times 60 \times 25} = 106.1 \ \Omega$

$I_C = \dfrac{V_C}{X_C} = \dfrac{240}{106.1} = 2.26 \text{ A}$

The total current is the phasor sum of the branch currents. Combining I_L and I_C, which are in opposition, we have

$I_L - I_C = 4.24 - 2.26 = 1.98 \text{ A}$

and the total current is

$I_T = \sqrt{I_R^2 + (I_L - I_C)^2} = \sqrt{3^2 + 1.98^2} = 3.6 \text{ A}$

(b) Power factor $= \cos \theta = \dfrac{I_R}{I_T} = \dfrac{3}{3.6} = 0.833$

As I_L is larger than I_C, the total current lags voltage by the angle θ.

(c) $P = EI_T \cos \theta = 240 \times 3.6 \times 0.833 = 720 \text{ W}$

also $P = (I_R)^2 R = 3^2 \times 80 = 720 \text{ W}$ (check)

(d) $Z = \dfrac{E}{I_T} = \dfrac{240}{3.6} = 66.7 \ \Omega$

Example 11-7

A resistance of 30 Ω is connected in parallel with a coil that has a resistance of 12 Ω and an inductive reactance of 16 Ω. Find (a) the line current, and (b) the power taken by the circuit when it is connected to a 240-V supply as in Fig. 11-14.

(a) $$Z_2 = \sqrt{R^2 + X_L^2} = \sqrt{12^2 + 16^2} = 20\ \Omega$$

$$I_2 = \frac{E}{Z_2} = \frac{240}{20} = 12\ A$$

$$I_1 = \frac{E}{Z_1} = \frac{240}{30} = 8\ A$$

The phasor diagram is drawn in Fig. 11-14(b). The current I_1 is in phase with the voltage, while I_2 lags the voltage by an angle ϕ whose cosine is R_2/Z_2, or

$$\cos\phi = \frac{R_2}{Z_2} = \frac{12}{20} = 0.6$$

$$\phi = 53.13° \qquad \text{(from tables or by calculator)}$$

The phasor addition of I_1 and I_2 is performed by completing the triangle OBC as shown in Fig. 11-14(b).

$$OA = 8$$

$$AC = 12$$

$$AB = 12\cos 53.13° = 12 \times 0.6 = 7.2$$

FIGURE **11-14**
Circuit and phasor diagram for Example 11-7.

(a)   (b)

$$OB = OA + AB = 8 + 7.2 = 15.2$$

$$BC = 12 \sin 53.13° = 12 \times 0.8 = 9.6$$

$$I = OC = \sqrt{(OB)^2 + (BC)^2}$$

$$= \sqrt{15.2^2 + 9.6^2} = 18 \text{ A}$$

(b) $\text{Power factor} = \cos \theta = \dfrac{OB}{OC} = \dfrac{15.2}{18} = 0.8444$

$$P = EI \cos \theta = 240 \times 18 \times 0.8444$$

$$= 3648 \text{ W}$$

also $P_1 = I_1^2 R_1 = (8)^2 \times 20 = 1920 \text{ W}$

$$P_2 = I_2^2 R_2 = (12)^2 \times 12 = 1728 \text{ W}$$

$$P = P_1 + P_2 = 1920 + 1728$$

$$= 3648 \text{ W} \quad \text{(check)}$$

Using **polar rectangular conversion** the solution for Example 11-7 would follow the steps shown below.

(a) $I_1 = \dfrac{240}{30} = 8\underline{/0°} \text{ A}$

$$I_2 = \frac{240}{(12 + j16)} = \frac{240}{20} \underline{/-5313°}$$

$$= 12\underline{/-53.13°} \text{ A}$$

$$I_t = I_1 + I_2 = 8\underline{/0°} + 12\underline{/-53.13°}$$

$$8\underline{/0°} \text{ A} = 80 + j\,0$$

$$12\underline{/-53.13°} \text{ A} = \frac{7.2 - j\,9.6}{15.2 - j\,9.6} = 18\underline{/-32.3°} \text{ A}$$

(b) $\text{Power factor} = \cos\underline{/32.3°} = 0.84$

Resonance occurs in a parallel circuit when the reactive current in the inductive branches is equal to the reactive current in the capacitive branches. Since inductive and capacitive reactive currents are equal and opposite in phase, they cancel each other at parallel resonance.

If a coil and a capacitor, each with negligible resistance, were connected in parallel to an ac source and the reactances were adjusted so that at the frequency of the supply they were exactly equal, current would flow in the coil and in the capacitor but the total current drawn from the supply would be negligible. Stating this another way, the parallel circuit would present an almost infinite impedance to the source. For this condition, the circuit is said to be oscillating; that is, the capacitor is alternately charging and discharging through the coil. This condition may be approached but not actually achieved in practical circuits because all coils and capacitors have some resistance and some current will always be drawn from the supply as determined by the amount of this resistance, even though the net reactance of the circuit is zero.

The expression for the resonant frequency in a parallel circuit in which the branch resistances are zero or very small is

$$f = \frac{1}{2\pi\sqrt{LC}}$$

which is identical to Eq. (11-7) for series resonant circuits.

Parallel resonant circuits are used extensively in communication equipment circuits.

11-9
Parallel Resonance

More current is required to supply a given kilowatt load at a low power factor than at unity power factor. Since both voltage drop and line losses in any power line supplying a load are proportional to the line current, it follows that the lower the power factor, the higher are the line drop and losses to transmit a given kilowatt load. Because of the large number of induction motors and other inductive devices used on modern power systems, the power factors of many such systems are quite low, resulting in substantial voltage drops and line losses.

Many power suppliers correct for low power factors by the use of power-factor-corrective capacitors connected to their systems at various points. Since the current drawn by a capacitor leads the applied voltage by 90° (neglecting the small amount of resistance in the capacitor), the current drawn by such a device effectively cancels the effect of the inductive reactive component of the load

11-10
Power-Factor Correction

devices on the same circuit. An installation of power-factor-corrective capacitors on a distribution system is shown in Fig. 11-15.

To illustrate the effect of a power-factor-corrective capacitor, consider the circuit of Example 11-7. The total current drawn by the circuit is 18 A, and the current lags the applied voltage by an angle whose cosine is 0.8444. From the phasor diagram in Fig. 11-14(*b*), this current has an active component *OB* of 15.2 A in phase with the voltage and a reactive component *BC* of 9.6 A lagging the voltage by 90°. If a capacitor with a current rating of 9.6 A is connected parallel with the resistor and coil, the resulting circuit power factor is unity. This is because the current drawn by the capacitor leads the voltage by 90° and, therefore, is 180° out of phase with the reactive component of the load current. Since there is no net reactive component in the circuit, the total line current is thus reduced from 18 to 15.2 A. Even though the total line current has been reduced, the resistor and coil are still supplied the same currents as before and the kilowatt load on the circuit is unchanged. The following example further illustrates the application of power-factor-corrective capacitors.

F I G U R E **11-15**
Assembly of power-factor corrective capacitors.
(Cooper Power Systems.)

E x a m p l e   1 1 - 8

A single-phase circuit has a load of 600 kVA at a power factor
of 75 percent. If capacitors are to be added to the circuit to
improve the power factor to 100 percent, what will be the rating
of the capacitors in kilovars?

$$\text{Circuit kW} = \text{kVA} \times \text{power factor}$$

$$= 600 \times 0.75 = 450 \text{ kW}$$

$$\text{kVA}^2 = \text{kW}^2 + \text{kvar}^2$$

$$\text{kvar} = \sqrt{\text{kVA}^2 - \text{kW}^2}$$

$$= \sqrt{600^2 - 450^2} = 397 \text{ kvar}$$

Since the load reactive is 397 kvar, the capacitor bank rating
must be 397 kvar to correct the circuit power factor to 100
percent.

Additional information on power-factor correction, including
the use of synchronous motors for this purpose, is included in Sec.
16-8.

R E V I E W   Q U E S T I O N S

1 In an ac circuit, how may the power at any instant be calculated? Is the instantaneous power a constant value over an entire cycle?
2 Draw a sine-wave voltage in phase with a sine-wave current. Is
   the instantaneous power zero at any time during a complete
   cycle? When is the instantaneous power at a maximum?
3 Under what condition is the power in an ac circuit equal to
   VI?
4 In general, what unit is used to express the product of volts
   and amperes in an ac circuit?
5 Define power factor. How is it used in finding the power of an
   ac circuit? What are its maximum and minimum values?
6 What is meant when it is said that an alternating current has
   an active and a reactive component?
7 In a circuit in which the current and voltage are in phase, what
   is the value of the reactive component of the current? What is
   the value of the reactive voltamperes, or vars, of the circuit?

8 What is the phase angle in degrees of a circuit in which the vars are equal to the watts? What is the phase angle of a circuit in which the volt-amperes are equal to the watts?

9 When the resistance and current of an ac circuit are known, how may power be calculated regardless of power factor?

10 Give the current and voltage rules for an ac series circuit.

11 When a series circuit contains inductance and resistance, does the current lead or lag the applied voltage? What is the phase relation between the voltage across the inductance and the current through the inductance?

12 How may the power factor of a series ac circuit be calculated from the circuit constants?

13 What is the phase relation between current and voltage in an *RC* series circuit?

14 Describe the procedure for finding the current, power factor, and power of a resistance-inductance-capacitance series circuit when the circuit constants, the frequency, and the voltage are given. Under what conditions in this circuit will the current lead the voltage?

15 When several impedances are connected in series, how is the combined impedance found?

16 Give the current and voltage rules for a parallel ac circuit.

17 Is the line current necessarily the arithmetic sum of the branch currents in a parallel ac circuit? When is this the case?

18 If the applied voltage and the branch currents of a parallel circuit are known, explain how the equivalent impedance of the circuit might be found.

19 Explain how the power factor of an inductive circuit may be improved.

20 Describe what effect a change in frequency from resonance will have in: (*a*) a series circuit; (*b*) a parallel circuit.

PROBLEMS

11-1 When a voltage of 416 V is applied to a certain load, the current that flows is 20 A. What are (*a*) the voltamperes of the circuit, (*b*) the kilovoltamperes?

11-2 The power taken by a motor is 800 W when the current is 9 A. If the line voltage is 120 V, at what power factor is the motor operating?

11-3 A certain load draws 85 kW and 105 kVA from an ac supply. At what power factor is it operating?

11-4 What full-load power can a 5-kVA single-phase generator supply at a power factor of 90 percent? What is the full-load line current if the terminal voltage is 120 V?

11-5 A single-phase motor operates at a power factor of 70 percent lagging. The line voltage is 240 V and the line current is 20 A. Find the voltamperes and the actual power in watts taken by the motor.

11-6 A single-phase circuit has a unity power factor. The applied voltage is 120 V. The line current is 30 A. Find the actual power in watts.

11-7 The power consumed in a single-phase circuit is 4 kW. The line current is 40 A and the voltage is 120 V. Find the voltamperes and the power factor of the circuit.

11-8 A single-phase motor is operating at a power factor of 0.8 lagging on a 240-V line. The motor consumes 8 kW. Find the motor line current.

11-9 A motor draws 1000 W and 1500 VA from a single-phase line. What is the value of the reactive voltamperes, or vars, drawn by the motor? What is the power factor?

11-10 Find the kilovoltamperes of a circuit when the actual power is 1200 W and the reactive voltamperes are 600 vars. What is the power factor?

11-11 An inductive reactance of 12 Ω is connected in series with a resistance of 16 Ω. A 115-V 60-Hz voltage is applied. Find (*a*) the impedance, (*b*) the current flowing, (*c*) the power factor, (*d*) the voltamperes, and (*e*) the power.

11-12 Find the voltage applied to a coil that has a reactance of 8 Ω and a resistance of 3 Ω when a current of 11 A is flowing through the coil. What is the power used by the coil?

11-13 A resistance of 40 Ω and a capacitance of 50 μF are connected in series across a 120-V 60-Hz line. Find (*a*) the impedance, (*b*) the current, (*c*) the power factor, (*d*) the voltamperes, and (*e*) the power.

11-14 A circuit consisting of a capacitor and a resistance in series takes 60 W at a power factor of 28 percent (leading) from a 120-V 60-Hz line. Find (*a*) the current, (*b*) the impedance, (*c*) the resistance, and (*d*) the capacitance of the circuit.

11-15 A 100-μF capacitor is connected to a 120-V 60-Hz line. Find the current that will flow. If a resistance of 10 Ω is connected in series with the capacitor, what will be the new value of current?

11-16 A series circuit consists of a resistance of 10 Ω, an 80-μF capacitor, and an inductance of 0.1 H. What current will flow when the circuit is connected to a 240-V 60-Hz supply?

11-17 A capacitor, a resistor, and a coil with negligible resistance are connected in series. The voltage drop across the capacitor is 50 V, across the resistor 80 V, and across the coil 20 V. Find the voltage drop across the entire circuit.

11-18 A resistance of 40 Ω and a capacitive reactance of 60 Ω are connected in series across 120-V circuit. Find (*a*) the current, (*b*) the power factor, and (*c*) the power.

11-19 When a resistance of 4 Ω and an inductance of unknown value are connected in series across 120-V 60-Hz supply lines, the current is 20 A. Find the value of the inductance.

11-20 The following meter readings were taken in an inductive single-phase circuit: wattmeter, 2400 W; voltmeter, 240 V; ammeter, 15 A; frequency meter, 60 Hz. Find (*a*) the volt-amperes, (*b*) the power factor, (*c*) the impedance, (*d*) the resistance, (*e*) the inductive reactance, (*f*) the inductance, and (*g*) the value of a series capacitor that will make the power factor 100 percent.

11-21 A 120-V ac motor delivers 5 hp at an efficiency of 85 percent. The motor operates at a power factor of 80 percent lagging. Find (*a*) the power input and (*b*) the current drawn by the motor.

11-22 Find the total current required by a circuit having a resistance of 20 Ω, an inductive reactance of 10 Ω, and a capacitive reactance of 15 Ω, all connected in parallel to a 120-V line.

11-23 A resistance of 16 Ω is connected in parallel with a coil that has a resistance of 4 Ω and a reactance of 12 Ω. The supply voltage is 120 V. Find (*a*) the total current, (*b*) the power factor, and (*c*) the power taken by the circuit.

11-24 A resistance of 20 Ω is connected in parallel with an inductive reactance of 10 Ω to a 100-V 60-Hz line. Find (*a*) the current through the resistance, (*b*) the current through the reactance, and (*c*) the reactance of a capacitor which, when connected in parallel with the circuit, will improve the power factor of the circuit to 100 percent.

11-25 A coil with a resistance of 5 Ω and an inductive reactance of 12 Ω is connected in parallel with a capacitor which has a capacitive reactance of 10 Ω and negligible resistance. When the parallel combination of coil and capacitor is connected to a 120-V 60-Hz supply, find (*a*) the current in each branch, (*b*) the total line current, (*c*) the total power in watts, and (*d*) the circuit power factor.

11-26 A coil having an inductive reactance of 8 Ω and a resistance of 0.5 Ω is connected in series with a 5.5-Ω resistor. The coil and the 5.5-Ω series resistor are connected in parallel with a 20-Ω resistor to a 120-V 60-Hz supply. Determine (*a*) the current flowing through the coil, (*b*) the current flowing through the 20-Ω resistor, (*c*) the total line current, (*d*) the power taken by the circuit, and (*e*) the power factor of the circuit.

11-27 The input to a motor is 5.5 VA at 80 percent power factor. What must be the reactive voltampere rating of a capacitor connected across the motor terminals to correct the power factor to 100 percent?

11-28 A 2-hp 60-Hz motor has a full-load input of 2200 W and 12 A at 230 V. (*a*) Find the reactive voltampere rating of a capacitor to be connected across the terminals of the motor to correct the full-load power factor to 100 percent. (*b*) What is the size of the capacitor in microfarads? (*c*) What is the total current drawn by the motor and the capacitor?

11-29 A 5-kvar (5000 var) capacitor added in parallel to a given 440-V load corrects the circuit power factor to unity, and the resulting line current is 5 A. (*a*) What was the line current drawn by the load before the addition of the capacitor? (*b*) What was the power factor of the original 440-V load?

11-30 A single-phase circuit has a variable load. At light-load periods the load is 200 kVA at 75 percent power factor, and at peak-load periods it is 500 kVA at 85 percent power factor. What is the rating in kilovars of a capacitor bank that will raise the light-load power factor to unity? What will be the peak-load power factor with this capacitor bank added to the circuit?

11-31 A 100-μF capacitor, a 5-henry (H) inductor, and 100-Ω resistor are connected in series across a 100-V ac source. (*a*) At what frequency will maximum circuit current flow? (*b*) What is the current in (*a*)?

11-32 If the devices in Prob. 11-31 were reconnected in parallel, what would be the: (*a*) current through three individual branches; (*b*) current supplied by the source at resonant frequency?

Three-Phase Circuits

A three-phase circuit is merely a combination of three single-phase circuits. Because of this fact, current, voltage, and power relations of balanced three-phase circuits may be studied by the application of single-phase rules to the component parts of the three-phase circuit. Viewed in this light, it will be found that the analysis of three-phase circuits is only a little more difficult than that of single-phase circuits.

12-1
Reasons for Use of Three-Phase Circuits

In a single-phase circuit, the power is of a pulsating nature. At unity power factor the power in a single-phase circuit is zero twice each cycle. When the power factor is less than unity, the power is negative during parts of each cycle. Although the power supplied to each of the three phases of a three-phase circuit is pulsating, it may be shown that the total three-phase power supplied to a balanced three-phase circuit is constant. Because of this, the operating characteristics of three-phase apparatus, in general, are superior to those of similar single-phase apparatus.

Three-phase machinery and control equipment are smaller, lighter in weight, and more efficient than single-phase equipment of the same rated capacity. In addition to the above-mentioned advantages offered by a three-phase system, the distribution of three-phase power requires only three-fourths as much line conductor material as does the single-phase distribution of the same amount of power.

12-2
Generation of Three-Phase EMFs

A three-phase electric circuit is energized by three alternating emfs of the same frequency and differing in time phase by 120 electrical degrees. Three such sine-wave emfs are shown in Fig. 12-1. These emfs are generated in three separate sets of armature coils in an ac generator. These three sets of coils are mounted 120 electrical degrees apart on the generator armature. The coil ends may all be brought out of the generator to form three separate single-phase circuits. However, the coils are ordinarily interconnected either internally or externally to form a three-wire or four-wire three-phase system.

Three sine-wave emfs differing in phase by 120 electrical degrees such as are used for energizing a three-phase circuit.

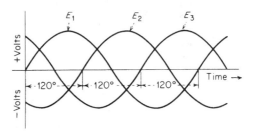

There are two ways of connecting the coils of three-phase generators and, in general, there are two ways of connecting devices of any sort to a three-phase circuit. These are the **wye connection** and the **delta connection**. Most generators are wye-connected, but loads may be either wye-connected or delta-connected.

12-**3**

Voltage Relations in a Wye-Connected Generator

Fig. 12-2(*a*) represents the three coils or phase windings of a generator. These windings are so spaced on the armature surface that the emfs generated in them are 120° apart in time phase. Each coil is lettered *S* and *F* (start and finish). In Fig. 12-2(*a*), all the coil ends marked *S* are connected to a common point *N*, called the neutral, and the three coil ends marked *F* are brought out to the line terminals *A*, *B*, and *C* to form a three-wire three-phase supply. This type of connection is called the *wye connection* (sometimes called the **star connection**). Often the neutral connection is brought out to the terminal board, as shown by the dotted line in Fig. 12-2(*a*), to form a four-wire three-phase system.

The voltages generated in each phase of an ac generator are called the **phase voltages** (symbol E_P or V_P). If the neutral connection is brought out of the generator, the voltage from any one of the line terminals *A*, *B*, or *C* to the neutral connection *N* is a phase voltage. The voltage between any two of the three line terminals *A*, *B*, or *C* is called a line-to-line voltage or, simply, a **line voltage** (symbol E_L or V_L).

The order in which the three voltages of a three-phase system succeed one another is called the **phase sequence** or the phase rotation of the voltages. This is determined by the direction of rotation of the generator but may be reversed outside the generator by interchanging any two of the three line wires (not a line wire and a neutral wire).

It is helpful when drawing circuit diagrams of a wye connection to arrange the three phases in the shape of a *Y* as shown in Fig. 12-2(*b*). Note that the circuit of Fig. 12-2(*b*) is exactly the same as

FIGURE **12-2**

(a) Connection of the phase windings in a wye-connected generator. (b) Conventional diagram of a wye connection. (c) Phasor diagram showing the relation between phase and line voltages.

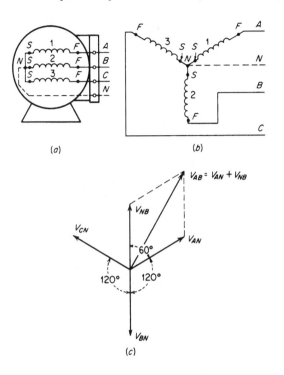

(a)   (b)

(c)

that of Fig. 12-2(a), with the S end of each coil connected to the neutral point and the F end brought out to the terminal in each case. After a circuit diagram has been drawn with all intersections lettered, a phasor diagram may be drawn as in Fig. 12-2(c). The phasor diagram shows the three phase voltages V_{AN}, V_{BN}, and V_{CN} which are 120° apart.

It should be noted in Fig. 12-2 that each phasor is lettered with two subscripts. The two letters indicate the two points between which the voltage exists, and the order of the letters indicates the relative polarity of the voltage during its positive half-cycle. For example, the symbol V_{AN} indicates a voltage V between the points A and N with the point A being positive with respect to point N during its positive half-cycle. In the phasor diagram shown, it has been assumed that the generator terminals were positive with respect to the neutral during the positive half-cycle. Since the voltage reverses every half-cycle, either polarity may be assumed if this polarity is assumed consistently for all three phases. It should be noted that if the polarity of point A with respect to N (V_{AN}) is assumed for the positive half-cycle, then V_{NA} when used in the same phasor diagram should be drawn opposite to, or 180° out of phase with, V_{AN}.

The voltage between any two line terminals of a wye-connected generator is the difference between the potentials of these two terminals with respect to the neutral. For example, the line voltage V_{AB} is equal to the voltage A with respect to neutral (V_{AN}) minus the voltage B with respect to neutral (V_{BN}). To subtract V_{BN} from V_{AN}, it is necessary to reverse V_{BN} and add this phasor to V_{AN}. The two phasors V_{AN} and V_{NB} are equal in length and are 60° apart, as shown in Fig. 12-2(c). It may be shown graphically or proven by geometry that V_{AB} is equal to $\sqrt{3}$, or 1.73, multiplied by the value of either V_{AN} or V_{NB}. The derivation of $\sqrt{3}$ is illustrated in Fig. 12-3. The graphical construction is shown in the phasor diagram. Therefore, in a balanced wye connection

$$V_L = \sqrt{3}V_P = 1.73V_P \qquad \text{[12-1]}$$

12-4
Current Relations in a Wye-Connected Generator

The current flowing out to the line wires from the generator terminals A, B, and C (Fig. 12-2) must flow from the neutral point N out through the generator coils. Thus, the current in each line wire (I_L) must equal the current in the phase (I_P) to which it is connected. In a wye connection

$$I_L = I_P \qquad \text{[12-2]}$$

12-5
Voltage Relations in a Delta-Connected Generator

A **delta-connected** generator is shown in Fig. 12-4(a). This connection is formed by connecting the S terminal of one phase to the F terminal of the adjacent phase. The line connections are then made at the common points between phases as shown. The conventional circuit diagram in which the three coils are arranged in the shape of the Greek letter delta (Δ) is shown in Fig. 12-4(b). An

---

FIGURE **12-3**

$0.866V_{NB} + 0.866V_{NB} = V_{AB}$
$\therefore 1.732V_{NB} = V_{AB}$
$\therefore \sqrt{3}\ V/\text{PHASE} = V_{AB}$

(WYE SYSTEM)

FIGURE **12-4**

(*a*) Connection of the phase windings in a delta-connected generator. (*b*) Conventional diagram of a delta connection. (*c*) Phasor diagram showing the relation between phase and line currents.

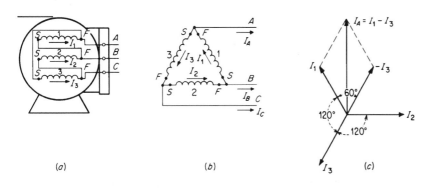

(*a*)   (*b*)   (*c*)

inspection of the diagram shows that the voltage generated in each phase is also the voltage between two line wires. For example, the voltage generated in phase 1 is also the voltage between lines A and B. Therefore, in a delta connection

$$V_L = V_P \qquad\qquad [12\text{-}3]$$

The phase currents in the delta connection of Fig. 12-4(*b*) are I_1, I_2, and I_3. The phasor diagram representing these currents is shown in Fig. 12-4(*c*). To find the current in any of the three line wires it is necessary to add as phasors the currents flowing in the two phases to which that line is connected. For example, the current flowing out toward the load through line A must be

$$I_A = I_1 + (-I_3)$$

Since I_1 and $-I_3$ are two equal phasors 60° apart, their phasor sum is $\sqrt{3}$, or 1.73, times the value of either I_1 or $-I_3$ as seen in Fig. 12-4(*c*). Therefore, in a delta connection

$$I_L = \sqrt{3}I_P = 1.73I_P \qquad\qquad [12\text{-}4]$$

From the formula for power in a single-phase circuit, the power developed in each phase (P_P) of either a delta or wye connection is

$$P_P = V_P I_P \cos\theta$$

where θ is the angle between the phase current and the phase voltage. The power developed in all three phases of a balanced three-phase connection is then

$$P = 3P_P = 3V_P I_P \cos\theta \qquad\qquad [12\text{-}5]$$

|12-6

Current Relations in a Delta-Connected Generator

|12-7

Power in Three-Phase Circuits

But in a wye connection

$$I_P = I_L \quad \text{and} \quad V_P = \frac{V_L}{\sqrt{3}}$$

Thus, the three-phase power in a wye-connected system in terms of line voltage and current is

$$P = 3 \frac{V_L}{\sqrt{3}} I_L \cos \theta$$

$$= \sqrt{3} V_L I_L \cos \theta$$

$$= 1.73 V_L I_L \cos \theta$$

In a delta connection

$$V_P = V_L \quad \text{and} \quad I_P = \frac{I_L}{\sqrt{3}}$$

Again, the three-phase power in terms of both line current and voltage is

$$P = 3 V_L \frac{I_L}{\sqrt{3}} \cos \theta$$

$$= \sqrt{3} V_L I_L \cos \theta$$

$$= 1.73 V_L I_L \cos \theta$$

Thus, the expression for three-phase power in a balanced system, either wye- or delta-connected, is equal to

$$P = \sqrt{3} V_L I_L \cos \theta \qquad \text{[12-6]}$$

$$P = 1.73 V_L I_L \cos \theta$$

If $V_P I_P \cos \theta$ is the power per phase in watts, then $V_P I_P$ represents the voltamperes per phase. It follows, then, that the three-phase voltamperes are equal to $3 V_P I_P$, or $1.73 V_L I_L$. The total three-phase kilovoltamperes in either a wye or delta system may be found by

$$\text{kVA} = \frac{1.73 V_L I_L}{1000} \qquad \text{[12-7]}$$

The power factor of a balanced three-phase system, either wye- or delta-connected, is defined as the cosine of the angle between the phase voltage and the phase current. From Eq. (12-6) also, the power factor is seen to be

$$\text{Power factor} = \cos \theta = \frac{P}{1.73 V_L I_L} \qquad \text{[12-8]}$$

or is equal to the ratio of the three-phase power to the three-phase voltamperes.

E x a m p l e   1 2 - 1

A three-phase wye-connected generator has a terminal voltage of 480 V and delivers a full-load current of 300 A per terminal at a lagging power factor of 75 percent. Find (a) the voltage per phase, (b) the full-load current per phase, (c) the kilovoltampere rating, and (d) the full-load power in kilowatts.

(a) $V_P = \dfrac{V_L}{1.73} = \dfrac{480}{1.73} = 277$ V

(b) As the generator is wye-connected, the phase current is equal to the line current.
$$I_P = I_L = 300 \text{ A}$$

(c) $\qquad \text{kVA} = \dfrac{1.73 V_L I_L}{1000}$

$\qquad\qquad = \dfrac{1.73 \times 480 \times 300}{1000} = 249.1$ kVA

(d) $\qquad P(\text{kW}) = \dfrac{1.73 V_L I_L \times \text{power factor}}{1000}$

$\qquad\qquad = \text{kVA} \times \text{power factor} = 249.1 \times 0.75$
$\qquad\qquad = 186.8 \text{ kW}$

E x a m p l e   1 2 - 2

Each phase of a three-phase delta-connected generator supplies a full-load current of 100 A at a voltage of 240 V and at a power factor of 0.6, lagging. Find (a) the line voltage, (b) the line current, (c) the three-phase kilovoltamperes, and (d) the three-phase power in kilowatts.

(a) The line voltage is equal to the phase voltage in a delta system.

$$V_L = V_P = 240 \text{ V}$$

(b) $I_L = 1.73 I_P = 1.73 \times 100 = 173$ A

(c) $\text{kVA} = \dfrac{1.73 V_L I_L}{1000} = \dfrac{1.73 \times 240 \times 173}{1000} = 72 \text{ kVA}$

(d) $P = \text{kVA} \times \text{power factor}$

$$= 72 \times 0.6 = 43.2 \text{ kW}$$

12-8

Wye- and Delta-Connected Loads

Not only may generators be connected in either wye or delta, but various types of loads such as motor windings, lamps, or transformers may also be wye- or delta-connected. The same current, voltage, and power relations that are used for three-phase generators are used for three-phase load connections. The following examples will illustrate these relations for load connections. (See also Sec. 13-16 for additional discussion of three-phase load connections.)

E x a m p l e   1 2 - 3

Three resistances of 15 Ω each (power factor = 100 percent) are wye-connected to a 240 V three-phase line. Find (a) the current through each resistance, (b) the line current, and (c) the power taken by the three resistances.

The circuit diagram is shown in Fig. 12-5. The phase voltage or the voltage applied to each resistance is

$$V_P = \frac{V_L}{1.73} = \frac{240}{1.73} = 138.7 \text{ V}$$

(a) The current in each resistance is (no reactance present)

$$I_P = \frac{V_P}{Z_P} = \frac{V_P}{R_P} = \frac{138.7}{15} = 9.25 \text{ A}$$

(b) As the line and phase currents are equal,

$$I_L = I_P = 9.25 \text{ A}$$

F I G U R E **12-5**
Circuit diagram for Example 12-3.

(c) The power taken by one resistance is

$$P_P = V_P I_P \times \text{power factor} = 138.7 \times 9.25 \times 1 = 1280 \text{ W}$$

The three-phase power is

$$P = 3P_P = 3 \times 1280 = 3840 \text{ W}$$

or $P = 1.73 V_L I_L \times \text{power factor}$

$$= 1.73 \times 240 \times 9.25 \times 1 = 3840 \text{ W} \qquad (\text{check})$$

Example 12-4

Repeat the preceding problem if the three resistances are re-connected in delta.

(a) The circuit diagram is shown in Fig. 12-6. Now the voltage applied to each phase is equal to the line voltage, or 240 V.

$$I_P = \frac{V_P}{Z_P} = \frac{V_P}{R_P} = \frac{240}{15} = 16 \text{ A}$$

(b) The line current is

$$I_L = 1.73 I_P = 1.73 \times 16 = 27.7 \text{ A}$$

(c) The three-phase power is

$$P = 1.73 V_L I_L \times \text{power factor}$$

$$= 1.73 \times 240 \times 27.7 \times 1 = 11\ 520 \text{ W}$$

or $P = 3V_P I_P \times \text{power factor}$

$$= 3 \times 240 \times 16 \times 1 = 11\ 520 \text{ W} \qquad (\text{check})$$

FIGURE **12-6**
Circuit diagram for Example 12-4.

CHAPTER 12

Example 12-5

A 15 hp 230 V three-phrase induction motor has a full-load current of 42 A per terminal. (*a*) What is the full-load kilovolt-ampere input? (*b*) If the full-load power factor is 85 percent, what is the kilowatt input?

(*a*)
$$\text{kVA} = \frac{1.73 V_{\text{L}} I_{\text{L}}}{1000}$$
$$= \frac{1.73 \times 230 \times 42}{1000} = 16.71 \text{ kVA}$$

(*b*) $P(\text{in kW}) = \text{kVA} \times \text{power factor}$
$$= 16.71 \times 0.85 = 14.21 \text{ kW}$$

SUMMARY OF THREE-PHASE RELATIONSHIPS

Wye Connection	*Delta Connection*

(*a*)   (*b*)

$V_{\text{L}} = 1.73 V_{\text{P}}$	$V_{\text{L}} = V_{\text{P}}$
$I_{\text{L}} = I_{\text{P}}$	$I_{\text{L}} = 1.73 I_{\text{P}}$
$I_{\text{P}} = \dfrac{V_{\text{P}}}{Z_{\text{P}}}$	$I_{\text{P}} = \dfrac{V_{\text{P}}}{Z_{\text{P}}}$

For Either Connection

Voltamperes per phase $= V_{\text{P}} I_{\text{P}}$

Kilovoltamperes per phase $= \dfrac{V_{\text{P}} I_{\text{P}}}{1000}$

Three-phase voltamperes $= 3 V_{\text{P}} I_{\text{P}}$
$$= 1.73 V_{\text{L}} I_{\text{L}}$$

Three-phase kilovoltamperes $= \dfrac{3 V_{\text{P}} I_{\text{P}}}{1000}$
$$= \dfrac{1.73 V_{\text{L}} I_{\text{L}}}{1000}$$

$$\text{Power factor} = \text{cosine of angle between } V_P \text{ and } I_P$$

$$= \frac{P}{1.73 V_L I_L}$$

$$\text{Power per phase} = V_P I_P \cos\theta \quad \text{(in watts)}$$

$$= \frac{V_P I_P \cos\theta}{1000} \quad \text{(in kilowatts)}$$

$$\text{Three-phase power} = 3 V_P I_P \cos\theta \quad \text{(in watts)}$$

$$= 1.73 V_L I_L \cos\theta \quad \text{(in watts)}$$

$$\text{Also} = 3 V_P I_P \times \text{power factor} \quad \text{(in watts)}$$

$$= 1.73 V_L I_L \times \text{power factor} \quad \text{(in watts)}$$

$$\text{Reactive Power} = V_P I_P \sin\theta \quad \text{(vars)}$$

REVIEW QUESTIONS

1 What is a three-phase circuit?

2 What are some advantages of three-phase systems over single-phase systems?

3 In the three-phase generator, how many electrical degrees out of phase are the three emfs generated?

4 What are two commonly used connections in a three-phase circuit?

5 Explain briefly how generator phase windings are connected in wye.

6 How is a wye-connected generator connected to supply (a) a three-wire three-phase system? (b) a four-wire three-phase system?

7 In a wye connection, what is the line-to-neutral voltage called? What is meant by a line voltage?

8 What is meant by phase sequence? How may it be reversed?

9 If V_{AB} represents a line voltage in a phasor diagram, what would be the symbol for the voltage that is equal and opposite to V_{AB} in the same diagram?

10 Give the relationship between phase and line voltages in a wye connection. How are the phase and line circuits related?

11 Show how the phase windings of an ac generator may be connected in delta.

12 What is the relation between phase and line voltages in a delta connection? Between phase and line currents?

13 Give two three-phase power formulas. Since power in a single-phase circuit is equal to $I^2 R$, how could this relationship be used in finding three-phase power?

14 Give the formula for finding three-phase voltamperes.

15 If the three-phase watts and voltamperes of a circuit are known, how could the three-phase vars be found?

PROBLEMS

Note: Balanced three-phase connections are assumed in all the following problems.

12-1 The phase voltage of a wye-connected generator is 120 V. What is the line voltage?

12-2 If the terminal voltage of a wye-connected generator is 13 200 V, what is the voltage generated in each of the phases?

12-3 What is the *maximum* value of the line voltage of a wye connection if the effective value of the phase voltage is 127 V?

12-4 For a given load, the phase current of a wye-connected generator is 50 A. What is the current flowing in the line wires?

12-5 Each phase of a wye-connected generator delivers a current of 30 A at a phase voltage of 254 V and a power factor of 80 percent, lagging. What is the generator terminal voltage? What is the power developed in each phase? What is the three-phase power developed?

12-6 At full load, each of the three phases of a wye-connected generator delivers 150 A at 1329 V at a power factor of 75 percent, the current lagging. Find (*a*) the terminal voltage rating, (*b*) the kilovoltampere rating, and (*c*) the kilowatt rating.

12-7 It is desired that a 10 000-kVA three-phase 60-Hz generator have a rated terminal voltage of 13 800 V when it is wye-connected. What must be the voltage rating of each phase? Find the kilovoltampere rating per phase and the rated current per terminal.

12-8 The line current of a delta connection is 40 A. What is the phase current?

12-9 The phase current in a delta connection is 50 A. Find the line current.

12-10 The voltage per phase of a delta-connected generator is 450 V. What is the terminal or line voltage?

12-11 If the generator of Prob. 12-6 is reconnected for delta operation, what is the new voltage rating? What is the new kilovoltampere rating?

12-12 A three-phase motor takes a current of 20 A per terminal. The line voltage is 480 V, and the power factor is 80 percent, lagging. What is the power used by the motor?

12-13 In a three-phase delta-connected load, the phase current is 20 A and the phase voltage is 240 V. The power factor is 90 percent, lagging. Find the total three-phase power in kilowatts.

12-14 A three-phase load consumes 60 kW when connected to a 480-V line. The line current is 100 A. Find the kilovoltamperes and the power factor of the load.

12-15 A wye-connected load draws 20 kW from a 416 V line. The line current is 30 A. Find the phase voltage and the power factor.

12-16 A three-phase generator delivers 150 A at 7200 V. What is the kilovoltampere output? If the power output is 1500 kW, what is the power factor?

12-17 Find the current rating of a three-phase 460-V 60-Hz 50-hp induction motor, if it operates at an 85 percent lagging power factor. The full-load input is 38.8 kW.

12-18 If a generator delivers 26 000 kW at a power factor of 80 percent, lagging, what is its kilovoltampere output?

12-19 A wye-connected load of three 10-Ω resistors (power factor = 100 percent) is connected to a 208-V three-phase supply. Find (*a*) the voltage applied to each resistor, (*b*) the line current, and (*c*) the total power used.

12-20 Three loads, each having a resistance of 16 Ω and an inductive reactance of 12 Ω, are wye-connected to a 240 V three-phase supply. Find (*a*) the impedance per phase, (*b*) the current per phase, (*c*) the three-phase kilovoltamperes, (*d*) the power factor, and (*e*) the three-phase power in kilowatts.

12-21 Work Prob. 12-19 if the resistors are delta-connected.

12-22 Work Prob. 12-20 if the loads are delta-connected.

12-23 A delta-connected load draws 28.8 kW from a three-phase supply. The line current is 69.2 A and the power factor is 80 percent, lagging. Find the resistance and the reactance of each phase.

Transformers and Regulators

Transformers provide a simple means of changing an alternating voltage from one value to another. If a transformer receives energy at a low voltage and delivers it at a higher voltage, it is called a **step-up** transformer. When a transformer is supplied energy at a given voltage and delivers it at some lower voltage, it is called a **step-down** transformer. Any transformer may be operated as either a step-up or step-down transformer; however, the voltage for which the transformer is designed must be applied in either case.

To transmit a given amount of energy, less current is required at a high voltage than at a low voltage. This means that energy may be transmitted with less I^2R or line loss when high transmission voltages are used. In order to secure high transmission voltages, such as 345 000 or 765 000 V, step-up transformers are used at the generating station, since it is not feasible to generate voltages this high. Then at the points where energy is to be used, step-down transformers are used to reduce the high transmission voltage to safe and usable values. Thus, transformers make possible the economical transmission of electric energy over long distances.

Since a basic transformer has no moving parts, it requires little attention and the maintenance expense is low. Transformer efficiencies are high, running as high as 98 or 99 percent at full load in the larger sizes.

13-1
Transformer Terminology

A simple transformer consists of two coils wound on a closed iron core as represented in Fig. 13-1. The coils are insulated from each other and from the core. Energy is supplied to one winding, called the **primary winding**, and is delivered to the load from the other winding, called the **secondary winding**. When the transformer is used as a step-up transformer, the low-voltage winding is the primary. In a step-down transformer, the high-voltage winding is the primary.

Standard markings have been adopted for transformer terminals. The terminals of the high-voltage winding are marked H_1, H_2, ...; the terminals of the low-voltage winding are marked X_1, X_2, ... It is convenient, therefore, to call high-voltage winding the

H winding and the low-voltage winding the X winding and to designate the number of turns of each winding as N_H and N_X.

13-2

Theory of Operation: No Load

When an alternating voltage V_H is applied to the primary (H) winding of the step-down transformer represented in Fig. 13-1, with the load switch open, a small current called the **exciting current** flows. As in any inductive circuit, the current is limited by the counter emf of self-induction which is induced in the winding. Transformer windings are designed to have an inductance high enough to make the counter emf practically equal to the applied voltage at no load. This limits the no-load or exciting current to a very low value.

The excitation current is an inductive component current that lags the source voltage by 90°. Fig. 13-2 shows the **no-load** relations of the transformer in Fig. 13-1.

The exciting current causes an alternating flux to be set up in the core. This alternating flux cuts across the turns of both the primary and secondary windings as it increases and decreases in alternate directions, thereby inducing an emf in both windings. As noted previously, the emf induced in the primary winding opposes

F I G U R E **13-2**
Note the induced emf E_H and E_X are in phase with each other. This is a result of the mutual flux produced by the excitation current I_e. Therefore, the excitation current lags the source voltage by 90 degrees and leads the induced emf of both the primary and secondary windings by 90 degrees.

the applied voltage V_H. Since the turns of both windings are cut by the same flux, the emf induced in each turn of both windings is the same. If E_H is the emf induced in the primary winding and E_X is the emf induced in the secondary winding, then the voltage per turn in the two windings is E_H/N_H and E_X/N_X, respectively, and $E_H/N_H = E_X/N_X$.

If the resistance of the primary winding is small, as is usually the case, E_H will be very nearly equal to the applied voltage V_H. Neglecting this small difference and noting that the secondary terminal voltage V_X will be equal to E_X since there is no current flowing, then $V_H/N_H = V_X/N_X$. Cross-multiplying and dividing by $V_X N_X$ results in

$$\frac{V_H}{V_X} = \frac{N_H}{N_X} \qquad \text{[13-1]}$$

This equation shows that the voltages of each of the windings of a transformer are directly proportional to the number of turns in each winding.

Example 13-1

A transformer with 200 turns on the primary winding is to be wound to step the voltage down from 240 to 120 V. Find the number of turns required on the secondary winding.

$$\frac{V_H}{V_X} = \frac{N_H}{N_X}$$

$$\frac{240}{120} = \frac{200}{N_X}$$

$$240 N_X = 24\ 000$$

$$N_X = 100$$

13-3
Operation Under Load

When the load switch in the secondary circuit of the transformer in Fig. 13-1 is closed, a current, I_X, equal to V_X divided by the load impedance, will flow. By Lenz's law, any current caused to flow by an induced emf flows in such direction as to oppose the action that causes the emf to be induced. In the case of a transformer, this means that I_X will always flow in a direction such that its magnetizing action will oppose the magnetizing action of the primary winding. The current I_X, then, tends to reduce the flux in the transformer core. However, if the flux is reduced, the counter emf E_H is reduced, thereby permitting more primary current I_H to flow, which restores the flux to its original value.

If more load is added, causing I_X to increase further, its increased demagnetizing action lowers the flux again, which permits still more primary current to flow. Thus, the magnetizing action of the primary winding adjusts itself with each change in secondary current. The action is somewhat similar to the condition in a dc motor in which the amount of current drawn by the armature is dependent upon the amount of counter emf generated. An increase in motor load causes the counter emf to drop, which in turn permits more armature current to flow. Likewise, in the transformer, an addition of load to the secondary causes a decrease in primary counter emf that permits more primary current to flow.

Fig. 13-3 illustrates the relations of a loaded transformer connected to load impedances of (*a*) unity power factor, (*b*) lagging power factor, and (*c*) leading power factor.

From the above discussion the following relations are evident:

Primary ampere-turns = secondary ampere-turns

or $$I_H N_H = I_X N_X \qquad\qquad \text{[13-2]}$$

If both sides of Eq. (13-2) are divided by $I_H N_X$, then

$$\frac{I_X}{I_H} = \frac{N_H}{N_X} \qquad\qquad \text{[13-3]}$$

that is, the ratio of the currents in a transformer is inversely proportional to the ratio of the turns.

When a load current flows from the secondary winding of a transformer, there is a small potential drop in the transformer as a result of its impedance. Thus, the terminal voltage is slightly lower than the induced emf. However, this difference is often neglected, and V_X is assumed to be equal to E_X. Thus, Eq. (13-1) still applies. Combining Eqs. (13-1) and (13-3) results in

---

F I G U R E **13-3**

Primary relations of a loaded transformer. Current I_{LC} represents the load component current that flows in the primary winding with its corresponding phase angle.

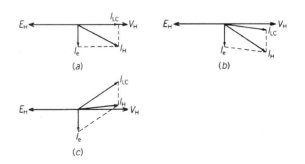

(a)   (b)

(c)

$$\frac{V_H}{V_X} = \frac{I_X}{I_H}$$

and $$V_H I_H = V_X I_X \qquad \text{[13-4]}$$

Eq. (13-4) shows that the voltampere input of a transformer is equal to the voltampere output.

It should be noted in connection with Eqs. (13-1) to (13-4) that they are approximate equations only. They are true only for an ideal transformer, that is, a transformer with no losses. However, they are sufficiently accurate for most practical purposes since the losses in most transformers are very small.

Example 13-2

A transformer supplies a load with 30 A at 240 V. If the primary voltage is 2400 V, find (a) the secondary voltamperes, (b) the primary voltamperes, and (c) the primary current.

(a) $V_X I_X = 30 \times 240 = 7200$ VA

(b) $V_H I_H = V_X I_X = 7200$ VA

(c) $2400 I_H = 7200$ VA

$$I_H = \frac{7200}{2400} = 3 \text{ A}$$

13-4
Polarity

It is sometimes desirable to operate two transformers in parallel. One of the requirements for successful parallel operation is that the instantaneous polarities of the two transformers must be the same. In addition to having identical polarities, the two transformers should have the same or very similar voltage ratings, transformation ratios, and impedances.

As indicated in Sec. 13-1, standard terminal designations have been adopted for transformers. The high-voltage terminals of a two-winding single-phase transformer are marked H_1 and H_2 and the low-voltage terminals X_1 and X_2. Furthermore, the lead **polarity** or the relative instantaneous direction of currents in the leads is standardized. In a standard single-phase transformer, at any given instant, if current enters the H_1 lead, current leaves the X_1 lead in the same direction as though the two leads formed a continuous circuit.

Thus, to parallel two correctly marked transformers, both H_1 terminals should be connected to one high-voltage line and both

FIGURE **13-4**
Two transformers connected for parallel operation.

H_2 terminals to the other high-voltage line. Then the X_1 terminals should be connected to the same low-voltage line and the X_2 terminals to the remaining low-voltage line. Two transformers connected for parallel operation in this manner are shown in Fig. 13-4. It should be noted that *if terminals of unlike polarity should be connected to the same line, the two secondary windings would be short-circuited on each other with a resulting excessive current flow.*

If the terminal markings of the transformers to be connected in parallel have been removed or damaged, a simple polarity test can be performed. Fig. 13-5 illustrates this test.

Fig. 13-5 illustrates the procedure used to polarity test a transformer. Here we have used a 4160/2400 volt distribution transformer. Note the transformer's rated voltage is not used for the test since it is a very dangerous potential. However, a reasonably safe 115 V is substituted. The transformer ratio: 4160/2400 = 1.733. Therefore, the secondary output when the primary is connected to 115 V would be 115/1.733 = 66 V. The marking of the

FIGURE **13-5**

(a)
Additive polarity

4160/2400 V 1ϕ TRANSFORMER

(b)
Subtractive polarity

H_1 and H_2 leads are done first as indicated: H_1 on the left and H_2 on the right. H_1 is now connected to one of the secondary leads and H_2 is connected to the other secondary lead through a voltmeter. Now the 115 V source is connected to H_1 and H_2. The secondary voltage should be approximately 66 V. The voltmeter connected between the primary and secondary terminals will either read the sums of the primary and secondary winding voltages (additive polarity) or the difference between the primary and secondary voltages (subtractive polarity). Figure 13-5(*a*) indicates the terminal markings for additive polarity and Fig. 13-5(*b*) indicates the terminal markings for subtractive polarity.

Distribution transformers are usually wound with the secondary or low-voltage winding in two sections, as shown in Fig. 13-6. When the two low-voltage sections are connected in series, as in Fig. 13-6(*a*), the transformer may be used to supply a two-wire 240 V load connected to terminals X_1 and X_4. Terminals X_3 and X_2 are connected together but are not connected to the load. The series connection may also be used to supply a three-wire 120/240 V system by connecting the third wire or neutral wire to the common X_2X_3 terminal of the transformer. Either 120 or 240 V loads may then be supplied from the three-wire system as described in Sec. 2-12. The two low-voltage sections alternatively may be connected in parallel as is shown in Fig. 13-6(*b*) to supply a two-wire 120 V load.

Earlier transformers were made with four insulated secondary leads brought out of the transformer tank, the series or parallel connection being made outside the tank. In modern transformers, the connections are made inside the tank, with only three secondary terminals being brought out of the transformer.

The transformer described above is commonly used for distribution applications in residential areas. The split secondary winding is useful to provide 115 V to convenience receptacles and lighting in the home, whereas the 230 V available is used in con-

13-5

Single-Phase Connections

FIGURE **13-6**
The divided low-voltage winding may be connected (*a*) in series to supply a three-wire 120/240-V system or (*b*) in parallel to supply a two-wire 120-V system.

junction with 115 V to supply the electric range and electric clothes dryer with a three-wire supply cable. Also many residential electric hot water heaters are supplied with 230 V over a two-wire cable.

13-**6**
Ratings

The output rating or capacity of a transformer is given in **kilovoltamperes** since this is equivalent to specifying the load current. The rated kilovoltamperes of a transformer is based on the maximum output that the transformer can deliver at rated secondary voltage and rated frequency without exceeding a given temperature rise. Since power in an ac circuit depends upon the power factor of the load as well as the current flowing, an output rating in kilowatts would have to be at some stated power factor. For this reason, transformers are rated in kilovoltamperes, which are independent of power factor.

E x a m p l e 1 3 - 3

What is the full-load kilowatt output of a 5 kVA 2400/120 V transformer at (*a*) 100 percent, (*b*) 80 percent, and (*c*) 30 percent power factor? (*d*) What is the full-load current output?

(*a*) $P = \text{kVA} \times \text{power factor} = 5 \times 1.0 = 5 \text{ kW}$

(*b*) $P = 5 \times 0.8 = 4 \text{ kW}$

(*c*) $P = 5 \times 0.3 = 1.5 \text{ kW}$

(*d*) $I = \dfrac{VA}{V} = \dfrac{5000}{120} = 41.7 \text{ A}$

Full-rated current of 41.7 A is supplied by the transformer at the three different power factors even though the kilowatt output is different in each case.

Included on a transformer nameplate in addition to capacity and voltage rating data are the connection diagrams, percent impedance, polarity data, cooling class, data on winding taps, and basic insulation level. Basic insulation level is an indication of the ability of the insulation system to withstand transient overvoltages.

Transformers may be classified as **distribution transformers** or as **power transformers**. The term distribution transformer, as generally accepted, is applied to transformers rated 500 kVA and smaller, with high-voltage ratings of 67 000 V and below and with low-voltage ratings of 15 000 V and below. Transformers with higher kilovoltamperes and voltage ratings are referred to as power transformers.

The efficiency of a transformer is the ratio of the useful power output to the total power input. Since the input to a transformer is equal to its useful output plus its losses, the efficiency equation may be written in either of the following forms:

$$\text{Percent efficiency} = \frac{\text{power output}}{\text{power input}} \times 100 \text{ percent} \qquad \text{[13-5]}$$

$$= \frac{\text{power output}}{\text{power output} + \text{losses}} \times 100 \text{ percent} \quad \text{[13-6]}$$

From the above, it is evident that the efficiency of a transformer can be determined for any given load by making a direct measurement of its power input and its power output and computing its efficiency using Eq. (13-5). Because of limitations of available testing facilities, it is sometimes difficult to perform direct input-output load measurements, especially for very large transformers. When input-output measurements are not feasible, the losses of a transformer may be measured or calculated and its efficiency determined by using Eq. (13-6).

Although transformers are highly efficient, some losses are present in all transformers. There are two classes of losses, namely, **load losses**, which are principally I^2R losses in the transformer windings, and **no-load losses**, which are primarily core losses.

Load or I^2R losses are present because power is used whenever a current is made to flow through a resistance. Load currents flowing through transformer windings produce a power or I^2R loss which varies with the load being supplied by the transformer. Load losses can be calculated for any given load if the resistances of both windings are known or can be measured. If R_H and R_X are the high- and low-voltage winding resistances, then the load loss is

$$\text{Load loss} = I_H^2 R_H + I_X^2 R_X \qquad \text{[13-7]}$$

No-load or core losses are due to the effects of hysteresis and eddy currents in the iron core of the transformer. These effects are similar to those occurring in generators and motors as described in Sec. 8-15. Core losses in a transformer can be determined by energizing one winding of the transformer with the other winding open. The power input to the open-circuited transformer as measured with a wattmeter supplemented with a frequency meter, voltmeter, and ammeter is then the no-load or core loss. The core loss of a transformer is essentially constant for all loads when rated frequency and voltage are applied to the transformer.

13-7

Transformer Losses and Efficiency

FIGURE **13-7**
Step-down autotransformer.

13-**8**

Autotransformers

A transformer in which the primary and secondary windings are connected **electrically** as well as **magnetically** is called an **autotransformer**. Fig. 13-7 shows a connection diagram of an autotransformer. If this transformer is to be used as a step-down transformer, the entire winding *ac* forms the primary winding and the section *ab* forms the secondary winding. In other words, the section *ab* is common to both primary and secondary. As in the standard two-winding transformer, the ratio of voltage transformation is equal to the ratio of primary to secondary turns if the losses and exciting currents are neglected and

$$\frac{V_{\mathrm{H}}}{V_{\mathrm{X}}} = \frac{N_{\mathrm{H}}}{N_{\mathrm{X}}} = \frac{I_{\mathrm{X}}}{I_{\mathrm{H}}}$$

Fig. 13-8 represents an autotransformer winding with a total of 220 turns, with the sections *ab* and *bc* having 150 and 70 turns, respectively. If a voltage of 440 V is applied to the winding *ac*, the voltage across each turn will be 2 V. The voltage from *a* to *b* will then be 150 × 2 or 300 V.

FIGURE **13-8**
Step-down autotransformer winding supplying load.

When a noninductive load of 30 Ω is connected to winding *ab*, a current, I_X, of 300/30 or 10 A flows and the power output of the transformer is 300 × 10 or 3000 W. Neglecting the transformer losses, the power input must be 3000 W and the primary current 3000/440 or 6.82 A.

An application of Kirchhoff's current law to point *a* shows that when I_X is 10 A and I_H is 6.82 A, then the current from *b* and *a*, I_C, must be 3.18 A. Similarly, the current from *b* to *c* must be 6.82 A.

Thus, the section of the winding that is common to both primary and secondary circuits carries only the difference in primary and secondary currents. In effect, the transformer in the example transforms only 3.18 × 300 = 954 W rather than the full circuit power of 3000 W. The percentage of power transformed is 100 × 954/3000 or 31.8 percent. This is the same as the percent voltage difference between the primary and secondary voltages or 100 × (440 − 300)/440 or 31.8 percent. Since only a part of the circuit power or kVA is transformed by an autotransformer, it is smaller and more efficient than a two-winding transformer having a similar rating.

The autotransformer is said to deliver kVA from the primary to its secondary by two means: kVA transformed, as discussed above, and kVA transferred conductively. Using the example from Fig. 13-8 (step-down) autotransformer,

$$\text{VA transformed} = 300 \times 3.18 = 954 \text{ VA}$$

$$\text{VA transferred} = 300 \times 6.82 = \underline{2046 \text{ VA}}$$
$$\text{TOTAL VA} = 3000$$

This now would indicate the standard isolation transformer reconnected as an autotransformer would have a kVA capacity greater than its isolation transformer rating.

FIGURE **13-9**
Step-up autotransformer winding supplying load.

FIGURE **13-10**
2300/230 V isolation transformer reconnected as an autotransformer step-down (subtractive polarities).

Example 13-4

The isolation transformer in Fig. 13-10 has a 10 kVA rating. Determine:

a) the original current capacity of the 2300 V and 230 V windings.
b) the kVA rating of the autotransformer using the current rating of the 230 V winding determined in (*a*) above.
c) the increase in kVA capacity (in percent) of the autotransformer as compared to the isolation transformer.

SOLUTION:

a) $I_H = \dfrac{10\ 000}{2300} = 4.35$ A $I_X = \dfrac{10\ 000}{230} = 43.5$ A

b) The 230 V winding is capable of carrying 43.5 A, therefore the autotransformer kVA rating is:

$$V_X I_X = \frac{2070 \times 43.5}{1000} = 90 \text{ kVA}$$

c) percent increase in capacity of autotransformer to isolation transformer is:
(kVA autotransformer)/(kVA isolation transformer) $\times$ 100
(90/10) $\times$ 100 = 900% increase

Note, however, to achieve this large percent increase the transformation ratio of the autotransformer must be close to one.

FIGURE **13-11**
2300/230 V isolation transformer reconnected as a step-up autotransformer (additive polarity).

For some applications that require a multivoltage supply, an autotransformer in which the winding is tapped at several points is used. The connections from the various taps are brought out of the tank to terminals or to a suitable switching device so that any one of several voltages may be selected.

Autotransformers are used when voltage transformations of near unity are required. Such an application of an autotransformer is in "boosting" a distribution voltage by a small percentage to compensate for line drop. Another common application is in the starting of ac motors, in which case the voltage applied to the motor is reduced during the starting period.

Autotransformers are not safe, however, for supplying a low voltage from a high-voltage source; for, if the winding that is common to both primary and secondary should accidentally become open, the full primary voltage will appear across the secondary terminals. The requirements of safety codes should always be followed whenever autotransformers are applied.

13-9
Instrument Transformers

It is not a safe practice to connect instruments, meters, or control apparatus directly to high-voltage circuits. Instrument transformers are universally used to reduce high voltages and currents to safe and usable values for the operation of such apparatus.

Instrument transformers perform two functions: (1) They act as **ratio devices**, making possible the use of standardized low-voltage and low-current meters and instruments. (2) They act as **insulating devices**, to protect the apparatus and the operating personnel from high voltages. There are two kinds of instrument transformers: **potential transformers** and **current transformers**.

13-10
Potential Transformers

Potential transformers supply a voltage to meters, instruments, or control devices which has a definite ratio to the line voltage. The potential transformer operates on the same principle as a power transformer. When the primary winding is connected across the line, a current flows which sets up a flux in the core. The flux linking the secondary winding induces an emf that is proportional to the ratio of primary to secondary turns. Potential transformers are commonly designed to have a rated voltage of 115 or 120 V at the secondary terminals when rated voltage is applied to the primary winding. Since the amount of load supplied by potential transformers is small, voltampere ratings are small, common ratings being 200, 600, and 1000 VA. A 7200 to 120 V 1000 VA potential transformer is shown in Fig. 13-12.

F I G U R E **13-12**
Indoor-type potential transformer.
(General Electric Company.)

13-**11**

Current Transformers

The purpose of a current transformer is to provide a means of reducing line current to values that may be used to operate standard low-current measuring and control devices, with these devices being completely insulated from the main circuits. As the current transformer is used in conjunction with current-measuring devices, its primary winding is designed to be connected in series with the line. It is therefore necessary that the impedance of the primary winding be made as low as possible. This is done by using a few turns of low-resistance wire capable of carrying rated line current.

Since a current transformer is used ordinarily to decrease current, the secondary contains more turns than the primary, the ratio of primary to secondary current being inversely proportional to the ratio of primary to secondary turns. Current transformers are usually designed so that when rated current flows in the primary, 5 A will flow in the secondary. A current transformer, having a ratio of 30 to 5 A, is shown in Fig. 13-13.

Since the impedance of the primary winding of a current transformer is low, the current through the primary depends primarily on the load connected to the primary circuit rather than on the secondary load of the transformer itself. When the secondary circuit is closed, the secondary current establishes an F_m that opposes the primary mmf, thereby limiting the flux density in the core. When the secondary circuit is opened while the primary is energized, the secondary demagnetizing F_m is no longer present. This means that the flux density may become very high, causing a dangerously high voltage to be induced in the open secondary winding. To prevent injury to the apparatus and operating personnel, it is necessary that the secondary terminals of a current transformer be short-circuited before removing or inserting an instrument in the secondary circuit while the primary winding is energized. Modern current transformers are provided with a device for short-circuiting the secondary winding when changes must be made in the secondary circuit. However, anyone working with a secondary circuit of a current transformer should always make certain that the short-circuiting device is closed before the secondary wiring is disturbed.

Fig. 13-14 illustrates the method of connecting instrument transformers into a high-voltage circuit. Note that the secondary circuits are shown connected to earth. This is a general safety practice when the transformers are connected in circuits that have a potential above the earth of 300 V or more.

FIGURE **13-14**
Instrument-transformer connections.

Example 13-5

Find the load current, voltage, power, and power factor in the circuit of Fig. 13-14, as indicated by the instrument readings.

$$\text{Current} = 3 \times 10 = 30 \text{ A}$$

$$\text{Voltage} = 120 \times 20 = 2400 \text{ V}$$

$$\text{Power} = \frac{250 \times 10 \times 20}{1000} = 72 \text{ kVA}$$

$$\text{Power factor} = \frac{50}{72} \times 100 = 69.4\%$$

13-**12**

Three Phase Transformer Connections

Chap. 12 described the fundamentals of three-phase distribution and the reasons for its use. As a result of the constant power characteristics of a three-phase system, generation at the source is three-phase. However, this voltage generated by the large alternators in a power generating plant usually does not exceed 25 kV. Therefore, distribution transformers must step up this voltage to a much higher value (230 kV to 500 kV) to keep distribution losses low. This three-phase transformation can be accomplished by using Δ-Δ, Y-Y, Y-Δ, Δ-Y connections. We will examine each one of these types of transformation.

13-**13**

Y-Y Transformer Connections

Fig. 13-15(*a*) illustrates the connection diagram for Y-Y transformation. Note all of the H_2 connections are common to the primary neutral connection (N) and all H_1 connections are connected to their respective line connections (A, B, C). This connection or the opposite to this (i.e., H_1 to N) must be followed for a proper Y connection. The same is true for the secondary connections. That is, all X_2 connections to be common to the secondary neutral connection (n) and all X_1 connections to their respective load terminals (a, b, c) or the complete reverse as described in the primary connection description. Note, however, if one transformer secondary connection is reversed, an unpredicted load terminal voltage will result. Fig. 13-16 illustrates this secondary coil reversal.

It can be noted from Fig. 13-16(*b*) what effect the reversal of transformer coil "*a*" has on the secondary load voltages.

FIGURE **13-15**

(a)

(b) Primary relations

(c) Secondary relations

FIGURE **13-16**

$V_{ca} = 132.8$
$\angle -150°$ V

(a)
Transformer coil
"a" reversed

(b)

F I G U R E **13-17**

(a)

(b) Primary relations

(c) Secondary relations

13-**14**

Δ-Δ Transformer Connections

Fig. 13-17(*a*) illustrates the connection diagram for Δ-Δ transformation. Unlike the *Y* connection, the Δ connection is a closed loop where the finish of one coil (H_2) connects to the start of the next coil (H_1) and so on until the loop is completely closed. This also applies to the transformer secondary coils. Fig. 13-17(*b*) and (*c*) show the phasor relations of the primary and secondary voltage relations. In Fig. 13-16 we saw the results of an incorrectly connected transformer coil in *Y-Y* transformation. Fig. 13-18 shows the result of an incorrectly connected transformer coil when connecting a delta transformer bank.

Fig. 13-18(*a*) illustrates the correct Δ-Δ connection where the closure voltage measured by the voltmeter is equal to the algebraic sums of the voltages at their respective angles is equal to zero. This implies, of course, there will be no circulating current flowing in this closed circuit until a secondary load is added.

Fig. 13-18(*b*), however, shows secondary coil "*a*" reversed. This incorrect connection creates a closure voltage of twice coil voltage at the closure point measured by the voltmeter indicating closure voltage. If the coils were interconnected with disregard to this error, a large circulating current would flow around all three secondary windings limited only by the coils' very low internal impedance. This large circulating current would flow independent of any connected load, and would quickly burn out the transformer windings.

F I G U R E **13-18**

(a) Correctly connected
secondary coils

(b) Incorrectly connected
secondary coils,
coil "a" reversed

One of the major advantages of the Δ-Δ transformation system is the ability to supply a three-phase load with one of the three transformers removed. However, when this occurs the capacity of the system is not reduced to 66.6 percent of the original bank as one might deduce, but to 57.7 percent of the original capacity. Fig. 13-19 illustrates this fact.

Fig. 13-19(d) illustrates the same resultant secondary voltage across coil "a" whether it is there or not. Therefore, the three-phase voltage output is present despite one transformer being removed from the system. Now examine the resultant capacity of the system with one transformer removed.

The system capacity when all three transformers are connected is

$$\text{Three-phase power full delta} = \sqrt{3}V_tI_L\cos\theta$$

$$= 3V_tI_P$$

where $I_L = \sqrt{3}I_P$

13-15

Open Delta Connection (V-V)

F I G U R E **13-19**
V-V transformation.

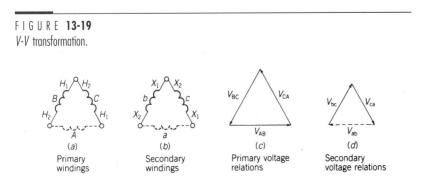

(a)
Primary
windings

(b)
Secondary
windings

(c)
Primary voltage
relations

(d)
Secondary
voltage relations

Now examine the resultant three-phase power when one transformer is removed.

Since one transformer is removed from the system I_L now is equal to I_p.

$$\text{Three-phase power open delta} = \sqrt{3}\,V_t I_L \cos\theta$$

Ratio of power, open delta as a percentage of full delta is:

$$\frac{\text{open delta}}{\text{full delta}} \times 100$$

$$= \frac{\sqrt{3}\,V_t I_p \cos\theta}{3 V_t I_p \cos\theta} = \frac{\sqrt{3}}{3} = 0.577 \text{ or } 57.7\%$$

| 13-**16**

Four-Wire Delta System

Although not commonly used, the four-wire delta distribution system provides for not only three-phase voltages necessary for rotating electrical equipment, but also provides for single-phase voltage required for lighting systems. Fig. 13-20 illustrates this type of delta connection and shows the inherent problems with such a system.

If one examines the connection diagram of Fig. 13-20(a) it might be difficult, at first glance, to determine any unusual voltage resultants from this type of connection. However, a close examination of Fig. 13-20(b) reveals all of the voltages available from this type of connection with the voltages determined at the secondary.

a) 3Φ 230 V is available at terminals (a, b, c)
b) 1Φ 230 V is available at terminals (a and b), (b and c), (c and a)
c) 1Φ 115 V is available at terminals (c and n), (n and b)
d) 1Φ 299 V is available at terminals (a and n)

F I G U R E **13-20**
Four-wire delta system 3Φ 230 V, 1Φ 230/115 V.

(a)
Secondary connection diagram

$$V_{an} = \sqrt{V_{ac}^2 - V_{cn}^2}$$
$$= \sqrt{230^2 - 115^2}$$
$$= 199.1 \text{ V}$$

$V_{ac} = 230 \angle -120°\text{V}$ $\quad V_{ab} = 230 \angle 120°$ V

$V_{cn} = 115 \angle 0°$ V
$V_{nb} = 115 \angle 0°$ V
$V_{cb} = 115 + 115 = 230 \angle 0°$ V

(b)

It should be evident that terminal "a" should be clearly identified to avoid this unexpected resultant voltage. It is also necessary to increase the capacity of transformer "c" in this illustration to allow the system to provide balanced three-phase power and unbalanced single-phase power from this configuration without overloading transformer "c".

This type of system is extremely popular in commercial buildings and industry. It provides for a commonly used three-phase voltage to operate rotating electrical equipment (208 V), and also provides for single-phase voltages of 208 V and 120 V for single-phase power circuits and lighting loads. Fig. 13-21 illustrates this system and its advantages.

Providing the connected load is balanced the neutral current would be zero. However, if the connected load is unbalanced, which is more likely, the neutral will carry the unbalanced load current distributed by the three lines. Described below are two methods of determine the quantity of neutral current based on the measured line currents.

13-17
Three-Phase Four-Wire Wye System

Example 13-6

A three-phase four-wire 208/120 V system has the following load currents: Line "a" = 27 A, Line "b" = 14 A, and Line "c" = 5 A. Determine the neutral current.

SOLUTION: Using a method derived from the Law of Cosines the following equation can be derived:

$$n = \sqrt{a^2 + b^2 + c^2 - (ab) - (bc) - (ca)}$$

$$n = \sqrt{27^2 + 14^2 + 5^2 - (27 \times 14) - (14 \times 5) - (5 \times 27)}$$

$$n = 19.16 \text{ A}$$

Using phasors to solve this problem, the illustration in Fig. 13-22 provides a step by step analysis of the solution.

FIGURE **13-21**
Three-phase four-wire system (208/120 V).

V_{ab} = 208 V
V_{bc} = 208 V
V_{ca} = 208 V
V_{an} = 208/$\sqrt{3}$ = 120 V
V_{bn} = 120 V
V_{cn} = 120 V

FIGURE **13-22**

$$n = I_a + I_b + I_c$$

Therefore: $n = 27\underline{/0°}$ A $+ 14\underline{/120°}$ A $+ 5\underline{/-120°}$ A

$27\underline{/0°}$ A to rectangular form $\quad = \quad 27 + j0$

$14\underline{/120°}$ A to rectangular form $= -7.0 + j12.12$

$5\underline{/-120°}$ A to rectangular form $= \underline{-2.5 - j4.33}$

Total neutral current $\qquad = 17.5 + j7.79$

Polar form $= 19.16\underline{/24°}$ A

13-**18**

The Scott "T" Transformer

This is another method of three-phase transformation with the use of a two winding transformer. This method differs from the (V-V) connection in that it uses two windings of unequal numbers of turns. Refer to the illustration (Fig. 13-23) of this concept and phasors to derive resultant voltages at the load terminals.

The (T-T) transformer contains two windings. (A and B/a and b) is the **main winding**, both primary and secondary respectively; windings (C and c) are called the **teaser** windings, both primary and secondary respectively. The teaser winding contains 86.6 percent of the number of turns of its respective main winding. Fig. 13-23(a) illustrates the connection diagram and Figs. 13-23(a) and (b) show the resultant phasor diagram. Note the resultant secondary voltages are equal in magnitude and displaced by 120 electrical degrees.

The Scott transformer connection also can be used to transform three-phase to two-phase by connecting the three-phase input as in the standard primary connection as shown in Fig. 13-23(a) and the secondary connected as in Fig. 13-24. The resultant is a true two-phase output with a 90° phase displaced voltages.

FIGURE **13-23**
(*T-T*) connection (480/230 V).

Although not a symmetrical connection, the T connection approximates the performance of the delta and wye connections with a less costly transformer.

If one examines the phasor diagrams of Secs. 13-14 and 13-15, it can be soon determined what the advantages would be of one system over another.

The delta-wye connection is well-adapted for stepping up voltages since the voltage is increased by the transformer ratio multiplied by the factor 1.73. Likewise, the wye-delta connection is used for stepping down voltages. The high-voltage windings of most transformers operating at above 100 000 V are wye-connected.

13-**19**
Y-Δ, and Δ-Y Transformation

FIGURE **13-24**
3Φ to 2Φ transformation.

Secondary relations

| 13-**20**

Three-Phase Transformers

Three-phase voltages may be transformed by means of three-phase transformers. The core of a three-phase transformer is normally designed with three legs, a primary and a secondary winding of one phase being placed on each leg. The three-legged-core transformer is adequate for all the more commonly used three-phase connections since the fluxes established by the three windings are 120° apart in time phase. At any time, two core legs act as the return path for the flux in the third leg and the net sum of the flux is zero. A core and coil assembly of a three-phase dry-type distribution transformer with a three-legged core is shown in Fig. 13-25.

During system-fault conditions or periods of highly unbalanced loads, the sum of the individual fluxes may not total zero in a transformer with a three-legged core. During such unbalanced conditions, some of the magnetic flux is forced to return through the transformer tank, resulting in severe overheating of the tank. This condition occurs most often in wye-wye-connected three-phase transformers operating with both neutrals connected to earth. To rectify this problem, transformers used for this service are designed with four- or five-legged cores which provide a return path for the unbalanced magnetic fluxes.

Because the three windings can be placed compactly on one core, the three-phase transformer occupies less space than do three single-phase transformers with the same total kilovoltampere rating. The three-phase transformer is slightly more efficient than the single-phase transformer and in the larger ratings has a lower first

---

F I G U R E **13-25**

Three-phase distribution transformer core and coil assembly.

(Westinghouse Electric Corporation.)

cost. A disadvantage of the three-phase transformer lies in the fact that when one phase becomes defective the entire three-phase unit must be removed from service. When one transformer in a bank of three single-phase transformers becomes defective, it may be removed from service and the other two transformers may often be reconnected to supply service on an emergency basis until repairs can be made.

Three-phase transformers may also be connected according to the four combinations mentioned for three single-phase transformers. These connections are made inside the tank, and for delta-delta connections only three high-voltage and three low-voltage leads need to be brought outside the tank. Four connections are brought out from wye-connected windings.

FEEDER-VOLTAGE REGULATORS

Much of the load on an electrical system is at some distance from the generating station. Because of this distance, there is a drop in voltage between the generating station and the point of utilization. Furthermore, this voltage drop is not constant but is proportional to the amount of load on the circuit at any one time. As the load varies, the voltage drop varies also.

Most electric equipment is designed to operate at a given voltage, and the efficiency of operation of this equipment is affected appreciably if the applied voltage deviates from the rated value. This is especially true with domestic loads such as incandescent lighting, electric ranges, and electric heaters. With 90 percent of rated voltage applied to an incandescent lamp, for example, the illumination output is only about 70 percent of rated value. Heating time of electric heaters and ranges is about 120 percent of normal when 90 percent of rated voltage is applied. While induction-motor operation is not affected as greatly by voltage variation as lamps and heaters, there are changes in efficiency, heating, and speed occasioned by variations in voltage.

Feeder-voltage regulators are used extensively as an aid to maintaining a reasonably constant voltage at the point of use on an electrical system. A voltage regulator is, in effect, an autotransformer with a variable ratio.

The basic principle of the voltage regulator is illustrated in Fig. 13-26. The transformer shown has a voltage ratio of 2400 to 240. By means of the reversing switch, the transformer may be connected as an autotransformer and, depending upon the switch position, the voltage induced in the low-voltage winding may be added to or subtracted from the voltage applied to the high-voltage

13-21
Voltage-Regulator Principle

FIGURE **13-26**
Circuit for illustrating the principle of the feeder-voltage regulator.

winding. Thus, when the generator voltage is 2400 V, as shown in Fig. 13-26, the output voltage of the transformer is either 2640 or 2160 V. When the generator voltage is 10 percent low, the transformer may be used to raise the voltage 10 percent. When the generator voltage is 10 percent high, the transformer may be used to lower the voltage by 10 percent.

FIGURE **13-27**
Single-phase step-type voltage regulator for pole mounting.
(Siemens-Allis, Inc.)

Feeder-voltage regulators are constructed with the two separate windings as shown in Fig. 13-26 and are provided with means for varying the amount of voltage induced in the low-voltage or series winding in small increments. These small increments of voltage may be added to or subtracted from the regulator input voltage, so that it is possible to maintain a nearly constant output voltage from the regulator.

As may be seen from Fig. 13-26, the autotransformer used as a voltage regulator actually transforms only 10 percent of the circuit kilovoltamperes, so the kilovoltampere rating of the regulator need be only 10 percent of the circuit kilovoltamperes. If, for example, the circuit full-load current in Fig. 13-26 were 100 A, the regulator kilovoltampere rating would be 240 × 100 or 24 000 VA (24 kVA), while the circuit rating would be 2400 × 100 or 240 000 VA (240 kVA). In general, the kilovoltampere rating of a single-phase regulator is the product of the rated load amperes and the percent regulation expressed in kilovolts. For a three-phase regulator this product is multiplied by 1.73.

13-**22**
Step-Voltage Regulators

Step-type voltage regulators are tapped autotransformers with a tap-changing-under-load switching mechanism to change tap settings and, thereby, change the ratio between the primary and secondary windings. Step regulators consist of three major parts: the transformer, the tap-changing mechanism, and the control mechanism. Views of a typical single-phase distribution-type step-voltage regulator are shown in Figs. 13-27 and 13-28.

The transformer section of a regulator is a conventional transformer with the primary (shunt) and secondary (series) windings wound on an iron core. The series winding is tapped at regular intervals, the number of taps depending upon the type of regulator. Pole-mounted regulators for regulating small loads may have taps arranged for 16 or 32 steps with a total range of regulation of 10 or 20 percent. Station-type regulators used for regulating entire feeders or substations usually have 32 steps with a 20 percent range in regulation. Voltage is adjusted in steps of 0.0625 percent in these regulators.

A schematic diagram of connections of a single-phase 32-step regulator is shown in Fig. 13-29. The taps of the series winding are connected to wide stationary contacts arranged physically in a circle on an insulating panel in the tap-changing mechanism. Two contacts mounted a fixed distance apart on the movable arm are used to make contact with the stationary contacts. The two moving contacts are so spaced that for each operating position either both of them are on the same stationary contact or one of them is on each of two adjacent stationary contacts.

F I G U R E **13-28**
Untanked step-type voltage regulator.
(Siemens-Allis, Inc.)

The operation of the tap-changing mechanism of a 32-step 20 percent regulator may be explained by referring to Fig. 13-29. The two movable contacts *A* and *B*, as shown in the diagram, are in contact with stationary contact number 1, the maximum LOWER position. The load current divides equally through the two halves of the reactor which is connected to the two movable contacts. The movable arm of the switch assembly is operated by a motor that drives a spring-loaded quick-operating mechanism for changing taps. The switch arm and movable contacts are latched in place until the driving springs are fully loaded, at which time the latch releases and the switch arm moves with a quick snap to the next position where it is latched in place again.

A change of the switch arm from tap 1 to tap 2 to raise voltage is made in two operations. First, the movable contact arm snaps to a point where contact *B* is on contact 2 but *A* is still on contact 1. In this position, the reactor acts as an autotransformer, and the

FIGURE **13-29**

Connections for a single-phase 32-step voltage regulator.

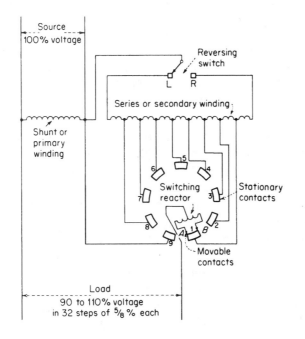

resulting voltage is halfway between the voltages of taps 1 and 2. It should be noted that the load current is not interrupted during the changing of the switch position, since the movable contact A is in contact with stationary contact 1 during the instant that the movable contact B is moving from 1 to 2. During this instant, all the load current is carried by one-half of the reactor. The next movement of the tap changer moves both A and B to contact 2, and the resulting voltage is that of tap 2. As the tap-changing switch arm is moved on around toward contact 9, the voltage is raised in 0.625 percent steps until the number 9 contact is reached. When the two movable contacts are on stationary contact 9, the regulator is in the NEUTRAL position, and the series winding is completely out of the circuit, so that voltage is neither raised nor lowered by the regulator. As the mechanism is moved through the neutral position to the RAISE positions, the reversing switch is operated automatically, reversing the polarity of the series winding. Thus, the first RAISE position is contact 1, and the voltage is raised in 0.625 percent steps as the contact arm moves around to contact 8, which is the maximum RAISE position. Thus, the full range of plus and minus 10 percent voltage regulation in thirty-two 0.625 percent steps with one neutral position is obtained with only eight taps in the series winding.

Step regulators are manufactured in both single- and three-phase units. The transformer section of the three-phase unit is assembled on a three-phase core, and the tap-changer switch is of a three-pole design, so that taps on all three phases are changed simultaneously. Step regulators are available in voltage ratings as high as 69 000 V but are normally used on lower voltage distribution circuits. Kilovoltampere ratings of single-phase regulators range from approximately 25 to 833 kVA. Three-phase regulators are available in even larger sizes.

13-23
Voltage-Regulator Control and Accessory Equipment

Voltage regulators ordinarily are equipped with controls and accessories that operate the regulator automatically to maintain a predetermined output voltage. Modern regulators have self-contained instrument and auxiliary transformers to supply the potential and current indications for the control system and the necessary power for the tap-changing operating motor.

The device that initiates any change in regulator position is the voltage control relay. This relay is a solid-state sensing device that is connected to the secondary terminals of the internally mounted potential transformer to sense the regulator output voltage. If the voltage of the circuit being regulated is below a predetermined set-point, the relay closes the operating motor circuit, causing the regulator to change taps to raise the output voltage. In a similar manner the control relay causes the regulator to decrease voltage if the line voltage rises above normal.

So that the regulator does not operate excessively to attempt to correct minor momentary voltage disturbances on the system, some type of time-delay or holding action is usually used with the regulator control equipment. Such a device is the so-called **voltage integrator** used on one type of step voltage regulator. This device integrates the system voltage variation by summing the lengths of time that the voltage is abnormal and, if the voltage is either high or low for a predetermined length of time, the integrator causes the regulator to operate. This results in the maintenance of correct average voltage even with widely fluctuating voltages. The amount of time delay introduced by the integrator is adjustable between the approximate limits of 10 and 90 s.

Regulators normally are equipped with **line-drop compensators**. The compensator consists of an adjustable resistance and a reactance inserted in series with the voltage-control relay. Current is supplied to the line-drop compensator from a current transformer in the load circuit of the regulator. This current produces a voltage drop in the control circuit that is proportional to the load current (and, therefore, proportional to the line-impedance drop). In this way the voltage regulator automatically increases the voltage as the load increases to compensate for the increasing drop in the line. Regulators equipped with line-drop compensators may be adjusted to maintain a constant voltage at a remote point on a feeder rather than at the point at which the regulator is installed.

Other control equipment and accessories used with voltage regulators include bypass surge arresters for the series winding, a control switch to change the regulator from manual to automatic operation, a manual raise-and-lower switch, test terminals for connecting a portable voltmeter, an auxiliary relay for the operating motor, limit switches to prevent overtravel of the regulator, a position indicator, and protective and switching equipment for the auxiliary operating power.

Tap-changing-under-load transformers, or load-ratio-control transformers, as they are sometimes called, are essentially combined transformers and voltage regulators. One winding of the transformer is tapped at various points, and these taps are connected to a tap-changing switch as in the step-type voltage regulator. These transformers are nearly always constructed as three-phase units.

One application of the tap-changing-under-load transformer is in a step-down station used to supply a load from a transmission line. In this application a constant voltage may be maintained for the load even though the transmission-line voltage varies considerably. One other common application of this transformer is in tie lines between two generating stations. A tap-changing-under-load transformer in such a tie line permits each station to maintain correct voltage at its own bus for supplying local loads, yet maintains the tie-line voltage at the correct value for interchange of power between the two stations. On many such interconnections it has been found that there has been a heavy interchange of reactive or wattless current over the tie line when the tie line is operated without tap-changing-under-load equipment. In effect, the variable-ratio transformer provides these interconnections with reactive voltampere control.

13-24
Tap-Changing-Under-Load Transformers

These are two different transformer core shapes in common use, namely, the **core type** and the **shell type** as shown in Fig. 13-30. The cores of both types are fabricated of special low-loss steel and are laminated to minimize core losses.

In the core-type construction shown in Fig. 13-30(a), the windings surround the laminated iron core. For the sake of simplicity, the primary winding of the core-type transformer represented in Fig. 13-1 is shown on one leg of the core and the secondary on the other. Commercial transformers are not constructed in this manner because a large amount of the flux produced by the

13-25
Transformer Construction

F I G U R E **13-30**

Single-phase transformer core configurations: (*a*) core type; (*b*) shell type.

primary winding does not cut the secondary winding, or it is said that the transformer has a large **leakage flux**. To keep the leakage flux to a minimum, the windings are divided with half of each winding being placed on each leg of the core. The completed core and coil assembly of a core-type transformer is shown in Fig. 13-31.

Transformer shell-type construction is represented in Fig. 13-30(*b*). In this construction the iron core surrounds the windings. A completed core and coil assembly of a shell-form distribution transformer is shown in Fig. 13-32.

The core and coil assemblies of the transformers shown in Figs. 13-31 and 13-32 are designed to be immersed in insulating oil in a steel tank. In addition to having insulating properties, the oil

F I G U R E **13-31**

Transformer core and coil assembly, core type.

(General Electric Company.)

conducts heat from the core and coils to the surface of the tank where it is given off to the surrounding air. Connections from the transformer coils to the external circuits are made through insulating bushings usually made of porcelain.

Coils of transformers are wound with copper or aluminum wire or strap. For heavy-current windings, several strands of conductor are paralleled to reduce eddy-current loss in the conductors. Coil insulation materials used are cotton, cellulose, special papers, polyester glass tapes, or other similar materials. Completed coils are dried in an oxygen-free atmosphere to remove all moisture. Coils of oil-immersed transformers are then impregnated with dry insulating oil while they are in a vacuum.

Two basic types of transformer windings are commonly used. These are the **concentric** and the **pancake** types. Concentric windings are cylindrical in form with one winding placed inside the other with the necessary insulation between them. The low-voltage winding is normally placed on the inside next to but insulated from the core. Pancake windings are built up with primary and secondary sections interleaved. In both types, spacers are provided between adjacent coils to permit ventilation or the circulation of the cooling liquid.

When a transformer is operating under load, heat is generated in both the windings and in the core owing to the losses mentioned in Sec. 13-7. Means must be provided to extract this heat from the transformer.

Transformers may be grouped into two general classifications depending upon the method of cooling used. Transformers may be

13-**26**
Transformer Cooling

the **liquid-immersed type** or the **dry type**. The liquid normally used in the liquid-immersed transformers is oil, except when the use of oil may present a fire hazard, in which case the liquid used is a nonflammable type. Dry-type transformers use air or an inert gas as a cooling medium. Both liquid-immersed and dry-type transformers are available with several different variations of the basic cooling method. Service conditions and economics dictate the selection of the specific cooling method for each application.

The simplest type of oil-immersed transformer is the self-cooled type. Heat generated in the core and coil assembly is conducted by convection through the surrounding oil to the tank, where it is given off to the surrounding atmosphere. In the larger sizes, fins or radiators are provided to present a larger tank surface to the air. Pole-type distribution transformers as well as smaller station-type power transformers are usually self-cooled.

In order to obtain more kVA capacity from a given core and coil assembly, supplemental cooling is used on larger power transformers. The **self-cooled**, **forced-air-cooled transformer** is provided with electrically operated, thermostatically controlled cooling fans to supplement the natural cooling system. The fans move air around fins or radiators through which the cooling oil circulates. The fans operate only when the oil temperature exceeds a certain value such as during high-transformer-load periods or during periods of high ambient-air temperature.

Still greater cooling may be obtained on large power transformers by the use of pumps to circulate the oil through radiators. The oil pumps may be the only type of supplemental cooling, or they may be arranged to supplement forced-air cooling.

A completed three-phase oil-immersed power transformer with supplemental cooling is shown in Fig. 13-33. Cooling fans can be seen mounted on the radiator at the rear of the transformer.

Smaller dry transformers are the ventilated self-cooled type which are cooled by the natural circulation of air around the core and coils. On larger dry-type transformers, fans thermostatically controlled by winding temperature are sometimes used to supplement the natural cooling. In extremely dusty, dirty, or hazardous locations, sealed dry-type transformers are used. The insulating gas in these self-cooled transformers may be air, nitrogen, or other inert gas.

13-**27**

Transformer Impedance

A characteristic of transformers on which data is needed for the calculation of transformer losses, voltage regulation, and system short-circuit currents is called the **percent impedance** of the transformer.

Transformer percent impedance is determined by a test normally made on a transformer immediately after it is manufactured.

FIGURE **13-33**
Three-phase oil-immersed transformer with supplemental cooling.
(Westinghouse Electric Corporation.)

The secondary winding is short-circuited, and a reduced voltage is applied to the primary winding. The primary voltage is then increased until rated secondary winding current flows. The voltage required to cause rated secondary current to flow is called the impedance voltage. This voltage when expressed as a percentage of the rated primary voltage is called the percent impedance of the transformer. Percent impedance of power transformers typically is 5 to 10 percent depending on the transformer voltage ratings.

The subject of system short-circuit currents and the relationship of transformer impedance to these currents is discussed later in Chap. 18.

For small adjustments of transformer ratio, to compensate for line drop, high-voltage windings of transformers are often equipped with tap-changing devices. The winding is tapped at several points, and connections from these points are made either to a tap-changing switch or to a terminal block inside the transformer tank. The transformers shown in Figs. 13-31 and 13-32 are both equipped with tap-changing switches which are mounted on an insulating block directly above the windings. By operating the switch, changes are made in the number of active turns in the high-voltage winding. These changes must be made with the transformer de-energized except in certain types of transformers in which special provision is made for tap changing under load.

13-**28**

No-Load Tap Changing

REVIEW QUESTIONS

1 What is the function of a transformer?
2 How does the efficiency of a transformer compare with rotating electric machinery studied thus far?
3 What is meant by (a) a primary winding, (b) a secondary winding?
4 How are transformer terminals marked?
5 What relationship exists between the voltages and the number of turns on the two windings of a transformer?
6 What relationship exists between the ratio of the voltages and the ratio of the currents in the high- and low-voltage windings?
7 Explain how a transformer regulates the amount of primary current required to supply a given secondary current.
8 What information is commonly found on a transformer nameplate?
9 What are two types of core construction used in transformers?
10 What is meant by leakage flux? How is it kept to a minimum?
11 What transformer losses vary with the amount of load on the transformer? Which losses are practically constant?
12 Why is oil placed in transformers?
13 Why are air-cooled transformers desirable in some locations?
14 Instrument transformers perform what two functions?
15 Are potential transformers connected in parallel or series with the load? How are current transformers connected?
16 What are some of the insulating materials used in transformer windings?
17 Why is the capacity of a transformer rated in kilovoltamperes?
18 What is the main difference between distribution and power transformers?
19 What are two general classifications of transformers based upon the method of cooling?
20 Describe what is meant by a self-cooled, forced air-cooled transformer?
21 What might be a typical application of a sealed dry-type transformer?
22 Why is it important to know the value of a transformer's impedance?
23 What precaution must be observed when working with current transformers?
24 What is an autotransformer? What are some of the advantages and disadvantages of the autotransformer?
25 Why must the transformer polarities be known when transformers are being connected for parallel operation?
26 What is meant by (a) additive polarity, (b) subtractive polarity?

27 What is a tap-changing switch? When might a transformer equipped with taps be desirable?

28 Why are single-phase distribution transformers made with the low-voltage winding in two sections?

29 What are four types of three-phase transformer connections?

30 What voltages are commonly provided by four-wire delta secondaries for light and power loads? By four-wire wye secondaries?

31 What are some advantages of using three-phase transformers in place of three single-phase transformers? What are some disadvantages?

32 Why is it necessary to maintain substantially constant voltage on an electrical system?

33 Describe how a transformer may be used to raise or lower voltage in a circuit.

34 How is the kilovoltampere rating determined for (*a*) a single-phase voltage regulator, (*b*) a three-phase voltage regulator?

35 Describe briefly the basic principle of operation of the step voltage regulator.

36 What is the purpose of the switching reactor in a step voltage regulator?

37 Describe briefly the operation of the voltage-control relay used with a voltage regulator.

38 What are some of the usual voltage-regulator accessories?

39 Can an isolation transformer be reconnected to make an autotransformer?

40 In an autotransformer, VA is conveyed from the primary to the secondary by two means. Describe them.

41 When connecting a three-phase delta connected secondary transformer bank, what precautions must be taken before closing the delta loop?

42 Are the secondary voltages of an open-delta system symmetrically displaced by 120 electrical degrees?

43 What prime factor reduces the capacity of an open-delta system to 57.7% of a full delta system?

44 What is the main advantage of the Scott T transformer over the conventional three-phase transformer?

45 Could two identical isolation transformers be easily converted to a Scott T connection? Why and how?

PROBLEMS

13-1 The high-voltage winding of a transformer has a voltage rating of 480 V and has 400 turns. How many turns are there on the low-voltage winding if its voltage rating is 120 V?

13-2 A 1000-kVA 24 000/2400-V transformer operates at 40 V per turn. Find the number of turns on each winding and the current rating of each winding.

13-3 A 5-Ω resistance is connected across the 120-V secondary winding of a step-down transformer. If the primary current is 6 A, what is the primary voltage?

13-4 The low-voltage winding of a step-down welding transformer has one turn and the high-voltage winding 600 turns. When the transformer delivers 100 A, what is the current in the high-voltage winding?

13-5 Find the current ratings of each winding of a 100-kVA 2400/120-V 60-Hz transformer.

13-6 A transformer is rated at 500 kVA, 60 Hz, and 2400/480 V. There are 200 turns on the 2400 V winding. When the transformer supplies rated load, find (*a*) the ampere-turns of each winding and (*b*) the current in each winding.

13-7 Find the size of wire in circular mils needed in each winding of a 10-kVA 2400/240-V 60-Hz transformer if the number of circular mils per ampere to be used in each winding is 1000. What is the closest gauge size in each case?

13-8 Following are data from a test of a 3 kVA 240/120 V 60 Hz transformer:

Resistance of 120 V winding	0.055 Ω
Resistance of 240 V winding	0.184 Ω
Core loss	28 W

Find the efficiency of the transformer when it delivers rated kilovoltamperes at unity power factor.

13-9 A voltmeter, ammeter, and wattmeter are connected with suitable instrument transformers into a single-phase circuit and the following data taken:

Current transformer ratio	5 to 1
Potential transformer ratio	20 to 1
Voltmeter reading	110 V
Ammeter reading	4 A
Wattmeter reading	360 W

Find the voltage, current, voltamperes, power factor, and power of the primary circuit.

13-10 A step-down 600/480-V autotransformer supplies a 10 kVA load. Find the primary and secondary line currents and the current in the winding common to both primary and secondary circuits.

13-11 An autotransformer starter used to start an induction motor on a 440-V line applies 65 percent of line voltage to the motor during the starting period. If the motor current is 140 A at starting, what is the current drawn from the line?

13-12 A 5-kVA 480/120-V transformer is equipped with high-voltage taps so that it may be operated at 480, 456, or 432 V depending on the tap setting. Find the current in the high-voltage winding for each tap setting, the transformer supplying rated kilovoltampere load at 120 V in each case.

13-13 A distribution transformer has two 120 V secondary windings that may be connected either in series or in parallel. The current rating of each winding is 41.7 A. What is the kilovoltampere rating of the transformer with the coils connected (*a*) in series and (*b*) in parallel?

13-14 Three single-phase transformers having a 20-to-1 ratio are delta-connected to a 2400-V three-phase line as step-down transformers. Find the voltage between the secondary terminals of each transformer. Find the secondary voltage of each transformer if the transformers are wye-connected to the same line.

13-15 The secondaries of a three-phase transformer bank supplying a three-phase 240 V motor are delta-connected. When the motor current is 10 A per terminal, find the current in each transformer winding.

13-16 A three-phase motor requires 80 kW at 80 percent power factor when operated at 240 V. If the motor is supplied from a 4160/240-V wye-delta step-down transformer bank, find the line currents on both the high- and low-voltage sides of the transformers.

13-17 The primary windings of three single-phase transformers are wye-connected and the secondary windings are delta-connected. The voltage applied to each primary winding is 2300 V, and the secondary line voltage is 230 V. Find the secondary line current when the primary line current is 20 A.

13-18 What is the kilovoltampere rating of a single-phase voltage regulator that has a rated voltage of 2400 V, a current rating of 200 A, and a total regulation range of 20 percent (10 percent raise and 10 percent lower)?

13-19 A 12 000-V three-phase step regulator has a rating of 208 kVA and has a range of regulation of 10 percent raise and 10 percent lower. What is the full-load current rating of this regulator? How much kilovoltampere load can be carried by a circuit in which this regulator is installed without overloading the regulator?

13-20 A polarity test is taken on a 5-kVA 480/120-V transformer. The test is done with a 120-V supply connected to the high voltage side of the transformer. While facing the transformer connections from the secondary side, the left side primary terminal is marked H_1 and the right side is marked H_2. With H_1 connected to its respective low voltage terminal and a voltmeter connected to H_2 and the other low voltage terminal, what would the voltmeter read if the secondary terminal common to H_1 was marked X_2?

13-21 What type of polarity is indicated by the polarity test in Prob. 13-20?

13-22 A step up autotransformer is used to boost the voltage of single-phase distribution line from 2 kV to 2.4 kV. Assuming efficiency of 100 percent, with a secondary load current of 150 A, determine:

a) input current (I_X)
b) output current (I_H)
c) common current (I_C)
d) transformer kVA rating
e) kVA rating of an equivalent isolation transformer to perform the same function.

13-23 Three secondary transformer windings are to be connected delta. The voltage output of each secondary winding is 440 V. Determine the voltage that should be present when completing the delta connection. What two possible voltages could be present?

13-24 A distribution system is supplied from a delta-delta connected transformer bank with a rating of 50 kVA, 4160/480 V. The connected plant load is 30 kVA. If one transformer becomes defective, determine:

a) the kVA of the system operating open-delta
b) the load, in kVA, on the two remaining transformers
c) the percentage overload on the two remaining transformers

13-25 A four-wire delta system operates with secondary phase voltages of 250 V. Transformer C is a centre-tapped transformer. Determine all the voltages available at the secondary terminals.

13-26 A three-phase four-wire system has unbalanced connected loads that draw 7 A from line A, 16 A from line B, and 9 A from line C. Determine the current flowing in the neutral conductor.

Alternating-Current Generators

Alternating-current generators, sometimes called synchronous generators or alternators, provide a vital link in the long process of converting the energy in coal, oil, gas, or uranium into a form that is useful in industry and home.

Large generators used for supplying modern national electric power grids are driven by steam or water turbines. The latter is referred to as **Hydro-Electric Generation.** Generators used to supply smaller, isolated power systems, or to furnish supplemental peak-load power to larger grids, or for emergency backup power supplies are often combustion-turbine or diesel-engine driven. An interior view of a generating station in which two 66 MW steam turbine-driven generators are installed is shown in Fig. 14-1. The direct-connected exciter can be seen on the unit in the foreground. A 3750 kW generator coupled directly to a diesel engine is shown in Fig. 14-2.

FIGURE **14-1**
Installation of two 66-MW steam-turbine-driven generators.
(Stanley Consultants, Inc.)

14-1

Construction

In dc generators the armature windings are placed on the rotating part of the machine in order to provide a way of converting the alternating voltage generated in the windings to a direct voltage at the terminals through the use of a rotating commutator. The field poles are placed on the stationary part of the machine. In all but small, low-voltage alternating-current generators, the field is placed on the rotating part, or **rotor**, and the armature winding on the stationary part, or **stator**, of the machine.

The revolving-field and stationary-armature construction simplifies the problems of insulation of an ac generator. Since voltages as high as 18 000 V to 24 000 V are commonly generated, this high voltage need not be brought out through slip rings and sliding contacts but can be brought directly to the switchgear through insulated leads from the stationary armature. This construction also has mechanical advantages in that armature windings are subjected to less vibration and centrifugal forces and can be braced better. The rotating field is supplied with direct current at 125, 250, or 375 V through slip rings and brushes, or through a direct cable connection between the field and the rotating rectifier if the brushless excitation system is used.

FIGURE **14-2**
Slow-speed ac generator connected to diesel engine.
(Cooper Industries.)

The armature or stator winding may be any one of many types, a widely used type being an open-circuited winding formed from separately insulated form-wound coils similar to the lap winding of the dc generator. Actually, such a winding is composed of three separate windings (on a three-phase generator), each displaced from the other two by 120 electrical degrees. The three windings may be either wye- or delta-connected. The wye connection is the more common since it lends itself well to the generation of high voltages directly, and a neutral wire can be brought out with the three lines to form a three-phase four-wire system as was shown in Chap. 12. An ac generator stator with windings in place is shown in Fig. 14-3.

A developed view of a simple three-phase winding is shown in Fig. 14-4. The winding shown in Fig. 14-4(*a*) is wye-connected; the method of connecting the terminals for a delta connection is shown in Fig. 14-4(*b*). The winding pictured is called a **concentrated winding** since all the conductors of each phase are included in one slot under each pole. Commercial windings such as that shown in Fig. 14-3 are distributed windings, with the conductors of each phase group occupying two or more slots under each pole. The distributed winding provides a more uniform heat distribution and results in the generation of a better emf wave.

There are two distinct types of synchronous-generator field structures: the **salient-pole type** and the **cylindrical type**.

Slow-speed generators such as those driven by diesel engines or water turbines have rotors with projecting or salient field poles like the rotor shown in Fig. 14-5. The laminated pole pieces with their field coils are mounted on the rim of the steel spider, which is, in turn, keyed to the shaft.

FIGURE **14-3**
AC generator stator.
(Kato Engineering.)

FIGURE **14-4**
(a) Developed view of a simple three-phase stator winding, wye-connected.
(b) Method of reconnecting the terminals for a delta connection.

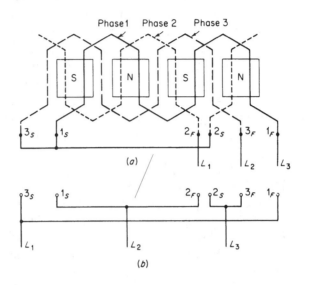

FIGURE **14-5**
Salient-pole rotor for slow-speed ac generator.
(Louis Allis Company.)

High-speed or turbo-type generators have cylindrical rotors such as that shown in Fig. 14-6. The rotor shown will be wound for two poles and is designed to operate at 3600 r/min (revolutions per minute). The cylindrical construction is essential in high-speed machines because the salient-pole type is difficult to build to withstand the stresses at high speeds. Furthermore, salient-pole rotors have high windage losses at high speeds. Alternating-current

FIGURE **14-6**
Rotor for 3600 r/min ac generator.
(General Electric Company.)

generators with the cylindrical-rotor construction are driven by steam or gas turbines. The steam turbine-driven generators shown in Fig. 14-1 have two-pole cylindrical rotors.

The conventional excitation system prior to about 1960 consisted of a direct-current source connected to the ac generator field through two slip rings and brushes. The dc source was normally a motor-driven dc generator or a dc generator driven by the same prime mover that powered the ac generator.

Following the advent of solid-state devices, several different excitation systems using these devices have been developed and applied. In one system, power is taken from the ac generator terminals, converted to dc power by a stationary solid-state rectifier, and then supplied to that ac generator field by means of conventional slip rings and brushes. In a similar system used in large steam turbine-driven generators, power is supplied to a solid-state rectifier from a separate three-phase winding located in the top of the generator stator slots. The sole function of this winding is to provide the excitation power for the generator.

Still another excitation system used with both salient-pole- and cylindrical-rotor-type synchronous generators is the brushless system, in which a small ac generator mounted on the same shaft as

14-2

AC Generator Excitation

the main generator is used as an exciter. The ac exciter has a rotating armature, the output of which is rectified by silicon diode rectifiers which are also mounted on the main shaft. The rectified output of the ac exciter is fed directly by means of insulated connections along the shaft to the rotating synchronous generator field. The field of the ac exciter is stationary and is supplied from a separate dc source. The output of the ac exciter and, consequently, the generated voltage of the synchronous generator, may thus be controlled by varying the field strength of the ac exciter. The brushless excitation system, therefore, has no commutator, slip rings, or brushes. This greatly improves reliability and simplifies maintenance of the machines.

14-**3**
Voltage Generation

After an ac generator is brought up to its proper speed by its prime mover, its field is excited from a dc supply. As the poles move under the armature conductors on the stator, the field flux cutting across the conductors induces an emf in them. This is an alternating emf, since poles of alternate polarity successively pass by a given conductor. Since no commutator is used, the alternating emf generated appears at the stator winding terminals.

The amount of any generated emf depends on the rate at which lines of force are cut or, in the case of the ac generator, the amount of emf depends on the field strength and the speed of the rotor. Since most generators are operated at a constant speed, the amount of emf generated becomes dependent on the field excitation. This means that the amount of emf generated can be controlled by adjusting the amount of field excitation supplied to the generator. The field excitation may be readily controlled by varying the amount of excitation voltage applied to the generator field.

The power factor at which the generator operates is determined by the characteristics of the load being supplied (unless the generator is operating in parallel with other generators as explained in Sec. 14-7).

The frequency of the generated emf depends on the number of field poles and on the speed at which the generator is operated. In a given coil, one complete cycle of emf is generated when a pair of rotor poles (a north and a south pole) is moved past the coil. Thus, the number of cycles generated in one revolution of the rotor will be equal to the number of pairs of poles on the rotor, or $p/2$ where p is the total number of poles. If n is the rotor speed in revolutions per minute, then $n/60$ is equal to the revolutions per second. The frequency in hertz or cycles per second is, therefore,

$$f = \frac{p}{2} \times \frac{n}{60} = \frac{pn}{120} \qquad \textbf{[14-1]}$$

By far the most common power frequency used in North America is 60 Hz, with 25 Hz being used to a much lesser extent. The frequency commonly used in Europe is 50 Hz.

As load is added to an ac generator operating at a constant speed and with a constant field excitation, the terminal voltage will change. The amount of change will depend on the machine design and on the power factor of the load. The effects of different load power factors on the change in the terminal voltage with changes of load on an ac generator are shown in Fig. 14-7.

Regulation of an ac generator is defined as the percentage rise in terminal voltage as load is reduced from the rated full-load current to zero, the speed and excitation being constant, or

Percent regulation (at a stated power factor)

$$= \frac{\text{no-load voltage} - \text{full-load voltage}}{\text{full-load voltage}} \times 100$$

Factors affecting generator regulation are as follows:

1. IR drop in the armature winding
2. IX_L drop in the armature winding
3. Armature reaction (magnetizing effect of the armature currents)

In a dc generator, the generated emf E is the sum of the terminal voltage V_t, and the IR drop in the armature circuit. In an ac generator, the voltage drop due to the inductive reactance of the winding must also be taken into account. Thus, the generated emf of an ac generator is equal to the terminal voltage plus both the IR and IX_L drops in the armature winding.

A simplified phasor diagram of an ac generator operating at unity power factor is shown in Fig. 14-8(*a*). The generated emf E

14-**4**

Generator Regulation

FIGURE **14-7**
Regulation curves of an ac generator at different power factors.

F I G U R E **14-8**
Simplified phasor diagrams of an ac generator operating at (*a*) unity power factor; (*b*) 0.8 lagging power factor; (*c*) 0.8 leading power factor.

is the phasor sum of the terminal voltage V_t, the *IR* drop which is in phase with the current *I*, and the IX_L drop, which leads *I* by 90°.

The phasor diagram of Fig. 14-8(*b*) represents the generator with the same load current as in Fig. 14-8(*a*) but with the current lagging the terminal voltage by 36.9° (power factor = 0.8 lag). As before, the generated emf is the phasor sum of V_t, the *IR* drop, and the IX_L drop in the armature winding. An inspection of Figs. 14-8(*a*) and 14-8(*b*) shows that, for a given generated emf, the terminal voltage is less in the case of the 0.8 lagging power factor. At lower lagging power factors, the *IR* and IX_L drops lower the terminal voltage still further.

Figure 14-8(*c*) represents a case in which a generator supplies a load with a leading power factor. When the *IR* and IX_L drops are added as phasors to the terminal voltage, it is found that the generated emf is less than the terminal voltage. This is possible because of the phase relations of the *IR* and IX_L drops with respect to the terminal voltage.

The phasor diagrams of Fig. 14-8(*a*), (*b*), and (*c*) show the effect of the *IR* and IX_L drops on the terminal voltage for a given *E*. However, *E* is *not* constant in an ac generator but varies with the amount of load and the power factor of the load due to the effect of armature reaction. At unity power factor, the effect of armature reaction is at a minimum, its effect being merely a distorting action on the main field flux. However, at lagging power factors, the magnetizing effect of the armature currents opposes the main field mmf, resulting in a weakened field flux and a lowered *E*. The lower the power factor in the lagging direction, the more the armature mmf demagnetizes the field.

At leading power factors, the armature mmf aids or strengthens the main field mmf, resulting in a higher generated emf with increases in load. This magnetizing effect increases as the power factor becomes more leading.

A further study of ac alternators and transformers under load conditions at varying power factors will show similar results as illustrated in Fig. 14-8.

Since the terminal voltage of an ac generator varies considerably with changes in load, some means must be provided to maintain the constant voltage required for the operation of most electric equipment. A common way of doing this is to use an auxiliary device called a **voltage regulator** to control the amount of dc field excitation supplied to the generator. When the generator terminal voltage drops because of changes in load, the voltage regulator automatically increases the field excitation, which restores normal rated voltage. Similarly, when the terminal voltage increases because of load changes, the regulator restores normal rated voltage by decreasing the field excitation.

Most voltage regulators control the field excitation of the generator indirectly by operating in the exciter field circuit. Much less current need be handled by the regulator in the exciter field circuit than in the general field circuit.

One type of generator voltage regulator is the direct-acting rheostatic type. Essentially, this regulator consists of an automatically controlled variable resistance in the exciter field circuit. The rheostatic element, which is connected in series with the exciter field, consists of stacks of nonmetallic resistance blocks or wafers, stacked so that the resistance of the stack is varied as it is tilted forward or backward by a torque element. The torque element is connected to the generator potential transformers. When the ac generator output voltage is constant, the torque element is stationary, holding the resistance elements stationary. However, should the generator voltage vary because of load changes from its preset value, the torque element acts to raise or lower the resistance of the rheostatic element and restores the generator voltage to its present value. This regulator has been largely replaced by the static type in which moving mechanical parts are replaced by solid-state devices.

The principle of operation of the static voltage regulator is the same as that of the direct-acting rheostatic type; that is, the voltage of the ac generator is regulated by varying the effective resistance in the exciter field circuit which, in turn, varies the voltage output of the exciter. A simplified elementary diagram of one type of static voltage regulator is shown in Fig. 14-9.

In the excitation system shown in Fig. 14-9, the effective resistance of the exciter field circuit is varied by power transistors which are connected in parallel with the exciter field rheostat. The transistors are switched from a conducting to a nonconducting state at a varying rate depending upon the amount of correction that is required in the ac generator voltage. This, in effect, alternately bypasses and inserts the rheostat into the exciter field circuit. The rate of on-off switching of the power transistors, which thereby regulates the exciter field current, is controlled by solid-state

14-5

Generator Voltage Regulators

F I G U R E **14-9**

Simplified diagram of a static voltage regulator.

auxiliary and sensing devices which are connected to the generator current and potential transformers.

Auxiliary apparatus includes stabilizing equipment to dampen out undue oscillations in the regulator and to prevent overshooting of the regulator on rapid changes in voltage. The current transformer connections are made to auxiliary apparatus which is used in connection with a cross-current compensation scheme to regulate automatically the division of kilovar load between generators operating in parallel.

14-**6**

Paralleling Generators; Synchronizing

If the load on a generating station becomes so large that the rating of the running generators is exceeded, it becomes necessary to add another generator in parallel to increase the power available (capacity) from the generating station.

Before two synchronous generators may be paralleled, the following conditions must be fulfilled:

1. Their phase sequence must be the same.
2. Their terminal voltages must be equal.
3. Their voltages must be in phase.
4. Their frequencies must be equal.

When two generators are operating so that these requirements are satisfied, they are said to be in **synchronism**. The operation of getting the machines into synchronism is called **synchronizing**.

Before a generator is synchronized with other generators for the first time, its phase sequence must be checked to determine that it has the same phase sequence as that of the other generators in the station. This normally is done with a test instrument called a phase-sequence indicator. One commonly used phase-sequence indicator is essentially a small three-phase motor that rotates in one direction for one phase sequence and in the opposite direction for the other phase sequence. The method of making the phase-sequence test and other synchronizing operations will be explained by making reference to the connection diagram shown in Fig. 14-10.

When a new generator has been installed and is ready for testing, the generator is operated at approximately rated speed and rated voltage with its circuit breaker open. The phase-sequence indicator is connected temporarily to the system bus potential transformers at points a, b, and c, and the system phase sequence is noted on the indicator.[1] The phase-sequence indicator connections are then transferred to the generator potential transformers, with temporary connections being made at points a', b', and c', and the phase sequence of the incoming generator is noted. If the sequences of the generator and of the system are the same, the generator is ready for the remaining steps in the synchronizing process. If, however, the phase sequence of the generator is opposite to that of the system, then any two of the three main leads of the generator must be interchanged to obtain the correct generator sequence. After it has been determined that the phase sequence of the generator matches that of the system and permanent connections have been made between the generator and its circuit breaker, it is not necessary to check phase sequence each time the generator is synchronized.

To determine that the remaining conditions for successful parallel operation are fulfilled, two voltmeters and a synchroscope are connected as shown in Fig. 14-10. A synchronizing switch is provided between both the bus and generator potential transformers and the synchronizing equipment, so that the synchronizing equipment may be switched on during the synchronizing operation.

With the incoming generator running at approximately rated speed, with its circuit breaker open, and with the synchronizing switch closed, the voltage of the generator, as indicated by the incoming voltmeter, is adjusted to match the bus voltage, as indicated by the running voltmeter. Generator voltage is raised or lowered by adjusting generator field excitation.

The synchroscope is then used to make certain that the generator voltage is in phase with the bus voltage and that the generator and bus frequencies are the same. The synchroscope is an instrument for indicating differences of phase and frequency between two voltages. It is essentially a split-phase motor in which torque is developed if the two voltages applied differ in frequency. Voltages from corresponding phases of the bus and the incoming

---

[1]The term "bus" refers to feeder or distribution conductors. These are often in the form of solid rectangular conductors from which secondary circuits are supplied.

F I G U R E **14-10**
Generator synchronizing connections.

generator are applied to the synchroscope. A pointer, which is attached to the rotor of the instrument, moves over the dial face in either a clockwise or a counterclockwise direction, depending on whether the incoming generator frequency is high or low with respect to the bus frequency. When the pointer stops, the frequencies of the two generators are equal. When the pointer stops in a vertical (12-o'clock) position, the synchroscope indicates that the frequencies are equal and the voltages are in phase. The dial markings of a synchroscope are as shown in Fig. 14-11.

In the synchronizing operation, the frequency of the incoming generator is raised or lowered to match that of the running generator or bus. Generator frequency is varied by increasing or decreasing the speed of the prime mover driving the generator. When the synchroscope pointer stops in the vertical position and the two voltmeters read the same, the generator circuit breaker may be closed to parallel the running and incoming generators.

In practice, it is sometimes difficult to adjust the speed of the incoming generator closely enough to stop the synchroscope pointer in the correct position. If this is the case, the frequency of the incoming generator should be adjusted as closely as possible to that of the bus, and the circuit breaker closed just before the

FIGURE **14-11**
Synchroscope dial.

pointer reaches the vertical position when traveling very slowly in the fast direction. This causes the incoming generator to take a small amount of load immediately after the closing of the circuit breaker and results in stable operation of the paralleled generators.

The process of synchronizing an incoming generator to a generating station bus is usually accomplished by automatic equipment rather than by the manual method just described. A typical complement of equipment required for automatic synchronizing includes a speed matching relay, a voltage matching relay, a synchronizing relay, auxiliary relays, and transfer relays or switches.

The automatic synchronizing equipment is energized as a part of a generating unit start-up sequence as in manual synchronizing. As the incoming unit approaches its rated speed, the speed matching relay provides "raise" or "lower" impulses to the generator prime mover to match the generator frequency to the bus frequency. Likewise, the voltage matching relay matches the generator and bus voltages by sending "raise" and "lower" impulses to the generator excitation system. When the frequencies and voltages are matched within predetermined limits and the voltages are in phase, all as determined by the synchronizing relay, the closing impulse is given automatically to the generator circuit breaker. The closing impulse is given at a phase angle slightly in advance of synchronism to take into account the time required for the generator breaker to close its contacts.

Each generator in a generating station may be equipped with a complete complement of automatic synchronizing equipment, or one common set of equipment may be switched from generator to generator by suitable transfer switches and equipment. Manual synchronizing equipment is usually provided as backup equipment for the automatic equipment.

14-**7**
Parallel Operation

After two synchronous generators have been paralleled, the load is usually divided between them in proportion to their ratings. That is, the larger the machine, the larger the share of the load it carries.

The proper division of load between generators is made by adjusting the governors of the prime movers on the generators. One prime-mover governor is opened while the other is closed slightly. in this way the system frequency is maintained at a constant value while the load is shifted from one machine to the other. Governor-control switches are mounted on the switchboard so that the operator is able to watch the switchboard instruments while making adjustments in load division.

The power factor of any ac distribution system depends on the load. A generator operating singly, then, must operate at the power factor of the load it supplies. However, when two or more generators operate in parallel, the power factor at which each operates is determined by its field excitation.

In general, the proper amount of field excitation for generators operating in parallel is the amount of excitation each generator would require if it were carrying its load alone at the same voltage and frequency.

If the excitation of a generator operating in parallel with other generators is increased above this normal value of excitation, its power factor changes in the lagging direction and its current output increases with no appreciable change in kilowatt load. Likewise, if the generator is under-excited, its power factor becomes more leading and its current output increases with no change in kilowatt output. The increased current in either case is not supplied to the load but circulates between the generators connected to the system, thereby increasing their losses and decreasing their useful capacity. It is desirable in most cases, therefore, to operate each generator at the same power factor, keeping the circulating current to a minimum.

Thus, a change in field excitation causes a change in *ampere* load but not in *kilowatt* load. *Kilowatt-load division between synchronous generators must be made by adjusting the prime mover governor controls.*

The voltage of a system supplied by several paralleled generators may be raised or lowered by increasing or decreasing, simultaneously, the field excitation of all generators. Likewise, system frequency can be raised or lowered by increasing or decreasing the speed of the several prime movers.

14-**8**
Hunting

Synchronous generators operating in parallel sometimes have a tendency to **hunt**. If the driving torque applied to a generator is pulsating, such as that produced by a diesel engine, the generator rotor may be pulled periodically ahead of or behind its normal position as it rotates. This oscillating action is called **hunting**.

Hunting causes generators to shift load from one to another. In some cases this oscillation of power becomes cumulative and violent enough to cause the generators to fall out of synchronism.

The tendency of diesel-driven generators to hunt is reduced by using a heavy flywheel to reduce torque variations. Damper windings, often called **amortisseur** windings, are placed on the surface of some generator rotors to decrease the tendency to hunt. The rotor shown in Fig. 14-5 is equipped with a damper winding consisting of short-circuited conductors embedded in the pole faces. When hunting occurs, there is a shifting of the armature flux across the pole faces, thereby inducing currents in the damper winding. Since any induced current opposes the action that produces it, the hunting action is opposed by the flow of the induced currents. Generators driven by steam turbines generally do not have a tendency to hunt since the torque applied does not pulsate.

14-**9**
Ratings

Generator capacity is rated in kilovoltamperes and usually in kilowatts at a specified power factor. Other generator nameplate data includes voltage, current, frequency, number of phases, and speed ratings. Maximum temperature rise is stated together with the method of temperature measurement to be used. Excitation requirements are also stated, including rated field voltage and field amperes.

14-**10**
Losses and Efficiency

Losses of a synchronous generator are similar to those of a dc generator and include mechanical and iron losses, armature copper loss, and field-excitation loss.

The efficiency of an ac generator may be determined by a direct measurement of input and output or by calculation after the losses have been determined. Because of the difficulty of providing suitable power supply and loading devices required for a direct measurement, the efficiencies of ac generators, especially of larger ratings, are usually determined from their losses.

Alternating-current generator efficiency varies with the power factor at which the generator operates, since the kilowatt output decreases with a decrease in power factor while the field excitation (and field loss) must be changed to maintain rated voltage.

R EVIEW **Q** UESTIONS

1 Why are ac generators built with a stationary armature and revolving field?
2 Name two types of ac generator construction.

3 How is the field of an ac generator excited?

4 Upon what does the amount of emf generated in an ac generator depend? In actual operation which of these is variable?

5 Write the formula for frequency of an ac generator. What is the common frequency in use in North America? In Europe?

6 What is meant by generator regulation?

7 What factors affect generator regulation?

8 How does the load power factor change the effect of armature reaction?

9 What is the purpose of a voltage regulator?

10 What requirements must be satisfied before ac generators may be paralleled?

11 What is meant when it is said that two ac generators are being synchronized?

12 Show how a phase-sequence indicator may be used to check the phase sequence of a generator.

13 When a generator is being synchronized, if the synchroscope pointer revolves once per second, what is the difference in frequency between the bus and the incoming generator?

14 How often must the phase sequence of an ac generator be checked?

15 What two things are indicated by a synchroscope? Is this the only instrument needed to indicate synchronism?

16 How is the kilowatt load divided in the desired proportion between two ac generators operating in parallel?

17 How is it possible to adjust the power factor of an ac generator that is operating in parallel with other generators?

18 What is meant by the term "hunting" as applied to generator operation?

19 What information is found on an ac generator nameplate?

20 Name three types of generator losses. Are ac generator losses the same at all power factors?

P R O B L E M S

14-1 A diesel-driven synchronous generator operates at 200 r/min and has a frequency rating of 60 Hz. How many poles does it have?

14-2 How many cycles are generated in one revolution of a 24-pole ac generator? How many revolutions per second must it make to generate a frequency of 60 Hz? How many revolutions per minute?

14-3 What must be the speed of a two-pole 25-Hz synchronous generator?

14-4 A three-phase generator has a load of 100 kW per phase at a power factor of 80 percent, lagging. What is (*a*) the three-phase kilowatt load, (*b*) the three-phase kilovoltampere load, (*c*) the current per terminal if the terminal voltage is 7200 V?

14-5 A wye-connected 2400-V 600-kVA unity power factor generator is reconnected for delta operation. What is the new voltage, current, and kilovoltampere rating?

14-6 Find the regulation of an ac generator that has a full-load voltage of 2400 V and no-load voltage of 3240 V at 80 percent lagging power factor. Will the percent regulation at unity power factor be larger than, smaller than, or the same as at 80 percent lagging power factor?

14-7 What is the kilowatt rating of a three-phase 875-kVA generator at (*a*) unity power factor, (*b*) 80 percent power factor, (*c*) 50 percent power factor? If the voltage rating is 2400 V, what is the current rating at each power factor?

14-8 A three-phase 480-V 1200-kVA synchronous generator supplies rated load at a lagging power factor of 75 percent. If the efficiency of the generator is 90 percent, what horsepower is the prime mover delivering to the generator?

Polyphase Induction Motors

Because of its simple, rugged construction and good operating characteristics, the induction motor is the most commonly used type of ac motor. It consists of two parts: the stator, or stationary part, and the rotor, or rotating part. The stator is connected to the ac supply. The rotor is not connected electrically to the supply but has current induced in it by transformer action from the stator. Because of this, the stator is sometimes referred to as the primary and the rotor as the secondary of the motor.

Two types of three-phase induction motors are discussed in this chapter, namely, squirrel-cage and wound-rotor motors. Both motors operate on the same basic principle and have the same stator construction but differ in rotor construction. Single-phase induction motors are discussed in Chap. 17.

15-1
Construction

A cutaway view of a typical three-phase squirrel-cage motor is shown in Fig. 15-2. Note the extremely simple construction as compared, for example, with a dc motor.

The stator core is built of slotted sheet-steel laminations that are supported in a stator frame of cast iron or fabricated steel plate. Windings, similar to the stator windings of a synchronous generator, are spaced in the stator slots 120 electrical degrees apart. The phase windings may be either wye- or delta-connected.

FIGURE **15-1**
Standard squirrel-cage induction motor.
(Courtesy of Reliance Electric.)

The rotor of a squirrel-cage motor is constructed of a laminated core with the conductors placed parallel, or approximately parallel, to the shaft and embedded in the surface of the core. The conductors are not insulated from the core, since the rotor currents naturally follow the path of least resistance, that is, the rotor conductors. At each end of the rotor, the rotor conductors are all short-circuited by continuous end rings. The rotor conductors and their end rings are similar to a revolving squirrel cage, thus explaining the name.

The rotor bars and end rings of smaller squirrel-cage motors are cast of copper or aluminum in one piece on the rotor core. In the larger motors, the rotor bars, instead of being cast, are wedged into the rotor slots and are then welded securely to the end rings. Squirrel-cage rotor bars are not always placed parallel to the motor shaft but are often skewed. This results in a more uniform torque and also reduces the magnetic humming noise when the motor is running.

Wound-rotor or slip-ring motors differ from the squirrel-cage motor in rotor construction. As the name implies, the rotor is wound with an insulated winding similar to the stator winding. The rotor phase windings are wye-connected with the open end of each phase brought out to a slip ring mounted on the rotor shaft. Fig. 15-3 shows a cutaway view of a wound-rotor motor. The three slip rings and brushes can be seen to the left of the rotor winding. The rotor winding is not connected to a supply, the slip rings and brushes merely providing a means of connecting an external variable-control resistance into the rotor circuit.

FIGURE **15-3**
Cutaway view of a wound-rotor induction motor.
(General Electric Company.)

Wound-rotor motors are less extensively used than squirrel-cage motors because of their higher manufacturing cost and greater maintenance costs.

Motors have been classified according to environmental protection and methods of cooling by the Canadian Electrical Manufacturers Association (CEMA). The three general classes are open motors, totally enclosed motors, and motors with encapsulated or sealed windings.

Enclosures for the so-called open motors are constructed to provide several degrees of protection. The open drip-proof motor is constructed so that operation is not interfered with when drops of liquid or solid particles strike to enter the enclosure at any angle from 1 to 15° downward from the vertical. Guarded motors have protected openings to prevent accidental contact with live metal or rotating parts. Weather-protected motors have ventilating openings constructed so that entrance of rain, snow, or airborne particles is minimized.

Totally enclosed motors are enclosed to prevent the free exchange of air between the inside and the outside of the enclosure. They are classified as totally enclosed nonventilated, totally enclosed fan-cooled, explosion-proof, waterproof, or any of a number of other similar subclassifications. See Fig. 15-4.

The encapsulated or sealed-winding motor has its windings encapsulated or sealed with insulating resins or similar materials to seal and to protect the windings from severe environmental conditions.

FIGURE **15-4**
Totally enclosed explosion-proof induction motor.
(Courtesy of Reliance Electric.)

15-**2**

The Rotating Magnetic Field

An induction motor depends, for its operation, on a rotating magnetic field which is established in the air gap of the motor by the stator currents. As mentioned above, a three-phase stator winding is wound with the phase windings spaced 120 electrical degrees apart.

A simplified stator winding layout of a two-pole wye-connected motor is shown in Fig. 15-5(*a*). When the winding is energized from a three-phase supply, the phase currents vary in time phase as shown in Fig. 15-5(*b*), and a pulsating flux is built up by each of the three windings. However, owing to the spacing of the windings and the phase difference of the currents in the windings, the flux produced by each phase combines to form a resultant flux that moves around the stator surface at a constant speed. This resultant flux is called the **rotating magnetic field**.

The manner in which the rotating magnetic field is established by a three-phase stator winding may be illustrated by considering the direction of current flow through the three phases at several successive instants. These different times are marked off at 60° intervals on the current waves in Fig. 15-5(*b*). It will be assumed that, when currents have positive values in Fig. 15-5(*b*), current is flowing in the direction of the arrows in Fig. 15-5(*a*). For example, at time 1 in Fig. 15-5(*b*), currents in phases *A* and *C* are positive and the current in phase *B* is negative. Therefore, current is flowing toward the motor or with the arrows in lines *A* and *C* away from the motor or against the arrow in line *B*.

Fig. 15-5(*c*) shows the current directions in the stator conductors and the resulting field at each of the six different instants chosen in Fig. 15-5(*b*). At time 1, the current is outward in the three coil sides on the upper half of the stator and is inward in the three

FIGURE **15-5**

(a) Simplified two-pole stator winding layout. (b) Variation of current in the phase windings. (c) Resulting flux distribution in the motor at the successive instants indicated by the numbers on the curves in (b).

(c)

coil sides on the lower half of the stator. The resulting field is established toward the right, creating a south pole on the stator surface at the right and a north pole in at the left as shown. At time 2, the current is still in the same direction in phases A and B but has reversed in phase C. This establishes a field of the same strength as at time 1 but in a position 60° in a clockwise direction from time 1. At time 3, the current in phase B has reversed, causing the resulting field to be moved another 60° in the clockwise direction. The remaining diagrams in Fig. 15-5(c) show the resultant field at times 4, 5, and 6.

It is evident from Fig. 15-5 that the field, resulting from the currents flowing in the three stator windings, shifts around the stator surface and moves through the definite distance in each of the time intervals considered. Use is made of the principle of this rotating magnetic field in both induction and synchronous motors.

15-**3**

Speed of the Rotating Magnetic Field

In the two-pole winding of Fig. 15-5, the field makes one complete revolution in one cycle of the current. In a four-pole winding in which each phase has two separate groups of coils connected in series, it may be shown that the rotating field makes one revolution in two cycles of the current. In a six-pole winding the field makes one revolution in three cycles of the current. In general, the field makes one revolution in $p/2$ cycles, or

$$\text{Cycles} = \frac{p}{2} \times \text{revolutions}$$

and $\quad$ $$\text{Cycles per second} = \frac{p}{2} \times \text{revolutions per second}$$

Since revolutions per second equal revolutions per minute, n, divided by 60 and the number of cycles per second is frequency, f,

$$f = \frac{p}{2} \times \frac{n}{60} = \frac{pn}{120}$$

$$n = \frac{120f}{p} \qquad\qquad \text{[15-1]}$$

The speed at which the rotating magnetic field revolves is called the **synchronous speed** of the motor. It will be noted that the same relation exists between the frequency, poles, and synchronous speed of a motor as exists between the frequency, poles, and speed of rotation of a synchronous generator. For a constant supply frequency, the synchronous speed is constant in any given motor.

If any two of the three supply lines to the stator winding in Fig. 15-5(a) are reversed, thereby reversing the phase sequence of the stator currents, an analysis similar to that of Sec. 15-2 will show the rotation of the magnetic field to be in the reverse direction, or counterclockwise. As will be shown in the following sections, the rotor turns in the same direction as the rotating flux. Therefore, *the direction of rotation of a three-phase motor may be reversed by interchanging any two of the three motor supply lines.*

15-**4**

Principle of Operation

In a dc motor, current is drawn from the supply and conducted into the armature conductors through the brushes and commutator. When the armature conductors carry current in the magnetic field established by the field circuit, a force is exerted on the conductors which tends to move them at right angles to the field.

In an induction motor, there is no electric connection to the rotor, the rotor currents being induced currents. However, the same condition exists as in the dc motor, that is, the rotor conductors carry current in a magnetic field and thereby have a force exerted upon them tending to move them at right angles to the field.

When the stator winding is energized from a three-phase supply a rotating magnetic field is established which rotates at synchronous speed. As the field sweeps across the rotor conductors, an emf is induced in these conductors just as an emf is induced in the secondary winding of a transformer by the flux of the primary currents. The rotor circuit being complete, either through end rings or an external resistance, the induced emf causes a current to flow in the rotor conductors. The rotor conductors carrying current in the stator field thus have a force exerted upon them.

Fig. 15-6 represents a section of an induction motor stator and rotor, with the magnetic field assumed to be rotating in a clockwise direction and with the rotor stationary, as at starting. For the flux direction and motion shown, an application of Fleming's right-hand rule shows the direction of the induced current in the rotor conductor to be toward the reader. At the instant being considered, with the current-carrying conductor in the magnetic field as shown, force is exerted upward upon the conductor since the magnetic field below the conductor is stronger than the field above. For simplicity, only one rotor conductor is shown. However, other adjacent rotor conductors in the stator field likewise carry current in the same direction as the conductor shown and also have an upward force exerted upon them. One-half cycle later, the stator field direction will have reversed, but the rotor current will have

FIGURE **15-6**
Section of an induction motor rotor and stator showing the magnetic field in the air gap.

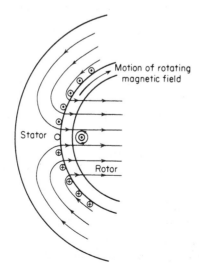

also reversed, so that the force on the rotor is still upward. Likewise, rotor conductors under other stator field poles will have a force exerted upon them all tending to turn the rotor in the clockwise direction. If the developed torque is great enough to overcome the resisting torque of the load, the motor will accelerate in the clockwise direction or in the same direction as the rotation of the stator magnetic field.

15-5
Speed and Slip

An induction motor cannot run at synchronous speed. If it were possible, by some means, for the rotor to attain synchronous speed, then the rotor would be standing still with respect to the rotating flux. Then no emf would be induced in the rotor, no rotor current would flow, and there would be no torque developed. The rotor speed even at no load must be slightly less than synchronous speed in order that current may be induced in the rotor, thereby producing a torque. This difference between rotor speed and synchronous speed is called **slip**. Slip may be expressed in revolutions per minute, but is more commonly expressed as a percent of synchronous speed.

$$\text{Percent slip} = \frac{\text{synchronous speed} - \text{rotor speed}}{\text{synchronous speed}} \times 100$$

Or, writing the above expression using symbols, results in

$$\text{Percent } s = \frac{N_s - N_r}{N_s} \times 100 \qquad \textbf{[15-2]}$$

E x a m p l e   1 5 - 1

A four-pole 60 Hz squirrel-cage motor has a full-load speed of 1740 r/min. What is the percent slip at full load?

The synchronous speed from Eq. (15-1) is

$$N_s = \frac{120f}{p} = \frac{120 \times 60}{4} = 1800 \text{ rpm}$$

Slip in revolutions per minute $= 1800 - 1740 = 60$ rpm

$$\text{Percent slip} = \frac{60}{1800} \times 100 = 3.33 \text{ percent}$$

15-6
Rotor Frequency

If a two-pole 60 Hz induction motor (synchronous speed = 3600 r/min) operates at 5 percent slip, the slip in revolutions per minute is 3600×0.05 or 180 r/min. This means that a pair of stator poles passes a given rotor conductor 180 times every minute, or three times every second. When a pair of poles moves across a conductor, one cycle of emf is induced in that conductor. Thus, the rotor conductor mentioned above will have induced in it an emf with a frequency of 3 Hz. If the slip is increased to 10 percent or 360 r/min, the frequency of the rotor emf and current is increased to 6 Hz. If the motor slip is increased to 100 percent, the rotor frequency will be 60 Hz.

It is obvious then that the rotor frequency depends on the slip — the greater the slip, the greater the rotor frequency. For any value of slip, the rotor frequency f_r is equal to the stator frequency f_s multiplied by the slip s expressed as a decimal, or

$$f_r = sf_s \qquad \text{[15-3]}$$

Rotor frequency is significant because as it varies, the rotor reactance ($X_r = 2\pi f_r L_r$) also varies, thus affecting both starting and running characteristics of the motor, as will be explained in following sections.

15-7
Torque and Speed of an Induction Motor

Torque is produced in an induction motor by the interaction of the stator and rotor fluxes. The flux produced by the stator currents revolves at synchronous speed. In order that rotor currents may be induced, making possible the production of a torque, the rotor must turn at a speed less than synchronous speed. At no load, the rotor lags behind the stator flux only a small amount, since the only torque required is that needed to overcome the motor losses. As mechanical load is added, the rotor speed decreases. A decrease in rotor speed allows the constant-speed rotating field to sweep across the rotor conductors at a faster rate, thereby inducing larger rotor currents. This results in a larger torque output at a reduced speed.

Since the rotor impedance is low, a small decrease in speed produces a large increase in rotor current. For this reason the speed regulation of a standard squirrel-cage motor is low, the full-load slip being 3 to 5 percent. Although the motor speed does decrease slightly with increased load, the speed regulation is good enough that the induction motor is classed as a constant-speed motor.

With increasing loads, the increased rotor currents are in such a direction as to decrease the stator flux, thereby temporarily decreasing the counter emf in the stator windings. The decreased counter emf allows more stator current flow, thereby increasing the power input to the motor. It will be noted that the action of the induction motor in adjusting its stator or primary current with changes of current in its rotor or secondary circuit is very similar to the changes occurring in a transformer with changes in load.

The torque of an induction motor being due to the interaction of the rotor and stator fields is dependent on the strength of those fields and the phase relations between them.

Mathematically, $$T = K\Phi I_r \cos \theta_r$$ [15-4]

where T = torque
    K = a constant
    Φ = rotating stator flux
    I_r = rotor current
    $\cos \theta_r$ = rotor power factor

Throughout the normal range of operation, K, Φ, and $\cos \theta_r$ are substantially constant, the torque increasing directly with the rotor current I_r. The rotor current, in turn, increases in almost direct proportion to the motor slip. The variation of torque with slip of a typical squirrel-cage motor of the standard type is shown in Fig. 15-7. Note that as slip increases from zero to about 10 percent the torque increases in an almost straight-line relationship with the slip.

As was explained in Sec. 15-6, an increase in slip causes an increase in rotor frequency and rotor reactance. Since the rotor-circuit resistance is constant, an increased rotor reactance means a decrease in rotor power factor (rotor power factor = R_r/Z_r). However, in the standard motor the change in slip is so small as load is increased from zero to full load, or even considerably above full load, that the change in rotor impedance is almost negligible.

However, as load and slip are increased much beyond the rated or full-load values, the increase in rotor reactance becomes appreciable. The increasing value of rotor impedance not only decreases the rotor power factor, but also lowers the rate of increase of rotor current so that the torque does not continue to increase directly with the slip. With the decreasing power factor and the lowered rate of increase in rotor current, the torque increase becomes less rapid and finally reaches maximum value at about 20 percent slip

---

F I G U R E **15-7**
Variation of torque with slip for a standard squirrel-cage motor.

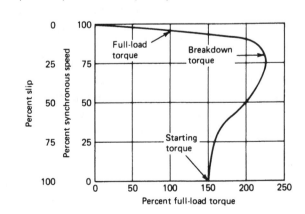

in the standard squirrel-cage motor. This maximum value of the torque is called the **pull-out** or **breakdown torque** of the motor. If load is increased beyond the breakdown point, the decrease in rotor power factor is greater than the increase in rotor current, resulting in a decreasing torque and the motor quickly coming to a stop.

The value of breakdown torque varies with the design of the motor but ranges from 200 to 300 percent of full-load torque in standard squirrel-cage motors. The value of slip at which the breakdown torque occurs depends on the value of rotor resistance: the higher the resistance, the higher the value of slip at breakdown. Some squirrel-cage motors for special applications are designed with high-resistance rotors so that the maximum torque occurs at 100 percent slip or at starting.

The maximum torque of an induction motor occurs when the rotor resistance (R_r) is equal to the variable rotor reactance $(sXlr)$ where (s) is the rotor slip expressed as a decimal and (Xlr) is the locked rotor reactance. This takes place when the rotor power factor is 0.707.

Therefore, maximum torque occurs when

$$R_r = sXlr$$

From this we can derive the slip of the rotor when maximum torque occurs.

$$spo = \frac{R_r}{Xlr} \qquad \text{[15-5]}$$

where spo = slip of rotor at pull-out torque
R_r = rotor resistance
Xlr = locked rotor reactance

The current drawn by an induction motor running at no load is largely a magnetizing current, the no-load current lagging the applied voltage by a large angle. Thus, the power factor of a lightly loaded induction motor is very low. Because of the air gap, the reluctance of the magnetic circuit is high, resulting in a relatively large value of no-load current as compared with a transformer.

As load is added, the active or power component of the current increases, resulting in a higher power factor. However, because of the large value of magnetizing current, which is present regardless of load, the power factor of an induction motor even at full load seldom exceeds 90 percent.

The variation of the power factor of a typical motor with load is shown in Fig. 15-9. Other performance curves also shown are

15-**8**
Effect of Load on Power Factor

FIGURE **15-8**

(a) No-load   (b) 50% Full load   (c) Full load

variations of speed, slip, efficiency, stator current, and torque for different values of load.

Fig. 15-8 shows the basic relationships that exist between the stators' energy component current and magnetizing component current for three different load conditions,

where I_e = energy component current
        I_m = magnetizing component current
        I_s = resultant stator current
        $\angle\theta$ = angle between in phase and quadrature (90° out of phase) component currents

Fig. 15-8(a) represents the no-load characteristics of an induction motor where the energy component current is very small with respect to the magnetizing component. This is due to the motor requiring only a small amount of energy component current to overcome the no-load losses of the motor.

Fig. 15-8(b) represents the half load characteristics. Note that the magnetizing current remains constant and only the energy component current increases as the load on the motor increases. This results in a decrease in angle theta, and an increase in the motor's power factor. Fig. 15-8(c) shows the full-load characteristics. Angle theta decreases further, while increasing the power factor. It could be assumed that further increases in load on the motor beyond full load would further increase the power factor. However, this does not happen due to high increases in slip; the rotor power factor decreases, thus reflecting this decreased rotor power factor back into the stator.

It should be noted, therefore, that an induction motor should operate at, or near, full load to be near optimal power factor. If an induction motor is run lightly loaded for prolonged periods of time, the system power factor will be dragged down and will require capacitive correcting as a result. See Sec. 16-8.

FIGURE **15-9**
Performance curves of a squirrel-cage motor.

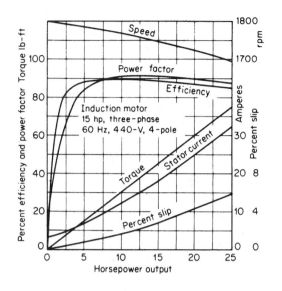

As stated in Sec. 15-6, the rotor frequency and reactance are high under starting conditions, that is, with 100 percent slip. Thus, in the highly reactive rotor circuit, the rotor currents lag the rotor emf by a large angle. This means that the maximum current flow occurs in a rotor conductor at some time after the maximum density of the stator flux has passed that conductor. This results in a high starting current at low power factor, which results in a low value of starting torque.

As the rotor accelerates, the rotor frequency and, hence, the rotor reactance, decreases, causing the torque to increase up to its maximum value. As the motor accelerates further, the torque decreases to the value required to carry the load on the motor at a constant speed.

The change in torque during the starting period is shown in Fig. 15-7, the starting torque being the value at the lower end of the curve at zero speed, or at 100 percent slip.

The high rotor reactance compared with the rotor resistance at starting results in a poor starting torque with a high starting current. One method of correcting this condition is to design the rotor circuit with a high resistance. This increases the rotor power factor and improves the motor starting characteristics but, under the running conditions, the motor operates at a reduced efficiency because of the high I^2R loss in the rotor circuit. Another effect of a high rotor resistance, which may or may not be a disadvantage, is the increased speed regulation. Standard squirrel-cage motors are a compromise design; that is, they have a rotor resistance high

15-9

Starting Conditions

enough to provide fair starting characteristics but that causes the motor to operate at a slightly reduced efficiency.

The standard or normal-torque normal-starting-current squirrel-cage motor has a starting torque of 80 to 200 percent of full-load value with a starting current of 500 to 700 percent of full-load current.

15-10

The Double-Squirrel-Cage Motor

The double-squirrel-cage motor is designed to provide a high starting torque at a low starting current. The rotor is so designed that the motor operates with the advantages of a high-resistance rotor circuit during starting and a low-resistance rotor circuit under running conditions.

As the name denotes, the double-squirrel-cage motor has two rotor windings, one inside the other. A sectional view of this type of rotor is shown in Fig. 15-10. The outer cage winding has a high resistance and, being close to the rotor surface, has a low inductance. The inner cage is a low-resistance winding and, being nearly surrounded by iron, has a high inductance.

During the starting period with the high rotor frequency, the impedance of the outer winding is less than that of the inner winding, resulting in a large proportion of the rotor currents flowing in the outer high-resistance winding. This provides the good starting characteristics of a high-resistance cage winding. As the motor accelerates, the rotor frequency decreases, thereby lowering the reactance of the inner winding and allowing it to carry a larger proportion of the total rotor current. At the normal operating speed of the motor, the rotor frequency is so low that nearly all the rotor current flows in the low-resistance inner cage, resulting in good operating efficiency and low speed regulation.

Thus, the outer winding produces the high starting and accelerating torque, while the inner winding provides the running torque at a high efficiency.

The starting torque of the double-squirrel-cage motor ranges from 200 to 250 percent of full-load torque, with a starting current of 400 to 600 percent of full-load value. It is classed as a high-torque low-starting-current motor.

F I G U R E **15-10**
Section of the rotor of a double-squirrel-cage motor.

There are several squirrel cage rotor designs not described here. CEMA (Canadian Electrical Manufacturing Association) designations provide for various combinations of **Speed and Torque** characteristics for special load applications.

The rotor of a **wound-rotor** or **slip-ring motor** is wound with insulated windings similar to the stator winding. This three-phase winding is wye-connected with the open ends of each phase winding being connected to three slip rings. Connected to the rotor circuit through the slip rings is a wye-connected external variable resistance. Fig. 15-3 shows the construction of the wound-rotor motor while the connection diagrams are shown in Fig. 15-11.

The rotor rheostat provides a means of increasing the rotor-circuit resistance during the starting period, resulting in a high value of starting torque. As the motor accelerates, the rheostat is gradually cut out, thereby lowering the rotor resistance as the rotor reactance decreases. By this means, the torque of the motor is controlled so that a maximum value of torque is provided throughout the accelerating period. The slip rings are short-circuited when the motor reaches full speed, its operation under running conditions being the same as the squirrel-cage motor.

Because the rotor-circuit resistance may be varied during operation, a means is provided for controlling the speed of a wound-rotor motor. As the rotor-circuit resistance is increased, a given torque is developed at a larger slip. Thus, with the control rheostat cut in, the motor operates at a reduced speed.

The effects of operating a motor with external resistance in the rotor circuit on the motor performance are a decreased efficiency due to the I^2R losses in the rheostat and a lowered value of speed regulation.

15-11
The Wound-Rotor Motor

FIGURE **15-11**
Circuits of a wound-rotor induction motor.

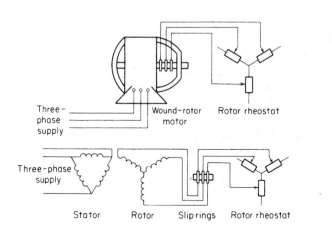

Three-phase supply — Wound-rotor motor — Rotor rheostat

Three-phase supply

Stator   Rotor   Slip rings   Rotor rheostat

15-**12**

Speed Control of Squirrel-Cage Motors

From Eq. (15-1), the formula for the synchronous speed of a motor, it is evident that the supply frequency and the number of stator poles are the only variable factors determining synchronous speed. A variation of frequency is impossible when a motor is connected directly to ordinary commercial supply lines, since such supplies are constant-frequency systems. However, when an ac generator supplies but one motor, as in some ship propulsion systems, the supply frequency may be varied by varying the speed of the generator prime mover, thereby varying the speed of the motor. Likewise, if an adjustable-frequency supply is installed between a constant-frequency system and a motor, the motor speed can be varied by varying the output frequency of the adjustable-frequency supply. Following the advent of semiconductor devices, static variable-frequency supplies were developed and are commercially available for this use.

Multispeed squirrel-cage motors, designed to be operated on constant-frequency systems, are provided with stator windings that may be reconnected to form different numbers of poles. Two-speed motors usually have one winding that may be switched through suitable control equipment to provide two speeds, one of which is half of the other. Four-speed motors are equipped with two separate stator windings each of which provides two speeds. While such motors do not have continuously adjustable speeds as do dc motors, or ac motors supplied from adjustable-frequency power supplies, they are suitable for such applications as ventilating fans, conveyors, machine tools, or other applications requiring several definite speeds but not necessarily a continuously adjustable speed drive.

The rotor speed of an induction motor is determined by the following equation:

$$N_r = \frac{120f}{p}(1 - s) \qquad \text{[15-6]}$$

Example 15-2

A three-phase 60-Hz induction motor stator is wound for two- or four-pole operation, and is connected to a variable frequency supply that has a frequency range of 30 to 90 Hz. Assuming a constant slip of 3 percent, determine the maximum and minimum speed range of this motor.

SOLUTION: Minimum speed is achieved when the motor is operating with four poles at a frequency of 30 Hz.

$$N_r = \frac{120 \times 30}{4}(1 - 0.03) = 873 \text{ rpm}$$

Maximum speed is achieved when the motor is operating with two poles at a frequency of 90 Hz.

$$N_r = \frac{120 \times 90}{2} (1 - 0.03) = 5238 \text{ rpm}$$

There are other constraining factors to be considered when using a variable frequency source on an induction motor. These will be discussed in Sec. 15-19.

15-13

Starting Induction Motors

In general, induction motors may be started either by connecting the motor directly across the supply circuit or by applying a reduced voltage to the motor during the starting period. Controllers used for starting motors by either method may be operated either manually or magnetically.

Unlike dc motors, induction motors may be connected directly across the line without damage to the motor. However, because of the voltage disturbance created on the supply lines by their heavy starting currents, motors larger than 7.5 to 10 hp are often started at a reduced voltage. The maximum allowable horsepower rating to be started on full voltage depends, however, on the motor design, the supply capacity, and the rules and regulations of the owners of the supply lines.

A greater starting torque is exerted by a motor when it is started on full voltage than when it is started on reduced voltage. In fact, it may be shown that the torque of an induction motor is proportional to the square of the applied voltage. Thus, if the voltage is reduced to 80 percent of its rated value during starting, the starting torque is reduced to only 64 percent of that obtained by full-voltage starting. The reduced voltage applied to the motor during the starting period lowers the starting current but, at the same time, increases the accelerating time because of the reduced value of the starting torque. The type of load being started, then, also has a bearing on the method of starting to be used. If, for example, a particular load might be damaged by sudden starting and should be accelerated slowly, then reduced-voltage starting must be used.

Commonly used starters and those to be described here are the following:

1. Full-voltage or across-the-line starters
2. Reduced-voltage starters
    (a) Primary-resistor starters
    (b) Autotransformer starters
    (c) Solid-state starters
3. Part-winding starters
4. Wye-delta starters

As stated previously, the reduced starting voltage also reduces the starting torque of the motor.

The starting torque of an induction motor under reduced voltage can be determined in proportional terms to full voltage starting torque by the following equation.

$$T_s = kV_L^2 \qquad\qquad [15\text{-}7]$$

Example 15-3

The starting torque of a three-phase induction motor is 30 N·m when a rated voltage of 208 V is applied. What would be the starting torque if the voltage at start is reduced to 125 V?

SOLUTION:

$$\frac{T_s}{T_s'} = \frac{kV_L^2}{kV_L'^2}$$

$$\therefore T_s' = T_s \frac{V_L'^2}{V_L^2}$$

$$\therefore T_s' = 30 \times \left(\frac{125}{208}\right)^2 = 10.83 \text{ N·m}$$

FIGURE **15-12**
Three-pole magnetic across-the-line starter.
(Square D Company.)

Motors are started on full line voltage by means of across-the-line starters. A magnetically operated across-the-line starter is shown in Fig. 15-12, and a connection diagram of the starter, using three-wire push-button control, is shown in Fig. 15-13. The operation is the same as that of the dc magnetic contactor with three-wire push-button control described in Sec. 9-18, with the exception that a three-pole contactor is used in the ac starter.

Across-the-line starters are generally equipped with thermal overload relays and, when used with the three-wire push-button control as shown in Fig. 15-13, also provide undervoltage protection for the motor.

15-14
Across-the-Line Starters

Reduced voltage is obtained in the primary-resistor starter by means of resistances that are connected in series with each stator lead during the starting period. The voltage drop in the resistors produces a reduced voltage at the motor terminals. At a definite time after the motor is connected to the line through the resistors, accelerating contacts close which short-circuit the starting resistors and apply full voltage to the motor.

A magnetically operated primary-resistor starter with the cover removed is shown in Fig. 15-14, and a typical elementary wiring diagram of this type of starter is shown in Fig. 15-15. When the START button is closed, the main contactor M is closed, connecting

15-15
Primary-Resistor Starters

FIGURE **15-13**
Circuit diagram of across-the-line starter with a three-wire control circuit.

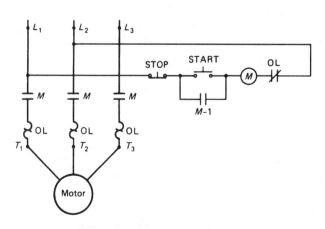

F I G U R E **15-14**
Primary-resistor starter.
(General Electric Company.)

the motor to the line through the starting resistors. At the same time, a timing relay *TR* is started. After a definite time has elapsed during which the motor has accelerated, the time-delay contact *TR* closes. This energizes the accelerating contactor A which short-circuits the starting resistors and applies full voltage to the motor.

In the starter just described, the starting resistance is cut out in one step. To obtain smoother acceleration with less line disturbance, starters are available in which the starting resistance is cut out in several steps.

Overload and undervoltage protection are provided in the same manner as in the across-the-line starter.

15-**16**
Autotransformer Starters

Autotransformer starters are used to reduce the voltage applied to the motor during the starting period through the use of a three-phase autotransformer. The autotransformer is provided with taps to provide a selection of 50, 65, or 80 percent of line voltage as a starting voltage with a corresponding reduction in supply line cur-

FIGURE **15-15**
Circuit diagram of a primary-resistor starter.

rents. Since motor starting torque varies as the square of the applied voltage, the resulting torque when using these taps will be 25, 42, and 64 percent, respectively, of full-voltage values. A tap, therefore, can be selected to match the starting torque required by a given motor and driven load.

Autotransformer starters may be either manually or magnetically operated. A magnetically operated starter is shown in Fig. 15-16 and an elementary diagram of a typical magnetic starter is shown in Fig. 15-17.

The starter shown in Fig. 15-17 has a two-pole starting contactor 1S, a three-pole starting contactor 2S, and a three-pole running contactor R. Contactors 1S and 2S are mechanically interlocked so that they cannot be closed simultaneously. Control relay TR has both time-opening and time-closing contacts TO and TC.

When the control relay TR is energized by closing the START button, contactors 1S and 2S are both energized through the TR contact connecting the motor to preselected taps on the autotransformer. After a time delay, during which the motor accelerates, timing relay contact TO opens and contact TC closes, which transfers the motor from the autotransformer to the line by dropping out starting contactors 1S and 2S and closing running contactor R. Starters of this type provide what is called closed-transition starting since the motor is not disconnected from the line at any time during the transition from reduced to full voltage.

Overload and undervoltage protection are provided by the thermal overload relay and the three-wire control circuit as shown.

FIGURE **15-16**
Magnetic autotransformer starter.
(Square D Company.)

FIGURE **15-17**
Circuit diagram of an autotransformer starter.

After solid-state power devices became readily available in the 1960s, solid-state motor starters were developed by a number of manufacturers. Although individual designs vary among manufacturers, all such starters, in effect, regulate motor starting current electronically to provide a smooth, stepless motor acceleration. A simplified block diagram of the power circuits of one such starter is shown in Fig. 15-18.

The basic solid-state power device used in this starter is a type of thyristor called the silicon controlled rectifier, or SCR. (SCRs are discussed in more detail in Chap. 20.) The SCR blocks the flow of current in one direction but allows current to flow in the other direction after it has received a "turn on" signal called a gate pulse. Six SCRs are arranged in what is called a full-wave rectifier configuration as shown in Fig. 15-18. With the appropriate solid-state control circuitry, control of motor current or acceleration time may be achieved by applying the gate pulses to the SCRs at different times within each half-cycle of the power-supply voltage. If the gate pulse is applied early in the half-cycle, the SCR output is high. If the gate pulse is applied late in the half-cycle, the output is low. Thus, input voltage to the motor can be varied from zero to full value during the starting period, causing the motor to accelerate smoothly from zero to full speed.

When the starter shown in Fig. 15-18 is energized, the START contacts are closed and the motor accelerates under the control of the SCRs. After the motor reaches full speed, the RUN contacts close, the SCRs are turned off, and the START contacts open.

Protective functions usually provided by the solid-state starter include detection and tripping for abnormal conditions such as a

15-17

Solid-State Reduced-Voltage Starters

FIGURE **15-18**
Solid-state starter, simplified diagram.

shorted SCR, phase-current unbalance, or motor overload. Current-limiting fuses or circuit breakers provide short-circuit protection for the starter and motor circuits.

15-18
Part-Winding and Wye-Delta Starters

Two starters that are not strictly reduced-voltage starters but which are used, however, to limit motor starting currents, are **part-winding** and **wye-delta starters**.

A requirement for the use of part-winding starting is that the motor must have two separate parallel windings with six leads brought out of the motor to the starter. The starter is designed to connect one of the three-phase motor windings to the supply when the starting impulse is received. After a time delay during which the motor accelerates, the starter automatically connects the second motor winding to the supply in parallel with the first. Although full voltage is applied to each of the motor windings, the initial motor starting current is considerably less than the starting current resulting from normal full-voltage starting of the standard motor. Care must be exercised in the application of this starting method, however, since the torque produced by the first half of the motor winding may be inadequate to accelerate some high-inertia loads.

Wye-delta starting, as the name implies, involves connecting a motor winding first in wye during the starting period and then in delta after the motor has begun to accelerate. Thus, during the starting period the supply phase voltage, which is only 57.7 percent of the line voltage, is applied to the motor winding and the starting inrush is reduced proportionally. Both ends of each phase of the motor winding must be brought out to the starter so that switching may be accomplished. This starter is often used for starting motors which drive loads having long acceleration times.

Fig. 15-19 shows a typical open transition wye-delta motor starter and control circuit. When the start button is initially operated the 1S and 1M contactors both energize, closing their respective contacts to the motor stator windings. This connects the stator winding in a wye configuration during the starting phase. After a time delay occurs the 1S contactor opens and the 2M contactor closes through the timing contacts from contactor 1M. At this point the motor's stator windings are connected in a delta configuration for its running phase.

15-19
AC Motor Drives

DC motor drives were the first to employ solid-state components. As a result the solid-state dc motor drive has dominated both the industrial and consumer markets in the past. However, solid-state ac drives have been developed to the point where they are competitive with the dc drives for many applications. In the solid-state ac drive, the induction or synchronous ac motor replaces the more complicated and less efficient dc motor used in the dc drives.

FIGURE **15-19**
Wye-delta starting.

Four of the more generally used types of solid-state ac drive systems are discussed briefly here, namely, the primary-voltage control drive, the cycloconverter drive, the inverter drive, and the wound-rotor drive.

Primary-Voltage Control AC Drives

This drive system, sometimes called the phase-controlled converter drive, is the simplest and least costly solid-state ac drive system. In this system, the voltage applied to a squirrel-cage induction motor is varied by controlling the firing time of SCRs connected between the ac supply and the motor as would be the case in a rheostat or a variable-voltage transformer.

When the voltage applied to a running induction motor is reduced, the strength of the rotating magnetic field in the air gap is reduced. This results in less voltage being induced in the rotor, less rotor current developed, and less torque developed, and so the motor slows down. It was shown in Eq. (15-7) that the torque reduces approximately as the square of the reduction in voltage. Standard squirrel-cage motors are not suited for primary voltage control service because they overheat when they are operated at the lower voltages. Because of this, the usual motor used with this drive is the CEMA design D motor, which has a high resistance rotor and a slip of 8 to 13 percent.

Several thyristor circuit configurations have been used to vary the voltage applied to the motor. Tests conducted by one research organization indicate that two phase-controlled thyristors in each of the three phases supplying a wye-connected motor resulted in the best motor performance. This is the configuration often used for this drive.

The primary-voltage control ac drive system has speed-torque characteristics that suit it for pump and fan drives in ratings generally below 125 hp. This drive has been used in single-pump drives and also in multiple pump drives. In these systems, a programmed control of several motors is used to maintain a constant liquid level in storage tanks or reservoirs.

Cycloconverter AC Motor Drive

The cycloconverter drive consists of a frequency converter with an adjustable-frequency output driving a synchronous or induction motor. Power conversion is accomplished by a set of thyristors in each phase of the three-phase input, a total of 36 thyristors being used in one system. Triggering of the thyristors is such that small increments of primary power are successively switched in a manner to simulate a lower-frequency sine wave in the output.

Advantages claimed for the cycloconverter are minimum heating, high efficiency, and the capability of motor regeneration and reversing. A major limitation is the low-frequency output when this system is operated from commercial 50 or 60 Hz systems. This drive is an economically attractive one for large low-speed loads such as papermaking machines, mine hoists, ball mills, or other machines having large slow-speed revolving drums. For some applications, a completely gearless ac drive using a single low-speed synchronous motor supplied from a cycloconverter can be used to replace earlier, much more complicated conventional drives.

Inverter AC Motor Drive

The inverter drive, like the cycloconverter, is an adjustable-frequency ac drive. However, unlike the cycloconverter, which provides a direct ac to ac conversion, the inverter drive consists of a rectifier that provides dc power from the ac line. An inverter then converts the dc power to an adjustable-frequency power supply for the motor. The elements of an inverter drive system are shown in Fig. 15-20.

FIGURE **15-20**
Block diagram of an inverter ac motor drive.

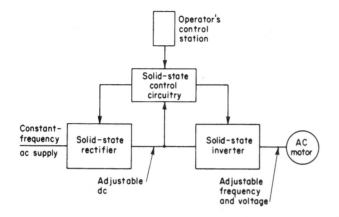

Several configurations are used for the components of the inverter drive, depending upon the manufacturer of the drive and the rating of the drive. For example, the drive represented in Fig. 15-20 is supplied by one manufacturer in a range of sizes from 1 to 5 hp. Incoming 230 V, single phase ac is rectified to a constant-voltage dc. The dc is then inverted by a transistor inverter section to an adjustable-frequency, three-phase output with a frequency range of 6 to 120 Hz. Output is suitable for operating standard three-phase squirrel cage induction motors. Special features that can be provided with the drive include reversing, dynamic braking, and several variations in the control devices supplied with the operator's station.

The inverter drive has a wider frequency and speed range than the cycloconverter and can be operated up to the supply frequency, and as high as 100 percent above that frequency in some systems. Applications of the inverter drive are for machine tools, conveyors, pumps, and air-handling systems. One important application of this drive has been in synthetic-fibre-spinning lines where a highly accurate power supply is required for variable-speed synchronous motors.

The Wound-Rotor Drive

As indicated in Sec. 15-11, the wound-rotor or slip-ring induction motor has an insulated three-phase rotor winding usually wye-connected and terminated in three slip rings. Three external variable resistors are connected through brushes to the rotor slip rings during the starting period, giving the motor a high starting torque with a low starting current. Conventionally, the external resistance is in the form of three rheostats, often manually operated. After the motor is accelerated to near full speed, the rheostats are usually bypassed. However, limited speed control can be provided by inserting rotor resistance during motor operation. This method of speed control is inefficient since power is wasted as heat in the rheostats. This method of control is illustrated in Fig. 15-11.

With the advent of solid-state power and control devices, developments have overcome some of the undesirable features of wound-rotor drives. Control systems are now available in which the external rotor resistance may be controlled electronically. This makes possible automatic control of both motor starting and motor speed. Slip power recovery systems have also been developed that improve wound-rotor-drive efficiency.

The components of one automatic control system in which rotor resistance is controlled electronically for motor starting and speed control are shown in Fig. 15-21. As shown, the three rotor currents are converted to a single direct current by a three-phase bridge rectifier. The dc is supplied to a single resistor through a smoothing reactor. Connected in parallel with the resistor is an electronic chopper consisting of one or more thyristors and solid-state circuitry. The chopper functions as an electronic switch that opens and closes at a rapid rate in response to the control circuitry. By varying the length of the ON and OFF periods, it is possible to obtain a variation in the value of the effective resistance between zero and its full value. Feedback control (not shown) from a speed-sensing device on the motor shaft can be used to vary the effective resistance to maintain a constant preset speed on the motor.

The efficiency of a wound-rotor motor operating at reduced speed can be improved by an arrangement in which the rotor slip power is returned to the ac supply rather than being wasted as heat in the rotor rheostat. The essentials of such a circuit are shown in Fig. 15-22.

F I G U R E **15-21**

Block diagram of an electronic starting and speed control system for a wound-rotor motor.

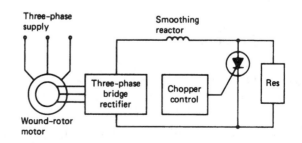

F I G U R E **15-22**
Slip power recovery system.

The slip power recovery system, when equipped with the necessary controls, is ideally suited for any application where a wound-rotor must be run at less than its rated speed. Water pump and fan drives are typical applications for this system.

Induction-motor losses include stator and rotor copper losses, stator and rotor core losses, and friction and windage losses. As in the transformer, the core losses are practically constant for all loads. For practical purposes, the friction and windage losses are also considered to be constant. The copper losses, of course, vary with the load.

The efficiency curve of a typical 15 hp squirrel-cage motor is shown in Fig. 15-9. Note that the efficiency increases with load up to about three-fourths full load; above this point it begins to decrease because of the relatively larger values of I^2R loss.

In general, the larger the motor, the higher the full-load efficiency. Average values of full-load efficiencies of squirrel-cage motors are about as follows: 5 hp, 83 percent; 25 hp, 88 percent; and 100 hp, 90 percent. Wound-rotor motor efficiencies are slightly lower.

A large part of the total electric energy used by modern industry is used by ac polyphase motors in the size range of 1 to 100 hp. Any increase in the efficiency of this class of motors, therefore, has the potential for effecting large energy-cost savings. Recognizing this, motor manufacturers have designed a series of **energy-efficient** motors having higher than standard efficiencies. This improved efficiency is obtained by the use of special low-loss lamination steel, longer stators and rotors, and by other similar design changes. These changes result in higher production costs and, in turn, a premium-priced motor. Motor users are thus offered the

|15-**20**

Induction-Motor Losses, Efficiency, and Ratings

opportunity, when purchasing a motor, to weigh the economics of a higher first cost of an energy-efficient motor against the savings in energy cost over the life of the motor.

Motor nameplate data usually includes the following in addition to the manufacturer's serial, frame, and type numbers: horsepower, speed, voltage, frequency, and temperature rise in a specified time. If a motor is designed to be used on more than one voltage or to operate at more than one speed by reconnecting the windings, a connection diagram is also often included on the nameplate.

A code letter which indicates the motor input in kilovoltamperes per horsepower with the rotor at a standstill is included on the nameplate of motors larger than 1/2 hp. This information is used in determining the size of fuses or circuit breakers to be used in the motor supply circuit.

Another item found on most motor nameplates is a number called the service factor. When rated voltage and frequency are maintained on the motor under standard specified operating conditions, the motor may be overloaded up to the horsepower obtained by multiplying the nameplate horsepower by the service factor. This means, for example, that a motor rated at 10 hp and having a service factor of 1.15, may be loaded to 11.5 hp when rated voltage and frequency are maintained at the motor terminals. The service factor for most motors is 1.15.

Squirrel-cage motors are designed to have a wide variety of starting and operating characteristics, the different characteristics being attained largely by different designs of the rotor circuits. The motor referred to in this chapter as the standard motor is a normal-torque normal-starting-current motor and is a general-purpose motor classified by CEMA as a design B motor. Other types of motors designed for special applications include the following: the CEMA design A motor, which has a higher breakdown torque and higher starting current than the design B motor; the CEMA design C motor, a high-starting-torque and normal-breakdown-torque motor; and the CEMA design D motor, which is a high-starting-torque, high-slip motor. The operating characteristics of each are denoted by the name.

REVIEW QUESTIONS

1 What are the two parts of an induction motor? How are the two circuits of an induction motor similar to the circuit of a transformer?

2 How does the construction of the squirrel-cage motor differ from that of the wound-rotor motor? Describe the rotor construction of each.

3 Describe briefly how the rotating magnetic field is produced by the three-phase stator currents. In a two-pole winding, how many revolutions does the rotating magnetic field make in one cycle of the current?

4 In general, what factors determine the synchronous speed of a motor?

5 How may the direction of rotation of a three-phase motor be reversed?

6 Upon what basic principle does the induction motor, like the dc motor, depend for its operation?

7 Describe briefly how torque is produced in an induction motor. Is the direction of rotation of the rotor the same as or opposite to that of the rotating field?

8 Why does an induction motor run at less than synchronous speed? What is the difference between synchronous and rotor speed called?

9 Show why the rotor frequency is equal to the slip multiplied by the stator frequency. To what is the rotor frequency equal when the rotor is at a standstill with the stator excited?

10 What effect does slip have on rotor reactance?

11 What is the order of magnitude of the full-load slip of a standard squirrel-cage motor?

12 Describe the changes in speed, rotor current, and torque as load is added to an induction motor. How is the motor able to adjust its stator current with changes in mechanical load?

13 Upon what factors does the torque of an induction motor depend?

14 What is the effect of the change in rotor frequency as load is increased from no load to full load? What is its effect when the load is increased considerably above full load?

15 What is meant by pull-out or breakdown torque? If load is increased beyond the breakdown torque, what happens to the speed of the motor?

16 In the standard squirrel-cage motor, at about what value of slip does breakdown torque occur? How does the value of rotor resistance affect the point at which breakdown torque occurs?

17 Why is the power factor of a lightly loaded induction motor very low? What happens to the power factor as load is increased on the motor?

18 As load is increased from no load to full load on an induction motor, what happens to the slip, speed, torque, stator current, power factor, and efficiency of the motor?

19 Why does a squirrel-cage motor have a poor starting torque?

20 What are objections to building a squirrel-cage motor with high enough rotor resistance to provide good starting torque?

21 Describe the action of the double-squirrel-cage motor. How does its starting torque and current compare with the standard squirrel-cage motor?

22 How is the rotor circuit of a wound-rotor motor excited?

23 Why does the wound-rotor motor have better starting characteristics than the squirrel-cage motor? What might be some reasons for the fact that wound-rotor motors are used less extensively than squirrel-cage motors?

24 How may the speed of a wound-rotor motor be varied? What are disadvantages of this method of speed control?

25 In what way may a squirrel-cage motor be made to operate over a wide range of continuously adjustable speeds? What are the limitations of this method of speed control?

26 How may the same squirrel-cage motor be made to operate at two definite speeds?

27 What are two general methods of starting squirrel-cage motors?

28 What determines the maximum size of a squirrel-cage motor that can be started on full voltage?

29 It is desired that an air-compressor motor be started automatically by an across-the-line starter that is controlled by a pressure switch on the air tank. Draw a connection diagram showing the starter and control wires. Use a two-wire control and include a thermal overload relay in the diagram.

30 Name three different types of reduced-voltage starters.

31 Describe the operation of a magnetically operated primary-resistor starter.

32 What is a major advantage of solid-state reduced-voltage starters over primary-resistor and autotransformer starters?

33 What are the special motor-design requirements if the motor is to be used with a part-winding or wye-delta starter?

34 What is meant by closed-transition starting?

35 Two motors are started at 50 percent of line voltage, one with a primary-resistor starter and the other with an autotransformer starter. The starting current taken by each motor is 100 A per terminal. What is the value of the current on the line side of the starters in each case?

36 Name four types of solid-state ac motor drives.

37 Why is a standard squirrel-cage motor not suitable for primary voltage control service? Which CEMA design type motor is usually used?

38 What is an advantage of the inverter ac-motor drive over the cycloconverter drive?

39 Draw a schematic diagram of a manually controlled wound-rotor drive.

40 Describe the essential features of a slip-power recovery system when used with a wound-rotor motor.

41 List the losses of an induction motor. Which are considered constant, and which are variable?

42 What is meant by the term motor service factor?

43 What are some of the data usually found on a motor name-plate?

P ROBLEMS

15-1 Find the synchronous speed of a 60-Hz motor that has an eight-pole stator winding.

15-2 Make a table showing the synchronous speeds of 2-, 4-, 6-, 8-, and 12-pole induction motors for frequencies of 25, 50, and 60 Hz.

15-3 A six-pole 60-Hz induction motor has a full-load slip of 5 percent. What is the full-load rotor speed?

15-4 A squirrel-cage-motor stator winding is wound for four poles. At full load, the motor operates at 1720 r/min with a slip speed of 80 r/min. What is the supply frequency?

15-5 What is the rotor frequency of an eight-pole 60-Hz squirrel-cage motor operating at 850 r/min?

15-6 How much larger is the rotor reactance of a squirrel-cage motor at starting (with the rotor at a standstill) than it is when the motor operates at 5 percent slip?

15-7 The three-phase induction motors driving an aircraft carrier have stators that may be connected for either 22 or 44 poles. The frequency of the supply may be varied from 20 to 65 Hz. What are the maximum and minimum synchronous speeds obtainable from the motors?

15-8 A 50-hp 230-V three-phase motor requires a full-load current of 130 A per terminal at a power factor of 88 percent. What is its full-load efficiency?

15-9 A 10-hp 460-V three-phase squirrel-cage motor at three-fourths rated load operates at an efficiency of 85 percent and at a power factor of 85 percent. What is the line current per terminal?

15-10 What are the rated full-load speeds of a 60-Hz motor that may be connected for either four- or eight-pole operation, assuming the motor to operate with a full-load slip of 5 percent for either connection?

15-11 What is the percentage of full-voltage starting torque developed by a motor when it is started at 65 percent of full voltage?

15-12 If the full voltage starting torque is 60 N·m, and rated voltage is 480 V, what would be the reduced starting voltage to provide 30 N·m of starting torque?

Synchronous Motors and Self-Synchronous Apparatus

Just as dc generators may be operated as motors, ac synchronous generators may be operated as motors. If, when two synchronous generators are operating in parallel, the prime mover is disconnected from one, it will continue to rotate, drawing power from the line to supply its losses. When mechanical load is added, the machine continues to operate at a constant speed. When operated in this manner, the machine is called a **synchronous motor**.

The construction of a synchronous motor, except for slight modifications, is the same as synchronous-generator construction. Salient-pole field construction is nearly always used for synchronous motors. Synchronous motors, like generators, may be classified as brush type or brushless type. The brush type, as the name denotes, has slip rings and brushes to connect the machine field to an external excitation supply. The brushless synchronous motor is similar to the brushless ac generator in which the field control and excitation systems are mounted on the rotor. The rotor of a salient-pole brushless synchronous motor is shown in Fig. 16-1.

The three-phase synchronous motor is discussed in this chapter. Single-phase synchronous motors are discussed in Chap. 17.

16-1

Operation of the Synchronous Motor

When an induction motor is connected to a three-phase supply, a rotating magnetic field is established which induces currents in the rotor windings, thereby producing a torque. The rotor can never turn at synchronous speed, since there must be relative motion between the rotating magnetic field and the rotor in order that currents can be induced in the rotor circuit.

When the stator windings of a synchronous motor are excited with three-phase voltages, a rotating magnetic field is established as in the induction motor. However, in the synchronous motor, the rotor circuit is not excited by induction but by a source of direct current as in the ac generator. If the rotor is brought up to synchronous speed by some means, with the rotor poles excited, the poles of the rotor are attracted by the poles of the rotating magnetic field and the rotor continues to turn at synchronous speed. In other words, the rotor is locked into step magnetically with the rotating magnetic field. If for any reason the rotor is pulled out of

F I G U R E **16-1**
Rotor of a slow-speed brushless synchronous motor.
(Cooper Industries.)

step with the rotating stator flux, the attraction is lost and torque is no longer developed. Therefore, a synchronous motor develops torque only when it is running at synchronous speed. With the stator of a motor energized and the magnetic field revolving at synchronous speed, and with the rotor at a standstill, the rotor poles are first attracted in one direction and then the other, resulting in a net torque of zero. It is evident, then, that a synchronous motor is not self-starting. See Fig. 16-3.

16-2

Starting a Synchronous Motor

Since a synchronous motor is not self-starting, some auxiliary means must be provided to start the motor. One starting method consists of using a small auxiliary induction motor to accelerate the rotor of the main motor to synchronous speed. This starting method is seldom used, however, and most synchronous motors are started by the use of a squirrel-cage winding which is embedded in the face of the rotor poles. The motor is then started as an induction motor and is accelerated to near synchronous speed by this means. At the proper instant, dc field excitation is applied and the motor pulls into synchronism. The squirrel-cage winding may be seen on the rotor shown in Fig. 16-1.

The amount of torque that a motor is able to exert when pulling into synchronism is called the **pull-in torque**. The value of pull-in torque developed by a synchronous motor varies widely with the application for which the motor is designed. For reciprocating compressors, a common application for synchronous-motor drive, the motor is designed to have a pull-in torque of about 50 percent of full-load value. Motors for other applications may be designed to have pull-in torques as high as 150 percent of full-load torque.

During the starting period, while the rotor is at a standstill, or is rotating at a speed much lower than synchronous speed, the rotating magnetic field rapidly cuts across the dc field coils, inducing an emf in them. Since each field coil is wound with many turns and the several coils are connected in series, the induced emf may become dangerously high. The usual method of limiting the value of field voltage during starting is to short-circuit the field winding through a field discharge resistor. This resistor is disconnected as the motor nears synchronous speed.

Low-speed synchronous motors equipped with squirrel-cage starting windings are usually started on full voltage. Reduced-voltage starting, using autotransformer or resistor-type starters, is very often used on high-speed motors or on other motors that require large amounts of starting current or where voltage fluctuations on the supply circuits must be kept to a minimum.

A starter designed for full-voltage starting of a brush-type synchronous motor is shown in Fig. 16-2. Starters of the type shown perform several functions in starting a motor and protecting it from damage during both the starting and running periods. These functions are described briefly in the following.

In the synchronous-motor starter, a line contactor similar to that used in induction-motor starters is used to energize the stator windings. To prevent damage from the voltage induced in the field windings, a field contactor in the starter short-circuits the field winding through a field-discharge resistor during the starting period and opens when the motor nears synchronous speed. After the motor accelerates to approximately 95 percent of synchronous speed, synchronizing equipment in the starter energizes the motor field. This function is usually controlled by a field-frequency relay which assures application of the field at the proper motor speed.

If the starting period of a synchronous motor is prolonged for any reason, the squirrel-cage winding may be overheated since it is designed for starting duty only. Likewise, the cage winding is subject to damage if the motor should pull out of synchronism and continue to run as an induction motor. Protective devices in the motor starter are used to detect these conditions and open the motor power supply.

As in an induction-motor starter, thermal overload relays are normally a part of the protective equipment in a synchronous-motor starter. Other operating and protective equipment usually

FIGURE **16-2**
Full-voltage synchronous motor starter.
(Square D Company.)

included are start-stop push buttons, a dc field ammeter, an ac ammeter, and a loss-of-field relay. In the starter shown in Fig. 16-2, a number of the synchronizing and protective functions are performed by a solid-state module which monitors motor operation during the starting and running periods.

16-3

Synchronous-Motor Excitation

As indicated earlier, excitation systems for synchronous motors may be external to the motor and connected to the motor field through slip rings and brushes or the motor may be the brushless type. The brushless type is largely supplanting the brush type primarily because many moving parts such as brushes, commutators, slip rings,

FIGURE **16-3**
The torque developed by the rotor is equal in alternate directions. No starting torque is produced.

and relays are replaced by static solid-state components mounted on the rotor of the brushless motor.

The brushless excitation system uses an ac exciter mounted on the main motor spider. The armature of the ac exciter may be seen in the photo of the brushless synchronous motor in Fig. 16-1. The output of the exciter is rectified by a silicon diode bridge-type rectifier which is also mounted on the main rotor. It is this rectifier output that is connected directly to the motor field. The need for brushes and slip rings is, therefore, eliminated. Also mounted on the rotor are the field-discharge resistor and the semiconductor control circuitry. This control circuitry automatically switches the field-discharge resistor during starting and automatically applies the field excitation to the motor at the proper time to cause it to pull into step. Protective equipment acts to de-energize the field circuit should the motor pull out of synchronism. A simplified block diagram of a brushless synchronous motor is shown in Fig. 16-4.

In dc motors and induction motors, an addition of load causes the motor speed to decrease. The decrease in speed reduces the counter emf enough so that additional current is drawn from the source to carry the increased load at a reduced speed. In the synchronous motor, this action cannot take place since the rotor is locked into step magnetically with the rotating magnetic field and must continue to rotate at synchronous speed for all loads.

The relative positions of a stator pole and a dc field pole of a synchronous motor running at no load are shown in Fig. 16-5(a).

16-4

Effect of Load on a Synchronous Motor

FIGURE 16-4
Simplified diagram of a brushless synchronous motor.

FIGURE **16-5**

(*a*) Relative positions of a dc field pole and a pole of the rotating magnetic field of a synchronous motor at no load. (*b*) As load is added, the dc field pole drops behind the rotating magnetic field.

The centre lines of the two poles coincide. However, when load is added to the motor, there is a backward shift of the rotor pole relative to the stator pole, as shown in Fig. 16-5(*b*). There is no change in speed; there is merely a shift in relative positions of the two poles, both of which continue to rotate at synchronous speed. The angular displacement between the rotor and stator poles is called the **torque angle**.

When a synchronous motor operates at no load or with a torque angle of practically 0°, the counter emf of the motor is equal and opposite to the applied or terminal voltage (neglecting the motor losses). With increasing loads and torque angles, the phase position of the counter emf changes with respect to the applied voltage, which allows more stator current to flow to carry the additional load. This can best be shown by phasor diagrams.

The phasor diagram in Fig. 16-6(*a*) represents the condition in a synchronous motor at no load, the counter emf E being equal

FIGURE **16-6**

Phasor diagrams of a synchronous motor for three different load conditions, all at the same field excitation.

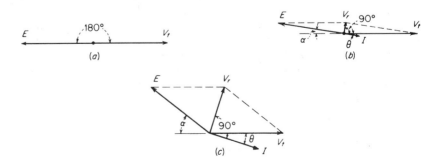

and opposite to the applied V_t. In Fig. 16-6(b), enough load has been added to cause E to drop behind its no-lead position by the angle α, corresponding to the change in torque angle similar to that shown in Fig. 16-5. The applied and counter voltages are no longer in direct opposition, their resultant being the voltage V_r, as shown. The resultant voltage V_r causes a current I to flow in the stator windings; I lags V_r, by nearly 90° owing to the high inductance of the stator windings. The power input to the motor is thus $V_t I \cos \theta$ (for one phase), θ being the angle between the terminal voltage V_t and the stator current I.

A further increase in load results in a larger torque angle which, in turn, increases the values of V_r and I as shown in Fig. 16-6(c). Thus, a synchronous motor is able to supply increasing mechanical loads, not by a decrease in speed but by a shift in relative positions of the rotor and the rotating magnetic field. Note in Fig. 16-6 that for increasing loads with a constant value of E the phase angle θ increases in the lagging direction.

If too great a mechanical load is placed on a synchronous motor, the rotor is pulled out of synchronism, after which it comes to a stop; or if it has a squirrel-cage winding, it continues to operate as an induction motor until protective devices operate to stop the motor. The maximum value of torque that a motor can develop without losing its synchronism is called its **pull-out torque**. Pull-out torque, like pull-in torque, may be designed for widely varying values, depending on the application of the motor. These values range from 125 to 350 percent of full-load torque values.

16-5
Power Factor; Effect of Changing Field Excitation

One of the outstanding characteristics of a synchronous motor is the fact that it may be made to operate over a wide range of power factors by adjustment of its field excitation.

Fig. 16-7(a) shows the phasor diagram of a synchronous motor with a mechanical load which results in the torque angle α and with the field excitation adjusted so that the motor operates at unity power factor. If, while the motor is carrying the same mechanical load, the field excitation is increased, the counter emf E increases to the value shown in Fig. 16-7(b). This results in a change in phase position of the stator current I with respect to the terminal voltage V_t, so that the motor then operates at a leading power factor. Since the power output is unchanged, the value of I must increase with the decrease in power factor. Further increases in field excitation cause the motor to operate at a still more leading power factor with corresponding increases in stator current.

Fig. 16-7(c) shows what happens if the field excitation is reduced below the value represented in Fig. 16-7(a). A reduction in excitation changes the power factor in the lagging direction, and as the

FIGURE **16-7**
Phasor diagrams of a synchronous motor with a constant mechanical load but with different amounts of field excitation. (*a*) Field excitation is adjusted for unity-power-factor operation. (*b*) Field is overexcited. (*c*) Field is underexcited.

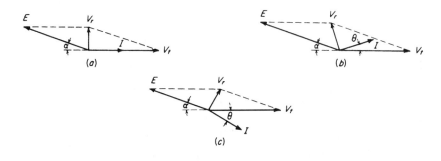

excitation is further reduced it becomes still more lagging with corresponding increases in stator current.

Hence, for a given load, the power factor of a synchronous motor may be varied from a low lagging value to a low leading value. Fig. 16-8 shows the variation of armature current and power factor of a synchronous motor with a variation of field excitation and for a constant load.

The normal value of field current for a given load is that value which results in unity power factor and a minimum stator current at that load. When the motor is overexcited, it operates at a leading power factor; when it is underexcited, it operates at a lagging power factor.

16-6
Efficiency and Ratings

The efficiency of synchronous motors is, in general, higher than that of induction motors of the same horsepower and speed rating. The losses are identical with those of synchronous generators.

Synchronous motors are divided into two distinct classifications as to speed: motors with speeds above 500 r/min are classed as high-speed motors, and those with speeds less than 500 r/min are classed as low-speed motors.

Synchronous motors are rated as unity-power-factor, 90 percent leading-power-factor, or 80 percent leading-power-factor motors. Other power-factor ratings may be used for special applications. While leading-power-factor motors provide more power-factor correction, they are more expensive than unity-power-factor motors since they must have larger current-carrying capacities.

Unity-power-factor motors may be operated at leading power factors but with less than rated horsepower output. This is because more than rated stator current must flow to carry the rated horsepower load at a reduced power factor. Likewise, field current must be increased above normal value.

FIGURE **16-8**
Variation of stator current and motor power factor with a variation of field excitation at a constant load.

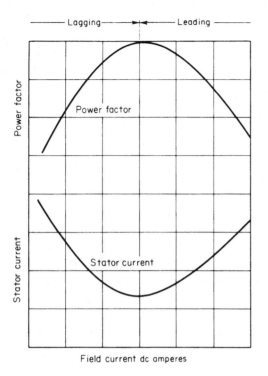

Synchronous-motor nameplate data include the same items found on ac generator nameplates with the kilovoltampere rating being replaced with a horsepower rating.

Synchronous motors are used for constant-speed power applications in sizes above 20 hp and more often in sizes larger than 100 hp. A very common application is for driving air or gas compressors. It is especially desirable that compressors be driven at a constant speed since their output and efficiency vary considerably with the speed at which they are operated.

Other common applications are in public-works pumping and for driving fans, blowers, and pulverizers. The advent of the brushless synchronous motor has increased the field of synchronous-motor application so that they are now used where formerly only induction motors were considered.

An outstanding advantage of synchronous motors is the fact that they operate at unity or leading power factors. When operated on the same electrical system with induction motors (or other devices that operate at lagging power factors), the leading reactive kilovoltamperes supplied by the synchronous motors compensate for

16-7
Application of Synchronous Motors

16-8
Power-Factor Correction

the lagging reactive kilovoltamperes of other devices; this results in an improvement in the overall power factor.

Low power factors are undesirable for several reasons. Generators, transformers, and supply circuits are limited in ratings by their current-carrying capacities. This means that the kilowatt load that they can deliver is directly proportional to the power factor of the loads that they supply. For example, a system can deliver only 70 percent of the kilowatt load at 0.7 power factor that it can deliver at unity power factor.

The voltage regulation of generators, transformers, and supply lines is also poorer at low power factors than at unity power factor.

Since line and equipment losses are proportional to I^2R, these losses are higher in an electrical system for a given kilowatt load at low power factors than at unity power factor. Thus, any improvement in power factor increases system efficiency and, in general, improves the operating characteristics of the system. For this reason electrical system operators often include power-factor clauses in industrial power contracts which place a penalty on a consumer for operating at a power factor below a certain value.

To gain some of the above-mentioned benefits from high power factors, very often synchronous motors are used to compensate for the lagging reactive kilovoltamperes taken by induction motors. The following example will be used to illustrate how a synchronous motor when used on the same system with induction motors improves the overall power factor.

Example 16-1

The load of an industrial site is 400 kVA at a power factor of 75 percent, lagging. An additional motor load of 100 kW is needed. Find the new kilovoltampere load and the power factor of the load if the motor to be added is (*a*) an induction motor with a power factor of 90 percent, lagging, and (*b*) an 80 percent power-factor (leading) synchronous motor.

Original load, 400 kVA at 75 percent power factor.

$$\text{kW} = 400 \times 0.75 = 300 \text{ kW}$$

$$(\text{kVA})^2 = (\text{kW})^2 + (\text{kvar})^2$$

$$\text{kvar} = \sqrt{(\text{kVA})^2 - (\text{kW})^2}$$

$$= \sqrt{400^2 - 300^2} = 264.6 \text{ kvar, lagging}$$

(*a*) Induction motor, 100 kW at 90 percent lagging power factor.

$$kVA = \frac{kW}{power\ factor} = \frac{100}{0.9}$$

$$= 111.1\ kVA$$

$$kvar = \sqrt{(111.1)^2 - (100)^2}$$

$$= 48.4\ kvar,\ lagging$$

$$Resultant\ kilowatt\ load = 300 + 100 = 400\ kW$$

$$Resultant\ kilovoltampere\ load = \sqrt{(kW)^2 + (kvar)^2}$$

$$= \sqrt{(400)^2 + (313)^2}$$

$$= 507.8\ kVA$$

$$Resultant\ power\ factor = \frac{kW}{kVA} = \frac{400}{507.8}$$

$$= 0.787 = 78.7\ \%,\ lagging$$

Since the relation between kilowatts, kilovars, and kilovolt-amperes of any load may be represented by a right triangle, the solution of the above problem may be made graphically as shown in Fig. 16-9. The triangle *OAE* represents the original load; $OE = 300$ kW, $EA = 264.6$ kvar, and $OA = 400$ kVA. The angle θ_1 is the power-factor angle of the original load. Triangle *ABC* represents the added induction-motor load, sides *AC*, *CB*, and *AB* representing 100 kW, 48.4 kvar, and 111.1 kVA,

FIGURE **16-9**
Graphical solution for Example 16-1(*a*).

Triangle *OAE* = Original load
Triangle *ABC* = Added load
Triangle *OBD* = Resultant load

respectively, with the phase angle represented as θ_2. Triangle *OBD* represents the resultant load with sides *OD*, *DB*, and *OB* representing 400 kW, 313 kvar, and 507.8 kVA, respectively. The resultant power-factor angle is θ_3.

(*b*) Synchronous motor, 100 kW at 80 percent leading power factor.

$$\text{kVA} = \frac{\text{kW}}{\text{power factor}} = \frac{100}{0.8} = 125 \text{ kVA}$$

$$\text{kvar} = \sqrt{(125)^2 - (100)^2} = 75 \text{ kvar (leading)}$$

$$\text{Resultant kilowatt load} = 300 + 100 = 400 \text{ kW}$$

$$\text{Resultant kilovar load} = 264.6 \text{ (lagging)}$$

$$- 75 \text{ (leading)}$$

$$= 189.6 \text{ kvar (lagging)}$$

$$\text{Resultant kilovoltampere load} = \sqrt{(\text{kW})^2 + (\text{kvar})^2}$$

$$= \sqrt{(400)^2 + (189.6)^2}$$

$$= 442.5 \text{ kVA}$$

$$\text{Resultant power factor} = \frac{\text{kW}}{\text{kVA}} = \frac{400}{442.5} = 0.903$$

$$= 90.3\%, \text{ lagging}$$

The graphical solution is shown in Fig. 16-10, with triangles *OEA*, *ABC*, and *OCD* representing the original load, the added load, and the resultant load, respectively.

F I G U R E **16-10**
Graphical solution for Example 16-1(*b*).

Triangle *OAE* = Original load
Triangle *ABC* = Added load
Triangle *OCD* = Resultant load

Synchronous motors when operated without mechanical load and for the purpose of improving power factor are called **synchronous condensers**. By considerably overexciting its field, a synchronous condenser is made to operate at a very low leading power factor, the only kilowatt input required being that necessary to supply its losses. When used at the end of a long transmission line, the synchronous condenser neutralizes the effects of lagging-power-factor loads, thereby improving the regulation of the transmission line.

SELF-SYNCHRONOUS APPARATUS

Self-synchronous devices are used to transmit motion electrically between two points. Self-synchronous indicating systems are used for transmitting messages or orders between two points, such as between the bridge and engine room of a ship. They are also used to provide an indication of some mechanical motion at distant points such as indications of wind direction, wind velocity, speed of a rotating shaft, the difference in speed of two rotating shafts, or the angular position of some mechanical device. Automatic control of operations remote from the point of control may also be accomplished by self-synchronous apparatus. As power-transmission devices, self-synchronous systems are used to maintain synchronism between several driving units such as between the driving units at each end of a lift bridge or between the many units of large newspaper presses.

Self-synchronous indicators are very similar in construction to small synchronous motors. A simple indicating system consists of a self-synchronous generator or transmitter, and a self-synchronous motor or receiver. The stators of each have three uniformly distributed windings very similar to the three-phase windings used in synchronous motors and generators. The rotors are of two-pole salient-pole construction. The transmitter and receiver rotors are similar in construction except that the receiver is equipped with a damper ring mounted on the shaft to prevent excessive oscillations and to prevent the receiver from starting as an induction motor. A typical receiver is shown in Fig. 16-11.

The rotor or primary circuits of both transmitter and receiver are excited from a single-phase ac supply, and the stator or secondary windings of the transmitter are connected to those of the receiver as shown in Fig. 16-12.

When the primary circuits are energized, emfs are induced in the secondary windings by transformer action. The value of the emf induced in each of the three secondary windings of both the transmitter and receiver depends on the angular positions of

16-9

Self-Synchronous Indicators

FIGURE **16-11**
Self-synchronous receiver assembly.
(General Electric Company.)

the rotors. When the rotors of the transmitter and receiver are in the same relative position, the secondary emfs induced in the transmitter are equal and opposite to those of the receiver and no secondary current flows. However, if the position of the transmitter rotor is changed, the secondary emfs are no longer balanced, resulting in the flow of current through the secondary circuits of both the transmitter and receiver. The action of the secondary currents is to produce torque in both the transmitter and receiver. The torque in the transmitter is a restraining torque, opposing the motion of the rotor, while that in the receiver attempts to move the receiver rotor to a new position where the secondary emfs are again balanced. Hence, if the receiver rotor is free to turn, it will follow any motion of the transmitter. If the transmitter rotor is moved, say, 30° clockwise, the receiver rotor also moves 30° in the clockwise direction. If the rotor of the transmitter is rotated at a speed of, say, 20 r/min, the receiver rotor follows in synchronism at 20 r/min. Thus, either angular motions or rotation may be transmitted by the system. The transmitter rotor may be moved automatically by means of gears from some mechanical motion or may be moved manually by an operator.

FIGURE **16-12**
Circuits of a simple self-synchronous system.

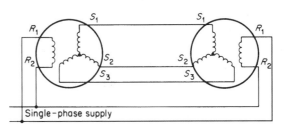

Single-phase supply

The simple indicating system shown in Fig. 16-12 may be extended so that one transmitter may be made to operate several receivers simultaneously. Selective operation may also be provided, with the transmitter being connected to any one of several receivers one at a time.

Self-synchronous motors used for synchronized power drives are very similar in construction to three-phase wound-rotor induction motors. The primary windings are excited from a three-phase supply and the secondary windings are interconnected.

The respective units of the system are synchronized by first applying single-phase excitation, the three-phase excitation being applied after a time delay of a few seconds. This is necessary since if three-phase excitation were applied when the rotors were not in synchronous positions the unbalanced secondary emfs might allow enough secondary current to flow to allow the motors to start as induction motors. Once synchronized, the various units all rotate at the same speed or at definite speed ratios over the required speed range.

16-**10**
Self-Synchronous Power Drives

R EVIEW QUESTIONS

1 How does the construction of a synchronous motor compare with that of a synchronous generator?

2 Describe the principle of operation of a synchronous motor. How does the principle of operation of a synchronous motor differ from that of an induction motor?

3 What determines the speed of a synchronous motor? How may the speed be varied?

4 How would it be possible to reverse the direction of rotation of a synchronous motor?

5 Why is a synchronous motor not self-starting? Name some ways in which they are started.

6 What is pull-in torque?

7 What precaution must be taken in regard to the field circuit of a synchronous motor during the starting period?

8 What types of controllers are used for starting synchronous motors? What forms of motor protection are generally provided?

9 How does a synchronous motor adjust its electric input with changes in mechanical output?

10 For a constant field excitation, what is the effect on the motor power factor of an increasing load?

11 What is meant by the pull-out torque of a synchronous motor?

12 For a constant mechanical output, how may the power factor at which a synchronous motor operates be changed?

13 Compare the method of adjusting the power factor of a synchronous motor with the method of adjusting the power factor of a synchronous generator operating in parallel with other synchronous generators.

14 When is a synchronous motor said to be (*a*) overexcited, (*b*) underexcited?

15 How are synchronous motors classified as to speed?

16 What are the standard power-factor ratings of synchronous motors?

17 What precaution must be taken in operating a synchronous motor at a power factor that is more leading than its rated power factor?

18 Under what operating condition would the field circuit be apt to heat abnormally?

19 What are some applications of synchronous motors?

20 Why is a low power factor undesirable?

21 Explain how a synchronous motor can improve the power factor of a load with a low lagging power factor.

22 What is a synchronous condenser?

23 What are some uses of self-synchronous devices?

24 Describe the construction of the self-synchronous receiver. How does it differ from the transmitter?

25 Describe the operation of the simple self-synchronous indicating system. Compare its operation with that of two single-phase transformers operating in parallel.

PROBLEMS

16-1 What is the speed of a 30-pole 60-Hz 440-V synchronous motor? Is this motor classed as a high- or low-speed motor?

16-2 What is the percent speed regulation of the motor in Prob. 16-1?

16-3 A motor-generator set used for frequency conversion consists of a 10-pole 25-Hz synchronous motor and a direct-connected 24-pole synchronous generator. What is the generator frequency?

16-4 If a six-pole induction motor electrically connected to the generator terminals in Prob. 16-3 has a full-load slip of 5 percent, what is its full-load speed in revolutions per minute?

16-5 The propulsion motors used on a naval vessel are rated 5900 hp, three-phase, 2400 V, 62.5 Hz, and 139 r/min. How many poles do they have? The speed of the above motors may be varied by a variation of the supply frequency between 16 and 62.5 Hz. What are the maximum and minimum speeds? Assuming a full-load efficiency of 85 percent and unity power factor, what is the full-load current input per terminal?

16-6 In Example 16-1, what must be the power factor of the added 100 kW load if it improves the overall plant power factor to 100 percent?

16-7 A transmission line delivers a load of 7500 kVA at a power factor of 70 percent, lagging. If a synchronous condenser is to be located at the end of the line to improve the load power factor to 100 percent, how many kilovoltamperes must it draw from the line, assuming it to operate at 0 percent leading power factor?

16-8 A synchronous motor which has an input of 480 kW is added to a system which has an existing load of 700 kW at 80 percent lagging power factor. What will be the next system kilowatt load, kilovoltampere load, and power factor if the new motor is operated at (*a*) 80 percent lagging power factor, (*b*) 100 percent power factor, and (*c*) 80 percent leading power factor?

Single-Phase Motors

Single-phase motors may be classified by electrical type into three general classes: (1) series motors, (2) induction motors, and (3) synchronous motors. These three classes of motors are discussed in this chapter.

17-1

The AC Series Motor

Direct-current shunt or series motors rotate in the same direction regardless of the polarity of the supply. Thus, it might be expected that either motor would operate on alternating current. It has been found, however, that the shunt motor develops very little torque when it is connected to an ac supply. The high inductance of the field winding causes the field current to lag the armature current by such a large angle that a very low net torque results. However, in the series motor, the field and armature currents are the same, so that the main field and armature field are in phase. Therefore, about the same torque is developed with a given alternating current as with a like amount of direct current in a series motor.

However, some changes must be made in a dc series motor that is to operate satisfactorily on alternating current. When an ordinary dc series motor is connected to an ac supply, the current drawn by the motor is limited to a relatively low value by the high series-field impedance. Consequently, the power developed is small. To reduce the field reactance to a minimum, ac series motors are built with as few field turns as possible, sufficient field flux being obtained by using a low-reluctance magnetic circuit. The effect of armature reaction in the series motor is overcome by the use of compensating windings in the pole faces. The compensating winding may be short-circuited on itself, in which case the motor is said to be *inductively* compensated, or it may be connected in series with the armature and field, in which case the motor is *conductively* compensated. All parts of the magnetic circuit of an ac series motor must be laminated to reduce the eddy-current losses.

The operating characteristics of the ac series motor are very similar to those of dc series motors. The speed increases to a high value with a decrease in load. In the very small series motors, the losses are usually large enough at no load to limit the speed to a definite value. The torque is high for high armature currents, thus giving the motor a good starting torque.

Since inductive reactance is directly proportional to frequency, ac series-motor operating characteristics are better at lower frequencies. Some series motors are built in large sizes for traction service and are designed to operate at low frequencies, 25 Hz or less. However, fractional horsepower sizes may be designed to operate satisfactorily at 50 or 60 Hz. For some applications, it is desirable to use a motor that will operate on either ac or dc circuits. By a compromise design, fractional-horsepower series motors may be built to operate satisfactorily either on 50 or 60 Hz or on direct current at 115 or 230 V. These motors are called **universal** motors. Common applications for the universal motor are in vacuum cleaners, sewing machines, and portable tools. As in the series dc motor, its rotation may be reversed by changing the source polarity of either the series field or the armature.

17-**2**

The Single-Phase Induction-Motor Principle

In a two-phase induction motor, the phase coils are spaced 90 electrical degrees apart on the stator surface. When these coils are excited by two-phase voltages, that is, voltages which differ in time phase by 90°, the resulting phase currents are out of phase by 90°. Each of the two currents establishes a pulsating or alternating field, but these fields combine to produce a single rotating field as in the three-phase motor (Chap. 15). The rotating field sweeping across the rotor conductors induces a current in these conductors that causes a torque to be developed in the direction of the rotation of the field. This is the basic principle of operation of the two-phase motor. It is briefly reviewed here because conditions in a single-phase motor are similar to those of a two-phase motor.

If a single-phase voltage is applied to the stator winding of a single-phase induction motor, alternating current will flow in that winding. This stator current establishes a field similar to that shown in Fig. 17-1. During the half-cycle that the stator current is flowing in the direction indicated, a south pole is established on the stator surface at A and a north pole at C. During the next half-cycle, the stator poles are reversed. Although the stator field strength is varying and reversing its polarity periodically, its action is always along the line AC. This field, then, does not rotate but it is a pulsating stationary field.

As in a transformer, voltages are induced in the secondary circuit, in this case the rotor. Since single-phase induction-motor rotors are of the squirrel-cage type similar to those of polyphase motors, rotor currents are caused to flow as shown in Fig. 17-1. These rotor currents establish poles on the rotor surface, but since these poles are always in direct line (along the line AC) with the

FIGURE **17-1**

The stator field pulsates along the line *AC*. No torque is developed.

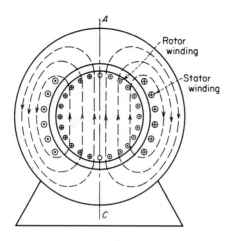

stator poles, no torque is developed in either direction. Therefore, a *single-phase induction motor is not self-starting* and requires some special starting means.

When, however, the single-phase stator winding in Fig. 17-1 is excited and the rotor is made to turn by some auxiliary device that will be described later, the rotor conductors cut across the stator field, causing an emf to be generated in them. This is illustrated in Fig. 17-2 which shows the rotor being turned in a clockwise direction. If the stator flux is upward at the instant shown, the

FIGURE **17-2**

The motor of Fig. 17-1, with the rotor turning, generates an emf in the rotor conductors in the direction shown by the dots and crosses.

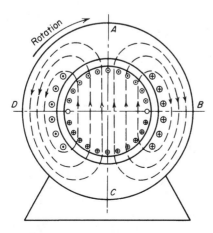

F I G U R E **17-3**
Phase relations of the stator current and flux, the generated rotor emf, and the rotor current and flux. The rotor flux lags the stator flux by 90°.

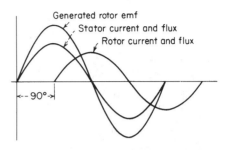

direction of the generated rotor emfs, as determined by Fleming's right-hand rule, will be outward in the upper half of the rotor and inward in the lower half of the rotor, as indicated by the dots and crosses. One-half cycle later the direction of the generated emfs will be reversed. The generated rotor emfs vary *in phase* with the stator current and flux. Because of the low resistance and high inductance of the rotor, however, the resulting rotor current *lags* the generated rotor emf by nearly 90°. Fig. 17-3 shows the phase relations of the stator current and flux, the rotor emf, and the rotor current and flux.

The maximum value of the field produced by the rotor currents, as shown in Fig. 17-4, occurs nearly one-fourth cycle after the generated rotor emf has reached its maximum value. Because this

F I G U R E **17-4**
Cross field established by the rotor currents one-fourth cycle later than the stator field shown in Fig. 17-2.

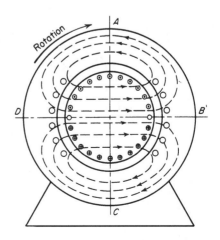

rotor field is at right angles to the stator field, it is called a **cross field**. Since the rotor currents are caused to flow by an alternating emf, the field resulting from these currents also alternates and its action is always along the line *DB*, Fig. 17-4. The cross field is very similar to a field that would be produced by another coil placed on the stator in the spaces at *A* and *C* in Fig. 17-4 and excited by a voltage 90° behind the voltage applied to the coil in place, as in a two-phase motor. Since the cross field acts at right angles to the stator field and also lags the stator field by 90° in **time phase**, the two fields combine to form a resultant rotating field that revolves at synchronous speed.

It should be kept in mind, however, that the cross field is produced by a *generator action* and, therefore, is present only when the rotor is turning. It also follows that the strength and the cross field must be proportional to the rotor speed. At synchronous speed the cross field is nearly the same strength as the stator field. But, since an induction motor must operate at some speed lower than synchronous speed, the cross field is somewhat weaker than the stator field at actual operating speeds. This means that the rotating field in a single-phase induction motor is irregular and is not of constant strength as is the field of a polyphase motor. Therefore, the torque developed by a single-phase induction motor is irregular or pulsating. This is the reason why many single-phase motors are set on rubber or spring mounts to reduce the vibration and noise which are inherent in such motors.

Fig. 17-5 provides a phasor illustration of the cross field theory. The reference oscillogram is graduated every 45 electrical degrees. The resultant phasor is shown for each graduation on the oscillogram. It can be seen that the phasor resultants at each graduation shift 45°, thereby illustrating the rotating magnetic field set up by the stator and rotor fields when the rotor is in motion.

17-**3** Split-Phase Starting

It was shown in the preceding section that, when two windings are spaced 90 electrical degrees apart on the stator of a motor and are excited by two alternating emfs that are 90° displaced in time phase, a rotating magnetic field is produced. If two windings so spaced are connected in parallel to a single-phase source, the field produced will alternate but will not revolve since the two windings are equivalent to but one single-phase winding. If, however, an impedance is connected in series with one of these windings, the currents may be made to differ in time phase. By the proper selection of such an impedance, the currents may be made to differ by as much as 90°, thereby producing a rotating field very much like the field of a two-phase motor. This is the principle of **phase splitting**.

FIGURE **17-5**

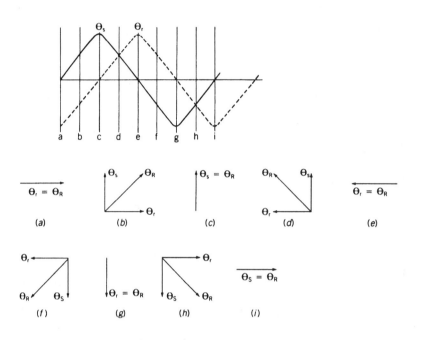

17-**4**

The Resistance-Start Split-Phase Motor

When two similar motor stator windings that are spaced 90 electrical degrees apart are connected in parallel to a single-phase source, the currents through the two windings lag the applied voltage by the same angle. By connecting a resistance in series with one winding, the current through that winding is caused to be more nearly in phase with the applied voltage. Since the current in the first winding is not affected by the addition of the resistance, the currents through the two windings are displaced in time phase. This is the condition necessary to produce a revolving field. A motor using this method of phase splitting is called a **resistance-start motor**. The resistance-start split-phase motor is commonly known as the **split-phase motor** even though there are other forms of split-phase motors.

In practice, instead of using an external series resistor, one winding is designed to have a higher resistance and lower reactance than the other winding. The high-resistance winding is called the **starting** or **auxiliary winding**, and the low-resistance winding is called the **main winding**.

The phase relations of the applied voltage E, the main-winding current I_m, and the starting-winding current I_s at the instant of

FIGURE **17-6**
(a) Phase relations in and (b) connection diagram of the resistance-start motor.

(a)   (b)

starting are shown in Fig. 17-6(a). The angle Φ between the main
and starting winding current is small, being of the order of 30°,
but this is enough phase difference to provide a weak rotating magnetic field. Since the currents in the two windings are not equal in
magnitude, the rotating field is not uniform and the starting torque
produced is small.

Starting torque for a split phase motor is:

$$T = K\,\theta I_s \sin\,(\theta_s - \theta_r)$$

where $K\theta$ is previously defined
                          I_s = motor resultant starting current
       $\sin\,(\theta_s - \theta_r)$ = sine of angle between starting winding and
                          running winding currents

Example 17-1

A resistive-start split-phase motor has a start winding current
of $3.8\underline{/-15°}$ A, and a main (running) winding current of
$5.2\underline{/-45°}$ A.

Determine:

a) the current drawn from the line at the instant of motor start.
b) the angle of the resultant motor starting current.

SOLUTION:

$$I_S = 3.8\underline{/-15°}\ \text{A} = 3.67 - j0.985$$

$$I_m = 5.2\underline{/-45°}\ \text{A} = \underline{3.68 - j3.677}$$

$$7.35 - j4.662 = 8.70\underline{/-32.4°}\ \text{A}$$

Therefore, the resultant starting current is 8.70 A at an angle
of −32.4°.

Fig. 17-7 illustrates the phasor solution for Example 17-1.

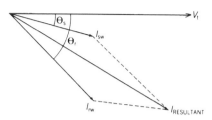

It was shown in the preceding section that a single-phase induction motor develops a torque once it has been started. For this reason, the starting winding of the resistance-start motor is disconnected when the motor reaches a predetermined speed, usually 70 to 80 percent of synchronous speed. This is accomplished by a centrifugally operated or a solid-state switch. A connection diagram showing the main and starting windings of a resistant-start motor is shown in Fig. 17-6(*b*).

The resistance-start split-phase motor is very widely used for easily started loads. Common applications are for driving fans, woodworking tools, grinders, oil burners, and various other low-starting-torque applications. Because of its low starting torque, this motor is seldom used in sizes larger than 1/3 hp. To reverse the direction of rotation of this motor the start winding connections are reversed with respect to the main winding connections.

17-**5**
The Capacitor-Start Motor

An improvement can be made in the starting characteristics of a split-phase motor by connecting a capacitor in series with the starting winding as shown in the connection diagram in Fig. 17-8. A motor of this type is called a **capacitor-start motor**. The current through the main winding lags the applied voltage as in the resistance-start motor. By choosing a capacitor of the proper size, the current in the starting winding may be made to *lead* the voltage. Thus, the time-phase difference Φ in the currents of the two windings at starting may be made nearly 90° as is shown in Fig. 17-8. This more nearly approximates the action of the two-phase revolving field than did the resistance-start motor, thereby resulting in a relatively higher starting torque and a significantly lower starting current.

To provide adequate starting winding current and optimum phase shift, the starting capacitor must have a large microfarad rating. The electrolytic capacitor has a large capacity rating with a relatively small size and low cost and, therefore, is used extensively

FIGURE **17-8**

(a) Phase relations in and (b) connection diagram of the capacitor-start motor.

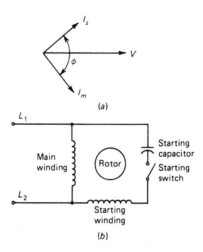

(a)

(b)

for motor-starting duty. This type of capacitor, however, is not suitable to be left permanently connected in the circuit. The capacitor-start motor, like the resistance-start motor, has a starting switch which disconnects the starting winding as the motor approaches synchronous speed.

Starting torque of the general-purpose capacitor-start motor is approximately 350 percent of full-load torque as compared with about 150 percent for the resistance-start split-phase motor.

It can be shown that the starting torque is proportional to the sine of the angle between the running and starting currents.

Therefore, the ratio of starting torque of the capacitor start motor to the resistive start motor is:

$$\frac{\sin \approx 90°}{\sin \approx 30°} = \frac{1}{0.5} = 2 \text{ to } 1 \text{ ratio}$$

This raises the starting torque of the capacitor start motor to approximately the ratio computed above times the starting torque of the resistive-start motor. This is approximately equal to 2×150 = 300 percent of full-load torque or greater. In many cases the cap start induction run motor has starting torques of up to 450 percent full-load torque.

This motor is used for heavy-duty drives such as refrigerators, compressors, pumps, and air conditioners. The usual size range is from 0.125 to 0.75 hp, but sizes up to 2 hp are available. Rotation reversal for this motor is the same procedure as the **resistive-start split phase motor** described in Sec. 17-4.

17-**6**

The Permanent-Split Capacitor Motor

The permanent-split capacitor motor, as the name indicates, has a capacitor permanently connected in series with the starting or auxiliary winding and in parallel with the main winding. The connection diagram, therefore, is the same as that of a capacitor-start motor with the starting switch omitted since both windings remain continuously energized. The operation of the motor is similar to that of a two-phase motor since a rotating magnetic field is established by the two windings for both the starting and running conditions.

It has been found that the size of the capacitor needed to provide the best running conditions for a motor is much smaller than that required to give good starting torque. The permanent-split capacitor motor is, therefore, a compromise design which uses a relatively small oil-filled capacitor rated for continuous duty. This results in a motor which has a very low starting torque but which is quieter and more efficient than the capacitor-start motor.

The permanent-split capacitor motor is used primarily for direct-connected fans and blowers where the motor can be matched accurately with the driven load. Sizes used are generally smaller than 1/3 hp.

Due to the low torque characteristics of the permanent-split capacitor motor, it lends itself to easy rotation reversal. By placing the capacitor in series with one or the other windings will reverse its rotation. This can be accomplished by using a single-pole, double-throw switch as shown in Fig. 17-9.

17-**7**

The Two-Value Capacitor Motor

The two-value capacitor motor is a motor in which a different value of capacitances is used for starting and for running conditions. In the usual switching arrangement, a starting capacitor in series with a starting switch is connected in parallel with a running capacitor and the parallel capacitors are in series with the auxiliary winding as shown in Fig. 17-10. A cutaway view of a two-value capacitor motor is shown in Fig. 17-11.

F I G U R E **17-9**

Permanent-split capacitor motor connected to a single-pole, double-throw switch for the purpose of reversing the rotation of the rotor.

FIGURE **17-10**
Connection diagram of a two-value capacitor motor.

The use of separate starting and running capacitors permits the motor designer to select an optimum size for each, which results in excellent starting torque and good running performance. The starting and running capacitors normally used are electrolytic and oil-filled types, respectively. This motor design is used normally only for larger single-phase motor applications where particularly high-starting torque is required.

A shading coil is a low-resistance short-circuited copper loop which is placed around a part of each pole of a motor. Fig. 17-12 shows one pole of a motor which is equipped with shading coils. As the flux begins its increase at the beginning of the cycle, an emf is induced in the short-circuited coil which causes a current to flow. The field produced by the flow of current is in such a direction as to oppose the change in the main field flux. Thus, the increase in flux is less rapid through the shading coil than in the main part of the pole, as is shown in Fig. 17-12(*a*). Fig. 17-12(*b*) represents the

17-**8**

The Shaded-Pole Motor

FIGURE **17-11**
Cutaway view of a totally enclosed two-value capacitor motor.
(Century Electric Inc.)

F I G U R E **17-12**
Effect of the shading coil on the air-gap flux in a shaded-pole motor.

same pole when the flux has reached a maximum value and is not changing in value. The flux is distributed uniformly across the pole face, since no current is flowing in the shading coil. As the flux decreases, the induced current in the coil is in a direction such that its magnetic effect opposes the decrease in flux. Consequently, the flux decreases less rapidly through the coil than through the other part of the pole as shown in Fig. 17-12(*c*).

The effect of the shading coil is to cause the field flux to shift across the pole face from the unshaded to the shaded portion. This shifting flux, somewhat like a rotating magnetic field, produces a small starting torque. This method of motor starting is used only on very small motors up to about 0.25 hp in size, such as may be used for driving small fans or blowers.

17-**9**

Single-Phase Synchronous Motors

There are three general types of single-phase synchronous motors classified by the type of rotor used: the dc-excited type, the reluctance type, and the hysteresis type. Stator windings used with any of these different rotors may be similar to those of single-phase induction motors; that is, they may be split-phase resistance, capacitor, or shaded-pole windings.

The **single-phase dc-excited synchronous motor**, like the larger synchronous motors described in Chap. 16, requires a dc supply to energize the rotor winding. Rotor poles lock into step with the stator rotating magnetic field, and the rotor turns at synchronous speed. Because of its high cost and the need for a separate dc field excitation supply, this motor is seldom used except for a few precision drive applications.

Reluctance-type single-phase synchronous motors have modified squirrel-cage rotors. The laminated steel part of the rotor is cut away at evenly spaced areas forming salient poles on the rotor surface. The number of poles formed corresponds to the number of poles for which the stator is wound. Rotor bars of conducting material are spaced around the entire rotor circumference as in the induction-motor rotor.

When the stator winding of the reluctance motor is energized, a magnetic field is established as in the single-phase induction motor; currents are induced in the rotor cage winding, and the rotor accelerates to near synchronous speed. Since the salient poles on the rotor provide the lowest reluctance path for the stator flux, they are attracted to the poles of the stator magnetic field and the rotor pulls into step with the rotating stator field.

The amount of torque that a reluctance motor, or any synchronous motor, is able to exert to pull the rotor and driven load into synchronism is called the pull-in torque. Load torque is produced by an angular shift between stator and rotor poles as described for the three-phase synchronous motor in Chap. 16. If load is added to the motor beyond its capability, the rotor is pulled out of synchronism. The torque developed at this point is called the pull-out torque.

Because of their inherently low pull-out torque, low power factor, and poor efficiency, reluctance motors are used only in small fractional sizes where constant speed is essential.

The rotor of the **hysteresis motor** is made of permanent magnet steel. In one construction used, the rotor is made in the form of a hollow, thin-shelled cylinder supported by nonmagnetic material so that its axis coincides with the centre line of the rotor shaft. Contrasted with the reluctance rotor, there are no well-defined poles on the rotor surface, nor is there a separate cage winding.

When the stator winding of the hysteresis motor is energized, eddy currents are induced in the rotor surface. These eddy currents, flowing in complex paths, induce poles on the rotor surface. The hardened steel rotor, in effect, acts as a squirrel-cage to accelerate the rotor. At synchronous speed, the rotor poles formed by the eddy currents take up fixed positions and the rotor locks into step with the stator magnetic field.

Load torque of the hysteresis motor at synchronous speed is produced by an angular shift between stator and rotor poles as in any synchronous motor. The pull-out torque of this type of motor is a measure of the ability of the rotor steel to retain its magnetism or, in other words, the amount of hysteresis effect present in the rotor steel. Hence, the name *hysteresis motor*.

Because the torque of a hysteresis motor is constant, very smooth and uniform, this motor was formerly used as a drive for phonographs and tape-reel drives. But it has been largely replaced by transistor-driven permanent-magnet dc motor drives. Likewise, it was universally used as a clock drive but now has been displaced by solid-state circuits with digital readouts.

17-**10**

Single-Phase Motor Control

Solid-state power devices such as diodes, diacs, SCRs, and triacs are widely used in control circuits for small single-phase motors. Typically these motors are used in household appliances, workshop tools, and fan or blower drives. Two motor control circuits are described in this section to illustrate typical applications of several solid-state devices.

A popular variable-speed control circuit for controlling a universal motor and using an SCR is shown in Fig. 17-13. As described in Sec. 17-1, the series ac-dc, or universal motor, is widely used in small domestic appliances and portable tools. This motor has a high torque for high armature currents, giving it a good starting torque. However, it has a widely varying speed from a very high speed at no load to a very low speed at full load. Speed control in the circuit shown in Fig. 17-13 is by varying the triggering time or angle of the SCR which is in series with the motor. The angle at which the SCR fires is controlled by the cathode-to-gate voltage. This voltage is determined at any time both by the setting of the variable resistance R and by the counter emf of the motor, which is proportional to motor speed. For example, after the motor has reached a stable operating speed for a given setting of the resistor R, if load is added to the motor, the rotor speed momentarily decreases, which reduces the counter emf. The resulting reduced cathode-to-gate voltage causes the gate of the SCR to fire earlier, which applies more voltage to the motor, which in turn causes its speed to increase. The counter emf of the motor thus provides a speed-regulative action which results in stable operation of the motor.

The circuit shown in Fig. 17-14 is a basic triac phase-control circuit in which the triac is triggered with a diac. The circuit shown

F I G U R E **17-13**
Circuit diagram of a universal motor drive.

FIGURE **17-14**
Single-phase induction motor control circuit.
(RCA.)

is suitable for controlling single-phase shaded-pole or two-value capacitor fan-drive motors. With minor modifications, the circuit can be used for other purposes such as lamp dimming or heat control.

The capacitor C_1 in Fig. 17-14 is charged first in one direction and then the other during each cycle of the applied voltage. As the charge on the capacitor increases in either direction to a value high enough to cause the diac to break over, the capacitor discharges through the diac into the gate of the triac. Either a positive or a negative pulse triggers the triac into conduction, and full line voltage is applied to the motor for the remainder of that half-cycle.

If the resistance of R_1 is increased, the time required for C_1 to charge during each half-cycle is increased. This delays the triggering of the triac, and a smaller percentage of the line voltage is applied to the motor and the motor slows down. Conversely, lowering the resistance of R_1 increases motor speed. The resistor R_2 and capacitor C_2 are connected across the triac as shown to assure reliable turn-off of the triac when this circuit is used for controlling an induction motor or other highly inductive load.

REVIEW QUESTIONS

1 What are the three general classes of single-phase motors?
2 Name three types of single-phase induction motors.
3 Why is the shunt motor unsatisfactory for ac operation?
4 How does an ac series motor differ in construction from a dc series motor?
5 Is an ac series motor classed as a constant- or variable-speed motor?

6 What is a universal motor?

7 Does a single-phase induction motor develop torque when the rotor is stationary? Why?

8 What causes the rotating magnetic field to be established in a single-phase induction motor? What determines its direction of rotation?

9 What is the split-phase method of motor starting? Name two methods of phase splitting.

10 Why is the starting winding of a split-phase resistance-start motor disconnected after the motor has been started?

11 Which has the better starting characteristics, the resistance-start or the capacitor-start induction motor?

12 What is a permanent-split capacitor motor?

13 What is an application of the permanent-split capacitor motor?

14 What kind of loads might require the use of a two-value capacitor motor?

15 What is the effect of the shading coil when it is used in starting induction motors? Motors using this method of starting are built in sizes up to about what horsepower?

16 Name three types of single-phase synchronous motors.

17 What is a typical application for the hysteresis motor?

18 Compare the speed-regulative action of the motor shown in Fig.17-13 with that of a dc motor.

19 What is the function of the diac in the motor control circuit shown in Fig. 17-14.

PROBLEMS

17-1 Determine the amount of current a resistive-start split-phase motor will draw from the line at the moment of start if the start winding current is $3.0/\!-15°$ A and the run winding current is $5.6/\!-40°$ A.

17-2 Assuming the running winding current does not change at speed, what is the power factor of the motor in Prob. 17-1 at start and at speed?

17-3 If a capacitor is added to the motor in Prob. 17-1, thereby causing the start winding current to lead the source voltage by 40°, determine the current drawn from the line at the instant of start. Compare these results with the starting current of Prob. 17-1.

17-4 A permanent-split capacitor motor has a starting winding and running winding current of $5/\!-45°$ A and $5/45°$ A respectively. What is the power factor of this motor while at speed under the above conditions?

Circuit-Protective and Switching Equipment

Protective and switching equipment plays a very important part in the operation of a modern electrical system. Since modern economy is so dependent upon the availability of electric energy, it is the goal of those who design, operate, and maintain electrical supply systems to provide as nearly as possible a continuous, uninterrupted supply of electric energy to all consumers at a reasonable price. To provide this service, heavy investments must be made in generating, transmitting, and distributing equipment. Protective and switching equipment is necessary to protect this investment — to provide flexibility in operation of the system and to assure a dependable supply of energy to all consumers. Some of this equipment and the function it performs in modern power systems is described in this chapter.

18-1
Short Circuits and Interrupting Rating

Short circuits are the greatest hazard to the continuity of service. Since protective and switching equipment must either isolate or withstand the effects of short circuits, it is desirable to know what short circuits are, what causes them, and what their effects are.

All circuits consist of conductors that are isolated from other conductors by insulating materials. Conductors are necessary to carry the current and insulators are necessary to confine the current to the conductor. Conductor materials commonly used are copper and aluminum. Insulating materials may be air, rubber, porcelain, thermoplastic materials, and other similar materials.

Conductors used indoors are usually insulated with rubber, varnished cambric, or thermoplastic materials coated directly over the conductor material so that the conductor may be placed in a confined area such as a conduit or raceway. Conductors used on outdoor overhead lines are very often bare and are supported on glass or porcelain insulators. Such circuits depend upon physical separation in air for their insulation, air being the insulator.

Regardless of the construction of an electric circuit, the two basic components are present, the conductor and the insulator. However, regardless of the care used in constructing an electric circuit, the circuit is subject to damage such that the insulator between two or more conductors is destroyed and a **short circuit** or a **fault** is said to exist. A short circuit is then merely an insulation failure in an electric circuit; this failure in insulation provides a low-resistance current path in the circuit.

Insulation failures or short circuits in an electric circuit may be caused by inherent defects or by external causes. Inherent defects result from improper design or installation of equipment. Insulation may fail because of external causes such as lightning surges, switching surges, mechanical damages, or operating errors. Many short circuits are the result of overloads. Overloads cause a deterioration of insulation and, if sustained, may cause a complete failure of insulation resulting in a short circuit.

The amount of current flowing in a circuit is determined by the applied voltage and the impedance of the circuit. This is true in a normal circuit as well as in a faulty circuit. In the circuit shown in Fig. 18-1, the normal load current is the phase voltage divided by the phase impedance or, assuming the load is wye-connected,

$$I_{\text{norm}} = \frac{480/1.73}{2} = 139 \text{ A}$$

However, if a three-phase short circuit should occur at the point X, the flow of current in the circuit will be much larger since the only impedance to limit the flow of current is then the impedance of the system itself. The total system impedance for the circuit shown in Fig. 18-1 includes the impedance of the step-down transformer and the impedance of the three-phase power system back to the generators. The impedance of the power system is normally very small relative to that of the step-down transformer.

When a transformer impedance is known in ohms, then the short-circuit current for a fault on the secondary side of the transformer may be calculated by dividing the transformer phase voltage

FIGURE **18-1**
Circuit to illustrate magnitudes of short-circuit currents.

by the transformer phase impedance. However, usually the transformer impedance is known in percent as indicated on the transformer nameplate (see Sec. 13-8). When the transformer percent impedance is known and the system impedance is so small that it may be neglected, as it often is, transformer secondary short-circuit current I_{sc} may be computed by the following:

$$I_{sc} = \frac{\text{kVA}_T \times 100}{\%Z \times 1.73 \times \text{kV}} \qquad \text{[18-1]}$$

where kVA_T = transformer rating, kilovoltamperes
           $\%Z$ = transformer percent impedance
           kV = transformer secondary voltage, kilovolts

Thus, for the circuit shown in Fig. 18-1, if the transformer is rated 500 kVA and has an impedance of 5 percent, the short-circuit current for a fault at point X will be

$$I_{sc} = \frac{500 \times 100}{5 \times 1.73 \times 0.48} = 12\ 000 \text{ A}$$

Larger supply systems and supply transformers normally produce higher fault currents. If, for example, the 500-kVA transformer in Fig. 18-1 were replaced by a 2500-kVA 5 percent impedance transformer, then the short-circuit current for a fault at point X, again neglecting the system impedance, would be

$$I_{sc} = \frac{2500 \times 100}{5 \times 1.73 \times 0.48} = 60\ 000 \text{ A}$$

As may be seen from the foregoing examples, insulation failures cause abnormally high currents to flow. Such high values of current may damage equipment or property unless the faulty circuit or equipment is removed promptly from the supply system. It is further desirable to remove only the faulty circuit or equipment from the system so that service may be maintained to the remainder of the system.

A circuit-protective and switching device such as the one shown in Fig. 18-1 has two purposes:

1. It carries the normal load current and is used to open and close the circuit when necessary.
2. It is used to open the circuit to interrupt the flow of abnormal or short-circuit current.

Circuit-protective and switching devices in general have two ratings: a **continuous** rating and an **interrupting** rating. The continuous rating is usually in amperes and is the amount of current that a device can carry continuously without overheating. The interrupting rating of a device is based on the ability of that device to interrupt the flow of short-circuit current. Interrupting ratings of low-voltage devices are usually in amperes and of high-voltage devices either in amperes or in kilovoltamperes at a given voltage.

The amount of current that will flow during a short circuit and the time that short-circuit current is permitted to flow will determine the amount of *let through energy*. This can be stated in units of ampere squared seconds.

$$I^2t \qquad \text{(amperes squared-seconds)} \qquad \text{[18-2]}$$

Fig. 18-2 illustrates the destructive damage that can occur when the short-circuit current is allowed to reach its full value.

18-2

Electrical Distribution Systems

The distribution of electric energy is accomplished by dividing and subdividing large-capacity feeders into feeders of smaller and smaller capacity. At each change in circuit capacity on an electrical system there is a distribution centre at which is grouped circuit-protective and switching equipment. In general, this is true throughout a system from the generators to the loads.

The system represented in one-line-diagram form in Fig. 18-3 is a simple radial system in which all circuits radiate from the generating station. Typical groups of protective and switching equipment are shown in the diagram. An assembly of metal-clad switchgear and a step-up outdoor substation are shown at the generating station. Another section of metal-clad switchgear is shown at the 34 500- to 4160-V step-down substation. At the load are

---

F I G U R E **18-2**
Quantity of *let through energy* as a result of a short circuit not being cleared in sufficient time to minimize system damage.

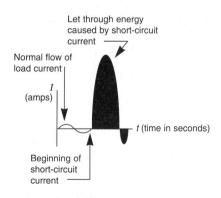

FIGURE **18-3**
Electrical system one-line diagram to illustrate the use of circuit-protective and switching equipment.

shown the load-centre unit substation, low-voltage metal-enclosed switchgear (which is a part of the unit substation), and lighting and power panelboards. This equipment has been grouped in this chapter into two main groups: low-voltage equipment for circuits operating at 600 V and below, and high-voltage equipment for circuits operating at voltages above 600 V.

LOW-VOLTAGE PROTECTIVE AND SWITCHING EQUIPMENT

The classification of low-voltage protective and switching equipment as used here applies to that equipment used on circuits rated at 600 V or less. This voltage classification includes a large percentage of the utilization systems such as in homes, commercial establishments, and industries since most of these systems utilize power at 120, 208, 240, 415, 480, or 550 V. Protective and switching equipment used on such systems is used for normal-load switching, for protection of circuits and equipment against overload, and for protection against short circuits.

18-3

Low-Voltage Fuses

A fuse is an overcurrent protective device that has a circuit-opening fusible member directly heated and destroyed by the passage of overcurrent through it. See Fig. 18-4. As indicated by the definition, a fuse contains a current-carrying element so sized that the heat created by the flow of normal current through it is not sufficient to fuse or melt the element. However, when short-circuit or overload currents flow through the fuse, the fusible element melts and opens the circuit. The fusible element of an indoor fuse is enclosed in a protective housing to prevent the heat generated during the clearing of a short circuit from damaging adjacent equipment.

The **plug fuse** is used on low-capacity circuits rated 125 V or less to ground. This fuse consists of a zinc alloy strip fusible element enclosed in a porcelain or glass housing which is fitted with a screw base. The maximum continuous current-carrying capacity of plug fuses is 30 A, and the commonly used standard sizes are 10, 15, 20, 25, and 30 A. These fuses do not have published interrupting capacities since they are ordinarily used on circuits that have relatively low values of available short-circuit current.

Cartridge fuses are used on circuits with voltage ratings up to 600 V, the common voltage ratings of these fuses being 250 and 600 V. Cartridge fuses are constructed with a zinc alloy fusible element enclosed in a cylindrical tube or cartridge. The ends of the fusible element are attached to metallic contact pieces at the ends of the tube. The tube is filled with an insulating arc-quenching powder which surrounds the fusible element. On overloads or short circuits, the fusible element is heated to a high temperature, causing it to vaporize. The powder in the fuse cartridge cools and condenses the vapour and quenches the arc, thereby interrupting the flow of current.

Cartridge fuses both in the 250- and 600-V ratings are made to fit standardized fuse-clip sizes. These are 30-, 60-, 100-, 200-, 400-, and 600-A sizes. There are several continuous current ratings for each fuse-clip size. For example, the 100-A size is available in the continuous ratings of 70, 80, 90, and 100 A. Many general-

FIGURE **18-4**

Cutaway view of a standard, single element cartridge fuse.

(Courtesy of Bussmann, Cooper Industries.)

FIGURE **18-5**
High-speed response of a current-limiting fuse that can interrupt the available short-circuit current before it is allowed to build up to its full value.

Let through energy permitted
when a current-limiting fuse
clears the short circuit in
less than 1/2 cycle.

purpose cartridge fuses do not have published interrupting ratings. However, for application on systems having high values of available short-circuit current certain classes or fuses are available which have rated interrupting ratings of 50 000, 100 000, or 200 000 A. *Some cartridge fuses are now being developed that have published interrupting ratings of 300 000* A. Fig. 18-5 illustrates the capability of a current-limiting fuse to minimizing the amount of damaging let through energy produced by a short circuit. Fig. 18-6 shows a cutaway view of a current limiting fuse that has the capability of interrupting up to 200 kA of fault current in less than 1/4 of a cycle.

Time-delay fuses are made in both the plug and cartridge types. These fuses are constructed so as to have a longer operating time than ordinary fuses, especially for overload currents. They do operate, however, to clear short-circuit currents in about the same time as do the standard fuses. Time-delay fuses have two parts, a

FIGURE **18-6**
Low-peak, time-delay, current-limiting fuse contains short-circuit and overload protection.
(Courtesy of Bussmann, Cooper Industries.)

F I G U R E **18-7**
Dual-element time-delay cartridge fuse showing the *time-delay element* and the *short-circuit element*.
(Courtesy of Bussmann, Cooper Industries.)

Short-circuit element   Overload element

thermal-cutout part and a fuse link (Fig. 18-7). The thermal cutout, with its long time delay, operates on overload currents up to about 500 percent of normal current. Currents above this value are interrupted by the fuse link. Time-delay fuses find their greatest application in motor circuits where it is desirable that the fuse provide protection for the circuit and yet not operate because of a momentary high current during the starting period of the motor.

A basic purpose of an overcurrent protective device is to interrupt the flow of short-circuit current before the protected circuit conductors or other components have been damaged by the high

F I G U R E **18-8**
The operation of the true dual-element fuse with its distinct and separate overload and short-circuit elements.
(Courtesy of Bussmann, Cooper Industries.)

(a) Under sustained overload conditions, the trigger spring fractures the calibrated fusing alloy and releases the "connector".

(b) The "open" dual element fuse after opening under an overload condition.

(c) A short-circuit causes the short-circuit elements to melt. The arcs are suppressed by the arc quenching material surrounding the fuse element.

(d) The "open" dual element fuse after opening under a short-circuit condition.

levels of let through energy that are released by the flow of the short-circuit current. **Current-limiting fuses** are designed to interrupt the flow of fault current in less than one-half cycle (8.0 milliseconds on a 60-Hz system). These fuses interrupt the fault current before it can build up to its full peak and damaging value.

Several types of fuses are classified by electrical standards as current-limiting fuses. Ratings for these fuses, in addition to their current-limiting capability, include a voltage, a continuous-current rating, and an interrupting rating. Several current-limiting fuses are shown in Fig. 18-9.

Since a fuse is a device that is destroyed in the process of interrupting the flow of abnormal current, it must be easily replaceable. Plug fuses have a screw-type base and can be inserted into sockets designed for their use. Cartridge fuses are inserted into fuse clips which make contact with the two ends of the fuse. Fuse sockets and clips usually are assembled into a supporting insulating base provided with means for connecting the fuse into the circuit. The assemblies of fuse, fuse clips, and supports are manufactured and used in many different ways. Two devices in which fuses are generally used are **safety switches** and **panelboards**.

FIGURE **18-9**
Current-limiting fuses.
(General Electric Company.)

18-4
Safety Switches

A switch is a device used for isolating parts of an electric circuit or for changing connections in a circuit or system. When a switch is mounted in a metal enclosure and is operable by means of an external hand, it is called a **safety switch**. The switch itself is not designed for interrupting the flow of short-circuit currents. However, switches and fuses are often incorporated into a single device called a **fusible disconnect switch**.

Safety switches are made in two-, three-, four-, or five-pole assemblies, either fused or unfused. They are made in single-throw and double-throw units and, depending upon their use, they have a variety of constructional features. One type has a quick-make, quick-break mechanism so arranged that regardless of the speed at which the operating handle is moved, a spring-loaded arrangement causes the contacts to open or close with a quick motion. This type of switch also has a door interlock to prevent the opening of the enclosure door when the switch is closed. A typical heavy-duty three-pole fusible disconnect switch with the door open and the fuses removed is shown in Fig. 18-10.

Enclosed switches, either fusible or nonfusible, are used as disconnecting devices for main services into buildings, for feeder and

---

FIGURE **18-10**
Three-pole safety switch.
(Square D Company.)

branch circuit-protective and switching devices, and for motor protection and switching.

Safety switches are available in two voltage ratings: 250 and 600 V ac. Current ratings are the same as the standard fuse-clip sizes.

18-5

Low-Voltage Air Circuit Breakers

A circuit breaker is a device designed for interrupting a circuit between separable contacts without injury to itself. Air circuit breakers are circuit breakers in which the circuit interruption occurs in air. The circuit breakers to be discussed here are the so-called low-voltage circuit breakers suitable for application on circuits rated 600 V or lower. Circuit breakers intended for application on high-voltage circuits are discussed in Sec. 18-10.

One commonly used low-voltage air circuit breaker is the **molded-case breaker**. The breaker is assembled as an integral unit in a housing of insulating material. The external appearance of a three-pole molded-case breaker is shown in Fig. 18-11, and a cutaway view of this type of breaker is shown in Fig. 18-12.

An electric circuit is completed or interrupted manually with a circuit breaker by moving the operating handle to the ON or OFF position. In all except the very small breakers, the linkage between the operating handle and the contacts is arranged for a quick-make, quick-break contact action regardless of the speed at which the

FIGURE **18-11**
Three-pole molded-case air circuit breaker.
(Square D Company.)

F I G U R E **18-12**
Cutaway view of a three-pole molded-case circuit breaker.
(Square D Company.)

handle is moved. The handle is also trip-free, which means that the contacts cannot be held closed against a short circuit or overload.

The breaker automatically trips when the current through it exceeds a certain value. In the lower current ratings, automatic tripping is accomplished by a thermal tripping device. The thermal trip consists of a bimetallic element so calibrated that the heat from the normal current through it does not cause it to deflect. However, an abnormally high current caused either by an overload or by a short circuit causes the element to deflect and trip the linkage holding the circuit-breaker contacts closed. The breaker contacts are opened by spring action.

The bimetallic tripping element, being responsive to heat from the current flowing through it, has an inverse-line characteristic. It operates quickly for heavy currents such as those resulting from short circuits and operates more slowly for moderate overload currents. This is a desirable characteristic for an overcurrent protective device that is used for protecting circuit conductors against overheating. The current-carrying ability of a conductor is limited by the temperature at which its insulation may be operated safely. The operating temperature of the conductor is the sum of the temperature of the air in which the conductor is operating and the temperature rise due to the I^2R loss in the conductor. A circuit breaker that uses a thermal element for tripping depends upon these same two sources of heat for its operation and, therefore, affords good conductor protection. Thus, when circuit-breaker sizes are properly selected, they have approximately the same response to temperature as do the conductors which they protect, and they will act to trip the circuit before dangerous overheating can occur in the conductors.

In the larger current ratings of molded-case breakers, the thermal trip element is supplemented by a magnetic trip element. The magnetic unit uses the magnetic force surrounding the conductor to operate the breaker-tripping linkage. Breakers which have the combination thermal-magnetic trip have inverse-line tripping characteristic for overcurrents up to about 10 times the nameplate rating of the breaker and instantaneous tripping for currents above that value. Stated another way, these breakers have inverse-time thermal tripping for overload currents and instantaneous magnetic tripping for short-circuit currents.

Arc interruption in an air circuit breaker takes place between the separable contacts. Many variations in design and arrangement of contacts and the surrounding chamber are used by different manufacturers. One commonly used design is the placing of the contacts in an arc chute made in such a way that the arc formed as the contacts part is drawn out into the arc chute. As the arc is drawn into the chute, it is divided into small segments and quenched.

Molded-case breakers are manufactured in a wide range of sizes and ratings. Frame sizes range from 50 to 4000 A, each with a standard range of continuous-current ratings. The physical size, rating of the contacts, and interrupting rating are the same for all breakers of a given frame size. The continuous-current rating of any breaker is determined by the rating of its trip elements. Voltage ratings available range from 120 to 600 V, and interrupting capacities range as high as 100 000 A.

Large air circuit breakers are used in industrial and large commercial distribution systems since these breakers are usually available in higher continuous-current and interrupting ratings than are the molded-case breakers. Circuit breakers of this type are available with continuous-current ratings as high as 4000 A and interrupting ratings as high as 130 000 A.

Most modern, large air circuit breakers use a closing device called a **stored energy mechanism** to assure a fast, positive closing action. In a commonly used breaker-closing mechanism, energy is stored by compressing powerful coil springs that are linked through a latching mechanism to the contact assembly of the breaker. After the springs have been compressed the latch may be operated to release the springs to provide a quick closing action of the breaker contacts.

Breaker-closing springs may be compressed manually by means of a hand crank or they may be compressed by a small electric motor. Thus, the breaker may be classified as either a manually or an electrically operated breaker. In either type, however, the speed and force of closing the breaker contacts are independent of the action of a human operator.

When a large air circuit breaker is closed, the operating mechanism is latched closed. As the breaker is closed, a set of tripping springs is compressed. The breaker may then be tripped by operating a trip latch manually at the breaker or by energizing a solenoid trip coil by means of a remote-control circuit. When the trip latch is operated either manually or electrically, the breaker contacts are opened quickly by the tripping springs.

As indicated previously, breakers may be either manually or electrically operated. Manually operated breakers have a lower first cost than do electrically operated breakers and are used when infrequent operation is required. Electrically operated breakers are used when breakers need to be operated frequently or when remote control is required. Electrically operated breakers may be closed and tripped from a push-button or control switch mounted in a convenient location remote from the breaker.

As soon as an electrically operated stored energy breaker is tripped, the spring-charging motor is started automatically and the closing springs are compressed so that the breaker is ready for the next closing operation. The closing springs of a manually operated breaker are normally compressed by the hand-cranking operation just prior to the closing of the breaker.

The breaker shown in Fig. 18-13 is a manually operated, stored energy, large air circuit breaker. The closing springs in the breaker are compressed by a downward stroke of the large operating handle on the front of the breaker, after which the breaker is closed by manual operation of the small closing lever. The breaker is tripped by the operation of the trip lever on the front of the breaker.

Automatic tripping of large air circuit breakers is accomplished on some breakers by a direct-acting series overcurrent tripping device. The operating coil of the tripping device is connected in series with the power circuit in which the breaker is installed. The flow of an abnormally high current in the circuit causes a plunger of the tripping unit to come in contact with the latch of the breaker-operating mechanism to open the breaker. One other type of trip-

FIGURE **18-13**
Three-pole large air circuit breaker.
(Siemens-Allis.)

ping system is used with large air circuit breakers in which the tripping function is performed by a static overcurrent trip unit. This tripping unit is supplied energy from the power circuit through current transformers mounted in the breaker. When the tripping unit detects the flow of an overcurrent, a trip coil is energized to trip the breaker. The breaker shown in Fig. 18-13 is equipped with a static trip device, which may be seen on the lower right-hand side of the breaker.

Overcurrent tripping devices for large air circuit breakers may be designed to have different tripping characteristics to fit different application requirements. The tripping device used on many breakers is a dual device having a long-time-delay element for moderate overload currents and an instantaneous element for short-circuit and severe overload currents. The tripping characteristics of these devices are similar to those of tripping devices used with molded-case breakers. One other tripping device often used has both a long-time-delay and a short-time delay element. Moderate sustained overloads cause the breaker to trip after a relatively long time delay and short circuits cause the breaker to trip after an intentional short time delay. This device is used in selective protection systems.

By the proper selection of ratings and types of tripping units, a completely selective system may be designed. On such a system, the breaker nearest the fault is caused to trip and remove the faulty circuit or equipment from service while the other breakers on the system, closer to the source, remain closed to carry normal load current to the unfaulted parts of the system.

Arc extinction in large air circuit breakers during the interruption of short circuits is accomplished by different methods by different manufacturers. The method used by one manufacturer is the de-ionization or physical removal of the conduction particles from the arc path. In breakers using this principle, the arc is forced upward into an arc chute by strong magnetic fields so that rising gas blasts carry the ionized air particles out of the arc path.

Large air circuit breakers are manufactured in several physical sizes as determined by their continuous-current and interrupting ratings. Standard frame sizes are 800, 1600, 2000, 3200, and 4000 A. Each frame size has a short-circuit or interrupting rating at 240, 480, and 600 V. Furthermore, each frame size is available in several continuous-current ratings, the continuous-current rating being determined by the rating of the series trip device used on the breaker.

In general, overcurrent protection is required at every point in a distribution system where wire sizes are reduced. As a consequence, circuit breakers are used at service entrances, on feeder circuits, and on branch circuits for the protection and switching of the various components of the system.

Circuit breakers used for the protection and switching of motor circuits are selected from breaker-application tables prepared by the circuit-breaker manufacturers. In general, such breakers are selected to have a continuous-current rating not to exceed approximately 250 percent of the full-load current of the motor. For circuits other than motor circuits, circuit breakers are selected to have the same rating as the continuous rating of the conductor used in the circuit they are protecting.

Large air circuit breakers are often assembled in groups together with other control and metering equipment into **metal-enclosed low-voltage air-circuit-breakers switchgear**. This type of switchgear is discussed in Sec. 18-7.

A **panelboard** consists of a group of overcurrent-protective de-vices, with or without switches, including buses, assembled into a cabinet which is accessible only from the front. As shown in Fig. 18-3, panelboards are located between the secondary feeders and the branch circuits that supply the utilization equipment. So lo-cated, they are the means of control and protection for lighting and power circuits and the equipment supplied by them.

Panelboard overcurrent-protective devices may be fuses or cir-cuit breakers. Fusible panelboards used for lighting and small-appliance loads often have a switch in series with each of the branch-circuit fuses and are called **switch-and-fuse panelboards**.

The panel assembly itself consists of a set of bus bars to which the several branch circuits are connected through the overcurrent or switching devices. The main-supply conductors for the panel-board may connect directly to lugs on the bus bars or may connect to the bus bars through a main circuit breaker, main fuses, or a fused disconnect switch. The panel assembly is enclosed in a sheet-steel cabinet of the dead-front type so that no live parts are exposed when the cabinet door is open.

Fusible and circuit-breaker lighting panelboards are available in several voltage ratings. Two of the more common ratings are the 120/240 V three-wire single-phase grounded neutral and the 120/208 V four-wire three-phase grounded neutral panelboards. Panelboards with these ratings are supplied from four-wire delta- or wye-connected transformers, as described in Sec. 13-16. A partially assembled circuit-breaker lighting panelboard is shown in Fig. 18-14.

For distribution or power circuits with voltage ratings up to 600 V, both fusible and circuit-breaker-type panelboards are avail-able. One commonly used panelboard of this type is the convertible distribution panelboard. Convertible panelboards are of the sec-tionalized type made up in multiples of standardized circuit-breaker dimensions so that it is possible to interchange circuit breakers with different ratings or with different numbers of poles. With this type of panelboard it is possible to provide space in the panelboard cabinet for future additional circuits. These panel-boards will accommodate circuit breakers in frame sizes up to 600 A.

A metal-enclosed low-voltage air-circuit-breaker switchgear, as the name indicates, is a metal-enclosed assembly containing air circuit breakers, together with bare buses, connections, control wiring, and accessory devices. Air circuit breakers are mounted in individ-ual metal compartments and may be either the stationary or drawout type.

18-**6**
Panelboards

18-**7**
Metal-Enclosed Low-Voltage Air-Circuit-Breaker Switchgear

F I G U R E **18-14**
Circuit-breaker lighting panelboard assembly.
(Square D Company.)

The stationary-type switchgear contains air circuit breakers which are mounted rigidly on bases and have no special arrangement for a quick removal from the structure.

Drawout-type switchgear contains breakers so arranged that they may be easily withdrawn from or inserted into their housing. As breakers are removed or inserted, they are automatically disconnected from or connected to their power and control circuits by means of self-aligning contacts. Interlocking is provided so that breakers cannot be inserted or removed when they are closed. Drawout-type switchgear is more flexible and is more easily maintained than the stationary type. Service interruptions are minimized when drawout switchgear is used since a breaker in need of maintenance can be replaced by a spare breaker in a very short time.

A section of low-voltage metal-enclosed switchgear containing several drawout air circuit breakers is shown at the right-hand end of the load-centre unit substation in Fig. 18-15. The housing of

FIGURE **18-15**
Load-centre unit substation.
(Westinghouse Electric Corporation.)

the switchgear includes the breaker compartments, breaker supporting rails, buses, connections, and instrument transformers. This switchgear is dead front; that is, no live parts are exposed at any time. Interlocks are provided to prevent inadvertent access to the live parts.

Both manually and electrically operated circuit breakers are used in metal-enclosed low-voltage switchgear. The application of circuit breakers in switchgear is the same as when breakers are used individually as described in Sec. 18-5. The rating of switchgear is dependent upon the rating of the circuit breakers used in the switchgear.

Load-centre unit substations are combinations of transformers and metal-enclosed switchgear assembled as a unit. These substations may have switchgear either on the high-voltage or low-voltage side, or on both sides of the transformer. The unit substation shown in Fig. 18-15 has a high-voltage incoming-line section on the left consisting of an air interrupter switch, a ventilated dry-type transformer section in the centre, and a low-voltage metal-enclosed switchgear section on the right. The usual voltage ratings of unit substations are 15 000 V or less for the high-voltage section and 600 V or less for the low-voltage section. Transformers are usually rated 2000 kVA or less.

18-**8**

Load-Centre Unit Substations

Modern practices in power-system design include the extensive use of the load-centre system of power distribution with distribution voltages of from 2400 to 13 800 V. In this system of distribution, power is distributed to the point of utilization at the distribution centre unit substation and distributed by short low-voltage feeders. In this way, good system voltage regulation is obtained with relatively small conductor sizes. The use of several small transformers at the load centres rather than one large transformer centrally located on the system also allows the use of smaller circuit breakers at the utilization-voltage level. Breakers are smaller for the load-centre type of system because less load current is carried by the breakers, and the available short-circuit current is less because of the higher impedance of the small transformers. Another advantage of the load-centre system of distribution is its adaptability to changes in loads. Since the unit substation is factory-assembled as a compact unit, it is readily moved if load centres change.

Load-centre unit substations find their greatest application in manufacturing plants and other large, industrial, power-distribution systems.

18-9
Ground-Fault Circuit Interrupters (GFCIs)

With the wide use of solid-state technology, the principle and application of ground fault circuit interruption is commonly used for protection from electric shock through ground faulted equipment.

The GFCI is a current sensing device that monitors the quantity of current entering and leaving an electrically operated device. Ideally, the circuit and connected device should be free of any ground faults. Therefore, the quantity of the current flowing from the circuit source to the device should be equal to the quantity of the current returning from the device to the circuit source. If, however, a ground fault exist in either the circuit conductors or the electrical device, the ground will provide an alternate path for the circuit current to flow. When the difference between the current entering and leaving the connected device exceeds approximately five milliamperes, the GFCI will trip or open the circuit protecting the user from receiving a lethal electrical shock.

The differential transformer in Fig. 18-16 senses the difference in the magnetic fields between the two conductors supplying the load impedance. Under ideal conditions with no ground fault present, the fields about the conductors produced by equal and opposite currents will cancel each other and the transformer will have no output. However, if a ground is present then the current flowing in the two circuit conductors will not be equal due to some of the current being shunted through ground. This produces unequal magnetic fields about the conductors producing a resultant field to

FIGURE **18-16**
Basic diagram of a GFCI.

create a secondary output signal voltage to the sensing circuit. This potential will cause the sensing circuit to output a voltage to the trip relay which in turn will open the circuits line contacts.

The circuit illustrated in Fig. 18-16 is incorporated in GFCI circuit breakers and receptacles. The Canadian Electrical Code requires the use of GFCIs in many electrical equipment installations where shock hazard could be lethal to the user of ground faulted connected equipment.

HIGH-VOLTAGE PROTECTIVE AND SWITCHING EQUIPMENT

High-voltage fuses are used both indoors and outdoors for the protection of circuits and equipment with voltage ratings above 600 V. There are many types of fuses and they are mounted in many different ways. Some of the more generally used fuses and mountings are mentioned briefly in the following paragraphs.

Expulsion fuses consist of a fusible element mounted in a fuse tube and depend upon the vaporization of the fuse element and the fuse-tube liner to expel conducting vapours and metals from the fuse tube, thereby extinguishing the arc formed when current is interrupted. Another type of fuse, called the **liquid fuse**, depends on a spring mechanism to separate quickly the ends of the melted fuse element in a nonflammable liquid to extinguish the arc. Still another type of fuse is the **solid-material fuse**, in which the arc is extinguished in a hole in a solid material. In one type of solid-material fuse a spring mechanism similar to that of the liquid fuse is used to separate the arcing terminals when the fuse blows. In this fuse, overload and low fault currents are interrupted in a small cylindrical chamber in the solid arc-extinguishing materials, and

18-**10**

High-Voltage Fuses

large fault currents are interrupted in a larger chamber in the same fuse holder.

High-voltage fuses are often mounted in the same enclosure with disconnect switches to provide short-circuit protection and switching facilities for circuits and equipment. Typical equipment of this type removed from its enclosure is shown in Fig. 18-17. The equipment shown is for use on 13 800-V circuits and consists of a three-pole load-interrupter switch above and three solid-material fuses below.

Outdoor high-voltage fuses for low-capacity overhead lines are mounted in distribution fuse **cutouts**. Cutouts consist of a fuse support and fuse holder in which the fuse link is installed. An often-used type of cutout is the open cutout illustrated in Fig. 18-18. The cutout shown is designed to be attached to an overhead pole or structure by means of the mounting insert which protrudes from the centre of the insulator. The fuse link is enclosed in the fuse tube which, when in the closed position shown, completes the protected circuit between the upper and lower contacts of the cut-

F I G U R E **18-17**
Combination load-interrupter switch and solid-material fuses.
(S & C Electric Company.)

FIGURE **18-18**
Distribution fuse cutout, open type.
(S & C Electric Company.)

out. When the fuse link is melted by fault current, a spring-loaded "flipper" quickly expels the severed link from the tube. This action also causes the upper end of the tube to swing out and down to an open position, thereby providing a visual indication of the blown fuse. The cutout is placed back in service by inserting a new fuse in the tube and moving the tube back into the closed position.

The term **high-voltage circuit breaker** as used here applies to circuit breakers intended for service on circuits with voltage ratings higher than 600 V. High-voltage circuit breakers have standard voltage ratings of from 4160 to 765 000 V and interrupting ratings as high as 63 000 A. Breakers with even higher ratings are being developed.

During the early development of electrical systems, the vast majority of high-voltage breakers used were oil circuit breakers. More recently, however, magnetic air, compressed air, vacuum, and sulfur hexafluoride breakers have been developed and are now used instead of oil circuit breakers.

The **magnetic air circuit breaker** is available in ratings up to and including 750 000 kVA at 13 800 V. In this type of breaker the current is interrupted between separable contacts in air with the aid of magnetic blowout coils. As the main current-carrying contacts part during the interruption of a fault, the arc is drawn out in a horizontal direction and transferred to arcing contacts. At

18-11
High-Voltage Circuit Breakers

the same time, the blowout coil is connected into the circuit to provide a magnetic field to draw the arc upward into arc chutes. The arc accelerates upward, aided by the magnetic field and natural thermal effects, into the arc chutes where it is elongated and divided into small segments. The arc resistance increases until, as the current passes through zero, the arc is broken; after this it does not reestablish itself.

The general construction of the magnetic power circuit breaker is somewhat similar to the large air circuit breaker used on low-voltage circuits except that they are all electrically operated. These breakers are used extensively in metal-clad switchgear assemblies in industrial plants, steel mills, and power plants.

Compressed-air breakers (sometimes called **air-blast breakers**) depend upon a stream of compressed air directed toward the interrupting contacts of the breaker to interrupt the arc formed when current is interrupted. This type of breaker was introduced to the North American market in 1940, and since that time it has become universally accepted for use in heavy-duty indoor applications. More recently, air-blast breakers have been developed for use in extra-high-voltage outdoor stations with standard ratings up to 765 000 V.

Oil-circuit-breaker contacts are immersed in oil so that the current interruption takes place under oil which by its cooling effect helps quench the arc. Since oil is an insulator, the live parts of oil circuit breakers may be placed closer together than they could be in air. The poles of small oil circuit breakers are all placed in one oil tank, but in the large high-voltage breakers each pole is in a separate oil tank. Tanks of small breakers are suspended from a framework so that the tanks may be lowered for inspection of the contacts. The tanks of very large oil circuit breakers rest directly on a foundation and have handholes for access to the contact assembly.

The oil tanks of oil circuit breakers are sealed, the electric connections between the external circuit and the contacts in the tank being made through porcelain bushings. The breaker contacts are opened and closed by means of insulated lift rods on which the movable contacts are mounted. The lift rods are connected to the operating mechanism by means of a mechanical linkage, so that the contacts of all poles of the breaker are opened and closed together.

Only the very small oil circuit breakers are manually operated. The larger oil-circuit-breaker mechanisms are either pneumatically operated or spring-operated. Pneumatic operators obtain the closing and tripping energy from compressed air provided by a small, automatically controlled air compressor that maintains enough compressed air for several operations of the breaker in an air receiver. Spring operators derive their energy from a spring that is compressed by a small electric motor.

Sulfur hexafluoride breakers use the gas sulfur hexafluoride (SF_6) as an insulating and arc-quenching medium. This gas has been found to have excellent insulating properties as well as being nonflammable, nontoxic, and odorless. A three-pole outdoor frame-mounted SF_6 breaker designed for use on circuits rated 121 kV to 145 kV is shown in Fig. 18-19. The breaker shown has three cylindrical interrupting modules which may be seen mounted on the frame behind the cabinet which houses the breaker operating mechanism. These modules are filled with SF_6 gas maintained under a pressure of 517 kPa (75 lb/in²). Each gas-filled interrupting module contains the main contacts and a "puffer" mechanism which momentarily increases the gas pressure in the space immediately surrounding the breaker main contacts during arc interruption. As the contacts part during a fault interruption, the compressed gas flows along the arc, sweeping the hot gases formed

FIGURE **18-19**
Outdoor SF₆ circuit breaker.
(WM Power Products, Inc.)

by the arc from between the parting contacts, which extinguishes the arc. After the arc is quenched, the SF_6 gas reverts to the original lower pressure in the module, ready for the next operation.

The operating mechanism of the SF_6 breaker is now pneumatically operated. As the breaker contacts are closed by the pneumatic mechanism, a spring is compressed, which provides the energy for opening the breaker.

Puffer SF_6 breakers have been used in voltage ratings as high as 765 kV and with interrupting ratings as high as 63 000 A. To obtain the required interrupting capability at voltages higher than 362 kV, two or more interrupter modules are connected in series in each phase of the breaker as is done in other types of high-voltage breakers.

Vacuum breakers interrupt the flow of short-circuit current by separating their contacts in a vacuum chamber. Vacuum interrupters used in these breakers are enclosed in ceramic and steel envelopes or cylinders. Two butt contacts, one stationary and one movable, are used in each phase. A flexible stainless steel bellows is brazed to the stem of the movable contact. This allows the contact to move during operation of the interrupter without breaking the vacuum seal.

Since the current interruption takes place in a vacuum in the vacuum breaker, there is no ionization of the arc products to sustain the arc as is the case when an arc is formed in the air. Thus, the separation of the contacts in the interrupter can be very small.

Specialized manufacturing processes are required to assure proper sealing of the vacuum interrupter. One manufacturer performs the entire operation of evacuating, brazing, and sealing in a vacuum furnace.

The vacuum interrupter has been used in both indoor and outdoor 5- and 15-kV-class breakers. To obtain the insulation levels and interrupting capacity required at higher voltage levels, several vacuum interrupter contacts are used in series in each phase of high-voltage breakers.

18-**12**

Protective Relays

Low-voltage air circuit breakers ordinarily have self-contained series trip coils of either the instantaneous or time-delay types. The tripping energy is supplied by the flow of the short-circuit current through the trip coil. Power circuit breakers seldom use series trip coils but are equipped with trip coils designed to operate from a storage battery or a reliable source of alternating current. Auxiliary devices called **protective relays**, designed to detect the presence of short circuits on a system, are used to connect the breaker trip coils to the source of tripping power and thereby trip the breaker.

Protective relays are said to be selective when they trip only the circuit breakers directly supplying the defective part of the system and no other circuit breakers. When relays and circuit breakers are selective, short circuits are removed from a system with a minimum of service interruption. Of course, it is also desirable to isolate the defective system element as quickly as possible. To this end, relays and circuit breakers have been developed that will clear a short circuit in less than 0.1 s. However, selectivity being more important than speed, the tripping of some circuit breakers on a system is delayed intentionally to gain selectivity in clearing faults at certain locations on a system.

Protective-relay operating elements are connected to high-voltage circuit by means of current and potential transformers so that they, in effect, "measure" the quantities of current, voltage, or phase angle or combinations of these quantities to determine whether or not an abnormal condition exists in the circuit being protected. Relays with widely different operating characteristics have been developed for specific applications in protective schemes for rotating machines, transformers, buses, and lines.

Protective relays have traditionally been electromechanical relays. They have electrical connections to operating coil(s) that magnetically move induction disks to which contacts are attached. The contacts may open or close circuits that operate the protective devices. These electromechanical relays are being replaced by electronic or solid-state relays and, in some instances, directly by computers. Regardless of construction, protective relays perform the same functions. Two of the more frequently used protective relay types are **overcurrent** and **differential** relays.

Overcurrent relays, as the name indicates, operate to close their contacts when current through the relay operating coil exceeds a predetermined value. Overcurrent relays are connected to the protected circuit through current transformers so that the current-transformer secondary current through the relay is proportional to the current in the primary circuit.

The most generally used electromechanical overcurrent relay is the induction overcurrent relay. This relay is similar in principle to the induction watt-hour meter and has a movable disk driven by an electromagnet. However, the induction overcurrent relay disk is not free to revolve continuously as in the watt-hour meter since the operating torque is opposed by a restraining spring. Furthermore, a movable contact is attached to the disk shaft so that after a partial revolution the movable contact makes contact with the stationary contact and further rotation is impossible.

The pickup current of an overcurrent relay is the current that will just cause the contacts to close. The operating coil of the relay is tapped to provide a means for adjusting the relay for different values of pickup current. Several tap ranges are available for induction relays, a commonly used range being from 4 to 16 A.

Induction overcurrent relays have inverse-time characteristics; that is, the contact closing is fast for high operating-coil currents and slow for low operating-coil currents. Moreover, the operating time for a given current is adjustable, the time of operation being proportional to the distance that the disk is allowed to travel before the contacts close.

With both the pickup current and the operating time being adjustable, induction overcurrent relays may be applied in selective systems with relays close to the generator adjusted for long operating times and with progressively shorter time settings for relays farther away from the generator. Induction overcurrent relays are relatively inexpensive, are reliable, and are easily calibrated and maintained. Consequently, they are widely used for the protection of transmission and distribution lines and equipment. An induction overcurrent relay withdrawn from its case is shown in Fig. 18-20. This relay has an instantaneous attachment in addition to the basic inverse time section. The instantaneous element responds only to extremely high fault currents.

F I G U R E **18-20**
Induction overcurrent relay removed from drawout case.
(General Electric Company.)

Solid-state overcurrent relays have a different appearance but perform the same function.

Electromechanical differential relays, like overcurrent relays, have an induction disk assembly on which is mounted a movable contact. However, the differential relay has, in addition to its operating electromagnet, a restraining electromagnet so connected that the flow of current through it provides a restraining torque or a contact-opening torque on the relay during the normal functioning of the equipment being protected by the relay.

Differential relays are used for the protection of rotating machines, transformers, and buses. Differential relays compare the currents entering and leaving each phase winding of the apparatus being protected. Normally, the currents entering and leaving the apparatus are equal or are directly proportional to each other. However, on the occurrence of an internal fault in the apparatus, the two currents are no longer equal or proportional, since short-circuit current is fed into the apparatus from one or both sides. Under this condition, the difference of the two currents passes through the operating coil of the relay, causing the relay to close its contacts and trip the necessary circuit breakers to isolate the apparatus from the system. An elementary diagram showing typical connections for a transformer differential relay is shown in Fig. 18-21.

A complete installation of three-phase transformer differential relays consists of three relays, one for each phase. For simplicity the diagram in Fig. 18-21 shows the connections for only one relay. The flow of normal currents is shown in the diagram, the current on the 69 000-V side of the transformer being 100 A and on the 6900-V side being 1000 A. With current-transformer ratios as shown, the secondary currents are balanced, each being 5 A. The

---

FIGURE **18-21**
Connections for a transformer differential relay.

5 A then circulates in the series circuit consisting of the two current transformers and the two relay-restraining windings R and R'. For this normal condition, there is no current in the relay-operating winding O, and the current in the two restraining windings creates a torque that holds the relay-operating contacts open. However, when a fault develops within the transformer, short-circuit current is fed into the transformer from one or both sides, depending upon the system arrangement. This causes the current in one restraining winding either to reverse or to increase out of proportion to the current in the other restraining winding. The restraining winding currents are no longer balanced, and the unbalanced current flows through the operating winding of the relay, developing a contact-closing torque which causes the relay contacts to close.

Differential relays for the protection of generators and motors are similar to transformer differential relays except that they are ordinarily more sensitive and will operate on a smaller unbalanced current than will transformer relays. A high-speed differential relay designed for the protection of large ac generators is shown in Fig. 18-22. Bus differential relays are also similar to transformer relays except that the current transformer secondaries of all incoming lines to the bus are paralleled and connected to one relay-

F I G U R E **18-22**
Differential relay in drawout case.
(General Electric Company.)

restraining winding, and the current transformer secondaries of the outgoing lines are paralleled and connected to the other restraining winding.

Metal-clad switchgear is a type of switchgear assembly defined by ANSI standards, in which all parts are completely enclosed in grounded metal enclosures. Circuit breakers used in metal-clad switchgear usually incorporate vacuum or SF_6 interrupting technology, although much of the installed base uses older, air-magnetic breakers. The breakers are equipped with self-coupling primary and secondary disconnecting devices and are removable so that maintenance can be performed away from energized switchgear—a key advantage in comparison with fixed-mount outdoor substation breakers. All buses, connections, and joints are insulated and are completely isolated from the secondary wiring and control devices. Instruments, relays, and control switches are mounted on the front panels of the switchgear.

Metal-clad switchgear is available in both indoor and outdoor types for use in circuits with voltage ratings below 38 000 V, the most common ratings being 4160 and 13 800 V. Interrupting and continuous-current ratings are based on the ratings of the circuit breakers used in the switchgear.

A typical assembly of metal-clad switchgear with one circuit breaker removed from the switchgear is shown in Fig. 18-23. Instruments, control switches, and protective relays required for con-

18-**13**
Metal-Clad Switchgear

FIGURE **18-23**
Metal-clad switchgear assembly.
(ABB Power T&D Company Inc., Sanford, Florida.)

trolling and monitoring the circuit breakers are mounted on the compartment doors. Vacuum and SF_6 interrupting technologies result in smaller, lighter circuit breakers that can be stacked in two-high arrangements for more compact switchgear with lower installation costs. Microprocessor-based protection devices integrate 3-phase protection and metering functions into a single unit with user-selectable protection and alarm features and remote communications capability.

Some manufacturers have now gone beyond ANSI standards to provide metal-clad switchgear that can also meet international standards, such as IEC or EEMAC, for protection against internal arc faults. This arc-resistant switchgear (Fig. 18-24) controls the effects of an internal arc fault by directing the resulting pressure and flames up through the roof, rather than allowing explosive forces and hot gasses to injure nearby personnel.

18-**14**

Outdoor Substations

Outdoor substations consist of structural frameworks on which switches, fuses, buses, and surge arresters are mounted and from which connections are made to circuit breakers, transformers, and other heavy equipment installed on the ground under the structure. Structures are usually constructed of galvanized structural steel, but some low-voltage structures are made of wood. Buses, jumpers, and

F I G U R E **18-24**

SafeGear™ arc-resistant metal-clad switchgear assembly.

(ABB Power T&D Company Inc., Sanford, Florida.)

connections are supported on insulators that are attached to the structural framework.

There are no limitations to electrical capacity in outdoor substations since equipment of almost any rating or capacity can be installed in stations of this type. Spacings of buses and equipment and arrangement of station are dependent upon the voltage of the station. Arrangement, of course, is also influenced by the function for which the station is intended. Substations are usually designed to fit individual requirements, although some standardization is possible in certain types of substations.

Outdoor substations may be of the step-up type used to connect generating plants to transmission systems or they may be step-down stations for supplying loads from a high-voltage transmission system. Step-down stations for supplying loads or distribution systems at 15 000 V or less often consist of an open-type steel framework for terminating the high-voltage circuit, a three-phase transformer, and an assembly of outdoor metal-clad switchgear for the protection and switching of the low-voltage circuits.

Voltage transformations are not always involved in outdoor substations. Switching stations in which only circuit breakers and other switching equipment are installed are used at junctions and taps in transmission systems.

A typical outdoor substation is shown in Fig. 18-25. This is a step-down substation with a high-voltage rating of 161 kV and a

FIGURE **18-25**
Outdoor substation.
(Stanley Consultants, Inc.)

low-voltage rating of 69 kV. The bus, overhead lines, and oil circuit breaker in the foreground are a part of the 69 kV section of the station.

18-15
Surge Arresters

Transient overvoltage surges on an electrical system may be caused by lightning, switching operations, or other disturbances. If these overvoltages exceed the insulation level of the system, flashovers occur which can destroy the insulation of transformers or other apparatus connected to the system. It is the function of surge arresters to provide a path by which these surges are conducted to earth before system flashovers can occur.

The **valve-type surge arrester** was a commonly used type up until a few years ago. These arresters may be likened to a normally open circuit breaker connected from the protected circuit to the earth, which closes when a high-voltage surge appears and then reopens when the surge disappears. This arrester consists of two elements, a series gap and a valve assembly, both enclosed in a porcelain housing. The spacing of the series gap is such that it will withstand normal circuit voltage. However, an overvoltage such as may be caused by a lightning surge causes the gap to break down, with a resulting flow of current through the valve assembly to ground. The valve assembly is constructed of a ceramic compound

FIGURE **18-26**
Installation of surge arresters.
(Westinghouse Electric Corporation.)

that has the peculiar property of offering a high resistance to current flow when normal system voltage is applied, but a low resistance to the flow of high-surge currents. Thus, it operates as a current valve and allows the surge current to pass but assumes its former high resistance to stop the flow of current as soon as the voltage drops to its normal value. An installation of heavy-duty station-type valve arresters is shown in Fig. 18-26. These arresters have been largely replaced by metal oxide-based varistors, which have the same physical appearance. They perform the same function but have no parts to burn or wear out. Their principle of operation is described in Sec. 20-11.

REVIEW QUESTIONS

1 What is a short circuit?
2 What are two commonly used automatic circuit-protective devices?
3 In general, where is circuit-protective and switching equipment grouped on an electrical system?
4 What is a fuse? What are two types of low-voltage fuses?
5 What are the standard fuse-clip sizes for cartridge fuses?
6 Describe a time-lag fuse.
7 Where might a current-limiting fuse be used?
8 What is a safety switch? Where is it used?
9 Describe the operation of a molded-case circuit breaker.
10 What is meant when it is said that a circuit breaker has a thermal-magnetic trip element?
11 When is electrical operation of a circuit breaker desirable?
12 What type of automatic tripping is used on large low-voltage air circuit breakers?
13 How do the ratings of large low-voltage air circuit breakers differ from the ratings of molded-case breakers?
14 What is a panelboard? What type of overcurrent devices are used in panelboards?
15 What are two types of construction used in metal-enclosed low-voltage air-circuit-breaker switchgear? What are some advantages of drawout switchgear?
16 What is a load-centre unit substation?
17 Name three types of high-voltage fuses.
18 What is a fuse cutout? Where is it used?
19 Name several types of high-voltage circuit breakers.
20 What are some different types of operating mechanisms used with high-voltage circuit breakers?

21 What is the function of protective relays?

22 Describe the principle of operation of overcurrent and differential relays.

23 What is metal-clad switchgear? What are the maximum standard current, voltage, and interrupting ratings?

24 What are the essential features of outdoor substations?

25 Describe briefly the operation of the valve-type surge arrester.

Electrical Instruments and Measurements

Electrical measurements play an important role in the design, development, manufacturing, and maintenance of modern industrial equipment. The devices that perform the measurements and indicate values electrically have evolved from very simple meters that move a pointer in response to currents in coils to highly complex, sophisticated, multifunction, solid-state, electronic equipment. The indicating parts have changed from pointers and dials to light-emitting diodes to miniature video display terminals. Regardless of construction, basic knowledge of the principles of operation of the devices is essential to the understanding and interpretation of their readings.

This chapter discusses the basics of electric measurements by describing the operation of many of the electromagnetic-based devices. The functions of the electronic types are the same.

19-1
Galvanometers

As was learned from the study of electric motors, when a current-carrying conductor is placed in a magnetic field, a force is developed on the conductor which tends to move the conductor at right angles to the field. This principle is used in current-detecting instruments. A sensitive current-detecting instrument called a **galvanometer** operating on this principle is shown diagrammatically in Fig. 19-1.

A coil of very fine insulated wire, usually wound on an aluminum frame or bobbin, is suspended as shown between the poles of a permanent magnet. The coil is suspended by a phosphor-bronze filament which acts as one lead-in wire for the coil. The other lead-in wire is a very flexible spiral wire at the bottom of the coil. When current flows through the coil, a deflecting force proportional to the flux density, the current, and the dimensions of the coil rotates the coil on its vertical axis. The deflecting force is opposed by the restraining force of the suspension filament so that the coil does not continue to rotate as in a motor but turns until the deflecting force is balanced by the restraining force of the suspension filament. Since the deflecting force is directly proportional to the current flowing in the coil, the amount of angular rotation may be used as an indication of the valve of the current flowing in the coil.

F I G U R E **19-1**

Diagram of the essentials of a galvanometer. The deflection of the movable coil is proportional to the current flowing.

The amount of deflection and hence the amount of current flowing through the coil may be indicated by a pointer which is attached to the moving element and moves over a calibrated scale.

On the more sensitive galvanometers a mirror is attached to the moving coil as shown in Fig. 19-1. A light beam is reflected from the mirror onto a ground-glass scale. As the coil is deflected, the light beam moves over the scale.

The restoring force of the suspension filament acts to return the coil and indicating system to the normal or zero position when the current flow through the coil is interrupted.

After a reading is taken and the restoring force acts to return the coil to its normal position, the coil tends to oscillate about the normal position for some time before coming to rest. To prevent excessive oscillation of the coil, a system of damping must be employed. The aluminum frame upon which the coil is wound provides the damping force in the galvanometer just described. Whenever the frame moves in the magnetic field, induced currents are produced which flow around the closed circuit formed by the frame. The induced currents oppose the motion that produces them, thereby bringing the moving element immediately to a standstill.

19-2

The Permanent-Magnet Moving-Coil Instrument

The permanent-magnet moving-coil instrument is universally used for the measurement of direct currents and voltages. It is essentially a galvanometer made for switchboard mounting or for portable use. The moving coil is supported in the magnetic structure in two different ways: by the pivot-and-jewel system or by the taut-band suspension system.

In the pivot-and-jewel construction, the moving coil is wound on a light aluminum frame and the frame turns on steel pivots that rotate in jeweled bearings at each end of the coil. A pointer is

FIGURE **19-2**
Moving element of a permanent-magnet moving-coil instrument, pivot-and-jewel construction.
(Weston Instruments.)

attached rigidly to the frame so that as the coil moves, the pointer moves over a graduated scale. Current is brought into the coil through spiral springs, one at each end of the coil. The springs also provide the restoring force for the instrument. The movable coil, springs, and pointer of a permanent-magnet moving-coil instrument with the pivot-and-jewel construction are shown in Fig. 19-2.

The magnetic circuit consists of a permanent horseshoe magnet to which are attached soft-iron pole pieces. To form a uniform air gap through which the coil may turn, a cylinder of soft iron is supported between the pole pieces. The method of assembly of the magnetic circuit and moving element is shown in Fig. 19-3. It will be noted that a uniform air gap is provided for the coil for a wide range of deflection of the coil. The use of the uniform air gap results in a deflection of the pointer that is almost directly proportional to the current flowing in the coil. Thus, the scale used with this type of instrument may be made very uniform. The aluminum frame upon which the coil is wound provides the damping force.

The taut-band suspension system for a permanent-magnet moving-coil instrument is illustrated in Fig. 19-4. As shown, the moving coil and pointer are suspended by a taut band at either end of the moving mechanism. The taut bands serve three functions:

FIGURE **19-3**
Permanent-magnet moving-coil mechanism.
(Weston Instruments.)

FIGURE **19-4**
Moving element of a taut-band suspension instrument.
(Westinghouse Electric Corporation.)

1. They support the moving element.
2. They provide the restoring force for the moving element.
3. They carry the current to the coil.

The permanent magnet for the taut-band suspension instrument is a core-type magnet. This is a cylindrical magnet with a hollow centre, and the coil thus surrounds the magnet. The return path for the flux is provided by a tubular piece of soft iron placed concentrically with respect to the magnet and forming an air gap through which the coil moves.

Since no bearings are used in the taut-band suspension instrument, the system has no friction and the instrument is highly shock- and vibration-resistant. The instrument is capable of retaining its calibration and accuracy over long periods of time with little maintenance.

19-3
DC Voltmeters

A voltmeter must be designed to be connected *across* the line. Since the coil of a permanent-magnet moving-coil instrument has a low resistance, it must have in series with it a high value of resistance when it is used as a voltmeter. The value of the series resistance must be high enough that the rated current of the coil is not exceeded. In portable testing voltmeters, several voltage ranges may be provided by using different values of series resistance for each range. The series resistance is usually contained in the instrument case itself.

So that the voltmeter will read upscale, the positive (+) terminal of the voltmeter must be connected to the positive line.

19-4
DC Ammeters

An ammeter is connected in **series** with the line in which current is to be measured. Since the moving coil and the spiral springs used as coil connections can be designed for a maximum of only about 50 mA (0.05 A), the permanent-magnet moving-coil instrument when used for the measurement of cur-rent higher than this value must be equipped with a **shunt**. A shunt is merely a low resistance that is placed in parallel with the coil circuit. The greater part of the current in the main circuit is then diverted around the coil through the shunt.

Portable testing ammeters are equipped with self-contained shunts in ranges up to about 50 A. For measurement of higher values of current, millivoltmeters are used with external shunts. The millivoltmeter together with the shunt then constitute the ammeter. Shunts used with millivoltmeters are usually designed so that when rated current flows through them the voltage drop across the shunt is 50 mV (0.05 V). Millivoltmeters used with 50 mV shunts are designed to give a full-scale reading at 50 mV. Switchboard-type instruments or portable instruments always used with the same shunt are generally scaled to read directly in amperes.

F I G U R E **19-5**
Diagram showing the method of connecting a shunt and a millivoltmeter for measuring current.

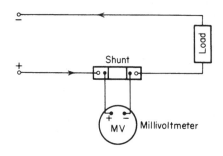

The method of connecting a shunt and millivoltmeter for measuring current is shown in Fig. 19-5. Note the polarity marking of the millivoltmeter with respect to the line polarity.

19-**5**

Moving-Iron Vane Instruments

When two soft-iron bars are placed parallel to each other inside a current-carrying coil, the bars become magnetized, with adjacent ends of the bars behaving like magnetic poles. The bars being similarly magnetized repel each other, the amount of repulsion being dependent on the amount of magnetizing force of the coil. Repulsion occurs between the bars for either direction of current through the coil, and thus they are repelled when an alternating current is passed through the coil.

The moving-iron vane instrument, widely used for the measurement of alternating currents and voltages, operates on the above-described principle. Two iron vanes, one stationary and one securely attached to the central shaft of the moving element, are placed inside the coil through which the current to be measured is passed. In one type of moving-iron vane instrument, the vanes are concentric, the movable vane being placed inside the stationary vane. This type of construction is shown in Fig. 19-6. Another version of this type of instrument uses flat vanes, one attached to the shaft like a flag, the other one fixed. This so-called **radial vane** type of instrument has certain advantages in sensitivity and scale distribution.

When current flows in the coil surrounding the vanes, the movable vane is repelled by the stationary vane and moves the entire moving element clockwise, the amount of movement being dependent on the amount of current flowing in the coil. Restraining action is provided by the spiral spring at the top of the moving element. It should be noted that in this instrument the springs do not carry current. The damping device is an aluminum vane at-

FIGURE **19-6**
Moving element of the moving-iron vane instrument with the stationary vane shown at the right. (Weston Instruments.)

tached to the moving element, as shown in Fig. 19-6, which moves in a closed chamber. The motion of the vane against the air in the chamber prevents excessive oscillation of the pointer. Fig. 19-7 shows a phantom view of an assembled moving-iron vane mechanism.

When used as a voltmeter, the moving-iron vane instrument is used with a series resistance. Portable voltmeters are made with self-contained resistors in ranges up to 750 V. Higher ranges may be obtained by using external multipliers or, as is usually the case, potential transformers (Sec. 13-11). Since the standard low-voltage rating of potential transformers is 115 or 120 V, voltmeters when used with potential transformers generally have a full-scale value of 150 V.

When used as an ammeter, the moving-iron vane instrument is wound with wire heavy enough to carry the rated current. Usual practice, however, is to use a 5 A ammeter in conjunction with a current transformer for measuring values of current larger than 5 A.

The electrodynamometer instrument operates on the same principle as the permanent-magnet moving-coil instrument in that deflection of the moving element is obtained from the interaction of two magnetic fields. However, in the electrodynamometer instrument, two stationary coils are used in place of the permanent magnet. The movable coil is attached to the central shaft so that it may

19-6

Electro-dynamometer Voltmeters and Ammeters

F I G U R E **19-7**
Moving-iron vane mechanism.
(Weston Instruments.)

rotate inside the two stationary coils as shown in Fig. 19-8. Connections are made to the movable coil through the two spiral springs at the top of the mechanism. The springs also provide the restoring force for the moving element. Air damping is obtained by means of the aluminum vanes that move in the enclosed chambers shown at the bottom of the mechanism.

When used as a voltmeter, or as an ammeter for measuring small values of current, the stationary and movable coils are connected in series. Since the polarity of the fields produced by both the stationary and movable coils is reversed by a reversal of current, the deflection of the moving element is always in the same direction, regardless of the direction of current through the coils. For this reason, electrodynamometer instruments may be used with practically equal precision for either dc or ac measurements.

Since the movable coil and its flexible connections can be made to carry but a small amount of current, the electrodynamometer-type instrument is seldom used as an ammeter except for lower current ranges. The permanent-magnet moving-coil and the moving-iron vane instruments are more widely used for the measurement of direct and alternating currents, respectively.

FIGURE **19-8**
Electrodynamometer mechanism.
(Weston Instruments.)

Power is measured by means of the wattmeter. Since power is a function of both current and voltage, two elements are necessary in a wattmeter. For this reason, wattmeters are generally of the electrodynamometer type. The movable coil with a series resistance forms the potential element, while the stationary coils are used as the current element. Connection is as shown in Fig. 19-9, with the potential and current elements in parallel and series, respectively, with the circuit in which the power is to be measured.

Electrodynamometer wattmeters may be used for the measurement of either ac or dc power. Since power in a dc circuit is always a product of current and voltage, however, it is seldom necessary to use a wattmeter in a dc circuit. The power can be calculated easily from the voltmeter and ammeter readings.

Power in an ac circuit depends on the power factor of the circuit as well as the current and the voltage. At unity power factor, the current in both the current and potential coils of a wattmeter reverses at the same time, resulting in a deflecting force on the moving element which is always in the same direction. However, at power factors less than unity, the current in one element reverses

19-**7**

Power Measurements

FIGURE **19-9**
Connection of the electrodynamometer instrument for use as a wattmeter.

before the current reverses in the other element, resulting in a reverse torque during the time that the two currents are in opposite directions. The inertia of the moving element prevents its following the torque reversals, however, so that the resulting indication of the instrument is a resultant of the two torques. For a phase angle of 90°, the two torques are equal and the wattmeter indicates zero power. Thus, the wattmeter indicates the true or actual power of an ac circuit.

Power in a three-phase three-wire circuit may be measured by means of two wattmeters W_1 and W_2 connected as shown in Fig. 19-10. The algebraic sum of the readings of the two wattmeters will be the total three-phase power of the circuit for either balanced or unbalanced loads or voltages. For balanced loads at unity power factor, the readings of the two wattmeters will be identical. When the load power factor is 50 percent, W_2 will read zero and

FIGURE **19-10**
Diagram of connections of two wattmeters for measuring power in a three-wire three-phase circuit.

W_1 will read the total three-phase power. At power factors between 50 and 100 percent, W_1 will read higher than W_2. At power factors lower than 50 percent, the reading of W_2 will be negative and the total three-phase power will be $W_1 - W_2$. At zero power factor, the wattmeters will have identical readings but of opposite signs, indicating zero power. Thus, there is a definite ratio of W_1 to W_2 for each value of circuit power factor.

The two-element or polyphase wattmeter may be used in place of the two single-phase wattmeters shown in Fig. 19-10. Two complete elements are mounted on the same shaft and connected in the same manner as two single-phase wattmeters. The deflection of the pointer indicates total three-phase power directly.

In a three-phase four-wire system, three wattmeters or the three elements of a polyphase wattmeter connected as shown in Fig. 19-11 are necessary for a true indication of power under all conditions of unbalance. Total three-phase power is the sum of the readings of the three wattmeters or is indicated directly by the three-element wattmeter. In general, power may be measured in any polyphase system with the number of wattmeters or elements one less than the number of wires in the system.

19-**8**

The Varmeter

A standard wattmeter can be used to measure reactive voltamperes, or vars, by applying a voltage to it which is displaced 90° in time phase from the voltage that would normally be used for the measurement of watts. The phase shifting required for measuring vars in a single-phase circuit is accomplished by connecting a combination of resistors and capacitors in series with the potential coil of the meter. For three-phase var measurement, a phase-shifting transformer can be used to shift the phase of the voltages applied to each of the elements of the meter.

F I G U R E **19-11**

Connection of three wattmeters to measure power in a four-wire three-phase circuit.

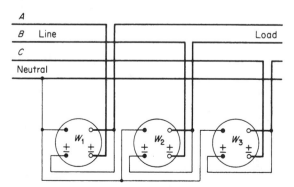

FIGURE **19-12**
Connections of a three-phase varmeter.

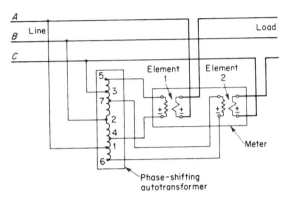

The connection of a two-element varmeter and its auxiliary phase-shifting autotransformers is shown in Fig. 19-12. Analysis of the circuit will show that the voltages V_{45} and V_{67} lag the voltages V_{12} and V_{32}, respectively, by 90°.

Varmeter scales are usually the zero-centre type and are marked IN and OUT at their left- and right-hand ends, respectively. When the meter reads vars OUT, it indicates by convention that magnetizing vars are flowing from the supply to the load. This would be the case when a generator is supplying an inductive load such as an induction motor. Likewise, a var IN reading would indicate that the load was capacitive in nature and that the load was causing magnetizing vars to flow back to the supply.

19-9

Energy Measurements in AC Circuits

Energy is measured by means of the watthour meter. Since energy is a product of power and time, both quantities must be taken into account in energy measurements. Watthour meters are small motors in which the speed of rotation at any time is proportional to the power at that time. The total number of revolutions made by the rotating element in a given time is then a measure of the energy consumption during that time.

The induction watthour meter is used for measuring and recording energy in ac circuits. The essential parts are an electromagnet, a rotating element, a damping or retarding system, and a register. A modern watthour meter is shown in Fig. 19-13.

The induction watthour meter operates essentially as a split-phase induction motor. The rotating element is an aluminum disk mounted on a vertical shaft. Friction is reduced to a minimum by the use of jeweled or magnetically suspended bearings. Driving

FIGURE **19-13**
Single-phase induction watthour meter.
(General Electric Company.)

torque is obtained from the electromagnet, which consists of a potential coil and two current coils mounted on an iron core but mechanically displaced from each other. The arrangement of the coils of a typical electromagnet is shown in Fig. 19-14. The current coils, being connected in series with the line, are wound with a few turns of relatively heavy wire since they must carry the full line current. Flux produced by the current coils is proportional to and in phase with the line current.

So that it may be connected directly across the circuit in which the energy is to be measured, the potential coil is wound with many turns of fine wire. Because of the high inductance of the coil, the

FIGURE **19-14**
Single-phase watthour-meter electromagnet and connections.

current lags behind the applied voltage by nearly 90°. To cause the potential coil flux to be exactly 90° behind the current coil flux, a short-circuited coil is placed around the core below the potential coil. Induced currents in this coil act to retard the potential coil flux to the desired phase position.

The flux produced by the potential and current coils, being displaced both in space and time phase, as in the split-phase motor, induce eddy currents in the disk of the rotating element. The motor action so produced is greatest at unity power factor and is zero at zero power factor and, for given values of current and voltage, is proportional to any value of power factor. Hence the speed of the rotating element is proportional to $VI \cos \theta$.

To prevent the armature from racing at a high speed when a torque is applied and to make the speed proportional to the power supplied the meter, a retarding torque is necessary. This is obtained by placing a permanent magnet near the rotating element so that the disk rotates in the field established by the magnet. Eddy currents induced in the disk produce a field that reacts with the field of the magnet, thereby causing a damping action that is proportional to the speed of the disk; that is, the faster the disk is turned, the greater the eddy currents and the greater the retarding action. Hence, the speed of the rotating element of a watthour meter is made directly proportional to the power in the circuit.

Since the speed of the rotating element is proportional to the power, every revolution represents a definite amount of energy. Geared to the rotating element is a register, the reading of which is an indication of the energy consumed over any given period. Register dials are calibrated to read directly in kilowatthours.

Friction compensation is obtained by means of a shading coil placed in the air gap of the magnetic circuit so as to produce a forward torque sufficiently great to overcome any friction normally encountered by the rotating element.

Single-phase watthour-meter connections are the same as single-phase wattmeter connections in that the potential coil is connected in parallel and the current coil in series with the circuit in which energy is being measured.

Polyphase energy measurements are similar to polyphase power measurements; that is, the number of watthour meters required for correct energy measurements is one less than the number of wires in the system. Multi-element watthour meters are generally used, however, the required number of electromagnets being mounted so as to drive one rotating element that records the total polyphase energy on one register.

Several schemes of metering polyphase energy are in use whereby the number of elements is less than required for absolutely correct measurement. For reasonably balanced loads and voltages, these meters are sufficiently accurate for commercial measurements.

Watthour meters can be equipped with special solid-state, microprocessor-based registers to record not only the total monthly kilowatthours, but also kilowatthours for certain periods of time (such as off-peak times). These registers can also be programmed to record kilowatt demand and the time that the demand occurred during each month. As a further step in the trend toward solid-state measuring equipment, many induction-type watthour meters are being replaced with electronic-type meters that are completely solid-state.

The electrodynamometer-type instrument when made with two movable coils set at right angles to each other may be used to measure power factor. The method of connection of this type of power-factor meter in a three-phase circuit is shown in Fig. 19-15. The two stationary coils S and S' are connected in series in line B. Mounted on the central shaft and free to move without restraining or control springs are coils M and M'. Coils M and M' are connected with their series resistors from lines B to A and B to C, respectively. At unity power factor, one potential-coil current leads and one lags the current in line B by 30° so that the coils are balanced in the position shown in Fig. 19-15. A change in power factor causes the current of one potential coil to become more in phase and the other to be more out of phase with the current in line B so that the moving element and pointer take a new position of balance to indicate the new power factor.

The power-factor meter shown in Fig. 19-15, when used with a special reactance-resistance network auxiliary, may be used to measure power factor in a single-phase circuit.

19-**10**

Power-Factor Meter

FIGURE **19-15**
Connection diagram of a three-phase power-factor meter of the electrodynamometer type.

19-11

Phase-Angle Meters

The phase-angle meter is a test instrument that is almost indispensable in power circuit testing work, particularly in the testing of metering and protective relaying circuits. It is used to indicate the phase angle between an alternating current and voltage, between two voltages, or between two currents. Since many meters, relays, and other control devices depend upon the proper phase relationships between two or more electrical quantities for their proper operation, the phase-angle meter may be used for installation or maintenance testing of such circuits and equipment. A portable phase-angle meter is shown in Fig. 19-16.

The movable element of the meter shown consists of iron vanes, but unlike the moving-iron instrument described in Sec. 19-5, the vanes are magnetized by a coil on the moving element. Furthermore, the moving element is free to turn a full 360°. When the stationary and moving coils are energized from two sources of the same frequency, the moving element takes a position where the pole strength of the vanes is greatest. This position of greatest pole strength is determined by the phase angle between the sources energizing the two coils. Therefore, the meter may be calibrated so that the phase angle between the two sources is indicated directly upon the meter dial.

The electrodynamometer-type instrument may also be used as a phase-angle meter, and one commercially available meter uses this principle.

F I G U R E **19-16**
Phase-angle meter.
(Westinghouse Electric Corporation.)

A very simple method of measuring resistance is by the voltmeter-ammeter method. A direct current is passed through the unknown resistance, the current being measured by an ammeter and the voltage drop across the resistance being measured by a voltmeter. By Ohm's law, the resistance is

$$R = \frac{V}{I}$$

Although this method of resistance measurement is relatively simple, care should be taken so that the currents taken by the instruments themselves do not introduce errors in the results of the measurements. When low values of resistance, such as an armature-circuit resistance, are being measured, the connections for the least amount of error are as shown in Fig. 19-17. To ensure that the voltage drop across the armature is large enough to be read on the voltmeter, a large value of current must be used, with care being taken of course not to exceed the current rating of the armature. For the connection shown in Fig. 19-17, the ammeter reads the sum of the currents through the armature and the voltmeter. However, the current taken by the voltmeter is so small compared with the current through the armature that the error introduced is practically negligible.

When higher values of resistance are being measured and where the value of test current is quite small, the instrument connections should be as shown in Fig. 19-18. Note that the voltmeter is connected across both the ammeter and the unknown resistance. The ammeter reads the true value of the current through the resistance, but the voltmeter reading includes the IR drop in the ammeter. Since the test current required is quite low, the ammeter IR drop is very low, resulting in an almost negligible error in the measurements.

19-**12**

Measurement of Resistance; Voltmeter-Ammeter Method

FIGURE **19-17**
Connection of a voltmeter and ammeter for measuring a low value of resistance.

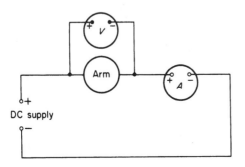

FIGURE **19-18**
Connection of a voltmeter and ammeter for measuring a high value of resistance.

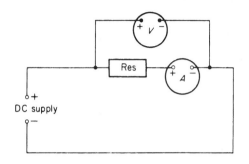

For precise measurements with either of the two above methods of resistance determination, corrections should be made for the currents taken by the instruments. This is not necessary in most ordinary commercial measurements, however.

19-**13**

Wheatstone Bridge

The most commonly used device for accurate resistance measurements in the range of 1 to 100 000 Ω is the Wheatstone bridge. As shown in Fig. 19-19, it is composed of resistances R_1, R_2, and R_3, which are accurately known adjustable resistances. The unknown resistance R_x is connected between points D and B. The resistors are arranged in two parallel circuits through which current from the battery can flow. A galvanometer is bridged across the two circuits between the points C and D.

Balancing the bridge consists of closing the battery switch S_1 and adjusting R_1, R_2, and R_3 to such values that, when the galvanometer switch S_2 is closed, the galvanometer shows no deflection.

FIGURE **19-19**
Schematic diagram of connections of the Wheatstone bridge.

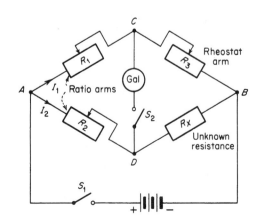

With the bridge balanced, the points C and D are at the same potential. This means that the voltage drops from A to C and A to D must be equal and that the drops from C to B and D to B are also equal. Hence

$$I_1 R_1 = I_2 R_2 \qquad\qquad \text{[19-1]}$$

and

$$I_1 R_3 = I_2 R_x \qquad\qquad \text{[19-2]}$$

Dividing Eq. (19-1) by Eq. (19-2) and solving for R_x results in

$$R_x = \frac{R_2}{R_1} R_3 \qquad\qquad \text{[19-3]}$$

Example 19-1

The Wheatstone bridge represented in Fig. 19-19 when used for determining the value of an unknown resistance R_x is balanced when R_3 is 124 Ω, R_1 is 10 Ω, R_2 is 100 Ω. What is the value of R_x?

$$R_x = \frac{R_2}{R_1} R_3$$

$$R_x = \frac{100}{10} \times 124$$

$$R_x = 1240 \ \Omega$$

Resistances R_1 and R_2 are called the ratio arms of the bridge and are usually made to equal a definite ratio such as 1 to 1, 10 to 1, or 100 to 1. Resistance R_3 is called the rheostat arm and is made continuously variable from 1 to 1000 or from 1 to 10 000 Ω. When the bridge is balanced, the value of the unknown resistance is equal to the value of R_3 multiplied by the ratio of R_2 to R_1.

On commercial "dial"-type bridges, the ratio of R_2 to R_1 is selected by means of a rotary switch, the setting being indicated on a dial. The rheostat arm R_3 is adjusted by four or more rotary switches, one of which varies the resistance in steps of 1 Ω, another in steps of 10 Ω, another in steps of 100 Ω, and so on. The value of the rheostat arm R_3 then may be read directly from the setting of the several dials on the rotary switches when the bridge is balanced.

In the portable bridge shown in Fig. 19-20, an adjustable slide wire controlled by the knob in the centre of the panel forms the ratio arms. The rheostat arm consists of six fixed standard resistors, one of which may be selected by means of the rotary range switch

FIGURE **19-20**
Portable-type Wheatstone bridge.
(Leeds & Northrup Company.)

located in the lower right-hand corner of the bridge. The unknown resistance is connected to the two terminals in the upper right-hand corner. The bridge is balanced by selecting the proper fixed resistor with the rotary selector switch and then adjusting the ratio arm slide wire until the galvanometer reads zero. The value of the unknown resistance is then the setting of the slide wire as indicated on its scale, multiplied by the multiplier as set on the rotary selector switch.

|19-**14**

Insulation Resistance

Insulating materials are materials that offer a high resistance to the flow of an electric current. The materials and the dimensions of the materials used for insulating electric circuits must be such that a very high resistance, usually in the order of megaohms, is offered to the flow of current. (One megaohm [MΩ] equals 1 000 000 Ω.) For example, the armature coils of a generator must have sufficient insulation to prevent the leakage of current to adjacent coils or to the iron armature core. The operation of electric equipment such as transformers, motors, generators, and cables depends on the maintenance of the proper value of insulation resistance for the circuits involved.

In many cases it is desirable to measure periodically the insulation resistance of electric circuits, so that defective insulation may be found before it causes failure of the equipment. Defective insulation may occur from the effects of heat, the presence of moisture, mechanical injuries, chemical action, or other causes. Of the several known methods for measuring insulation resistance, the voltmeter method (Sec. 19-15) and the Megger method (Sec. 19-16) are the most commonly used.

A voltmeter may be used for measuring insulation resistance or other high resistances. A high-resistance voltmeter is preferable, and the voltmeter resistance R_v must be known. A reading is first taken with the voltmeter across a constant source of voltage E. The voltmeter and the unknown resistance are then connected in series to the same source of voltage E, as in Fig. 19-21, and a second reading is taken. From these readings, the value of the unknown resistance may be calculated as shown below.

In Fig. 19-21 the current is

$$I = \frac{E_s}{R_v + R_x} \qquad \text{[19-4]}$$

The voltmeter reading V when the voltmeter is connected in the circuit of Fig. 19-21 is the voltage drop in its own resistance, or

$$V = IR_v \qquad \text{[19-5]}$$

Substituting for I from Eq. (19-4) into Eq. (19-5) and solving for R_x results in

$$R_x = R_v \left(\frac{E_s}{V} - 1 \right) \qquad \text{[19-6]}$$

The value of the unknown resistance R_x may thus be calculated by substituting the two voltmeter readings in Eq. (19-6).

19-15

Measurement of Resistance; Voltmeter Method

FIGURE **19-21**
Voltmeter method of measuring resistance.

DC supply

Example 19-2

It is desired to measure the resistance of the insulation between a motor winding and the motor frame. A 300-V, 30 000-Ω voltmeter is used in making the measurements. The voltmeter when connected across the source reads 230 V and when connected in series with the insulation reads 5 V. Find the insulation resistance.

$$R_x = R_v \left(\frac{E_s}{V} - 1 \right)$$

$$= 30\ 000 \left(\frac{230}{5} - 1 \right) = 30\ 000 \times 45$$

$$= 1\ 350\ 000\ \Omega, \text{ or } 1.35\ M\Omega$$

19-16

The Megger Insulation Tester

The Megger insulation tester is extensively used for measuring insulation resistance. One model of this line of insulation testers is shown in Fig. 19-22.

Essentially, the Megger insulation tester consists of a hand-driven generator and a direct-reading true ohmmeter. A simplified diagram of the electric connections of the instrument is shown in Fig. 19-23. A permanent magnet provides the field for the ohmmeter.

FIGURE **19-22**
Megger® insulation tester.
(AVO International)

FIGURE **19-23**
Simplified circuit diagram of the Megger® insulation tester.
(AVO International)

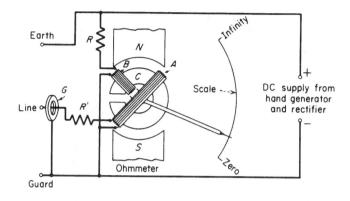

The moving element of the ohmmeter consists of two coils, *A* and *B*, which are mounted rigidly to a pivoted central shaft and which are free to rotate over a stationary C-shaped iron cage. The coils are connected to the circuit by means of flexible leads that exert no restoring force on the moving element. Hence, the moving element may stand in any position over the scale when the generator is not in operation. Coil *B* is connected in series with the resistance *R* across the generator terminals, while coil *A* is connected in series with the resistance *R'* between one generator terminal and the test terminal marked LINE.

When current flows from the generator through coil *B*, the coil tends to set itself at right angles to the field of the permanent magnet. With the test terminals open, corresponding to infinite resistance, no current flows in coil *A*. Coil *B* thus governs the motion of the rotating element, causing it to move to its extreme counterclockwise position. The point on the scale indicated by the pointer under this condition is marked infinite resistance.

Coil *A* is wound to produce a clockwise torque on the moving element. With the test terminals marked LINE and EARTH short-circuited, corresponding to zero external resistance, the current flowing through coil *A* is large enough to produce enough torque to overcome the counterclockwise torque of coil *B*. This moves the pointer to its extreme clockwise position, and this point is marked zero resistance on the scale. The resistance *R'* protects coil *A* from the flow of excessive current when the test terminals are short-circuited.

When an unknown value of resistance is connected between the test terminals LINE and EARTH, the opposing torques of the coil balance each other so that the pointer comes to rest at some intermediate point on the scale. The scale is calibrated so that the pointer indicates directly the value of the resistance being measured.

The purpose of the guard ring G is to prevent errors in reading due to leakage currents between the LINE and EARTH terminals of the instrument. The GUARD terminal is provided so that unwanted leakage currents in the apparatus under test may also be eliminated.

19-**17**
The Ohmmeter

The series ohmmeter makes use of the principle of using a voltmeter for measuring resistance as described in Sec. 19-15. Fig. 19-24 shows the circuit of the series ohmmeter. A battery, a current-detecting instrument G, and a series resistance R are connected in series between the two terminals A and B. With terminals A and B open (infinite resistance), the pointer of the instrument is at rest at the left-hand end of the scale. The value of the series resistance R is chosen so that with the test terminals A and B short-circuited (zero resistance) the pointer comes to rest at the right-hand end of the scale. Thus, an inverse scale is used, zero resistance being indicated on the right-hand end with increasing values of resistance marked on the scale from right to left.

Before a resistance measurement is made, the test terminals are short-circuited and the instrument pointer is adjusted to the zero position by means of the variable-shunt resistance R_s. This is necessary since the battery voltage may vary from time to time and thus affect the readings. The resistance R_x to be measured is then connected between terminals A and B, the value of the resistance being read directly from the scale.

Ohmmeters are very often included as a part of a multifunction, multirange test instrument.

F I G U R E **19-24**
Connections of the ohmmeter.

Electric instruments or meters maybe classified as being either passive or active. The permanent-magnet moving-coil, moving-iron vane, and electrodynamometer instruments described earlier in this chapter are examples of the passive type. Instruments of this type must extract energy from the circuit under test to deflect the meter movement. This loading effect of the meter is of no great consequence in normal 50- or 60-Hz power circuits since the current drawn by the meter is usually very small relative to the current in the circuit being tested. However, in sensitive high-impedance or high-frequency circuits the use of such meters may affect appreciably the operation of the circuit being tested.

Active instruments have their own power supplies, and the energy required to operate the instrument display is obtained from this internal power supply. The loading effect of such instruments therefore is minimal, resulting in very little disturbance of the circuits in which measurements are being made. Electronic voltmeters are active instruments and may be either the **analog** or the **digital** type.

In the **analog electronic voltmeter**, tiny currents flow from an internal power source through two vacuum tubes or transistors. With the instrument energized and with zero voltage at its input terminals, these two currents are balanced by the operation of a zero-adjustment knob on the instrument so that the pointer reads exactly zero on the meter scale. When a voltage to be measured is then applied to the input terminals of the meter, an unbalance is caused in the flow of current in the two voltmeter tubes or transistors. This causes a deflection of the meter pointer which is proportional to the unbalance in the currents and to the magnitude of the voltage being measured.

The **digital electronic voltmeter** displays the measured voltages on a multidigit numeric display as lighted figures or digits. This is in contrast to a pointer moving over a fixed scale as in the analog voltmeter. However, since voltage is an analog quantity — that is, it can vary from zero to its maximum value with an infinite number of values — its form must be changed to be displayed by a digital voltmeter. This is accomplished by the use of an analog-to-digital converter built into the voltmeter.

A digital voltmeter consists essentially of a signal conditioner or buffer, an analog-to-digital converter, and a display system. A built-in power supply is included also to provide a reference voltage for the analog-to-digital converter and to power the electronic circuits. A voltage to be measured is applied to the signal conditioner, where it is amplified, reduced in value, or passed unchanged to the analog-to-digital converter. The converter changes the input analog voltage to digital form by using one of several standardized techniques. The signal is then decoded and displayed in its digital form by the voltmeter's digital circuits. A range switch is provided so that different full-scale values of voltage may be selected by moving the displayed decimal point. Thus, full-scale values may be, for example, 9.999, 99.99, or 999.9 V.

19-19
Multimeters

Voltmeters, ammeters, and ohmmeters are often combined into multifunction, multirange test instruments called **multimeters**. Multimeters may be equipped with either an analog or a digital display system.

Analog multimeters may be either the passive type or the electronic type. The display system for either is the pointer-type movement, usually the permanent-magnet moving-coil type. A typical passive-type combination volt-ohm-milliammeter (usually referred to as a VOM) is shown in Fig. 19-25. This portable meter has self-contained dry cells to provide the source of emf for the ohmmeter. Both dc and ac currents and voltages, as well as resistance, can be measured with this meter.

Analog electronic multimeters have features similar to those of the passive analog VOM except that lower voltage ranges are pro-

FIGURE **19-25**
A portable volt-ohm-milliammeter, or VOM.
(Simpson Electric Company.)

FIGURE **19-26**
A digital multimeter, or DMM.
(Simpson Electric Company.)

vided on the electronic type. These meters are made portable by the use of self-contained battery supplies for the ohmmeter and the electronic circuits.

Digital multimeters (DMMs) are active electronic meters that offer some advantages over the analog types for certain applications. The use of the numeric display makes reading easier and eliminates interpretation errors which can occur with the use of multiscale analog meters. Digital multimeters are available in many styles, ratings, and levels of accuracy. A typical DMM is shown in Fig. 19-26. This meter is powered by rechargeable nickel-cadmium batteries, making it suitable for portable use. Measurements of dc and ac currents and voltages as well as resistance all in several ranges can be made with this compact instrument.

Fig. 19-27 is a more compact or pocket version of the instrument illustrated in Fig. 19-26. This type of multimeter is becoming very popular due to its compactness and durability since it contains no moving coil to be jarred out of calibration.

Fig. 19-28 is another type of multimeter that is designed to measure quite large ac currents as well as being capable of making voltage and resistance measurements. This instrument is quite often referred to as a **clamp-on** ammeter, so named due to its method of making ac current measurements. The large jaws at the end of the meter act as a secondary of a transformer and the conductor from which the current measurement is taken acts as the primary of a transformer. Since the strength of the field about the conductor is proportional to the current flowing through it and the rate of change of magnetic field is proportional to the

FIGURE **19-27**
A portable digital multimeter.
(Simpson Electric Company.)

FIGURE **19-28**
A clamp-on ammeter with volt-ohm measurement capabilities.
(Simpson Electric Company.)

frequency of the ac line, a voltage is induced into the instrument's secondary circuit. This induced emf is then measured and reflected in units of amperes on either a moving coil meter or a digital readout. Certainly the most unique feature of this type of instrument is its ability to measure circuit current without disconnecting the current carrying conductor and connecting it to the meter. The measurement is taken by simply opening up the jaws at the end of the instrument and closing them around the current carrying conductor making a safe measurement. Some variations of this type of meter can make ac current measurements up to 1000 A.

The cathode-ray oscilloscope is a very useful general-purpose electronic measuring instrument. It is used for studying waveshapes of alternating currents and voltages as well as for measuring voltage, current, power, and frequency, in fact, almost any quantity that involves amplitude and waveform.

The cathode-ray oscilloscope is built around the cathode-ray tube. This is a high-vacuum glass tube containing a cathode, a cathode heater, a control grid, an anode, and two pairs of deflecting plates, all as shown in simplified form in Fig. 19-29. The cathode is fabricated with a material that, when heated, liberates or emits electrons.

When the cathode of the cathode-ray tube is heated to its emitting temperature and a voltage of the proper magnitude and polarity is applied between the anode and the cathode, the emitted electrons are drawn toward the anode at a high velocity. The anode has an opening in it so that some of the electrons pass on through it. These electrons, because of the velocity attained by their movement from the cathode to the anode, continue to move through the highly evacuated tube until they strike the end wall of the tube. This part of the tube is covered with a fluorescent material that glows when it is struck by the stream of electrons and forms the

19-**20**

The Cathode-Ray Oscilloscope

FIGURE **19-29**
Diagram of a cathode-ray tube.

viewing screen of the tube. A stream of electrons passing from the cathode through the opening in the anode and in a straight line to the screen appears as a stationary spot on the screen.

Between the anode and the viewing screen and adjacent to the electron stream are placed two pairs of deflecting plates, one horizontal pair and one vertical pair. By applying a voltage to either pair of plates, the electron stream may be deflected from its straight-line path, the amount of deflection being in proportion to the voltage applied. If, for example, an alternating voltage is applied across the two vertical deflecting plates, the electron stream is deflected back and forth along a horizontal line on the viewing screen as the voltage changes in magnitude and direction. Unless the frequency of the applied voltage is very low, the back-and-forth movement of the electron stream appears as a stationary horizontal line on the screen. Likewise, an alternating voltage applied to the horizontal plates appears as a stationary vertical line.

When the oscilloscope is being used to study the waveshape of, say, an alternating voltage, the voltage under test is applied to one set of plates while a second voltage, called a sweep voltage, is applied to the other set of plates. The sweep voltage is of special waveform and is generated in an oscillator that is usually a part of the oscilloscope. The sweep voltage is adjusted until it is synchronized with the voltage under test. With the two voltages properly synchronized, a stationary wave of the exact shape of the voltage under test appears in the form of a graph on the viewing screen. Thus, both the waveshape and magnitude of the test voltage may be observed on the screen. The brilliance of the image on the screen may be controlled by means of a control grid placed between the cathode and the deflecting plates.

Because of its versatility in high-frequency measurements, the cathode-ray oscilloscope is almost indispensable in communications research work and in the service of communications equipment. It is used in the study of transient phenomena due to lightning and switching surges on power systems. It is also used in the studies of electric arcs and commutation; for the measurements of impedance, transformer ratios, and phase angle; for mechanical measurements; and in many other applications.

Fig. 19-30 is an illustration of a general purpose 15 Mhz dual trace oscilloscope. This instrument is capable of displaying two wave forms on the same CRT (cathode ray tube). This enables the technician to observe and compare two signals. Oscilloscopes are highly multifunctional instruments and should be carefully selected when applying to any given application.

F I G U R E **19-30**
15 Mhz dual trace oscilloscope.
(Simpson Electric Company.)

R EVIEW QUESTIONS

1 What is a galvanometer? What is the functional principle upon which it operates?

2 How is the restoring or restraining action produced in a galvanometer? How is damping accomplished?

3 Describe the construction of a permanent-magnet moving-coil instrument. For what kind of measurements is it used?

4 How are voltmeters and ammeters connected to a circuit?

5 How may the range of a voltmeter be extended so that high values of voltage may be measured?

6 How are high values of current measured with a permanent-magnet moving-coil instrument?

7 Describe the principle of the moving-iron vane instrument. How is damping provided? For what kind of measurements is it used?

8 What is an electrodynamometer instrument? Why can this instrument be used for either ac or dc measurements while the permanent-magnet moving-coil instrument is suitable only for dc measurements?

9 How is the electrodynamometer instrument connected when used as a wattmeter? Will this instrument correctly measure power in a circuit in which the current and voltage are out of phase?

10 How many single-phase wattmeters are necessary for accurate measurements of power in a three-wire three-phase circuit? How are the wattmeters connected?

11 How is driving torque obtained in the induction watthour meter? How is retarding torque provided?

12 How do watthour-meter connections compare with wattmeter connections?

13 What type of instrument is used for power-factor measurement?

14 Show how an ammeter and voltmeter should be connected for determining the resistance of a 115-V 10-W lamp. How does this connection differ from that used for measuring a motor armature resistance?

15 Draw a sketch showing the essential circuits of a Wheatstone bridge. Show the relation between the four resistances when the bridge is balanced.

16 What is meant by insulation resistance? Why is it important to know the value of insulation resistance?

17 Describe the method of measuring resistance with a voltmeter.

18 What are the essential parts of the Megger insulation tester? Describe its operation.

19 How is a series ohmmeter adjusted for a zero reading? Why is this adjustment necessary?

20 How do passive test instruments differ from active ones?

21 Why is an analog-to-digital converter a necessary part of a digital electronic voltmeter?

22 What is the basic function of an oscilloscope?

23 Describe how a clamp-on ammeter takes a current measurement, and give at least two advantages of this type of current measurement over more conventional methods.

P R O B L E M S

19-1 A 150-V dc voltmeter has a resistance of 15 000 Ω. Find the current flowing through the voltmeter when it is connected to a 120-V line. What will be the voltmeter current for full-scale (150-V) deflection?

19-2 What must be the value of an external resistance used with the voltmeter in Prob. 19-1 if it is desired to use the voltmeter for measuring a maximum of 300 V?

19-3 What is the resistance of a 50-A shunt if the voltage drop across it is 50 mV at rated shunt current?

19-4 A 50-mV millivoltmeter is used with a 100-A 50-mV shunt for measuring the current taken by a dc motor. What is the motor current when the instrument indicates 30 mV? By what factor must any reading of the above millivoltmeter be multiplied to give the motor current in amperes?

19-5 If a 100-mV instrument is used with the shunt in Prob. 19-4, what will be the scale-multiplying factor?

19-6 A millivoltmeter used with a 200-A 50-mV shunt has a 0 to 200 scale marked to read directly in amperes. If the 200-A shunt is replaced by a 100-A 50-mV shunt, by what factor must the instrument readings be multiplied to obtain true values of current?

19-7 A permanent-magnet moving-coil instrument has a coil resistance of 2 Ω and requires a current of 0.025 A for full-scale deflection. The scale reads 0 to 300. Find the value of a series resistance required to make the instrument suitable for use as a 300 V voltmeter.

19-8 Three impedances having resistances of 5 Ω and inductive reactances of 8.66 Ω are wye-connected to a 480-V three-phase three-wire system. Three ammeters and two single-phase watt-meters are connected to read currents and power in the circuit. What will be the readings of each of the ammeters and of each wattmeter?

19-9 A 15 000-Ω voltmeter is to be used for an insulation-resistance measurement. The supply voltage is 120 V. When connected in series with the supply and the insulation under test, the voltmeter reads 10 V. What is the resistance of the insulation?

19-10 With the ratio arms of a Wheatstone bridge set at a ratio of 10-to-1, the bridge balances with the rheostat arm set at 23 Ω. What is the value of the unknown resistance?

Industrial Electronics

The general subject of electronics related to the principles of semiconductors is too broad to be treated in any detail in a power-oriented text such as this one. Industrial and power engineers and technicians are, however, becoming more and more involved with electronic circuits and equipment. The purpose of this chapter is to give a very brief introduction to some of the semiconductor devices used in power electronics together with a few typical examples of circuits and devices in which electronics play an important part.

The reader desiring to pursue this subject in depth may refer to the many excellent texts and journals available.

20-1
Semiconductors

Materials such as copper and aluminum have many free electrons and are good conductors of electricity. Materials such as quartz or porcelain have few free electrons and are called insulators. Some materials having a conductivity that falls between that of good conductors and good insulators are called **semiconductors**. Some of these semiconductor materials can, by careful processing, be made suitable for use in solid-state electronic devices. Silicon, germanium, selenium, and certain oxides have been used in the manufacturing of solid-state electronic devices, but silicon is by far the most popular material.

To make a material having properties suitable for use in solid-state electronic devices, very minute amounts of other elements are added to pure silicon (or germanium) crystals during the manufacturing process. The process of adding other elements to the silicon is called **doping**. These other elements or **impurities** have atomic structures which differ from the silicon atomic structure. When these impurities are added in closely controlled amounts, they modify the electrical properties of the silicon, particularly its resistivity.

When silicon crystals are doped with impurity atoms of materials such as phosphorus or arsenic, the resulting material has an excess of loosely bound electrons. Since electrons are negative charge carriers, the material is called an **N-type semiconductor** (N for negative).

Pure silicon may, on the other hand, be doped with another type of impurity atom which has a deficiency of electrons with respect to silicon. Impurity elements of this type that have been used include boron, aluminum, and gallium. Since the resulting material has gaps or **holes** in its atomic structure, electrons, under certain conditions, can move into these holes. This leaves new holes in the material for other electrons to move into, and so on. The effect is just as if the holes were moving in a direction opposite to the electron movement. Thus, the holes may be considered to have a positive charge since they represent an absence of electrons. It is convenient then to speak of holes in this type of semiconductor material as positive charge carriers and to refer to the material as a **P-type semiconductor** (P for positive).

In a conductor, the flow of electric current is considered to be the movement of free electrons. In a semiconductor, the current may be considered to be either the movement of electrons or the movement of holes. If the material is P-type material, that is, deficient in electrons, conduction is by holes. If the material is N-type material, which has an excess of electrons, conduction is by electrons.

The conventions used in the discussion of current flow in solid-state electric devices thus may be stated briefly as follows:

1. In N-type semiconductors, current is carried by negative charge carriers or electrons, which move in a direction opposite to the conventional current flow.
2. In P-type semiconductors, current is carried by positive charge carriers or holes, which move in the same direction as the conventional current flow.

20-**2**
The Semiconductor Diode

When a section of P-type semiconductor is joined to a section of N-type semiconductor, it has been found that the junction so formed will pass current easily in one direction but will offer considerable resistance to the flow of current in the reverse direction. A two-electrode semiconductor device having a P-type electrode and an N-type electrode is called a **semiconductor diode**, a **junction diode**, or a **semiconductor rectifier**.

A semiconductor diode is in a state of equilibrium when there is no external voltage applied to the diode. When the junction is formed initially, some of the free charges from both the P-type and N-type materials diffuse across the junction and recombine. This forms a neutral barrier called the **depletion layer** between the two regions. This depletion layer prevents a further exchange of charge carriers between the two regions of the diode. Thus, the diode is said to be in equilibrium.

When a diode is connected to an external battery as in Fig. 20-1 with the battery positive terminal connected to the P terminal

FIGURE 20-1
Semiconductor diode with forward bias.

of the diode and the negative terminal to the N terminal of the diode, the diode is said to be **forward-biased**. The bias voltage overcomes the small potential barrier of the depletion layer, allowing electrons to be attracted across the diode junction by the positive terminal of the battery. Likewise, holes are attracted in the opposite direction across the junction by the negative terminal of the battery. Electrons constantly enter the N terminal of the diode and leave the P terminal, and current flows in the circuit.

When the battery polarity is reversed as in Fig. 20-2, the diode is said to be **reverse-biased** and the excess electrons in the N-type material are attracted away from the injunction by the positive terminal of the battery. Likewise, the holes are attracted away from the junction. This leaves the section of the diode near the junction practically void of charge carriers, and only an extremely small current called the **leakage current** can flow through the junction or in the external circuit. Since a forward-biased junction offers a low resistance to the flow of current and a reverse-biased junction offers a high resistance to the flow of current, the junction has the properties of a rectifier.

A semiconductor diode is represented by the symbol shown in Fig. 20-3. Note that the terminal identified as the cathode connects

FIGURE 20-2
Semiconductor diode with reverse bias.

F I G U R E **20-3**
Symbol for semiconductor diode.

to the N-type material. Note also that the arrow in the symbol points in the direction of conventional current flow. This is true in the symbols used for other solid-state devices also. (See Appendix A.)

|20-**3**
Silicon Rectifiers

A rectifier is a device for changing an alternating current to pulses of direct current. As indicated in the previous section, the semiconductor diode has the properties of a rectifier.

When an alternating voltage is applied to a silicon rectifier, as shown in Fig. 20-4, the diode is alternately forward- and reverse-biased during each cycle of the applied voltage. When the diode is forward-biased during the positive half-cycle, electron current flows freely. During the next half-cycle when the diode is reverse-biased, the diode is nonconducting. The diode conducts current

F I G U R E **20-4**
Half-wave rectifier: (*a*) Output current circuit; (*b*) input voltage wave; (*c*) output current wave.

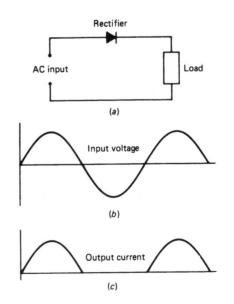

FIGURE **20-5**
Full-wave rectifier with centre-tapped transformer; (*a*) circuit; (*b*) input voltage wave; (*c*) output current wave.

only during the positive half-cycles of the applied voltage, resulting in a pulsating dc output with a waveshape like that shown in Fig. 20-4(*c*). A rectifier producing an output current of this type is called a *half-wave rectifier*.

To provide a smoother current output, two diodes and a centre-tapped transformer may be connected as shown in Fig. 20-5 to form what is known as a **full-wave rectifier**. With this arrangement, one diode conducts during each half-cycle, resulting in the output current waveform shown in Fig. 20-5(*c*).

Another commonly used rectifier connection, called the **full-wave bridge rectifier**, is shown in Fig. 20-6. This rectifier circuit avoids the need for a centre-tapped transformer and provides twice the output voltage obtained from the basic two-diode rectifier.

To provide the large amounts of direct current often required in industrial plants, three-phase rectifiers are usually used. A connection diagram of a three-phase full-wave bridge-type rectifier is shown in Fig. 20-7.

The pulsating output produced by rectifiers is suitable for some applications, but in most cases the pulsations must be reduced by

FIGURE **20-6**
Single-phase full-wave bridge rectifier.

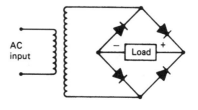

means of filter circuits. Filter circuits are combinations of inductance coils and capacitors arranged so that the pulsating energy is
stored alternately in the coils and capacitors, resulting in a much
smoother flow of current from the rectifier. Two typical filter circuits are shown in Fig. 20-8.

Silicon rectifiers are available commercially with current ratings
ranging from a few milliamperes to several hundred amperes and
with voltage ratings as high as 1000 V or more. They are highly
efficient, achieving rectification efficiencies as high as 99 percent.
Because of their many desirable characteristics, silicon rectifiers
find wide application as industrial dc supplies for battery charging,
electrochemical processes, variable-speed motor drives, and other
similar applications where formerly dc generators were used.

These high current diodes require a device to quickly remove
the heat produced by the large currents passed through them. This
device is called a **heat sink**. It is usually made of aluminum with
finned edges to provide a greater surface area. In some very large
diodes, the heat sink is hollow and water is passed through it for
cooling purposes.

FIGURE **20-7**
Three-phase full-wave bridge rectifier.

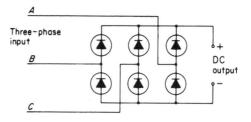

FIGURE **20-8**
Filter circuits used to reduce rectifier output pulsations.

The Zener diode is a special type of silicon junction diode often used as a voltage regulator or voltage stabilizer. Like the silicon rectifier diode, the Zener diode has a very low resistance to the flow of current when it is forward-biased. When it is reverse-biased at low voltages, it allows only a very minute current to flow. However, when an applied reverse-bias voltage is gradually increased, a point is reached at which the Zener diode breaks down and suddenly begins to conduct. The sharp break from nonconductance to conductance is called the Zener effect, so named for Dr. Zener who first proposed a theory explaining the effect.

The voltage level at which the breakdown occurs in a Zener diode may be controlled to within close limits during the manufacturing process. Thus, these devices may be designed to have a wide range of breakdown voltages with ratings as low as about 2 V to as high as several hundred volts.

At applied voltages greater than the breakdown point, the voltage drop across a conducting Zener diode remains essentially constant even though the current through the diode increases with the increased applied voltage. This makes the device well suited for use as a constant-voltage reference or control element.

The schematic symbol for a Zener diode is shown in Fig. 20-9(*a*), and a simple voltage-regulating circuit using a Zener diode

20-4

Zener Diodes

FIGURE **20-9**
Zener diode; (*a*) graphic symbol; (*b*) basic Zener diode dc regulator circuit.

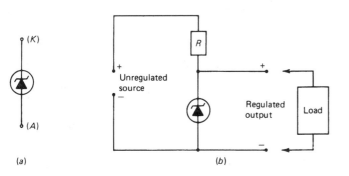

is illustrated in Fig. 20-9(*b*). In this circuit, the constant-voltage breakdown characteristic is used to provide a regulated dc output. The cathode of the diode is connected to the positive side of the supply to provide the reverse bias, and the current through the diode is limited by the series resistor *R*. Since the output voltage is the same as the voltage drop across the diode, the output voltage remains constant even though the input voltage and, hence, the diode current may vary.

The voltage-limiting characteristic is very useful to protect one circuit from excessive voltages caused by another circuit. For example, some computers may require that input voltages be held within certain ranges to prevent damage to the computer electronics.

In addition to their use as voltage references and voltage regulators, Zener diodes find use in what is known as intrinsically safe barriers. These devices are used in industrial applications where a field device such as a process transmitter must be located in an explosive atmosphere. The barrier limits voltage and current so that sufficient power is not available to ignite the surrounding atmosphere. A simplified diagram of such a barrier is shown in Fig. 20-10. The two diodes as shown provide functional redundancy and, in conjunction with the resistor network, perform both voltage and current limiting. The barrier itself is located in a nonexplosive atmosphere.

In addition to a breakdown voltage rating, Zener diodes have a power rating. This is the power that the diode can dissipate without being destroyed.

The alternating circuit equivalent to the Zener diode is the **Thyrector** (General Electric Company). This device performs a function equivalent to two Zener diodes connected back to back. This technique will allow transient suppression to be corrected for during both the positive and negative portions of the ac cycle. As a result, the load circuit is protected from sudden spikes in the line, whereby acting as a voltage regulator to the load circuit. See Fig. 20-11.

F I G U R E **20-10**
Safety barrier between hazardous and nonhazardous areas.

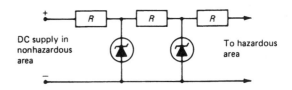

FIGURE 20-11
Thyrector application, voltage spike suppression.

20-5

Transistors

As described previously, a single-junction semiconductor device is capable of rectifying current. By adding a second junction, a semiconductor device is formed that is capable of amplification. Such a device is called a **transistor**.

The transistor consists of a sandwich of semiconductor metals containing alternate layers of N-type and P-type material. The transistor may be the PNP type consisting of two layers of P-type material separated by a thin layer of N-type material or the NPN type consisting of two layers of N-type material separated by a thin layer of P-type material. The arrangement of both types is shown in Fig. 20-12. In each type, one outer layer is called the **emitter**, the centre layer the **base**, and the other outer layer the **collector**. The function of the emitter is to supply charge carriers to its junction with the base. The function of the collector is to remove charge carriers from its junction with the base.

Transistor action may be described as the control of currents and voltages in one junction by the currents and voltages in another junction. In the normal operation of a transistor, the emitter-base junction is forward-biased and the collector-base junction is reverse-biased. When biased in this manner, the transistor has a

FIGURE 20-12
Pictorial and graphical representation of transistors; (a) PNP type; (b) NPN type.

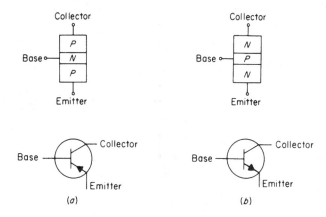

low-resistance emitter-base junction and a high-resistance collector-base junction. When the transistor is used as an amplifier, the
emitter-base circuit is used as the input circuit and the collector-
base circuit as the output circuit. The ability of the transistor to
transfer current from a low-resistance input to a high-resistance
output gives it its name, **transfer resistor**, which when contracted,
forms the word transistor.

A simplified circuit diagram of a basic NPN transistor amplifier
circuit is shown in Fig. 20-13. The circuit shown is called a common-emitter circuit since the emitter is common to both the input
and output circuits.

In the circuit shown, electrons move easily from the N-type
emitter material to the P-type material in the base because of the
forward bias. The electrons, upon entering the base, diffuse
through the thin base and are attracted to the collector by the
positive potential of battery V_C.

The characteristic of the transistor is such that nearly all the
electrons entering the base from the emitter flow into the collector
and out through its load resistance. The physical size, thickness,
and arrangement of the materials forming the transistor junctions
and the impurity concentrations in each are designed so that only
a very small part of the emitter current flows in the base circuit.
Hence, the collector current is almost equal to the emitter current.
In practical transistor circuits, the collector current may be as much
as 98 percent of the emitter current. Furthermore, the characteristics of the transistor are such that the ratio of collector current
to the base current remains nearly constant over a wide range of
currents.

If the voltage of the battery V_B in the emitter-base circuit of
Fig. 20-13 is raised or lowered, the result is an increase or decrease
in base current. The increase or decrease in base current causes a
corresponding increase or decrease in collector current.

In the above description it has been assumed that the only currents flowing in the circuit were those caused by the batteries V_B

FIGURE **20-13**
Basic transistor amplifier circuit, common-emitter configuration.

and V_C; that is, it has been assumed that the input signal has been zero.

If, in the circuit of Fig. 20-13, an ac voltage signal is applied to the circuit input, this signal alternately adds to and subtracts from the bias voltage V_B. As indicated previously, a change or variation in voltage in the emitter-base circuit results in a variation in base current. The variation in base current causes a corresponding variation in collector current. The collector current flowing in the load resistor results in an IR drop in this resistor, the magnitude of which is proportional to the current through it. Thus, it may be seen that the variation of input or signal voltage appears in amplified form across the load resistor or output terminals of the transistor amplifier circuit. Because of the polarities required for the proper biasing of the common-emitter circuit shown, there is a 180° phase shift between the input and the output voltages.

The above is a very much simplified description of the operation of an NPN transistor. The operation of the PNP transistor is similar except that bias-voltage polarities are reversed. A detailed analysis of transistor theory and operation involves consideration of advanced theories of physics and mathematics and is beyond the scope of this book.

Transistor amplifiers find a multitude of applications in communication equipment and in industrial control systems. Transistor amplifiers in communication systems may be used as radio and audio frequency amplifiers or as dc amplifiers.

There are three basic types of transistor amplifier circuits. These are: (a) common emitter, (b) common collector, (c) common base. The common emitter circuit is shown in Fig. 20-14. It is so termed because the emitter is common to both the base and collector.

When input voltage E_1 is zero as shown in the circuit in Fig. 20-14, the base-emitter voltage is zero and the transistor is "off." The voltage $+V$ is now effectively across the series combination

FIGURE **20-14**
Common emitter circuit.

(a)   (b)

of R_1 and the load. Since the ohmic value of R_1 is small compared to the load resistance nearly all of the voltage $+V$ will appear across the load. V_L will then be nearly equal to $+V$. When an input voltage E_1 is supplied of sufficient quantity to turn "on" the transistor, the collector-emitter voltage becomes nearly zero, and nearly all of $+V$ occurs as a voltage drop across R_1. As a result almost no voltage appears across the load. The above indicates that with no input voltage (E_1), there is an output voltage (V_L). When an input voltage (E_1) is present, there is no output voltage (V_L).

Fig. 20-15 shows a common collector circuit. This circuit is sometimes referred to as the **emitter follower** circuit because the voltage supplied to the load follows the base voltage. When E_1 is zero, the base voltage is zero, the transistor is "turned-off," and the voltage V_L is zero. When an input voltage E_1 is supplied that is sufficient to turn the transistor "fully on," the collector-emitter voltage drop becomes nearly zero and, therefore, the voltage V_L across the load becomes nearly equal to $+V$. The above indicates that with no input voltage there will be no output voltage, and with an input voltage there will be an output voltage. Fig. 20-15(*b*) illustrates this. Resistor R is required for high resistance loads. Since the output is separated from the input by the emitter to base connection and since there is only about a one volt drop between the base and emitter the output voltage will be only slightly lower than the input voltage. When the transistor is fully "on" by voltage E_1, the load current I_L will be much greater than the input current I_b because the $+V$ supplied is much greater than the input voltage E_1.

The common base circuit shown in Fig. 20-16 has its base common to the input and output circuits. When voltage E_1 is zero the transistor is turned "off," and the collector current I_c is zero. No load current is supplied and the output voltage V_L is zero. If a small

---

F I G U R E **20-15**
Common collector circuit.

(a)

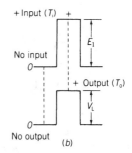

(b)

FIGURE **20-16**
Common base circuit.

(a)

(b)

negative voltage is supplied to the input terminal T_i of sufficient value to turn "on" the transistor, a small current I_b will flow which will produce a collector-emitter current. This current will be high due to the low collector-emitter voltage drop and the high relative $+V$ applied. The emitter current will be slightly greater than the collector because of the addition of the low base current. The common base circuit input and output voltages are reverse-biased but no inversion occurs. When the input voltage is zero the output voltage is also zero. When the input voltage is maximum negative the output voltage is maximum positive. At the same time that E_1 is maximum, the emitter current I_e is maximum as is the load current. This is indicated in Fig. 20-16(b).

As has been shown, a transistor conducts or amplifies when the emitter-base junction is forward-biased and the collector-base junction is reverse-biased. When both junctions are reverse-biased, the transistor will not conduct. Use is made of this characteristic of transistors in switching circuits.

   In the simplified circuit shown in Fig. 20-17, it can be seen that when the switch S is operated to connect battery A into the base-emitter circuit, the emitter-base junction will be forward-biased.

20-**6**

Transistors As Switching Devices

FIGURE **20-17**
Basic circuit to illustrate the use of a transistor as a switch.

For this condition the transistor will conduct and current will flow through the load. If, however, the switch is operated to connect battery *B* into the circuit, the emitter-base junction is reverse-biased and the transistor will not conduct and no current will flow through the load. Used in this way, then, the transistor performs the function of a switch.

The basic concept in any switching circuit is that a definite change of state, usually a voltage change, causes operation of the switching device. The circuit described above operates in this manner; that is, a change in voltage state in the emitter-base circuit in effect turns on or off the output or load current of the transistor.

Transistors used as switches offer several advantages over electromechanical types of switches or relays. They are small, have no moving parts, and are easily actuated from various electric inputs. Probably more important are their exceptionally fast operating times as compared with their electromechanical counterparts.

Perhaps the most important use of transistor switching is in the logic circuitry used in digital computers. Other uses are in pulse and switching circuits in radar, television, and other communication circuits and in commercial power rectifiers, inverters, and frequency-converting equipment control circuitry. More will be said about static switching in Sec. 20-16 — Basic Digital Control.

20-7
Thyristors

Thyristors are multilayer semiconductor devices which can be switched from the OFF state to the ON state by a pulse of control current. Once conduction commences, it continues until the voltage across the thyristor is decreased to zero, as occurs, for example, every cycle in ac circuits.

There are several kinds of thyristors, but only three will be considered here, namely, the reverse-blocking triode thyristor called the **silicon controlled rectifier**, the bidirectional triode thyristor called the **triac**, and the bidirectional diode called the **diac**.

20-8
The Silicon Controlled Rectifier (SCR)

The silicon controlled rectifier (SCR), like a diode, blocks reverse current. Unlike the diode, however, it is capable of blocking current under forward-voltage conditions also unless it has been switched electrically to the forward-current-conduction mode by a pulse of current flowing through its gate. As shown in Fig. 20-18, the SCR has three terminals: an anode, a cathode, and a gate. Also as shown, the SCR is composed of alternate layers of P- and N-type materials with three junctions. Junctions 1 and 3 are equivalent to those in ordinary PN semiconductor diodes. Both of these junctions will conduct current when they are biased in the forward direction, but conduction is blocked when they are reverse-biased.

FIGURE **20-18**

SCR thyristor: (*a*) junction diagram; (*b*) PNP-NPN equivalent diagram; (*c*) graphical symbol.

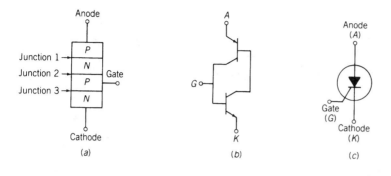

(*a*)   (*b*)   (*c*)

The NP junction 2 blocks conduction when the complete four-layer device is biased in the forward direction.

If, when an SCR is biased in the forward direction, a current pulse is injected into the P region of junction 2 by momentarily applying a positive voltage to the gate, junction 2 becomes forward-biased and conduction through the SCR begins. Once conduction has started it will continue even though the gate current is reduced to zero. Conduction can be interrupted only by means external to the SCR, such as by reducing the anode-to-cathode voltage to zero or by reducing the current flow to zero.

When the SCR is used as a rectifier, the average value of dc supplied by the rectifier to the load may be controlled by controlling the point in each cycle at which the gate voltage is applied to the SCR, or in other words, by controlling the time in each cycle at which the SCR is triggered. If zero gate signal is applied, the SCR blocks current flow for both positive and negative half-cycles of the sine wave and no current flows to the load. If the gate voltage is continuously applied, then the SCR performs as a conventional half-wave diode rectifier and it conducts for each positive half-cycle. If the SCR is triggered by application of the gate voltage at some point during each positive half-cycle, current will flow for the remainder of that half-cycle until the sine-wave voltage goes to zero. Thus, by adjusting the time in each positive half-cycle at which the gate voltage is applied to trigger the SCR, the average value of dc to the load may be controlled. The process of varying the point within the cycle at which forward conduction is permitted to begin is called **phase control** of the SCR.

Fig. 20-19 shows a simple SCR circuit application. With the switch (SW) being in the "off" position, no gate current flows, therefore no load current flows. When the switch is closed and a momentary + pulse current is supplied to the gate of the SCR as

FIGURE **20-19**
Simple SCR circuit connected to a resistive load.

indicated in Fig. 20-19(*b*), a current is supplied to the load during the half-cycles that the anode is positive only. Current is started through the SCR from anode to cathode when each gate pulse occurs. For a resistive load, the SCR turns "off" when the positive half-cycles change to negative (SCR is reverse-biased). The waveform of the current is indicated by the shaded areas in Fig. 20-19(*b*). This output is half-wave current supply.

It should be noted that if the trigger pulse is fired earlier or later in the positive half-cycle, the current flowing through the load will begin either earlier or later with respect to the timing of the trigger pulse. This, of course, will vary the power output of the connected load.

Fig. 20-20 shows a simple SCR circuit capable of producing a full-wave current supply. The SCRs are connected back to back or better known as inverse parallel. When L_1 is positive, and a trigger pulse occurs at the gate of SCR 1, a current is established through SCR 1, since it is forward-biased, and through the load. When L_2 is positive and a pulse occurs at the gate of SCR 2, a current will flow through SCR 2, now that it is forward-biased, and through

FIGURE **20-20**
Two SCRs connected inverse parallel to provide conduction during both + and − halves of ac input.

the load. This action will continue to repeat as long as the gate pulse is established at every half-cycle. As with the single SCR circuit shown in Fig. 20-19, the illustration in Fig. 20-20 output can be varied in time by providing the gate pulse either earlier or later in each respective half-cycle.

The bidirectional triode thyristor or **triac**, like the SCR, has three terminals, a main terminal no. 1, a main terminal no. 2, and a gate. The triac can block current flow in either direction between main terminal no. 1 and no. 2, or it can be triggered into conduction in either direction in response to positive or negative signals applied to the gate terminal. Once conduction has started in the triac it continues until it is stopped by external means, just as in the SCR. In effect, the triac behaves like two SCRs oriented one in each direction as indicated in the equivalent circuit diagram of Fig. 20-21(*a*). The standard symbol for the triac, shown in Fig. 20-21(*b*), also reflects the bidirectional property of the triac.

Because triacs can conduct in both directions, they are used basically as ac power devices for controlling ac loads, virtually superseding the rheostat for ac power control. Triacs are also used as static switches in ac circuits.

As an aid in visualizing the similarities and differences of diodes, SCRs, and triacs, the output waveforms (idealized) of these devices are shown in Fig. 20-22. As shown, the diode conducts for a full half of each cycle and blocks current flow for the other half-cycle. The SCR can conduct for a full half-cycle or for any part of that half-cycle depending upon the triggering time of its gate. It blocks current flow for the other half-cycle. The triac can be made to conduct in both halves of each cycle, the amount of conduction depending upon the time in each half-cycle that it is triggered by

20-**9**

The Triac

FIGURE **20-21**

(*a*) Two SCRS connected to operate the same as a triac; (*b*) graphical symbol for a triac.

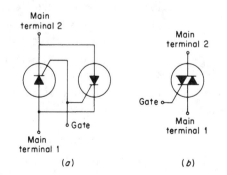

(a)   *(b)*

F I G U R E **20-22**
Output wave-forms of (*a*) diodes, (*b*) SCRs, and (*c*) triacs.

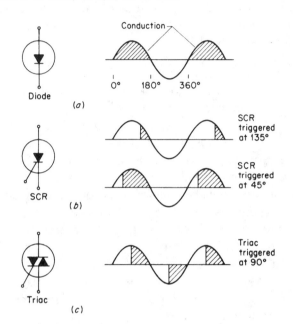

its gate. In summary, the output of diodes and SCRs is a form of dc; the output of triacs is a form of ac.

20-10

The Diac

The **diac**, sometimes called a bilateral trigger or a bidirectional trigger diode, as the names imply, is applied primarily as a trigger device for other thyristors. The diac blocks current flow in either direction until the voltage across it exceeds the breakover voltage. Typical breakover voltages of the diac are 28 to 36 V. When this breakover voltage is exceeded, the diac triggers or fires and conduction through it begins. Conduction continues, as in the SCR and triac, until the voltage across it is reduced to zero. A symbol for the diac is shown in Fig. 20-24. Examples of the application of the diac are included in a later section.

20-11

Varistors

Devices discussed immediately above require external pulses applied to gate elements to break down and initiate conduction. There are times when it is desirable to have circuit elements that can change their characteristics based upon the value of the voltage across them in the circuit. These characteristics are incorporated into semiconductor devices known as **varistors.** These devices change their resistance in a nonlinear manner depending upon voltage.

These devices have very high resistances (essentially, an open circuit) up to a given voltage. At that point, the varistor begins to conduct. Fig. 20-23 compares the voltage-current characteristics

A comparison of the voltage-current characteristics of a resistor and a varistor. The constant relationship between voltage and current based on Ohm's law is shown for a linear resistor.

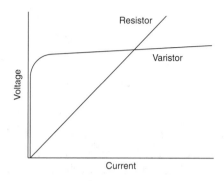

for a "normal" linear resistor (see Chap. 2) and a varistor. Note that the voltage and current for a linear resistor has a constant relationship given by Ohm's law. A varistor has the ability to change this relationship. The voltage where conduction begins and the amount of current it can withstand over a period of time depend upon the varistor's chemical components.

These devices have applications in a variety of circuits for protection against overvoltages such as lightning (see Sec. 18-15). The most common chemical composition for these varistors is a metal oxide such as zinc oxide.

Optoelectronic semiconductor devices are devices that interact with light. There are two general classifications of these devices: **light sensors**, those devices that convert radiant energy (light) into electric energy, and **light emitters**, those devices that convert electric energy into light. These devices, together with other semiconductor devices, are being used increasingly, in many industrial control applications. Symbols used for several optoelectronic devices are shown in Fig. 20-25.

Three important optoelectronic devices, classified as light-sensing or light-detecting devices, are the photodiode, the phototransistor, and the light-activated SCR (LASCR).

20-**12**

Optoelectronic Devices

Standard graphical symbol for a diac.

F I G U R E **20-25**
Graphical symbols for optoelectronic devices; (*a*) photodiode; (*b*) NPN phototransistor; (*c*) LASCR; (*d*) LED.

The **photodiode**, as the name implies, is a diode designed specifically to make use of the inherent characteristic of a PN junction to interact with light. As indicated earlier in this chapter, a PN junction without external bias has a very thin depletion layer. However, when the junction is reverse-biased, the depletion layer is increased in width in proportion to the value of the bias voltage. Only a minute leakage current can flow across the junction. However, when light is allowed to fall on a properly designed reverse-biased junction, a current in addition to the leakage current flows across the junction. Moreover, the amount of current that flows is proportional to the intensity of the light. The resulting current is very small, and for many control applications it must be amplified to make it useful.

Phototransistors combine in one device the ability to detect light and provide amplification of the resulting current as well. When light strikes the collector-base junction of a phototransistor, reverse leakage current flows as in the photodiode. The small emitter-base current is used to control a much larger emitter-collector current in the usual circuit arrangement. The effect is to switch on or off or to regulate and amplify a current in proportion to the amount of light striking the collector-base junction.

The **light-activated SCR** or **LASCR** is a light-sensing optoelectronic device which is used to detect light, convert that light to a current, and use the current to trigger an SCR section within the device.

Like the SCR, the LASCR has three junctions. It also has three terminals: an anode, a cathode, and a gate, all as indicated by the symbol shown in Fig. 20-25. In addition, the LASCR has a window through which light is admitted to activate the light-sensitive area.

As normally used, the LASCR gate is biased to near the triggering value. Then light energy, when added to the gate bias, triggers the unit into conduction. Provisions must be made in the circuit to turn off the current as in the control of the SCR. Thus, large currents can be switched on or off in the LASCR with small amounts of light energy.

The **light-emitting diode** or **LED** is a semiconductor diode that emits light when it is forward-biased. Different materials have been used in the formation of the P- and N-type materials for the LED junction. One producer of these devices uses gallium arsenide and gallium aluminum arsenide for the junction materials. A junction made of these materials emits an infrared light. Other materials used in differing proportions are combined to emit different light colours such as green or yellow.

When the LED is forward-biased, the bias current causes electrons to be injected into the P-type material and holes to be injected into the N-type material. In terms of energy levels, free electrons are at a higher level than are the holes. As the free electrons move through the region near the junction, they recombine with the holes. In the process of recombination, energy is released, some in the form of light and the remainder in the form of heat. The light output power efficiency is, however, very low — less than one percent.

Light-emitting diodes have several advantages over other kinds of light sources. They operate at low voltages, making them compatible with other semiconductor devices. They have very fast response times, they are small, and they have a long life. These attributes make the LED particularly well-suited for displaying information obtained from electronic equipment.

Probably the most familiar use of the LED is its use in an array form used to display numbers. For example, an array of seven rectangular LEDs, properly arranged, can be used to form any digit from zero to nine. Other arrays can display alphanumerics, or both letters and numbers. Such arrays are used as readouts for calculators, digital clocks, measuring instruments, and other similar equipment.

An increasingly important use of the LED is its use as a light source in optically-coupled systems as described in the next paragraphs.

Often it is necessary to isolate one electric circuit from another or one part of a circuit from another part of the circuit. Electrical isolation may be necessary to assure personal safety, to prevent equipment damage, to assure proper equipment functioning, or for other reasons. Electrical isolation of two ac circuits can be accomplished relatively easily by the use of transformers. This is not so, however, for dc circuits. Optically coupled systems provide an excellent solution for this problem.

A **semiconductor optically coupled system** may be used to provide complete electrical isolation between two circuits. Such a system consists of a light source and a light detector often assembled within the same package. One combination used is an LED light source and a photodiode detector as shown diagrammatically

F I G U R E **20-26**
LED-photodiode optical coupler.

in Fig. 20-26. When greater amplification is required, phototransistors or photo SCRs are used in the coupler output.

A typical example of the electrical isolation of circuits is the isolation used between functional modules of electronic control systems. This isolation prevents a minor electrical failure in one module or part of the system from cascading into adjacent parts and causing a catastrophic system failure. Signal information can still be transmitted between the various parts of the system even though the parts are electrically isolated by the optocouplers.

Optically coupled systems are not limited to use as electrical isolators. Many systems operate with the light source and the light detector in separate locations. These systems depend upon the interruption of the light beam to transmit information. The punched-card reader in which the data card is inserted between the light source and detector is an example of this type of system. Other applications include the sensing of the position of an object, fluid-level sensing, colour determination, and intrusion alarms.

20-**13**

Inverters

An inverter is used to change dc power to ac power, as contrasted with a rectifier, which changes ac power to dc power. Solid-state inverters provide an efficient and economical method for accomplishing the conversion of dc to ac.

An inverter circuit is basically a type of **chopper**. In a chopper circuit, a dc supply is alternately opened and closed or "chopped" by a switching device such as a transistor or SCR. By varying either the ratio of on to off time of the switching device, or the repetition rate of the switching, the average voltage and frequency of the chopper output may be controlled.

The basic principle of operation of the inverter may be illustrated in a simplified way by the circuit shown in Fig. 20-27, which shows two manually operated switches, A and B, in the circuit. With both switches open, no current flows in the circuit. When switch A is closed, current I_A flows in the direction shown, and when switch B is closed, I_B flows as shown. If switches A and B are

FIGURE **20-27**
(*a*) Circuit to illustrate the inverter principle, and (*b*) basic inverter circuit.

alternately opened and closed in sequence, it can be seen that
an alternating output can be generated at the load terminals of
the circuit. In practical inverter circuits, SCRs or transistors are
used to replace the mechanically operated switches shown in
Fig. 20-27.

One of the simplest inverter circuits is the centre-tapped transformer circuit using two SCRs as shown in Fig. 20-27. In this
circuit the two SCRs alternately connect the output transformer
to the dc supply, first with one polarity and then the other,
to produce a square-wave output similar to that shown. In the interest of simplicity, SCR gate trigger circuits are not shown in
Fig. 20-27.

It must be remembered that after an SCR has begun to conduct,
the gate loses control of the anode current. Thus, in order to use
SCRs on a dc system, special turn-off control circuitry must be
used to stop the SCR conduction at the right times. Circuits that
are used to turn off an SCR are called **commutating** circuits. In
the circuit shown in Fig. 20-27(*b*), turn-off is accomplished by the
action of the capacitor *C*. When SCR$_1$ is triggered and begins to
conduct, the voltage across it drops very rapidly because of the
voltage drop across the reactor *L*. This allows the capacitor to
charge to a positive polarity at point 2 and to a negative polarity
at point 1. Because of the autotransformer action of the output
transformer, the capacitor charge approaches twice the battery
voltage. At the beginning of the second half-cycle, when SCR$_2$ is
triggered, capacitor *C* is then connected across SCR$_1$ with a polarity to reverse-bias it and thus cause conduction in SCR$_1$ to cease.

With conduction in SCR$_2$ and with SCR$_1$ turned off, capacitor C charges to the opposite polarity and the cycle repeats, resulting in an alternating current in the output transformer. The diodes D_1 and D_2 prevent capacitor discharge current from flowing through the transformer.

There are several configurations of inverter circuits often used. Inverter configurations are somewhat analogous to rectifiers; that is, they may be half-wave, full-wave, single-phase bridge, or three-phase bridge circuits. Inverter circuits are also classified by the commutation method used. The inverter shown in Fig. 20-28 is a bridge-type inverter. The commutation is accomplished by the inductors L and the capacitor C. Turn-on is by SCR triggering circuitry, which is not shown. For high-capacity applications, three-phase bridge inverters are used. An elementary diagram of a three-phase bridge inverter is shown in Fig. 20-29. The commutating capacitors and related components are not shown.

If the ac output of an inverter is rectified to provide dc again, the overall circuit is called a **converter**. The usual use of the converter is to change the magnitude of a dc voltage. Applications of the converter include its use in power supplies for computers and telephone equipment.

Static inverters are used extensively in adjustable-speed ac motor drive systems and in standby power supplies. These applications are discussed in later sections. Other applications include power supplies for control and instrumentation circuits and in automotive electrical systems.

F I G U R E **20-28**
Single-phase bridge-type SCR inverter.

FIGURE 20-29
Three-phase bridge-type SCR inverter.

Devices and systems such as computers, airline and hotel reservation systems, process controllers, and boiler flame safeguard systems all require essentially uninterruptible power supplies for safety or for economic reasons. To supply backup power for these applications, various forms of **uninterruptible power supplies** (UPS) have been developed.

Static UPS systems have three basic parts; namely, a combination rectifier and battery charger, a battery, and an inverter. These basic parts or units may be combined in several different configurations. The simplest form of UPS is the continuous system shown in block-diagram form in Fig. 20-30. With this system the critical ac load is normally supplied through the rectifier, inverter, and the transfer switch. The rectifier converts commercial ac to dc, and the inverter changes the dc to closely regulated ac for the load. If there are power outages or transient disturbances in the commercial supply, the battery automatically picks up the load without any switching. The battery is maintained in a fully charged condition by the rectifier and is recharged by the rectifier after a power outage. The inverter output is locked into synchronism with the commercial ac supply as indicated by the dotted line in Fig. 20-30. This maintains exact clock timing for the critical load and

20-14
Uninterruptible Power Supplies

FIGURE 20-30
Block diagram of a continuous-type static UPS.

permits operation of the manual transfer switch to take the UPS out of service if necessary.

An often used variation of the system shown in Fig. 20-30 is called the static switching transfer system. In this system, a static transfer switch is added in the output section of the UPS. This system supplies the critical ac load in the same manner as the continuous system does under normal conditions. However, if the UPS system fails or if the critical load demand becomes larger than the UPS can deliver, the critical load is transferred to the commercial power supply automatically by the static transfer switch. Manual transfer is normally provided for this system also to permit the removal of the UPS for routine maintenance.

20-**15**

Harmonics

The generation of an alternating emf was discussed in Chap. 10. As shown in Fig. 10-1, the emf created by a generator has a waveform in the shape of a sine wave. The waveform repeats itself 60 times per second on a 60-Hz power system. However, under some circumstances, frequencies other than 60 Hz are generated by other equipment on the same system. These frequencies are whole number multiples of the fundamental frequency and are called **harmonics.** At 60 Hz, these frequencies include the following:

Harmonic	Frequency
1	60
2	120
3	180
4	240
5	300
6	360
7	420

In three-phase power systems, only odd-numbered frequencies are usually present.

When various waveforms of differing frequencies combine, the result shows the effects on a waveform of combining various harmonics. This particular wave shows the unique characteristic result of energizing a transformer that creates a rare, even second harmonic (120 Hz). Note that the resulting wave is greatly distorted.

Generators are designed to produce as close to a perfect sine wave as possible. As electronic devices can change the wave shape, they may be a source of harmonics. These harmonics then flow to other areas of the power system. For example, the inverter described above has historically been a harmonic source. The six-pulse inverter (see Fig. 20-29) produces harmonics according to the following formula:

$$h = np \pm 1$$

FIGURE **20-31**
The current fundamental wave, (a), is combined with the second harmonic, (b), to form the characteristic, (c).

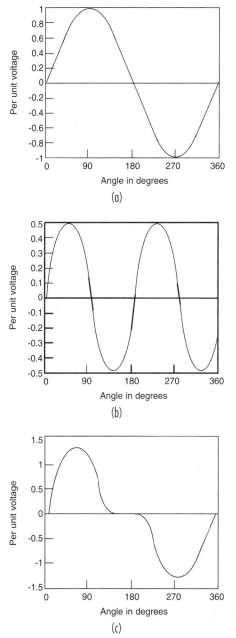

(a)

(b)

(c)

where b is the harmonic, n is the whole number (1,2,3, etc.), and p is the number of pulses (6). Fig. 20-32 illustrates some of the harmonic frequency waveshapes and the simplified resulting output wave.

F I G U R E **20-32**
The unfiltered current output of a six-pulse inverter (see Fig. 20-29) is a series of harmonic waves
that are combined to form the total output waveform.

Harmonics are of increasing concern in modern power systems as they can cause abnormal heating in electrical equipment, very high overvoltages, and interference with electronic operations due to distorted voltage inputs. Filters and newer types of circuits are used to make equipment less susceptible to these problems. The combined simplified current waveform is shown in (a).

Representative current harmonics are as follows:
(b) fundamental,
(c) fifth, and
(d) seventh.

Frequencies up to the nineteenth were used to construct the (a) waveform.

20-**16**

Basic Digital Control

Much of the switching, sequencing, and interlocking used in industrial control systems and in digital computers involves digital devices. Digital or switching-type control functions in a binary manner; that is, the devices used are permitted to exist in only two possible **states**. A switch, for example, is a digital device in that it may be either open or closed. Various other designations given to these two states are on-off, yes-no, high-low, or energized-de-energized. The designations most often used, however, particularly in the mathematical manipulation of switching or logic functions, are the symbols 1 (one) and 0 (zero).

Digital control can be performed and has been performed for many years by electromechanical relays which have moving contacts operated by electromagnets. Another type of digital control to be discussed briefly here is **static control**, or control by means of devices without moving parts. Static control has several advantages over electromechanical control, the main advantages being its relatively small size, its greater reliability, and its much higher speed of operation. While theoretically it would be possible to build a digital computer with electromechanical parts, the space and power requirements would be prohibitive.

Static switching building blocks called **logic gates** are composed of a functional grouping of electrical components such as resistors, capacitors, diodes, and transistors. The building blocks can be represented by symbols, and these symbols can be assembled into **logic diagrams**. The logic diagram is used to show signal or information circuits but not necessarily power sources or connections. Furthermore, the logic diagram does not indicate actual circuit details nor components used within the logic gate. The logic symbols and the logic diagram are nothing more than a shorthand method of representing control circuitry.

There are three basic building blocks or logic gates used in logic diagrams. They are called the AND, OR, and NOT gates. When these three basic gates are put together in the right combinations almost any control or mathematical problem can be solved.

The AND gate has two or more inputs and one output. In order to have an output, all inputs must be present. In accordance with the American National Standards Institute (ANSI) formal definition, *the output of an AND assumes the 1-state if and only if all the inputs assume the 1-state*. This, of course, is equivalent to the electromechanical series circuit. The standard symbol, its mechanical equivalent, and a table of combinations called a truth table for the AND are shown in Fig. 20-33.

As shown in Fig. 20-33, the truth table for a two-input AND gate has three columns, one for each input and one for the output. It should be kept in mind that the 1 and 0 are not numbers as used in the usual sense but are symbols representing "states." Thus, reading across in the table for the AND gate, if inputs *A* and *B* have

FIGURE **20-33**
Basic logic gates.

Function	Symbol	Truth Table		Output	Comments
		Inputs		Output	
AND		A	B	Y	Mechanical equivalent
		1	1	1	
		1	0	0	
		0	1	0	
		0	0	0	
OR		A	B	Y	Mechanical equivalent
		1	1	1	
		1	0	1	
		0	1	1	
		0	0	0	
NOT		A		Y	Inverter
		1		0	
		0		1	
NAND		A	B	Y	Same as AND with output inverted
		1	1	0	
		1	0	1	
		0	1	1	
		0	0	1	
NOR		A	B	Y	Same as OR with output inverted
		1	1	0	
		1	0	0	
		0	1	0	
		0	0	1	

the 1-state, the output state is 1. On the second line of the table, if A is 1 and B is 0, the output must be 0 since both inputs must be 1 to result in a 1 output. The same reasoning applies for line 3. Likewise, in line 4 if both A and B are 0, then the output obviously must be 0. The table shows all possible combinations of inputs and the resulting outputs for these combinations.

The OR gate symbol, truth table, and mechanical equivalents are shown in the second part of Fig. 20-33. As shown, the OR gate, like the AND gate, has two or more inputs and one output. However, the OR gate has an output only when any one of its inputs is present. The ANSI formal definition is: *the output of an OR assumes the 1-state if one or more of the inputs assume the 1-state.* This is equivalent to the parallel electromechanical circuit as shown. In the truth table, if A and B are 1, Y is 1. If either A or B is 1 and the other is 0, Y is 1. The output Y is 0 only if both A and B are 0.

The third basic logic gate is the NOT gate, which is usually called an inverter simply because its output is always the opposite of its input. This is defined by ANSI as logic negation as follows: *the output of a logic negation takes on the 1-state if and only if the input does not take on the 1-state.* The standard symbol and truth table are shown in the third part of Fig. 20-33. As indicated, when A is 0, Y is 1, and when A is 1, Y is 0.

Many gates other than the basic three described are used, but mostly these are derived from the basic three building blocks. For example, a combination of AND and NOT gates is called a NAND (meaning NOT-AND) and is merely the inverted output of an AND. If, for example, both inputs of a NAND are 1s, the output is 1 inverted, or 0. Similarly, the NOR (or NOT-OR) is made up of the NOT followed by an OR, so that an input of one or more 1s will result in an output of 0. The NAND and NOR gates are included in Fig. 20-33 for reference.

20-17

Logic Control Applications

As indicated in the previous section, two areas of application of logic control are in industrial control and in digital computers. The following examples illustrate, in an elementary way, some of the ways in which logic gates can be applied to control problems. Computer applications are beyond the scope of this brief discussion.

The **three-wire motor control circuit** shown in Fig. 20-34 may be used to illustrate the use of logic gates for control. The circuit, shown in its electromagnetic form in Fig. 20-34(*a*), is the standard three-wire circuit discussed in Sec. 9-18. The START push button is a momentary contact switch held normally open by a spring. The STOP button is held normally closed by a spring. When the START push button is depressed, the contactor coil M is energized and its contact M, which is connected in parallel with the START button, closes to "seal in" the contactor. The START button can then be released and the coil M remains energized. Depressing the stop button momentarily de-energizes coil M and opens contact M.

To accomplish the above-described operation with logic circuitry, an OR and an AND gate may be used connected as shown in

F I G U R E **20-34**
Three-wire motor control circuit; (*a*) electromagnetic circuit diagram, and (*b*) logic diagram.

the logic diagram of Fig. 20-34(*b*). When the START switch is operated, a 1-state input is provided to input *B* of the OR, and this provides a 1 output from the OR to the *A* input of the AND. Since the STOP switch is normally closed, it provides a 1 input to the *B* input of the AND. Thus, the output of the AND assumes the 1-state since it has two 1 inputs, and the coil *M* is energized. The 1 output of the AND is also used to "feed back" to the *A* input of the OR, which then maintains its 1 output even though the START button is released. When the STOP switch is operated, the *B* input to the AND becomes 0, causing the AND output to assume the 0-state and thereby de-energizing the coil *M*. This circuit is sometimes referred to as an off-return memory circuit.

A simple **three-way switching circuit** used for control of a light from two points is shown in Fig. 20-35. As shown, the light

F I G U R E **20-35**
Three-way switching circuit; (*a*) conventional diagram, and (*b*) logic diagram.

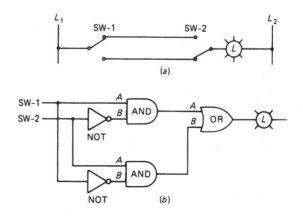

may be switched on or off by either SW 1 or SW 2. The logic diagram in Fig. 20-35(b) will further illustrate the use of logic gates in control circuits.

It will be assumed in analyzing the logic diagram in Fig. 20-35(b) that the switches SW 1 and SW 2 will provide a 1-state input when they are in the position shown in Fig. 20-35(a). Thus, if both switches provide a 1 input, the A input to each AND gate is 1 and the B input is 0. Therefore, both AND outputs and both OR inputs are 0. Since the resulting OR output is 0, the light is not energized for this position of SW 1 and SW 2. However, if the position of *either* SW 1 or SW 2 is changed, one OR gate input is changed resulting in a 1 output from the OR gate to energize the light. If the position of both switches is changed, the OR output is again 0 and the light is de-energized. The truth table for this logic diagram is as follows.

Input		
SW 1	SW 2	Output
1	1	0
0	1	1
1	0	1
0	0	0

It is interesting to note that the above truth table is also the truth table for another type of gate called the **exclusive** OR gate. This gate differs from the simple OR gate in that it has a 1 output when input *A or B* but *not both* are 1. The difference between the simple OR and the exclusive OR gates is evident when a comparison is made of the respective truth tables.

Another way in which logic gates may be used is illustrated by the circuit shown in Fig. 20-36. In this circuit, three contactor coils M are controlled by three control relays CR 1, CR 2, and CR 3. Indicating lights L connected as shown are mounted on a control panel to provide an operator a means of monitoring the operation of the contactors. The closing of a control relay contact CR energizes its contactor coil M and also provides a 1-state input to its OR gate. The resulting 1 output of the OR energizes the monitor light L for the contactor coil.

Also mounted on the control panel is a momentary-contact, spring-return monitor light test switch connected as shown. To test periodically for defective lights, an operator may depress the light test switch, which provides a 1 input to all the OR gates. The resulting 1 output from each of the OR gates energizes all the monitor lights, thereby giving the operator an indication of any defective light. The OR gates in effect isolate the test circuit from the

F I G U R E **20-36**
Control circuit with OR gates.

contactor coil circuits, permitting an input from either the CR contact or the test switch to energize a light, yet preventing the test switch from energizing the contactor coil. In actual practice the OR logic gates can be built into the monitor light socket.

The examples of logic circuits just described have been very simple control circuits, and consequently the logic diagrams offer little if any simplification in presentation over the conventional electromechanical diagrams. However, in industrial processes or automatic machine tool controls containing literally hundreds of switching devices, the logic diagram using combinations of standard digital building blocks and symbols can be used to great advantage in understanding, designing, and maintaining such systems.

CAUTION: When checking a transistor with a multimeter, too much current or voltage could be supplied from the instrument. Check the instrument's output. For example, the Simpson 260 multimeter will output 1.5 V and a maximum current of 1 mA on the R $\times$ 100 scale. These voltage and current values are safe for checking any transistor component.

The table on page 488 will give the resistance measurements expected when checking a transistor.

F I G U R E **20-37**
Testing methods for basic solid-state components.

SCR: 1)

2)

Jumper

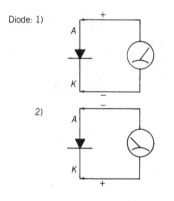

Diode: 1)

2)

(*a*) Determine the polarity of the ohmmeter leads.

(*b*) Connect the ohmmeter between the anode *A* and cathode *K* as shown. The resistance measured should exceed one megaohm.

(*c*) Reverse the ohmmeter leads as shown. The resistance again should exceed one megaohm.

(*d*) With the ohmmeter leads connected as in step (*b*), short the gate to the anode as shown. The resistance should now drop to less than 1 kΩ. Now remove the jumper. If the ohmmeter is on a low range (R × 10), the meter reading will remain low after the jumper from the gate to the anode was removed.

(*a*) Connect the ohmmeter between the anode *A* and cathode *K* as shown. The meter should measure a low resistance value, indicating continuity. If not, the diode is either open or the ohmmeter leads are reversed.

(*b*) Connect the ohmmeter between the anode *A* and cathode *K* as shown, leads reversed. The meter should measure a very high resistance value, indicating no continuity. If not, the diode is shorted or the ohmmeter leads are reversed.

Resistance between terminals of PNP type transistors (reverse probes for checking NPN types)
*Shorting the Base to the Collector should lower ohm reading.

Types of Transistors	Probe Contacts	*Ohms
Small Germanium	+ on Emitter − on Base	300-400
	+ on Emitter − on Collector	10 K-50 K
Power Germanium	+ on Emitter − on Base	30-50
	+ on Emitter − on Collector	several hundred
Small Silicon	+ on Emitter	1 K-2 K
	− on Base + on Emitter − on Collector	very high
Power Silicon	+ on Emitter − on Base	200-1 K
	+ on Emitter − on Collector	very high approx 1 M

Triac: 1)

(*a*) Connect the positive terminal of the ohmmeter on terminal T_2 and the negative terminal on T_1. The ohmmeter should measure a very high resistance, or no continuity. (*b*) Reverse the above procedure in (*a*) with respect to the polarity of the ohmmeter terminals to T_1 and T_2. The results should be the same.

(*a*) Connect the positive terminal of the ohmmeter on terminal T_2 and the negative terminal on T_1 and short the gate terminal to terminal T_2. The ohmmeter should measure a low resistance, or circuit continuity. (*b*) Reverse the ohmmeter connections to the triac without removing the short between terminal T_2 and the gate. The ohmmeter should once again measure a low resistance as before.

Testing of any semiconductor device should always be done with caution. The technician should always be aware of the device's characteristics and voltage/current capacities. A perfectly good semiconductor device can be destroyed by simply using an incorrect testing procedure.

REVIEW QUESTIONS

1 What are some materials used in the manufacture of semiconductor devices?

2 What is the effect of adding P-type and N-type impurities to semiconductor crystals?

3 Describe the conventions used when considering electric charge movement in semiconductor materials.

4 What important function can be performed by a semiconductor diode?

5 What is the depletion layer in a P-N junction?

6 What is meant by forward-biasing and reverse-biasing of a semiconductor junction?

7 What is a half-wave rectifier?

8 What advantage does a full-wave rectifier have over a half-wave rectifier?

9 How are the pulsations of the output of a rectifier "smoothed out"?

10 Give some applications for the Zener diode.

11 Name the three electrodes of a transistor.

12 How is the emitter-base junction biased in a transistor?

13 What characteristics of the transistor make it suitable for use as a switch?

14 Describe how a transistor functions as an amplifier.

15 Name three kinds of thyristors.

16 Give the names of the three terminals of the SCR.

17 Describe what is meant by phase control of an SCR.

18 Compare an SCR with a triac. What are their differences? Their similarities?

19 How many terminals does a triac have?

20 Describe the differences in the output waveforms obtainable with diodes, SCRs, and triacs.

21 What is a diac?

22 What are the two general classifications of optoelectronic devices?

23 What is a photodiode? A phototransistor? Describe briefly the action of each.

24 How many junctions does the LASCR have?

25 What is an LED?

26 Give an application of the optical coupler.
27 Define an inverter. What are some inverter configurations?
28 What are some harmful effects of harmonic currents?
29 What is a digital device?
30 What is a logic gate? A logic diagram?
31 Name the three basic logic gates and define each.
32 What are some applications of logic gates?

21 Introduction to Machine Control

Entire textbooks have been written on the subject of machine control. In this chapter we will examine the fundamental concepts of discrete control systems and related safety requirements for machine control. It is of utmost importance for the technician/electrician to completely understand what is to be controlled, and be totally familiar with the suggested machine cycle.

All control systems are constructed of three essential components (1) **information** (inputs), (2) **decision** (logic), and (3) **action** (outputs). Information (inputs) are sensors and/or transducers such as devices to detect position, temperature, pressure, flow, and level to name but a few. Decision (logic) is made up of electromechanical devices such as contactors and relays, or static switching and **programmable logic controller** programs. This is where the decisions are made in the control system. Given certain inputs in a pre-determined array, the logic system will decide what outputs should be turned ON or OFF. Action (outputs) are devices that produce the work the machine is intended to do. These may be devices or apparatus such as motors, solenoid valves to control compressed air or hydraulic fluids, pilot lights, and so on.

21-1

Low-Voltage Release versus Low-Voltage Protection

When the machine designer is making decisions regarding the method(s) of controlling the apparatus, safety must be a major consideration. If the machine cycle requires no human interaction, then the machine can be allowed to restart automatically after system failure. This is referred to as **Low Voltage Release.**

"When it is necessary or desirable that a motor stop on failure or reduction of voltage and automatically restart on return of voltage, the motor control device shall provide low-voltage release." [1]*(C.E.C. 28-400 (b))*

An example of this type of control is one that would be applied to a sump pump (Fig. 21-1). Usually this application would require three functions to control the operation of the pump:

---

[1] C.E.C. (CANADIAN ELECTRICAL CODE PART 1)

F I G U R E **21-1**

Low-voltage release for a sump pump control.

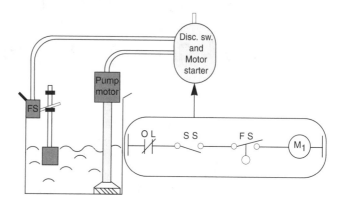

a) motor overload protection;

b) water level control (high/low level);

c) motor safety switch.

Note: For standard electrical symbols, see Appendix A.

It can be seen in Fig. 21-1 that the pump motor is controlled by a motor starter M_1. Providing the safety switch SS, float switch FS, and overload contacts OL are all in the closed state, coil M_1 will be energized. This will enable the sump pump motor to operate. If any one of the above mentioned devices opens for any reason, the pump will stop. These would be considered normal control functions. However, if a sudden drop in line voltage was experienced, the coil of motor starter M_1 would open the sump motor from its source. Upon restoration of power, and providing all of the indicated control functions were in the closed condition, the motor would restart automatically. This is an example of **low-voltage release**.

Since the starting and stopping of the sump pump motor is not operator controlled, and the pump motor itself is likely remote from any possibility of human interference, this type of control is acceptable. If, however, we now apply a control to a power saw, a very different approach must be used. First, we must realize that the saw is operated by a human operator. This, in itself, implies greater safety must be built into the electrical control of this saw. Let us assume this saw is of a very basic design and requires the following control functions:

a) motor overload protection;

b) start/stop control push buttons;

c) safety stop foot switch.

From Fig. 21-2 it can be seen that the start/stop buttons are of the momentary contact design. The safety foot switch is also a momentary contact switch. When the operator pushes the start button (providing the stop button and foot switch are not being operated and the overload relay is in the reset condition) the saw motor will start. The operator may now release the start button and proceed to cut. If the operator wishes to stop the motor, this may be done by either pushing the stop button or operating the foot switch to de-energize the motor starter coil M_1. If, however, while the saw is in operation the system voltage drops, the holding coil M_1 will de-energize and the saw will stop. Upon restoration of power, however, the saw will not restart until the operator once again pushes the start button. This safety feature protects the operator from a surprise or accidental start. The control technique described is providing **Low Voltage Protection.** This control technique **must** be employed where there is human interaction with the machine as this is a form of **Fail Safe** protection

"When automatic restarting is liable to create a hazard, the motor control device shall provide low-voltage protection." (C.E.C. 28-400 (a))

Most industrial electric machinery is operated from a three-phase voltage source of 208 V to 600 V. In the interest of operator safety it is advisable to have the control equipment operate at a potential of 24 V to 120 V. This, of course, will depend upon the nature of the control devices. A control transformer is used to step-down the higher three-phase potential to a safe single-phase potential. The rating of the control transformer will be dependent upon the number and sizes of the relays, motor starters and solenoid coils used, as well as pilot lights and other load devices in the control circuit. The secondary of the transformer should be protected with an over

21-**2**

Control Transformers — Ground Indication and Protection

FIGURE **21-2**
Low-voltage protection circuit for a power saw control.

current device to protect the transformer in the event of a faulty load device in the control system.

One important question that confronts the control designer is whether or not to ground the secondary of the control transformer. The Canadian Electrical Code 10-106 states:

"(1) Except as otherwise provided for in this code, alternating current systems shall be grounded if: (a) By so doing, their maximum voltage-to-ground does not exceed 150 V; or (b) The system incorporates a neutral conductor."

This would imply the secondary of the control transformer must be grounded. However, this section goes on to say:

"(2) Wiring systems supplied by an ungrounded supply shall be equipped with a suitable ground detection device to indicate the presence of a ground fault."

This code regulation allows a choice, whether or not to ground the control transformers secondary. Generally speaking, this decision can be made quite quickly by asking the machine owner whether he wishes the said piece of machinery to shut down immediately upon a ground fault or to remain running and be repaired at the earliest machine-down period. Figs. 21-3 (*a*) and (*b*) show these two alternatives.

If a ground occurs in line 1 of Fig. 21-3(*a*) the control transformer secondary would be shorted and the fuse in line 1 would open. This would immediately shut the machine down and the ground condition would have to be found and cleared before restarting. Note that the location of the intended ground on this transformer is in line 2. This convention is standard in the control industry and the grounded conductor is referred to as the **Identified Conductor**.

FIGURE **21-3**

(*a*) Grounded control transformer secondary. (*b*) Ungrounded control transformer secondary with appropriate ground detection lamps.

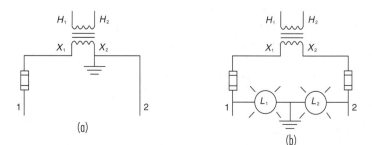

In Fig. 21-3(*b*), however, a ground could occur in either lines 1 or 2 without affecting the output of the control transformer. Under ground free conditions the ground detection lamps would glow dimly since they are in series across the transformers secondary. If a ground occurred in line 1, the lamp L_1 would go out and lamp L_2 would now be across the line and glow brightly. The lamp that is out would indicate on which side of the control system the ground is present. If, however, the ground was in line 2 and not line 1, then the lamp L_2 would go out and L_1 would glow brightly indicating the ground is present in line 2. If both lines 1 and 2 ground simultaneously the transformer secondary would now be shorted and the fuse in line 1 and/or line 2 would open. This method of isolation in the control circuit would allow a ground to be present in either lines 1 or 2 without affecting the operation of the machine. However, the presence of this ground would be indicated on the ground indicating lamps and could be cleared when the machine was not in operation.

The machine tool industry in North America has, for the most part, adopted JIC (Joint Industrial Conference) Standards. The acceptance of a set of uniform standards is of great importance when the machine designer(s) is communicating their design ideas. The conductor colour code standards are described in Fig. 21-4 and Table 21-1.

For many large and complex machines, the electrical schematic diagrams take up many pages in a machine manual. When maintaining and troubleshooting such a machine it is necessary to cross-reference relays and their associated contacts quickly, as well as other discrete devices in the system. All conductors must be numbered. Generally, numbers 1 and 2 are reserved for the vertical lines on the schematic from left to right or, if needed, odd numbers on the left vertical line and even numbers on the right vertical line. The horizontal lines, better known as rungs, are also numbered from start to finish of the circuit. Rung numbers indicating the rung locations of contacts associated with the relay device are located on the right hand side of the rungs. For an example, see Fig. 21-5.

When examining Fig. 21-5, we can see the vertical lines on the left have odd numbers (1 and 3) while the vertical lines on the right have even numbers (2 and 4). It should also be noted that there are four control line fuses, one for each vertical line. F_1 and F_2 are the overcurrent protection for the logic portion of the control circuit, while F_3 and F_4 are the overcurrent protection for the solenoid circuits. Either this method or individual fusing of solenoids is a common practice, since solenoids can be operated manually as well as electrically. The separation of fusing enables the

21-**3**

Wiring Systems Colour Coding Based on JIC Standards

21-**4**

Numbering and Cross-Referencing of a Control Circuit Schematic Diagram

F I G U R E **21-4**
Typical colour coding of power and control conductors.

TABLE **21-1**		**Conductor Colour Code Standards**
Black	Power conductors used for distribution and supply of electric motor equipment.	
Red	Ungrounded control conductors of a potential to ground not greater than 150 V.	
White	Grounded conductor (identified conductor).	
Blue	dc control circuit conductors.	
Yellow	Control conductors supplied from a different source and not de-energized when the main disconnect for the individual machine is off.	
Green	Equipment ground, fault current carrying conductor.	

logic portion of the control to continue to function independently of the solenoid circuit. Note also that this machine schematic has an isolated control transformer supply complete with ground detection lamps. Down the left side of the schematic, each rung is numbered from top to bottom. Down the right side of the schematic adjacent to the relay coils are rung reference numbers. These reference numbers refer to the rung numbers of the contacts for that relay. This enables the reader to determine quickly what lines are affected when a given relay energizes or de-energizes. For example, to the right of relay CR_3 on rung 11, we see the numbers

FIGURE **21-5**

Machine tool electrical schematic diagram using JIC Standard Symbols complete with line reference numbers and conductor numbers.

8, 12, 15, 15. This means that when CR_3 is energized a normally closed contact in rung 8 will open, a normally open contact in rung 12 will close, and two normally open contacts in rung 15 will close. From this, the technician/electrician can determine what the sequence of machine operation is or troubleshoot the machine during a breakdown. It can also be seen that all the conductors from device to device in this drawing are numbered. These are the wire numbers. The electrician would use these numbers to connect to the control panel, and as a means of troubleshooting. For instance, if it is suspected that the normally closed contacts of LS_2 in rung

F I G U R E **21-6**
Control panel terminal strip for schematic diagram in Fig. 21-5.

1	2	3	4	5	6	7	8	9	10	11	12	13	14	15

X1	X2	F1	F2	F3	F4	L1	L2	L3	T1	T2	T3

8 are faulty and not allowing CR_2 to energize, the electrician could use the voltmeter across wire terminals 15 and 16 in the control panel while the operator is operating the cycle start buttons. If the control transformer secondary voltage appears across these terminals this would indicate that LS_2 is open while everything else in the rung is closed. Fig. 21-6 shows the wire terminal strip layout for this drawing. Note that every one of these wires is accounted for at the terminal strip. This enables the tradesperson to be able to effectively troubleshoot the machine from one central location. Upon determining the machine fault, corrective action can be taken.

21-**5**

Control Relays (Electromechanical)

Relays generally can be divided into two types:

  i) nonretentive
 ii) retentive

The nonretentive relay is one that relies upon a maintained electrical signal input to keep the relay in its energized state. When the electrical signal input is removed, the relay will return to its normal (de-energized) state. Fig. 6-10 illustrates a basic electromechanical relay. Fig. 21-7 shows a variety of electromechanical relays, both of the plug-in and nonplug-in varieties.

A retentive (latch) relay is one that will retain its last state when the control system is turned OFF. With a standard relay, the de-energization of the control power would return all relays to the OFF state. However, the latch relay will remain in whatever state it was in when the control system was turned OFF. This type of relay is considered to be retentive. An application of this type of relay is a machine that must start up where it left off when it was shut down. Conveyorized machinery must remember its last state of operation when shut down at the end of a shift or perhaps during an accidental power interruption. There are essentially two different types of latch relays. The two-coil latch relay uses one coil to latch the relay's contacts and the second coil to unlatch them. However, some latch relay manufacturers use a split-coil arrangement. With the use of diodes and residual magnetism, this type of

FIGURE **21-7**
Variety of relays.
(Courtesy of Omron Canada Inc.)

latch relay has become very popular. Fig. 21-8(*a*) shows a circuit containing a two-coil latch relay application. A momentary contact push-button PB_1 (set) in rung #1, when operated momentarily, will energize the *CRL* (latch) coil. As soon as this coil is energized its own normally closed contact *CR* in series with *CRL* will open de-energizing *CRL*. However, since this is a latch relay, the mechanical latching mechanism contained within this relay will hold the relay latched even though PB_1 is no longer closed. Now, the normally open *CR* contact in rung #2 is closed, setting up the condition for

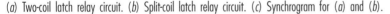

FIGURE **21-8**
(*a*) Two-coil latch relay circuit. (*b*) Split-coil latch relay circuit. (*c*) Synchrogram for (*a*) and (*b*).

unlatching the relay when PB_2 (reset) is closed. As can be seen by the synchrogram in Fig. 21-8(c), the light L_1 is on from the period when PB_1 was initiated to the period when PB_2 is initiated, thus resetting the latch relay. The dashed line from CRL (latch) to CRU (unlatch) is a symbol indicating that both of these relay coils are interlocked (belong to the same relay).

Fig. 21-8(b) is a schematic diagram similar to that in Fig. 21-8(a). The difference is that (b) is using a split-coil latch relay. Note the three connections to the relay coil CR. One from rung #1, the set or latch circuit, and one from rung #2, the reset or unlatch circuit. The third wire is common to both and connects to line #2 of the schematic. When PB_1 is momentarily operated, the diode D_1 provides a half-wave rectified signal to coil CR from line #1 to line #2. This signal will energize one-half of the split-coil latching relay. Once this latching signal has been removed, the relay will remain latched by a residual field contained within the armature of the relay. When PB_2 is momentarily energized, the diode D_2 will provide a half-wave signal from line #2 to line #1. The voltage provided by this unlatch signal will produce a magnetic field opposing the residual field in the relay's armature. This will unlatch the relay, thereby resetting it to its normal state. Note that this latch relay also contains the interlocking contacts to prevent the latch coils or the unlatch coils from being energized for an extended period.

21-6
Control Relays (Solid-State)

Solid-state relays perform a similar function to their electromechanical counterparts, but with no moving parts. They provide optical isolation between the relay input and output signals (see Figs. 20-26 and 22-2). Either power transistors or thyristors are used as

FIGURE **21-9**
Solid-state relays.
(Courtesy of Omron Canada Inc.)

FIGURE **21-10**

(*a*) ON delay timing contacts. (*b*) OFF delay timing contacts.

electronic switching devices to control dc or ac outputs respectively. (See Secs. 20-6 and 20-7.) The solid-state relay has a marked advantage over the electromechanical relay in terms of switching speed and high frequency switching of connected loads.

The basic timing relay is nothing more than a standard relay with timed contacts. These contacts may be normally closed or open, and may be ON or OFF delay contacts. Most relay manufacturers today manufacture timing head attachments for standard relays. This allows the flexibility of instantaneous contacts provided by the standard relay as well as timed contacts all operated by the same relay coil. The purpose of time contacts is to allow a portion of machine operation to take place after a set time of energization or de-energization of the control relay coil. This device is usually quite accurate with a high level of repeatability. The individual relay manufacturers list the timers' specifications in their catalogues.

The ON delay timing contacts operate after a present delay upon energization of the timing relay coil. With reference to Fig. 21-11, note that when PB_1 in rung #1 is not operated, lights L_1 and L_2 are off. However, when PB_1 is operated and held in the operated state, TR_1 will energize. The instantaneous contact TR_1 in rung #2 will close, immediately turning on L_1. L_2 will not come on until 5 s has elapsed. This is the present time of the relay setting of TR_1. Fig. 21-11 (*a*) and (*b*) illustrate this using a schematic diagram (*a*) and a synchrogram (*b*).

21-**7**

Standard Timing Relays

FIGURE **21-11**

(*a*) ON delay timing relay operating two outputs (lamps) using instantaneous and timing contacts.
(*b*) Synchrogram of lamp operation from schematic diagram in (*a*).

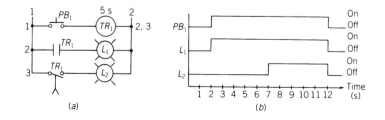

(*a*)   (*b*)

F I G U R E **21-12**

(*a*) OFF delay timing relay operating two outputs (lamps) using instantaneous and timing contacts.
(*b*) Synchrogram of lamp operation from schematic diagram in (*a*).

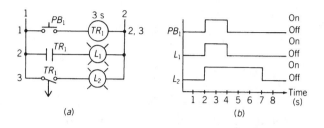

The OFF delay timer is a little more difficult to understand. Hopefully, with the use of the illustration in Fig. 21-12, its operation will become clear. Essentially, the OFF delay timer contacts begin timing only after the de-energization of the timing relay coil. Note that in Fig. 21-12(*a*) when PB_1 is not operated, the lamps L_1 and L_2 are off. However, when PB_1 is operated and held in this state, the timer's instantaneous contact TR_1 in rung #2 will close, immediately turning on output L_1. In rung #3 the timed contact TR_1 will also close, immediately turning on lamp output L_2. Therefore, L_1 and L_2 will come on at the same time when PB_1 is operated. When PB_1 is released and TR_1 de-energizes, contact TR_1 in rung #2 will open, immediately turning L_1 off. Timed contact TR_1 in rung #3 will remain closed for the timer's present time of 3 s, then it will open turning L_2 off. As a result, L_2 will remain on for 3 s longer than L_1 upon de-energization of timing relay TR_1. See Fig. 21-12 for the illustration of OFF delay timing.

Solid state timing relays possess similar characteristics to that of the solid-state relay. However, due to the flexibility of integrated circuits, they can perform many other functions than just the ON-Delay and OFF-Delay operations of the electromechanical timing relay. To become aquainted with the versatility of such timers, one needs only to acquire the product manuals of the many manufacturers of these devices.

The example problems in this chapter will include a respective solution. Note, however, that there are many solutions to any given systems problems. Read the problem, list the main functions that are the constraints the system must operate under, and then attempt your own solution before examining the ones given.

Example 21-1: Delay Starting of Motors

Three motors are to be started from one Start/Stop control station. The starting current inrush is too large for all three motors to be started simultaneously, therefore a delay of 5 seconds must occur between the start of each of the motors.

The ON-Delay timing contacts M_1 and M_2 in Fig. 21-13 are auxiliary timing contacts that can be attached to motor starters M_1 and M_2 respectively.

FIGURE **21-13**
Solution to Example 21-1.

Example 21-2: Pump Control Problem

A pumping system consists of three pump motors; M_1, M_2, and M_3. The system is to be designed so that pump M_1 must be running before pumps M_2 or M_3 can be started. Each pump control has its own momentary start/stop push-button control station. If pump M_2 is started while M_1 is running, M_2 can also be stopped without affecting the operation of pump M_1. Pump M_3 can also be started or stopped without affecting the running of pump M_1. However, if all three pumps are running, the stopping of any pump for any reason will stop all three.

FIGURE **21-14**
Solution to Example 21-2.

21-**8**

Timers and Counters

Timers differ from timing relays in that they coordinate the timing functions of their output contacts through very precise timing circuits in both analog and digital form. The timer can have a multiple of functions such as: ON-Delay, OFF-Delay, Interval Timing, Repeat Cycle Timing, One-Shot Timing, Daily and Weekly Timing, etc. Timing ranges on some products can vary from 0.001 seconds up to 9999 hours and can contain a multiple of the above functions. Most have the capability of being programmed to specify the ON-OFF duration of the output switching.

Counters keep track of the changes of state of input signals. Like the timer, they also can be programmed and display their readouts in digital form. For the most part, counters count in an UP direction or a DOWN direction, and can be capable of either count direction. The input pulse to a counter can come from a variety of devices such as switches, photo detectors, output pulse from other timers or counters, various TTL outputs, etc. The detection speed of the counter depends on the type; however, detection speeds of some counters can respond to an input signal in the range of 30 000 cycles per second. When the counter's count function is completed, an output pulse can be generated to reset the counter to zero or some preset value.

F I G U R E **21-15**
(a) Multi-range timer. (b) Programmable digital display counter.
(Courtesy of Omron Canada Inc.)

(a)   (b)

When a machine is operated by one or more persons and it must be so designed to prevent the operator(s) from being able to place any part of their body in the mechanism of the machine while cycling, it must contain an anti-tie down control. This is spelled out in Section 32 of the *Occupational Health and Safety Act for Industrial Establishments*.

First, let's determine what an anti-tie down control is. Using a single operator punch press machine for our example, we know that a ram or moving head will come in contact with a stationary part to be pressed when the machine is cycling. The operator's hands must be clear of the part to be pressed while the cycle is in progress. To satisfy this requirement, two push buttons are connected and located in such a manner that both of the operator's hands must be engaged to operate these buttons. This, of course, will ensure both of the operator's hands are occupied while the machine is going through a cycle. However, if one of these buttons is tied down for any reason the machine must not cycle upon operation of the untied button. This safety circuit is designed to prevent the operator from speeding up the cycle of the machine by allowing one hand free to load the machine while the other hand is cycling the machine control. Fig. 21-16 shows two acceptable methods of achieving anti-tie down control.

FIGURE **21-16**
Anti-tie down circuits: (*a*) OFF delay control. (*b*) RC network control.

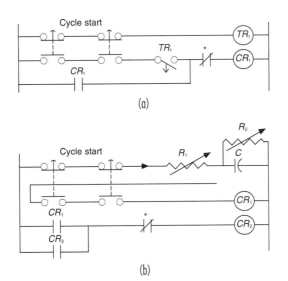

(a)

(b)

Fig. 21-16(*a*) employs the use of an OFF delay timer. When the two cycle start buttons are in their normal state, TR_1 is energized and the OFF delay TR_1 contact in rung #2 is closed. Upon operating the two cycle buttons simultaneously, TR_1 will de-energize. However, the TR_1 contact in rung #2 will delay in opening based on the preset adjustment of timer TR_1 (approximately 1 s). This is sufficient time for rung #2 continuity to be complete, energizing CR_1 and beginning the machine cycle. If one of the cycle buttons is tied down, TR_1 will de-energize, opening up the TR_1 OFF delay contact in rung #2. This will prevent any further machine cycles.

Fig. 21-16 (*b*) uses a **resistive/capacitive (RC)** network to achieve the anti-tie down cycle. If one of the cycle start buttons is tied down, the capacitor C will lose its charge and will not be able to supply sufficient energy to relay CR_1 to begin the cycle.

Certainly, many adaptations of these techniques can be employed depending on the individual application. If more than one operator is involved in the operation of the machine, then more pairs of cycle start buttons can be added to the control so all operators are sure to be clear when the machine begins its cycle.

Example 21-3: Automatic Drill Press

Using a momentary start/stop push-button control station, sequence the drill head so that if the drill is fully retracted and the start button is operated, the drill will advance downward and the drill motor will start. The downward motion will be produced by energizing solenoid valve *A*. This, in turn, will control the operation of an air cylinder used to raise or lower the drill mechanism. When the drill is fully lowered it will dwell for 5 s, still running, to clear cuttings from the piece being drilled. After the down dwell is complete, solenoid valve *A* is de-energized, returning the drill to the fully raised position and shutting down the drill motor. If the stop button is operated during any part of the drill cycle, the drill motor must stop and the drill head will return to its fully raised position. The cycle is now complete.

Try this same problem using an anti-tie down circuit that will ensure the operator's hands are occupied on the cycle buttons until the drill has reached the fully lowered position.

Fig. 21-17 shows a solution to this problem.

FIGURE **21-17**
Automatic drill press.

FIGURE **21-18**
(*a*) Drill problem solution without anti-tie down control. (*b*) Drill problem solution with anti-tie down control.

(*a*)

(*b*)

REVIEW QUESTIONS

1 Name the three basic components of a control circuit.

2 Compare a low-voltage release circuit with a low-voltage protection circuit.

3 With reference to Fig. 21-3(*b*), describe what the condition of the ground indicating lamps would be for the following conditions: (*a*) no grounds, (*b*) ground on line #2.

4 List the standard JIC colour code for conductors used in industry and give their respective application.

5 What is the purpose of a dual voltage relay?

6 With reference to Fig. 21-5, list the sequence of events that must take place to cycle the machine from the point of turning on the main disconnect switch. List all the events that occur after the cycle start buttons are operated.

7 With reference to Fig. 21-6, determine the number of individual conductors that must terminate on each respective terminal.

8 With reference to Fig. 21-5, determine what would take place if one of the cycle start buttons was tied down for the purpose of operator convenience.

9 Describe ON and OFF delay timing, and contrast the two types of timers with respect to some applications.

10 Describe the operation of a latch relay and give an application for same.

11 What is the purpose of the normally closed and normally open contacts in series with the latch and unlatch relay coils respectively?

12 Describe the difference between a timer and a counter.

13 What is the prime purpose of an anti-tie down circuit?

14 Describe the operation of the circuit in Fig. 21-16(*b*).

15 What is the maximum number of cycles a machine can operate after one of the cycle start buttons of an anti-tie down circuit has been tied down?

16 Name two advantages of solid-state relays over conventional electro-mechanical relays.

17 What is the prime consideration when designing a control circuit that will run a machine operated by a person?

PROBLEMS

21-1 With reference to Fig. 21-5, determine the troubleshooting procedure that would be used to correct the following fault in the machine cycle: When the tool head has reached the advanced position, the head will not return automatically.

21-2 Design a circuit using a timing relay, two momentary contact push buttons, and two pilot lights to perform the following functions: (*a*) when the start button is operated "L_1" will turn on and remain on after the start button is released. (*b*) The start button will also turn on "L_2" ten seconds after "L_1". (*c*) Pressing the stop button will reset the circuit (both lights off).

21-3 Design a circuit using a timing relay, a two-position selector switch and two pilot lights to perform the following functions: (*a*) when the selector switch is turned on "L_1" will turn on immediately and "L_2" will turn off immediately. (*b*) When the selector switch is turned off "L_1" will remain on for ten seconds and then turn off and "L_2" will remain off for ten seconds and then turn on.

21-4 Design a circuit that will, with the use of a latch relay, timing relay, momentary contact push-button, and pilot light perform the following functions: When the push-button is momentarily operated, the lamp will come on. Five seconds after the push-button is released, the lamp will turn off.

21-5 A system machine tool requires four motors. The running state of the motors must satisfy the following requirements:
(1) Motors one and two cannot operate simultaneously. However, they are started by momentary contact start/stop buttons.
(2) Motor number three must run when either motor one or two is running, but cannot run alone.
(3) Motor four starts only when motor one or two (whichever was running) is stopped. Motor number four will run for eight seconds and shut down automatically.
(4) The tripping of any of the motor's overload relays must shut down the entire system.
Design a control schematic to achieve the above requirements.

21-6 Determine the **minimum** number of conductors between the devices where indicated. Use the schematic diagram of Fig. 21-19 on page 510 for reference purposes.

FIGURE **21-19**
Diagrams associated with Prob. 21-6.

Introduction to Programmable Controllers

The **programmable controller** as we know it today was introduced in 1969. The original intent of the programmable controller was strictly for replacement of conventional relays with static switching that could be functionally programmed and reprogrammed without extensive wiring changes when machine re-tooling was required. The prime movers behind the advent of the programmable controller were the giant auto industries who, at this time, were going through annual model changes. The retooling costs for these changes were high and very labour-intensive. The programmable controller cut the time required to electrically retool a piece of equipment down to a fraction of the average retooling time. The ability, in many cases, to simply reprogram the electrical system to adapt it to its new task was a far cry from the days of completely rewiring a control panel for such a tooling change.

FIGURE **22-1**
SYSMAC C200H programmable controller.
(Courtesy of Omron Canada Inc.)

Today, of course, the programmable controller has evolved into far more than just a relay replacement control system.

A programmable controller is a microprocessor base system that can monitor input and output devices and control the switching of the outputs based upon a set of structured instructions called the user program.

With reference to Fig. 22-2, the inputs are shown as simple discrete switching devices connected to an input module. The voltage level at which these inputs can operate varies from very low dc voltages to 230 V ac or dc depending on the type of input module being used. The input module takes the input signal from the machine sensors and conditions it to a logic level that can be handled by the internal **Central Processing Unit** (CPU). This logic voltage is generally in the 5 V dc range. The outputs, in turn, are connected to an output module. The voltage levels of the output modules vary similar to the choices stated for input voltages. Both the input and output modules are equipped with optical isolation circuits to prevent the high voltage values used at input and output devices from being accidentally leaked into the processor's logic level voltage. Fig. 22-3 shows a partial opto-isolation circuit that is using a push button to produce and input signal. This input signal switches an LED which provides an optical input to a photosensitive transistor. The output is then turned ON/OFF with no electrical contact with the input device, only through the opto-isolator circuit.

The processor itself is programmed by the user through a programming panel. The program panel can be a dedicated terminal for this purpose or a computer containing appropriate software to enable the computer to provide instructions in the form of a user program to the processor in the CPU. After the program is entered, the input and output registers will be scanned by the pro-

22-1

What Is a Programmable Controller?

F I G U R E **22-2**

Block diagram of a very basic Programmable Controller System.

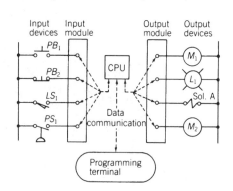

FIGURE **22-3**
Electrical isolation through optical coupling.

cessor for conditions stated in the program. These registers reflect the actual ON-OFF status of the connected inputs and outputs. Remember, the program is nothing more than a set of instructions for the system to operate on when given machine conditions are present. For example, if we want the output L_1 in Fig. 22-2 to turn ON when LS_1 is closed, we must instruct the processor to examine the status of LS_1, at its input register. When the contacts on LS_1 close, the input register for this point will become a logic 1. The processor will then scan the program to determine it's instruction. At this point the output register will be also be set at a logic 1 and turn on L_1 at the output. (See Fig. 22-4.)

FIGURE **22-4**
Inputs and outputs shown in Fig. 22-2 related to their respective input/output registers.

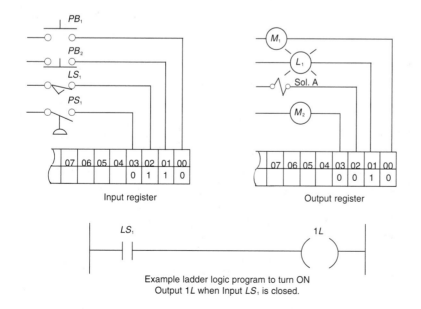

Input register

Output register

Example ladder logic program to turn ON
Output 1L when Input LS_1 is closed.

The processor will, after the program is entered and in the run mode, scan the conditions of the inputs and outputs every few milliseconds looking for the conditions required by the user program. If the programming terminal is connected while the machine is in operation, the program panel can be used to observe the program's operation while running. Therefore, debugging the system's program can be accomplished at the program terminal. As can be seen from Fig. 22-2, two-way communication or data flow occurs between the input modules to the CPU, the output modules to the CPU, and the programming terminal to the CPU. This complete free-flow of data allows the status of inputs and outputs to be updated at every scan of the processor. As a result, machine control logic can be controlled through programmed, high-speed static switching instead of mechanical switching requiring hard-wired magnetic relays that are subject to continuous wear and replacement schedules.

22-2
Terminology

The following chart contains some of the common terms encountered when working with programmable controllers.

Address	Memory location of a given instruction or set of instructions.
Analog	A continuous variation of some physical quantity. For example, a moving coil meter makes its measurement in the form of an analog readout.
BCD	(Binary Coded Decimal) Binary digits (bits) arranged in groups of four to produce a base ten number. See Appendix I.
BCO	(Binary Coded Octal) Binary digits arranged in groups of three to produce a base eight number. See Appendix I.
Binary Bit	A single-digit base two number that contains two possible states, 0 or 1 (OFF or ON).
Byte	A group of eight binary digits (bits) operated on as a unit.
EEPROM	Electrically Erasable Programmable Read Only Memory.
Hexadecimal	A numbering system with its base, sixteen.
Logic True	Logic switching condition(s) in an ON (1) state.
LSB	Least Significant Bit.
MSB	Most Significant Bit.
LSD	Least Significant Digit.
MD	Middle Digit.
MSD	Most Significant Digit.
Octal	A numbering system with a base of eight.

PROM	Programmable Read Only Memory.
RAM	(Random Access Memory) Storage area of the system that enables the user to obtain data from, or place data into, storage where the time required for such access is independent of the location of the data most recently obtained or placed in storage.
ROM	(Read Only Memory) Storage area of the system where data cannot be altered by user instructions.
Reset	To turn OFF or place condition to normal state.
Set	To turn ON.
Volatile Memory	Data stored in RAM that will be lost if the system loses its power source.
Word Length	A group of binary digits operated on as a unit (16 bits).

The Processor module, see Fig. 22-5(*a*), contains the systems intelligence. This unit houses the Central Processing Unit (CPU) and the memory organization. The CPU makes the decisions about what the processor is to do and when it should do it. The memory portion of this processor is broken down into three functions:

1) Data Table: stores information that the CPU will need to make its decisions.

22-**3**

The Processor

FIGURE **22-5**
(*a*) Processor module — Allen-Bradley PLC-2/16, 2/17 Processor. (*b*) Function block diagram of Processor PLC-2 Family.

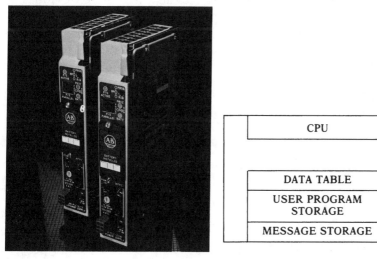

(a)   (b)

2) User Program Store: instructions are stored by the programmer to give logic to the machine operation.
3) Message Store: this area is reserved for the storage of messages and/or graphic characters.

The area of memory where data is controlled and utilized in this processor is called the data table. The data table is divided into smaller sections according to the type of information to be remembered. Fig. 22-6 illustrates the data table sections for the processors in Fig. 22-5.

The **output image** (status register) table reflects the status of output bits controlled by the user program. The **input image** (status register) table reflects the status of inputs at the terminals of the input module. When the processor detects a voltage at an input terminal it records that information by storing a binary "1" (on signal) in its respective bit location. If no voltage is present at that terminal, then the processor deems the input to be OFF and records that information by storing a binary "0" (OFF signal) in its respective bit location. The status of the outputs connected to the output module are similarly reflected by the presence of 1s or 0s in the output image table to indicate an output being ON or OFF, respectively. The processor also scans these input/output image tables for changes. If an input changes from OFF to ON, then the input image table for that particular bit would change from "0" to "1." During the next processor scan this change would be recognized and acted upon based upon the instructions in the program; for example, turn ON a predetermined output that was previously OFF. The processor I/O and program scan time is dependent upon the size of the program. However, it should not exceed 10 ms with the modern processor. Some processors' scan rate is less than 5 ms. The processor scan is simply the rate at which the CPU looks at the status of the I/O and user program. The larger the user program and connected I/O, the more lengthy the scan time. The scan time should, however, be quick enough to keep up to date with fast-acting inputs.

FIGURE **22-6**
Block organization of the data table for the processors shown in Fig. 22-5.

Data Table
Output Image Table
Input Image Table
Timer/Counter Storage

Data Memory (DM) Addressing (Omron CQM1 System)

The DM area in a CQM1 Omron processor can be divided into four sections with the General Purpose and PC Setup sections having subdivisions.

FIGURE **22-7**
Memory organization of the CQM1 processor.
(Courtesy of Omron Canada Inc.)

DM0000 DM1024	General Purpose Data Memory
DM1025 DM6134	General Purpose Data Memory *Not supported by CPU11 and CPU21*
DM6144 DM6568	Fixed Data Memory (Read Only)
DM6569 DM6599	Error Log (Read Only)
DM6600 DM6614	PC Setup (Standard Processing)
DM6615 DM6644	PC Setup (Pulse output/Scan time) (Interrupt Processing) (High-speed counter)
DM6645 DM6655	PC Setup (RS232 port settings) (Peripheral port settings)

22-4
The I/O and Power Supply

The power supply provides the low level dc voltage required for the electronic circuitry of the processors and the trigger circuits of the input and output modules. This is achieved by stepping-down the line level ac voltage and rectifying it for the logic circuits. Some power supplies come with battery back-up. This is used to hold memory in the processor in the event of a system power failure. Systems requiring this back-up have volatile memories. Some systems, however, do not require this back-up protection because they employ the use of EEPROM memory. If the back-up battery supply is used, it is scanned by the processor for sufficient battery potential, and is annunciated if it falls below an acceptable level.

The input/output modules are contained in a chassis known as the I/O rack. Each of these I/O modules plug into a back plane connector or side connection plugs. Each I/O module contains status lights for each input and output terminal on the module. The status lights are illuminated when a particular input or output

FIGURE **22-8**
Control panel containing PLC-3 processor and seven I/O racks.
(Courtesy of Allen-Bradley.)

is ON. This enables the observer to better diagnose faults at the panel location. The I/O racks vary in size depending upon the capacity of the system being used and the requirement of the connected machinery. Fig. 22-8 shows a very large system employing an Allen-Bradley PLC-3 processor containing seven I/O racks mounted in a system control panel. Note that the panel sections

FIGURE **22-9**
Processor system scan.

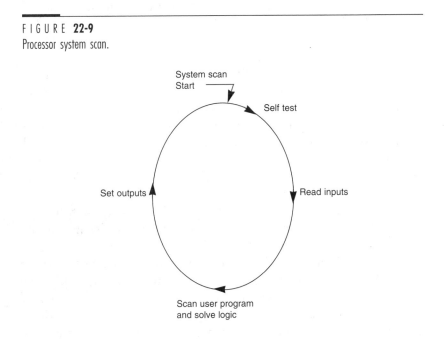

on the extreme left and right sides of the panel contain the connecting terminal strips for all the field wiring.

In order to effectively program and understand the controller, one must first have a general understanding of how the programmable controller works. The model in Fig. 22-9 is based on the Omron controller. However, this model is somewhat generic for most systems.

22-5

Programmable Controller Fundamentals

1. **Self Test:** The processor scans the I/O connections, resets watchdog timer, and examines the executive programming before putting the system ON-LINE.
2. **Input Scan:** All connected real world inputs are scanned and their ON/OFF status is entered into the input register.
3. **Logic Solve:** The program instructions will be scanned and executed using the I/O register information along with other word mapped data.
4. **Output Scan:** After the user program scan is completed, the connected real world outputs are updated from information derived from the output register.

Although there are several methods of programming the PLC, the most popular method is **Ladder Logic.** The Ladder Logic program is similar in structure to its relay logic counterpart. The program may be inserted into the central processor using either a dedicated programming terminal or a computer containing

22-6

Programming

F I G U R E **22-10**
System structure.
(Courtesy of Omron Canada Inc.)

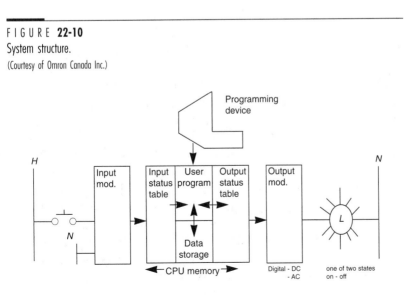

appropriate software. The logic instructions are arranged in a logic rung format where inputs occupy the left side of the rung and outputs the right side. Figs. 22-4 and 22-12 illustrate very simple logic rungs.

22-**7**

Memory Organization

The manner in which the processor scans the ON/OFF status of inputs and outputs is entirely dependent upon the manufacturer of the system in question. Generally speaking, most systems operate on a 16-bit word or memory register. Different numbering systems are used to interpret the ON/OFF status of the memory word. For instance, if decimal numbering is used, the least significant bit (LSB) is "0" and the most significant bit (MSB) is "15". Whereas, if an octal based numbering system is used, the LSB bit is "0" and the MSB bit is "17". Remember, there are no 8s and 9s in octal numbers.

The concept of "Addressing" the various inputs and outputs also depends upon the type and manufacturer of the system in question. The important thing to remember when studying any addressing code is that the location address is simply a method of telling the CPU the precise location of the memory bit or word. This concept can be likened to mailing a letter to a friend. The envelope must contain the receiver's name, street address, city, province, and country, not to mention a postal code. In the same manner, the bit or word address contains similar identification so the processor knows exactly what output should be turned ON/OFF when given inputs change state.

Fig. 22-11 illustrates the addressing method of the Omron CQM1 system.

Fig. 22-12 shows a small PLC system containing the processor; I/O modules; computer for programming and troubleshooting; connected discrete I/O and a very basic program example. It can be readily seen that the discrete input/output devices connected to their respective modules do not determine, in any way, how these devices will be controlled. However, at the lower portion of the illustration in Fig. 22-12, is a sample of a ladder logic program that will instruct the CPU to tie the inputs and outputs together in a manner prescribed by the program. In this example, if 2PB is NOT operated and 1PB plus 1LS is operated, the rung logic will be complete. The output 1M will turn ON. The 1M contact in parallel with 1PB in the program will now be logic 1 (ON). At this point the push button 1PB can be released by the operator and the output will remain ON until either 2PB is operated or 1LS opens. In the second rung of this program the output 1L will be ON as long as the contacts on pressure switch 1PS are open.

FIGURE **22-11**

(Courtesy of Omron Canada Inc.)

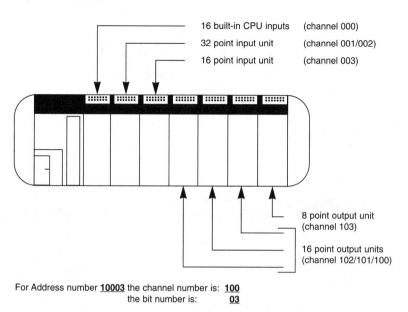

16 built-in CPU inputs   (channel 000)

32 point input unit   (channel 001/002)

16 point input unit   (channel 003)

8 point output unit
(channel 103)

16 point output units
(channel 102/101/100)

For Address number **10003** the channel number is: **100**
the bit number is: **03**

Where inputs start at channel **000** while outputs start at channel **100**.

The programming terminal (computer) in Fig. 22-12 can be used not only to install the program, but also to monitor that program while operating. The computer also has the ability to edit this program and document information relating to the program and the machine cycle.

The program is simply a list of instructions that guide the processor. These instructions can examine or change the status of bits in the memory of the processor. The status of these bits determines the operation of your outputs. When the program is written, you specify through the program the things you want controlled in your application, and conditions must be met before those things are done.

As described earlier, the actual discrete input devices or internal reference addresses are scanned by the processor for their ON/OFF condition. In the user program, the input device/internal reference can be operated on in either a closed or open state. When the logic programming symbol -] [- (normally open contact) is used, the processor scans the addressed input for a closed contact. If closed, the logic symbol -] [- becomes a 1 state in its respective rung. If however, the programming symbol -]/[- (normally closed contact) is used, the processor scans the addressed input/internal reference for an open contact. If open, the logic symbol -]/[- becomes a 1

22-8
Relay Type Instructions

FIGURE 22-12

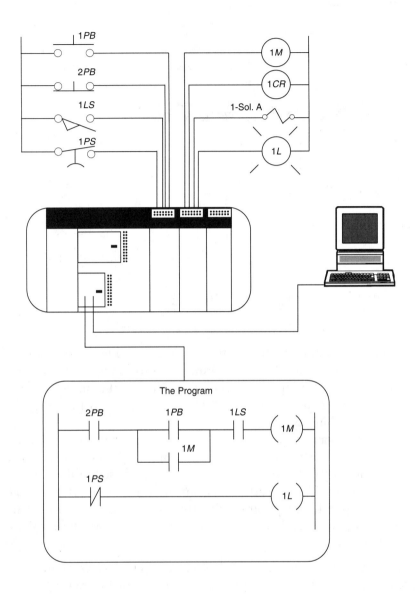

state in its respective rung. The -]/[- programming symbol is the complement of the -] [- .

In Fig. 22-12 it should be noted that the output coil 1M initially requires 1PB, 2PB and 1LS all to be in a closed state to be energized. However, output coil 1L requires pressure switch 1PS to be in an open state to be energized.

The output coil symbol -( )- is a programmed instruction that, when energized by complete rung continuity, will turn ON a real world output or an internal relay coil in the system memory. Many manufacturers also have provided the ability to program a NOT output. This symbol -(/)- will provide power flow to the coil when the logic rung is false.

The equivalent to a latch relay is also possible to program. This type of output is referred to as a retentive output. If the output is set/latched, and the initial signal is removed, the output will remain in the set/latched condition until a reset/unlatch signal is received. This type of output will remain in its previous state regardless of system power. As long as system memory is in place the output will remember its previous state. The retentive output's purpose is for programs that require memory regardless of the presence of system power.

Timers and Counters can also be programmed to operate much the same way as their relay logic counterparts and provide even a higher degree of accuracy and versatility.

With the rapid advancement of programmable controller technology, systems can control and manipulate data, perform basic and high level arithmetic functions, interchange and share information among multiples of interconnected systems, receive signals from analog inputs and drive analog outputs, and control and monitor very sophisticated processes that requires Proportional, Integral, and Derivative (PID) calculations.

The modern factory networks the various processes by interconnecting the PLCs controlling individual machines. Through these networks an entire factory process can be monitored and controlled from a central computer. Fig. 22-13 illustrates a small linked communication system tying together several controllers and a robot system. With this capability, the factory of today may access production information, quality statistics, equipment reliability data, and provide the manufacturing departments with production orders.

The operator/machine interface panels have progressed from simple push buttons to complex, programmable touch-sensitive displays (see Fig. 22-14) that not only provide the basic Start/Stop functions for the operator but, also, in graphic form display a high resolution picture of the machine being controlled. These interface panels can be programmed to supply the production operators with vital information about their machine's function. For example, in the event of a machine failure, the panel can display a diagnostic readout describing what has failed and how to rectify the fault. All of these capabilities lead to reduced machine downtime and lower production costs as a result.

22-**9**

Higher Level System Capabilities

FIGURE **22-13**

A small integrated network.

(Courtesy of Omron Canada Inc.)

System Configuration

FIGURE **22-14**

Operator interface programmable terminals.

(Courtesy of Omron Canada Inc.)

To keep abreast with this technology fifteen years ago was not a difficult task. Today, with many types of programmable controller systems on the market, offering many interesting and unique control capabilities, the ability to stay current is difficult to impossible. It is important, however, to learn the generic capabilities of these systems. Once mastered, the ability to select the appropriate system for your requirements becomes easier.

Some of the important things to look for when selecting a system for a single machine or factory is:

- Does the system manufacturer provide local support for their equipment?
- Does either the manufacturer or supplier offer training on their equipment?
- Does the manufacturer maintain a philosophy of system compatibility with new to older controllers as the technology evolves?
- Check out reliability references before moving to an unknown, untried system.
- Can your existing system be networked with a different manufacturer's system?

|22-**10**
Conclusion

R E V I E W Q U E S T I O N S

1 How does a programmable controller differ from a conventional relay control system?
2 If an input device such as a push button is required to operate an output device such as a motor starter, could this be done without additional wiring if both push button and motor starter are already connected to the I/O? Explain.
3 When using a standard relay control system, any functional changes of a machine cycle have to be done with hard wiring changes. Explain how this would be accomplished with a PLC.
4 Describe what an output/input image table register word provides in the operation of a PLC.
5 What is the purpose of the PLC power supply?
6 The processor's function is best described by subdividing its functions. Describe these functions.
7 What protection is provided to prevent line voltage values from inputs/outputs from entering the programmable controller's logic area?
8 Describe what is meant by a system having a volatile memory.

9 Describe the purpose of I/O addressing.

10 If the normally open and normally closed states of a limit switch are required to control outputs, how many wires would have to be connected to the limit switch

  a) using relay control?

  b) using PLC control?

11 The scan rate of a PLC is the rate at which the processor checks the status of the I/O and then runs through the written user program to execute the machine's operation. Name one of the determining factors of the scan rate.

Appendixes

Wiring Diagram Symbols

SWITCHES						
DISCONNECT	CIRCUIT INTERRUPTER	CIRCUIT BREAKER	LIMIT			
			NORMALLY OPEN	NORMALLY CLOSED	NEUTRAL POSITION	ACTUATED
			HELD CLOSED	HELD OPEN	NP	NP

LIMIT (CONTINUED)			LIQUID LEVEL		VACUUM & PRESSURE		TEMPERATURE	
MAINTAINED POSITION	PROXIMITY SWITCH		NORMALLY OPEN	NORMALLY CLOSED	NORMALLY OPEN	NORMALLY CLOSED	NORMALLY OPEN	NORMALLY CLOSED
	CLOSED	OPEN						

FLOW(AIR,WATER ETC.)		FOOT		TOGGLE	CABLE OPERATED (EMERG.) SWITCH	PLUGGING		NON-PLUG
NORMALLY OPEN	NORMALLY CLOSED	NORMALLY OPEN	NORMALLY CLOSED			F	F	F
						R	R	R

PLUGGING W/LOCK-OUT COIL	SELECTOR		ROTARY SELECTOR	
	2-POSITION	3-POSITION	† NON-BRIDGING CONTACTS	† BRIDGING CONTACTS
	1 2	1 2 3	OR	OR
			† TOTAL CONTACTS TO SUIT NEEDS	

THERMOCOUPLE SWITCH	PUSHBUTTONS			CONNECTIONS, ETC.
TCS	SINGLE CIRCUIT	DOUBLE CIRCUIT	MAINTAINED CONTACT	CONDUCTORS
OFF	NORMALLY OPEN	MUSHROOM HEAD		NOT CONNECTED / CONNECTED
1				
2	NORMALLY CLOSED			

Wiring Diagram Symbols continued:

CONNECTIONS, ETC. (CONT'D)			CONTACTS							
GROUND	CHASSIS OR FRAME NOT NECESSARILY GROUNDED	PLUG AND RECP.	TIME DELAY AFTER COIL				RELAY, ETC.		THERMAL OVER-LOAD
			ENERGIZED		DE-ENERGIZED		NORMALLY OPEN	NORMALLY CLOSED	
			NORMALLY OPEN	NORMALLY CLOSED	NORMALLY OPEN	NORMALLY CLOSED			

COILS							
RELAYS, TIMERS, ETC.	SOLENOIDS, BRAKES, ETC.				THERMAL OVERLOAD ELEMENT	CONTROL CIRCUIT TRANSFORMER	
	GENERAL	2-POSITION HYDRAULIC	3-POSITION PNEUMATIC	2-POSITION LUBRICATION			

COILS (CONTINUED)		
AUTO TRANSFORMER	LINEAR VARIABLE DIFFERENTIAL TRANSFORMER	VARIABLE AUTO-TRANSFORMER

COILS (CONTINUED)			
SATURABLE TRANSFORMER	REACTORS		
	SATURABLE CORE	IRON CORE	SATURABLE CORE

COILS (CONTINUED)			MOTORS	
REACTORS (CONTINUED)			3 PHASE MOTOR	DC MOTOR ARMATURE
ADJUSTABLE IRON CORE	AIR CORE	MAGNETIC AMPLIFIER WINDING		

MOTORS (CONT'D)	RESISTORS, CAPACITORS, ETC.				
DC MOTOR FIELD	RESISTOR	HEATING ELEMENT	TAPPED RESISTOR	RHEOSTAT	POTENTIOMETER

Wiring Diagram Symbols continued:

Device	Standard Symbol	Other Symbols in Use
Semiconductor diode		
PNP transistor		
NPN transistor		
Silicon controlled rectified (SCR)	(A) — (K) (G)	(A) — (G) (K)
Triac	(T_2) — (G) (T_1)	
Diac	(T) — (T)	(T) — (T)
Zener diode		(A) — (K)
Photodiode		
Light-emitting diode (LED)		
Phototransistor, PNP	(E) — (C) (B)	
Light activated SCR (LASCR)	(A) (G) (K)	

Dimensions, Mass, and Resistance of Bare Copper Wire, Solid, AWG Sizes

Size AWG	Diameter, mils	Area, cmils	Mass, lb per 1000 ft	Resistance, Ω per 1000 ft, 20°C Annealed Wire
0000	460.0	211 600	640.5	0.0490
000	409.6	167 800	507.8	0.0618
00	364.8	133 100	402.8	0.0779
0	324.9	105 600	319.5	0.0983
1	289.3	83 690	253.3	0.124
2	257.6	66 360	200.9	0.156
3	229.4	52 620	159.3	0.197
4	204.3	41 740	126.3	0.249
5	181.9	33 090	100.2	0.313
6	162.0	26 240	79.44	0.395
7	144.3	20 820	63.03	0.498
8	128.5	16 510	49.98	0.628
9	114.4	13 090	39.62	0.793
10	101.9	10 380	31.43	0.999
11	90.7	8 230	24.92	1.26
12	80.8	6 530	19.77	1.59
13	72.0	5 180	15.68	2.00
14	64.1	4 110	12.43	2.52
15	57.1	3 260	9.87	3.18
16	50.8	2 580	7.81	4.02
17	45.3	2 050	6.21	5.05
18	40.3	1 620	4.92	6.39
19	35.9	1 290	3.90	8.05
20	32.0	1 020	3.10	10.1
22	25.3	640	1.94	16.2

Dimensions, Mass, and Resistance of Bare Copper Wire, Stranded, AWG and cmil Sizes

Size, AWG or cmils	Overall Diameter, mils	Number of Strands Class B Stranding	Mass, lb per 1000 ft	Resistance, Ω per 1000 ft, 20°C Annealed Wire
2 000 000	1 630	127	6 175	0.00529
1 750 000	1 526	127	5 403	0.00605
1 500 000	1 411	91	4 631	0.00705
1 250 000	1 288	91	3 859	0.00846
1 000 000	1 152	61	3 088	0.0106
900 000	1 094	61	2 779	0.0118
800 000	1 031	61	2 470	0.0132
750 000	998	61	2 316	0.0141
700 000	964	61	2 161	0.0151
600 000	891	61	1 853	0.0176
500 000	813	37	1 544	0.0212
450 000	772	37	1 389	0.0235
400 000	726	37	1 235	0.0265
350 000	679	37	1 081	0.0302
300 000	629	37	925	0.0353
250 000	574	37	772	0.0423
0 000	552	19	653	0.0500
000	492	19	518	0.0631
00	414	19	411	0.0795
0	368	19	326	0.100
1	328	19	259	0.126
2	292	7	205	0.159
3	260	7	162	0.201
4	232	7	129	0.253
5	206	7	102	0.320
6	184	7	80.9	0.403
7	164	7	64.2	0.508
8	146	7	51.0	0.641
9	130	7	40.4	0.808
10	116	7	32.1	1.020

Dimensions, Mass, and Resistance of Bare Copper Wire, Metric Sizes

Nominal Area, mm²	Stranding and Wire Diameter, mm	Approx. Overall Diameter, mm	Nominal Mass, kg/km	Resistance at 20°C,* Ω/km
1000	91/3.73	41.1	9033	0.01765
800	91/3.35	36.9	7284	0.02188
625	91/2.97	32.7	5722	0.02786
500	61/3.25	29.3	4590	0.03472
400	61/2.90	26.1	3642	0.04377
300	61/2.51	22.6	2746	0.05803
240	61/2.26	20.3	2219	0.07181
185	37/2.54	17.8	1699	0.09375
150	37/2.29	16.0	1376	0.1157
120	37/2.06	14.4	1115	0.1429
95	37/1.83	12.8	881	0.1808
70	19/2.18	10.9	645	0.2467
50	19/1.85	9.27	464.8	0.3424
35	19/1.55	7.75	324.5	0.4904
25	19/1.32	6.60	235.8	0.6748
16	7/1.73	5.18	148.3	1.069
10	7/1.37	4.12	93.51	1.695
6	7/0.107	3.21	56.55	2.803
4	7/0.864	2.59	37.08	4.277
2.5	7/0.686	2.06	23.38	6.782
1.5	7/0.533	1.60	14.14	11.21
1.0	1/1.14	1.14	9.122	16.80
0.75	1/0.991	0.99	6.851	22.37
0.50	1/0.813	0.81	4.613	33.23

* The resistance values in this table are based on a conductivity of 100 percent of international annealed copper standard at 20°C.
Source: Based on data published by British Insulated Calendar's Cables, Limited.

Full-Load Currents of Motors

Horsepower Rating	Three-Phase Motors*						
	Induction-Type Squirrel-Cage and Wound-Rotor, A				Synchronous-Type, Unity Power Factor, A		
	200 V	230 V	460 V	575 V	230 V	460 V	575 V
½	2.3	2	1	0.8			
¾	3.2	2.8	1.4	1.1			
1	4.1	3.6	1.8	1.4			
1½	6.0	5.2	2.6	2.1			
2	7.4	6.4	3.2	2.6			
3	10.4	9.9	4.9	3.8			
5	16.0	14.4	7.2	5.9			
7½	23.0	22.0	1.1	8.5			
10	29.0	25.0	12.5	10.4			
15	46	40	20	16			
20	57	50	25	19			
25	80	70	35	26	56	28	23
30		74	37	29	67	34	27
40		98	49	40	88	44	35
50		124	62	50	110	55	44
60		140	70	56	131	66	53
75		174	87	70	162	81	65
100		232	116	95	214	107	86
125			145	116		134	107
150			170	136		160	128
200			230	185		213	171

* These values of full-load currents are approximate values. Actual currents may be higher or lower than those listed due to variations in torque characteristics, speed, or manufacturer's designs.

Full-Load Currents of Motors (continued)

Direct-Current Motors,* A			Single-Phase Motors,* A		
Horsepower Rating	120 V	240 V	HP Rating	115 V	230 V
¼	2.9	1.5	⅙	3.6	1.8
⅓	3.6	1.8	¼	5.0	2.5
½	5.2	2.6	⅓	6.4	3.2
¾	7.4	3.7	½	8.6	4.3
1	9.4	4.7	¾	10.6	5.3
1½	13.2	6.6	1	15.4	7.7
2	17	8.5	1½	16	8
3	25	12.2	2	27	13
5	40	20	3	34	17
7½	58	29	5	56	28
10	76	38	7	80	40
15	....	55	10	100	50
20	....	72			
25	....	89			
30	....	106			
40	....	140			
50	....	173			
60	....	206			
75	....	255			
100	....	341			
125	....	425			
150	....	506			
200	....	675			

* These values of full-load currents are approximate values. Actual currents may be higher or lower than those listed due to variations in torque characteristics, speed, or manufacturer's designs.

APPENDIX F

Trigonometric Definitions and Formulas

Right Triangles

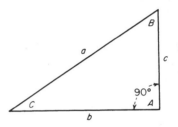

1. A right triangle is a triangle in which one angle is a right angle (90°).
2. The sum of the three angles (of any triangle) is 180°.
3. The side opposite the right angle is called the hypotenuse. Side a is the hypotenuse in the above figure.
4. The square of the hypotenuse is equal to the sum of the squares of the other two sides. In the above figure,

$$a^2 = b^2 + c^2$$

$$\text{or} \quad a = \sqrt{b^2 + c^2}$$

$$\text{also} \ b = \sqrt{a^2 - c^2}$$

$$\text{and} \ c = \sqrt{a^2 - b^2}$$

Several of the possible ratios between the sides of the right triangle shown in the above figure are listed below. These ratios are called **trigonometric functions**. An abbreviated table of values of the trigonometric functions is given in Appendix G.

5. The ratio of side c to side a is called the sine (sin) of angle C.

$$\sin C = \frac{c}{a} = \frac{\textbf{opposite} \text{ side}}{\text{hypotenuse}}$$

6. The ratio of side b to side a is called the cosine (cos) of angle C.

$$\cos C = \frac{b}{a} = \frac{\textbf{adjacent} \text{ side}}{\text{hypotenuse}}$$

7. The ratio of side c to side b is called the tangent (tan) of angle C.

$$\tan C = \frac{c}{b} = \frac{\text{opposite side}}{\text{adjacent side}}$$

8. The ratio of side b to side c is called the cotangent (cot) of angle C.

$$\cot C = \frac{b}{c} = \frac{\text{adjacent side}}{\text{opposite side}}$$

The following are examples using the above relationships:

Example F-1

If angle B in the triangle shown is 63°, find angle C.

$$A + B + C = 180° \qquad \text{(from relation 2)}$$

$$A = 90°$$

$$B + C = 90°$$

Therefore,

$$C = 90° - 63° = 27°$$

Example F-2

If side c in the figure represents 12 Ω and side b represents 16 Ω, find the angle C.

$$\tan C = \frac{c}{b} \qquad \text{(from relation 7)}$$

$$\tan C = \frac{12}{16} = 0.75$$

In the table of tangents (Appendix G), the number nearest 0.75 is 0.7536 which is the tangent of 37°. Thus, the angle C is approximately 37° (or by calculator, 36.87°).

Example F-3

If side a in the figure represents 200 V and angle C is 45°, find side c.

$$\sin C = \frac{c}{d} \quad \text{(from relation 5)}$$

or $$c = a \sin C$$

From the table of sines, sin 45° = 0.7071
Thus, $c = 200 \times 0.707$ or 141.4 V

Example F-4

If side a in the figure is 40 units long and angle C is 30°, find sides b and c.

$$b = a \cos C \quad \text{(from relation 6)}$$
$$b = 40 \times \cos 30°$$
$$= 40 \times 0.866 \text{ or } 34.64$$
$$c = a \sin C \quad \text{(from relation 5)}$$
$$c = 40 \times \sin 30°$$
$$= 40 \times 0.500 \text{ or } 20$$

Trigonometric Functions

Angle, degree	Sin	Cos	Tan	Cot	
0	0.0000	1.0000	0.0000	∞	90
1	0.0175	0.9998	0.0175	57.29	89
2	0.0349	0.9994	0.0349	28.64	88
3	0.0523	0.9986	0.0524	19.08	87
4	0.0698	0.9976	0.0699	14.30	86
5	0.0872	0.9962	0.0875	11.43	85
6	0.1045	0.9945	0.1051	9.514	84
7	0.1219	0.9925	0.1228	8.144	83
8	0.1392	0.9903	0.1405	7.115	82
9	0.1564	0.9877	0.1584	6.314	81
10	0.1736	0.9848	0.1763	5.671	80
11	0.1908	0.9816	0.1944	5.145	79
12	0.2079	0.9781	0.2126	4.705	78
13	0.2250	0.9744	0.2309	4.332	77
14	0.2419	0.9703	0.2493	4.011	76
15	0.2588	0.9659	0.2679	3.732	75
16	0.2756	0.9613	0.2867	3.487	74
17	0.2924	0.9563	0.3057	3.271	73
18	0.3090	0.9511	0.3249	3.078	72
19	0.3256	0.9455	0.3433	2.904	71
20	0.3420	0.9397	0.3640	2.748	70
21	0.3584	0.9336	0.3839	2.605	69
22	0.3746	0.9272	0.4040	2.475	68
23	0.3907	0.9205	0.4245	2.356	67
24	0.4067	0.9135	0.4452	2.246	66
25	0.4226	0.9063	0.4663	2.146	65
26	0.4384	0.8988	0.4877	2.050	64
27	0.4540	0.8910	0.5095	1.963	63
28	0.4695	0.8829	0.5317	1.881	62
29	0.4848	0.8746	0.5543	1.804	61
30	0.5000	0.8660	0.5774	1.732	60

Angle, degree	Sin	Cos	Tan	Cot	
31	0.5150	0.8572	0.6009	1.664	59
32	0.5299	0.8480	0.6249	1.600	58
33	0.5446	0.8387	0.6494	1.540	57
34	0.5592	0.8290	0.6745	1.483	56
35	0.5736	0.8192	0.7002	1.428	55
36	0.5878	0.8090	0.7265	1.376	54
37	0.6018	0.7986	0.7536	1.327	53
38	0.6157	0.7880	0.7813	1.280	52
39	0.6293	0.7771	0.8098	1.235	51
40	0.642	0.7660	0.8391	1.192	50
41	0.656	0.7547	0.8693	1.150	49
42	0.6691	0.7431	0.9004	1.111	48
43	0.6820	0.7314	0.9325	1.072	47
44	0.6947	0.7193	0.9657	1.036	46
45	0.7071	0.7071	1.0000	1.000	45
	Cos	Sin	Cot	Tan	Angle, degree

For angles over 45°, use titles at foot of table.

Complex Quantity Notation for Phasor Representation

Phasors when represented as complex quantities consist of two components, a **real** and a **quadrature** component. Graphically, the real components are represented by points along a horizontal axis, and the quadrature components are represented by points along a vertical axis, as shown in Fig. H-1. The point of intersection of the two axes is called the **origin point O**. Positive values of the real components are represented by points to the right of the origin and negative values to the left of the origin. Positive values of the quadrature components are represented by points above the origin and negative values by points below the origin.

The four sections of the plane as divided by the two axes are called **quadrants** and are numbered as shown. The horizontal line to the right of the origin is called the **reference line**. Starting at the reference line and proceeding in a counterclockwise direction, the first quadrant contains all angles from 0 to 90°; the second quadrant, 90 to 180°; the third quadrant, 180 to 270°; and the fourth, 270 to 360°.

FIGURE **H-1**

Diagram showing the four quadrants with the positive and negative values of phasor components in each.

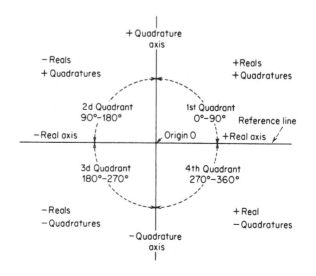

The real and quadrature components of a phasor in any quadrant are the projections of that phasor on the horizontal and vertical axes of the quadrant in which the phasor lies. For example, in Fig. H-2, the phasor C has a real component a (the projection on the horizontal axis) and a quadrature component jb (the projection on the vertical axis). The operator j is used with the quadrature component to indicate that this component is at right angles to the real component.

In accordance with the convention stated, both the real and quadrature components of phasors in the first quadrant have positive values. Mathematically, the phasor C can be written:

$$C = a + jb$$

Using the numerical values shown in Fig. H-2, the phasor C is

$$C = 4 + j3$$

As can be seen in Figs. H-1 and H-2, phasors in the second quadrant have negative real and positive quadrature components, those in the third quadrant have negative real and negative quadrature components, and those in the fourth quadrant have positive real and negative quadrature components. The phasors D, E, and F in Fig. H-2 are expressed numerically as

$$D = -4 + j4$$

$$E = -2 - j5$$

and $$F = +3 - j4$$

The angle that a phasor makes with the horizontal is the angle whose tangent is the quadrature component divided by the real component. For example, the angle θ between the phasor C and the horizontal in Fig. H-2 is

$$\tan \theta = \frac{b}{a} = \frac{3}{4} = 0.75$$

$$\theta = 36.87°$$

Similarly, the angle Φ for the phasor E is

$$\tan \phi = \frac{5}{2} = 2.5$$

$$\phi = 68.2°$$

FIGURE **H-2**
Diagram to illustrate phasor notation.

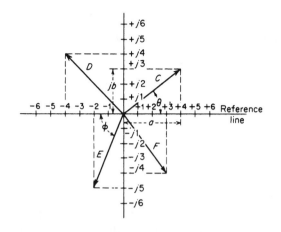

The magnitude of a phasor expressed in the $a + jb$ form is $\sqrt{a^2 + b^2}$. For example, in Fig. H-2 the magnitude (length) of each of the four phasors shown is

$$C = \sqrt{4^2 + 3^2} = 5.0$$

$$D = \sqrt{4^2 + 4^2} = 5.66$$

$$E = \sqrt{2^2 + 5^2} = 5.39$$

$$F = \sqrt{3^2 + 4^2} = 5.0$$

Thus, the magnitude and the angular position of any phasor are determined fully by the expression $a + jb$, the magnitude being $\sqrt{a^2 + b^2}$ and the angle from the horizontal being the angle whose tangent is b/a. The phasor form $a + jb$ is called the **rectangular form** of phasor notation.

Another way of expressing a phasor is the so-called **polar form** **c** $\underline{/\theta^\circ}$, where c is the magnitude of the phasor and θ is the angular position of the phasor with respect to the reference line. Using this notation, the phasor C in Fig. H-2 may be represented numerically as $5\underline{/36.87^\circ}$ and the phasor E as $5.39\underline{/248.2^\circ}$.

Both the rectangular and the polar forms are useful, and many times it is necessary to convert from one form to the other. In Fig. H-2, the two components of the phasor C may be written

$$a = C \cos \theta \qquad \text{and} \qquad b = C \sin \theta$$

Substituting these values in the $a + jb$ form results in

$$C(\cos \theta + j \sin \theta)$$

Again referring to Fig. H-2, if the phasor C is given as $5\underline{/36.87°}$, it can be changed to the $a + jb$ form by writing

$$C = 5(\cos 36.87° + j \sin 36.87°)$$

$$= 5(0.8 + j0.6)$$

$$= 4 + j3$$

Furthermore, if the phasor E is represented as $5.39\underline{/248.2°}$, it is known that this phasor is in the third quadrant, since the angle is between 180 and 270°. Thus, the phasor makes an angle of $248.2° - 180°$, or 68.2° with the horizontal. Since it is in the third quadrant, both the real and the quadrature components will have negative values. Thus,

$$E = 5.39(-\cos 68.2° - j \sin 68.2°)$$

$$= 5.39(-0.37 - j0.93)$$

$$= -2 - j5$$

As is shown in the text, currents and voltages are conveniently represented as phasors. Both currents and voltages, then, may be expressed as complex quantities. Although impedances are not strictly phasor quantities, it is convenient to express impedances as complex quantities. Resistances are represented as real components and reactances as quadrature components. In general, impedance is expressed in the rectangular form as

$$Z = R + j(X_L - X_C)$$

and in the polar form

$$Z \underline{/\theta°}$$

Complex quantities representing phasors in general may be subjected to the usual algebraic operations such as addition, subtraction, multiplication, and division. The $a + jb$ or rectangular form is the more convenient form when adding or subtracting phasors, while the $c\underline{/\theta°}$ or polar form is the more convenient form when multiplying or dividing phasors. The conversion from one form to the other and the algebraic operations using either form are easily accomplished using inexpensive hand-held electronic calculators.

Addition and Subtraction of Phasors

To add or subtract phasors expressed as complex quantities, the real and quadrature components are added or subtracted separately, and their sums or differences are combined to form the resultant phasor.

Example H-1

Find phasor sum of the two voltages $100\underline{/0°}$ V and $100\underline{/30°}$ V. (Refer to Example 10-4 and Fig. 10-7 in Sec. 10-8 in the text.)

The two phasors expressed in rectangular form are

$$100\underline{/0°} = 100(\cos \theta° + j \sin \theta°)$$

$$= 100(1 + j0)$$

$$= 100 + j0$$

$$\text{and } 100\underline{/30°} = 100(\cos 30° + j \sin 30°)$$

$$= 100(0.866 + j0.5)$$

$$= 86.6 + j50$$

Adding the two phasors results in

$$100 \quad + j0$$

$$\underline{86.6 + j50}$$

$$186.6 + j50$$

The magnitude of the resultant voltage is

$$\sqrt{(186.6)^2 + (50)^2} = 193.2 \text{ V}$$

The resultant angle is

$$\tan \theta = \frac{50}{186.6} = 0.268$$

$$\theta = 15°$$

The sum of the voltages is, therefore, $193.2\underline{/15°}$ V.

Example H-2

The total current supplied to two branches of a single-phase parallel circuit is $40\underline{/315°}$ A. The current in branch no. 1 is $20\underline{/0°}$ A. What is the current in branch no. 2? The circuit and phasor diagrams are shown in Fig H-3.

$$I_t + 40\underline{/315°} = 40(\cos 45° - j \sin 45°)$$

$$= 40(0.707 - j0.707)$$

$$= 28.28 - j28.28$$

$$I_1 = 20\underline{/0°} = 20(\cos 0° + j \sin 0°)$$

$$= 20(1 + j0)$$

$$= 20 + j0$$

Subtracting I_1 from I_t results in

$$
\begin{array}{r}
28.28 \quad - j28.28 \\
- (+20 \qquad + j0) \\
\hline
I_2 = +8.28 \quad - j28.28
\end{array}
$$

FIGURE **H-3**
Circuit and phasor diagrams for Example H-2.

(a)   (b)

The magnitude of the current I_2 in the second branch is

$$\sqrt{(8.28)^2 + (28.28)^2} = 29.5 \text{ A}$$

and the angle is

$$\tan \theta = \frac{-28.28}{8.28} = -3.416$$

$$\theta = -73.68°$$

It should be noted that the angle θ has a negative value. This indicates that the angular position of I_2 is 73.68° in the *clockwise* direction for the reference line since, by convention, positive angles are measured in a counterclockwise direction from the reference line. A phasor with an angle of 73.68° in the clockwise direction from the reference line is, of course, in the fourth quadrant. This is evident also from the fact that the real component of I_2 is positive and the quadrature component is negative. The angle $-73.68°$ may be expressed as a positive angle by subtracting from 360°:

$$360° - 73.68° = 286.32°$$

The current I_2 then may be expressed in the polar form either as

$$29.5 \,\underline{/-73.68°} \text{ or } 29.5 \underline{/286.32°} \text{ A.}$$

Multiplication of Phasors

The product of two phasors $A\underline{/\theta°}$ and $B\underline{/\Phi°}$ is $AB \,\underline{/\theta° + \Phi°}$.

Example H-3

What is the voltage across an impedance of $40\underline{/20°}$ when a current of $6\underline{/40°}$ A flows through it?

$$V = IZ = 6\underline{/40°} \times 40\underline{/20°}$$

$$= 6 \times 40\underline{/40° + 20°}$$

$$= 240\underline{/60°} \text{ V}$$

Division of Phasors

The quotient of two phasors $A\underline{/\theta°}$ and $B\underline{/\Phi°}$ is $\dfrac{A}{B}\underline{/\theta° - \Phi°}$.

Example H-4

What is the current in a circuit that has a resistance of 12 Ω and an inductive reactance of 16 Ω in series when a voltage of $120\underline{/0°}$ V is applied?

$$I = \frac{V}{Z}$$

$$V = 120\underline{/0°}$$

$$Z = 12 + j16 = 20\underline{/53.13°}$$

$$I = \frac{120\underline{/0°}}{20\underline{/53.13°}}$$

$$= \frac{120}{20}\ \underline{/0° - 53.13°}$$

$$= 6\underline{/-53.13°}\ \text{A}$$

This angle may be expressed as a positive angle by subtracting from 360°:

$$360° - 53.13° = 306.87°$$

Thus $\qquad\qquad\qquad I = 6\underline{/-53.13°}$

or $\qquad\qquad\qquad I = 6\underline{/306.87°}\ \text{A}$

Numbering Systems Used in Programmable Controllers

Timers, counters, and math operation word values use the decimal numbering system. This is a numbering system made up of ten digits: the numbers 0 through 9 (Table I.1). All decimal numbers are composed of these digits. The value of a decimal number depends upon the digits used and the place value of each digit.

Each place value in a decimal number represents a power of ten starting with ten raised to the zero power ($10^0 = 1$); see Fig. I-1. You can compute the decimal value of a number by multiplying each digit by its corresponding place value and adding these numbers together.

Byte word values use the octal numbering system. This is a numbering system made up of eight digits: the numbers 0 through 7 (Table I-1). All octal numbers are composed of these digits. The value of an octal number depends upon the digits used and the place value of each digit.

Each place value in an octal number represents a power of eight starting with eight raised to the zero power ($8^0 = 1$); see Fig. I-2.

TABLE I-1		Numbering System Conversion Chart	
Hexadecimal	**Binary**	**Decimal**	**Octal**
0	0000	0	000
1	0001	1	001
2	0010	2	002
3	0011	3	003
4	0100	4	004
5	0101	5	005
6	0110	6	006
7	0111	7	007
8	1000	8	010
9	1001	9	011
A	1010	10	012
B	1011	11	013
C	1100	12	014
D	1101	13	015
E	1110	14	016
F	1111	15	017

FIGURE I-1
Decimal numbering system.

$$2 \times 10^2 = 200_{10} \qquad 200$$
$$3 \times 10^1 = 30_{10} \qquad 30$$
$$9 \times 10^0 = 9_{10} \qquad \frac{9}{239_{10}}$$

| 2 | 3 | 9 | $_{10}$ |

You can compute the decimal value of an octal number by multiplying each octal digit by its corresponding place value and adding these numbers together.

Binary numbering is used in all digital systems to store and manipulate data. This is a numbering system made up of two numbers: 0 and 1 (Table I-1). All binary numbers are composed of these digits. Information in memory is stored as an arrangement of 1 and 0. The value of a binary number depends upon the digits used and the place value of each digit.

Each place value in a binary number represents a power of two starting with two raised to the zero power ($2^0 = 1$); see Fig. I-3. You can compute the decimal value of a binary number by multiplying each binary digit by its corresponding place value and adding these numbers together.

Binary coded decimal (BCD) format expresses a decimal value as an arrangement of binary digits. Each group of four binary digits is used to represent a decimal number from 0 to 9. All BCD numbers are composed of these digits. The value of BCD number depends upon the digits used and the place value of these digits.

FIGURE I-2
Octal numbering system.

$$3 \times 8^2 = 192 \qquad 192$$
$$5 \times 8^1 = 40 \qquad 40$$
$$7 \times 8^0 = 7 \qquad \frac{7}{239_{10}}$$

| 3 | 5 | 7 | $_8$ | $239_{10} = 357_8$

FIGURE **I-3**
Binary numbering system.

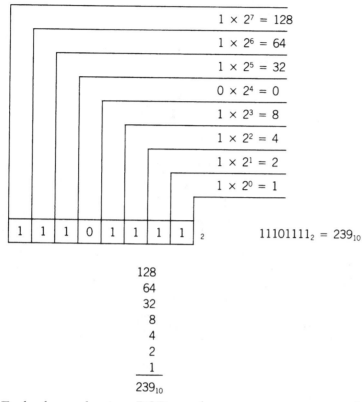

$$1 \times 2^7 = 128$$
$$1 \times 2^6 = 64$$
$$1 \times 2^5 = 32$$
$$0 \times 2^4 = 0$$
$$1 \times 2^3 = 8$$
$$1 \times 2^2 = 4$$
$$1 \times 2^1 = 2$$
$$1 \times 2^0 = 1$$

| 1 | 1 | 1 | 0 | 1 | 1 | 1 | 1 | $_2$ |

$$11101111_2 = 239_{10}$$

$$\begin{array}{r} 128 \\ 64 \\ 32 \\ 8 \\ 4 \\ 2 \\ \underline{1} \\ 239_{10} \end{array}$$

Each place value in a BCD number represents a power of two starting with two raised to the zero power ($2^0 = 1$); see Fig. I-4.

You can compute the decimal value of a binary number by multiplying each binary digit by its corresponding place value and adding these numbers together (Table I-2).

TABLE **I-2**   **BCD Representation**

	Place Value			
2^3 (8)	2^2 (4)	2^1 (2)	2^0 (1)	Decimal Equivalent
0	0	0	0	0
0	0	0	1	1
0	0	1	0	2
0	0	1	1	3
0	1	0	0	4
0	1	0	1	5
0	1	1	0	6
0	1	1	1	7
1	0	0	0	8
1	0	0	1	9

FIGURE **I-4**
Binary coded decimal.

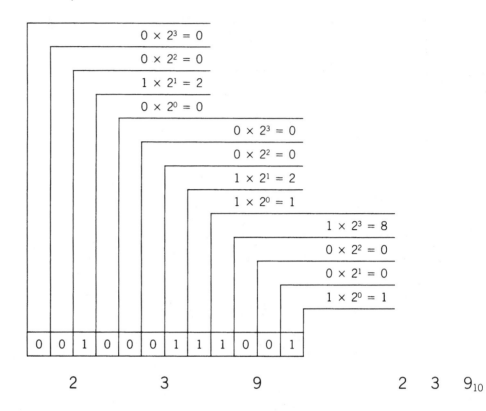

Binary coded octal (BCO) format expresses an octal value as an arrangement of binary digits (eight bits or one byte). The 8 bits are broken down into three groups: 2 bits, 3 bits, and 3 bits. Each group of binary digits is used to represent a decimal number from 0 to 9. All BCO numbers are composed of these digits.

Each place value in a BCO number represents a power of two starting with two raised to the zero power ($2^0 = 1$); see Fig. I-5.

You can compute the octal number for each group of bits by multiplying the binary digit by its corresponding place value and adding these numbers together (Table I-3).

Some operations use the hexadecimal numbering system. This is a numbering system made up of 16 digits: the numbers 0-9 and the letters A-F (Table I-3). The letters A-F represent the decimal

FIGURE **I-5**
Binary coded octal.

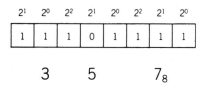

$$2^1 \quad 2^0 \quad 2^2 \quad 2^1 \quad 2^0 \quad 2^2 \quad 2^1 \quad 2^0$$

| 1 | 1 | 1 | 0 | 1 | 1 | 1 | 1 |

$$3 \qquad 5 \qquad 7_8$$

numbers 10–15, respectively. Four binary digits represent each hexadecimal character. You can convert between hexadecimal to a binary by writing out the patterns for each hexadecimal character or group of four binary digits; see Fig. 1-6.

Each place value in a hexadecimal character represents a power of 16 starting with 16 raised to the zero power ($16^0 = 1$); see Fig. I-6. You can compute a decimal number for each group of hexadecimal characters by multiplying the decimal digit equivalent of each hexadecimal character by its corresponding place value and adding these numbers together.

TABLE **I-3**   **Octal Representation**

Place Value			
2^2 (4)	2^1 (2)	2^0 (1)	Octal Equivalent
0	0	0	0
0	0	1	1
0	1	0	2
0	1	1	3
1	0	0	4
1	0	1	5
1	1	0	6
1	1	1	7

FIGURE **I-6**
Hexadecimal to decimal conversion.

$$0 \times 16^3 = 0$$
$$1 \times 16^2 = 256$$
$$10 \times 16^1 = 160$$
$$7 \times 16^0 = 7$$

| 0 | 1 | A | 7 |

256
160
  7
———————
$423_{10} = 01A7_{16}$

APPENDIX J

Three-Wire vs. Two-Wire Conductor Calculation Comparison

In Sec. 2-12 (Three-Wire Distribution Circuits) it was stated that, for an equivalent load, the three-wire circuit can supply the load with only three-eighths theline copper required for a two-wire system. Below is an example of how this is achieved.

With two 1-kW loads connected in parallel to a 100 V source (Fig. J-1), the line resistance $R_{AB} = 0.01\ \Omega$ and $R_{CD} = 0.01\ \Omega$

$$I_T = \frac{\text{Power}}{\text{Voltage}} = \frac{2000}{100} = 20\ \text{A}$$

The total power loss in the line conductors is:

$$P_L = I^2R = 20_2 \times 0.02 = 8\ \text{W}$$

The objective now is to determine the resistance of the three-line conductors that will produce an equivalent line loss to compare withthe 2-wire circuit. See Fig. J-2.

$$I_T = \frac{1000}{100} = 10\ \text{A} = I_{EF} = I_{HI}$$

Since the load is balanced, we will neglect the neutral conductor in determining the line resistance and then add it in later.

$$R_{EF} + R_{HI} = \frac{P}{10^2} = \frac{8}{10^2} = 0.08\ \Omega$$

$$R_{EF} = 0.04\ \Omega = R_{HI} = R_{GF}$$

FIGURE **J-1**
Two wire distribution circuit.

FIGURE J-2
Three-wire distribution circuit.

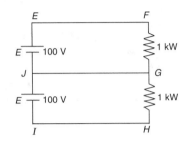

Since the supply conductors in the 2-wire circuit have 1/4 the re-sistance $\left(\dfrac{0.01}{0.04}\right)$ of the supply conductors in the 3-wire circuit, the crosssectional area of the 3-wire circuit conductors must be 1/4 of the 2-wire conductors.

Therefore, let the area of $R_{AB} = R_{CD} =$ "4" in the 2-wire circuit, and let the area of $R_{EF} = R_{HI} = R_{GJ} =$ "1" in the 3-wire circuit.

Therefore,

$$\frac{(1 + 1 + 1)}{(4 + 4)} = \frac{3}{8}$$

which is the conductor material ratio.

References

Handbooks and Reference Books

Beeman, Donald (ed.), *Industrial Power Systems Handbook*, McGraw-Hill Book Company, New York, 1955.

Central Station Engineers, *Electrical Transmission and Distribution Reference Book*, Westinghouse Electric Corporation, East Pittsburgh, PA, 1950.

Eshbach, Ovid W., and Mott Souders (eds.), *Handbook of Engineering Fundamentals*, 3d ed., John Wiley & Sons, Inc., New York, 1975.

Fink, Donald G., and H. Wayne Beaty (eds.), *Standard Handbook for Electrical Engineers*, 11th ed., McGraw-Hill Book Company, New York, 1978.

——— and Donald Christensen (eds.), *Electronics Engineer's Handbook*, 2d ed., McGraw-Hill Book Company, New York, 1982.

IEEE Standard Dictionary of Electrical and Electronics Terms, 2d ed., Institute of Electrical and Electronics Engineers, New York, 1977.

Institute of Electrical and Electronics Engineers, *National Electrical Safety Code*, 1981 edition, John Wiley & Sons, Inc., New York, 1981.

Kurtz, Edwin B., and Thomas M. Shoemaker, *The Lineman's and Cableman's Handbook*, 6th ed., McGraw-Hill Book Company, New York, 1982.

Ross, Joseph A. (ed.), *The National Electrical Code Handbook*, 2d ed., National Fire Protection Association, Quincy, MA, 1980.

Smeaton, R., *Switchgear and Control Handbook*, McGraw-Hill Book Company, New York, 1976.

Summers, Wilford I. (ed.), *American Electrician's Handbook*, 10th ed., McGraw-Hill Book Company, New York, 1981.

Principles and Circuits

Angus, Robert B. Jr., *Electrical Engineering Fundamentals*, 2d ed., Addison-Wesley Publishing Company, Reading, MA, 1968.

Boylestad, Robert L., *Introductory Circuit Analysis*, 7th ed., Merrill Publishing Company A Bell & Howell Company, Columbus, Ohio 1994.

Fitzgerald, A. E., Arvin Grabel, and David E. Higginbotham, *Basic Electrical Engineering*, 4th ed., McGraw-Hill Book Company, New York, 1975.

Morley, Arthur, and Edward Hughes, *Principles of Electricity in SI Units*, 3d ed., Longham Group Limited, London, 1970.

Oppenheimer, S. L., and J. P. Borchers, *Direct and Alternating Currents*, 2d ed., McGraw-Hill Book Company, New York, 1973.

Smith, Ralph J., *Circuits, Devices, and Systems*, 3d ed., John Wiley & Sons, Inc., New York, 1976.

Machinery and Equipment

Bose, Bimal K. (ed.), *Adjustable Speed AC Drive Systems*, Institute of Electrical and Electronics Engineers, New York, 1981.

Grant, Joseph C. (ed.), *Nickel-Cadmium Battery Application Engineering Handbook*, 2d ed., General Electric Company, Gainesville, FL, 1975.

Hubert, Charles I., *Electric Machines, Theory, Operation, Applications, Adjustment, and Control*, Merrill Publishing Company, A Bell & Howell Company, Columbus, Ohio 1991.

Kosow, Irving L., *Electric Machinery and Transformers*, Prentice-Hall Inc., Englewood Cliffs, New Jersey, 1992.

Lloyd, Tom Cox, *Electric Motors and Their Applications*, John Wiley & Sons, Inc., New York, 1969.

Mason, C. Russell, *The Art and Science of Protective Relaying*, John Wiley & Sons, Inc., New York, 1956.

Mueller, Gustav A. (ed.), *The Gould Battery Handbook*, Gould Inc., Mendota Heights, MN, 1973.

Veinott, Cyril G., *Fractional and Subfractional Horsepower Electric Motors*, 3d ed., McGraw-Hill Book Company, New York, 1970.

Control

Kissell, Thomas E., *Modern Industrial/Electrical Motor Controls*, Prentice Hall, Englewood Cliffs, New Jersey 1990.

McIntyre, R. L., *Electric Motor Control Fundamentals*, 3d ed., McGraw-Hill Book Company, New York, 1974.

Millermaster, Ralph A., *Harwood's Control of Electric Motors*, 4th ed., Wiley Interscience, New York, 1970.

Rexford, Kenneth B., *Electrical Control for Machines*, 2d ed., Delmar Publishers Inc., 2 Computer Drive, W. Box 15-015 Albany, New York.

Electrical Measurements

Bartholomew, Davis, *Electrical Measurements and Instrumentation*, Allyn and Bacon, Inc., Boston, 1963.

Cooper, William D., *Electronic Instrumentation and Measurement Techniques*, 2d ed., Prentice-Hall, Inc., Englewood Cliffs, NJ, 1978.

Nachtigal, Chester L., *Instrumentation and Control: Fundamentals and Applications*, John Wiley & Sons, Inc., New York, 1990.

Reissland, Martin U., *Electrical Measurements: Fundamentals, Concepts, Applications*, John Wiley & Sons, New York, 1989.

Electronics

Battle, Charles W. (ed.), *Understanding Optronics*, Texas Instruments Learning Center, Dallas, 1981.

Chute, George M., and Robert D. Chute, *Electronics in Industry*, 5th ed., McGraw-Hill Book Company, New York, 1979.

Deboo, Gordon J., and Clifford N. Burrous, *Integrated Circuits and Semiconductor Devices*, 2d ed., McGraw-Hill Book Company, New York, 1977.

Grafham, D. R., and F. B. Golden (eds.), *SCR Manual*, 6th ed., General Electric Company, Auburn, NY, 1979.

McWhorter, Gene, *Understanding Digital Electronics*, Texas Instruments Learning Center, Dallas, 1978.

Malvino, Albert Paul, *Electronic Principles*, 4th ed., McGraw-Hill Book Company, New York, 1989.

Malvino, Albert Paul, *Semiconductor Circuit Approximations*, 4th ed., Glencoe Division of Macmillan/McGraw-Hill, Columbus, OH, 1985.

———, *Transistor Circuit Approximations*, 3d ed., McGraw-Hill Book Company, New York, 1980.

Thyristor and Rectifier Manual, Publication No. TRM-445, RCA Corporation, Somerville, NJ, 1975.

Understanding Solid-State Electronics, 3d ed., Texas Instruments Learning Center, Dallas, 1978.

Young, George, *Digital Electronics*, Hayden Book Company, Inc., Rochelle Park, NJ, 1980.

Zbar, Paul B., *Industrial Electronics*, 3d ed., McGraw-Hill Book Company, New York, 1977.

Answers to Odd-Numbered Problems

2-1 50 V
2-3 4.5 A
2-5 0.5 A
2-7 1600 A
2-9 130 V
2-11 220 Ω
2-13 61 Ω
2-15 112 V
2-17 55 Ω
2-19 160 Ω

2-21 32.67 Ω
2-23 12.0 A; 3 A
2-25 47.5 Ω
2-27 3.75 Ω; 3.94 Ω
2-29 208 V
2-31 (a) 229 V
      (b) 235 V
2-33 (a) 4 A from A to B
          2 A from C to F
          2 A from D to E

      (b) 3.2 V in line AB
          1.6 V in line CF
          1.6 V in line DE
      (c) 115.2 V; 120 V
2-35 (a) 6 V
      (b) 12 V
      (c) 36 V

CHAPTER 3

3-1 2000 mils;
     750 mils;
     675 mils;
     430 mils;
     250 mils

3-3 No. 13; No. 10; No. 4;
     No. 0
3-5 2750 kg
3-7 33.6 mm^2
3-9 255 Ω

3-11 0.003 33
3-13 35.6°C
3-15 20 014.75 cmil;
      #7 AWG

CHAPTER 4

4-1 20 N
4-3 (a) 320 000 ft-lb per
         min;
     (b) 9.7 hp
4-5 (a) 0.823 kW;
     (b) 3.292 kWh

4-7 480 kWh; 20 kW
4-9 50.9 A
4-11 7.37 hp
4-13 23.04 Ω

4-15 (a) 406 V;
      (b) 180 W;
      (c) 288 kWh;
      (d) 4.32 kWh
4-17 $v_T = 0.539$ or 54
      percent

CHAPTER 8

8-1 208.3 A
8-3 133.3 V
8-5 120 V
8-7 1.6 A
8-9 26.33 A
8-11 0.2 Ω

8-13 0.0392 Ω
8-15 25 percent
8-17 2.5 V
8-19 83.8 percent
8-21 91.1 percent

8-23 (a) 501 W
      (b) 1331 W
8-25 (a) 1652 W
      (b) 382 W
      (c) 1960 W
      (d) 4810 W

CHAPTER 9

9-1 50 N·m
9-3 2.08 kW
9-5 2.4 A; 77.4 A; 18.57 kW
9-7 1167 r/min
9-9 1221 r/min
9-11 (a) 2.4 A
      (b) 35.6 A

      (c) 111.1 V
      (d) 0 V
9-13 3.02 kW
9-15 230 V
9-17 5.88 percent
9-19 (a) 146.3 A
      (b) 143.1 A

      (c) 568.5 V
      (d) 3.16 A
9-21 (a) 85.1 percent
      (b) 0 percent
9-23 (a) 112.6 V
      (b) 1.81 hp

CHAPTER 10

10-1	e = 105.6 V	10-13	0 V	10-25	60 Ω
10-3	i = 9.85 A	10-15	75.4 Ω; 150.8 Ω;	10-27	21.5 Ω
10-5	141.4 A		754 Ω	10-29	3 Ω
10-7	4.95 A	10-17	318.3 Hz	10-31	AB = 11.2 μF
10-9	44.72 A	10-19	1.02 A; 2.44 A		BC = 18.67 μF
10-11	240 V	10-21	33.2 μF		CA = 9.33 μF
		10-23	0.904 A		

CHAPTER 11

11-1	8320 VA; 8.32 kVA	11-13	(a) 66.5 Ω	11-23	(a) 13.83 A
11-3	81 percent		(b) 1.8 A		(b) 75.9 percent
11-5	4800 VA; 3360 W		(c) 60.2 percent		(c) 1260 W
11-7	4800 VA; 83.3 percent		(d) 216 VA	11-25	(a) 9.23 A; 12 A
11-9	1118 var; 66.7 percent		(e) 130 W		(b) 4.97 A
11-11	(a) 20 Ω	11-15	4.52 A; 4.23 A		(c) 426 W
	(b) 5.75 A	11-17	85.4 V		(d) 71.4 percent
	(c) 80 percent	11-19	0.012 H	11-27	3.3 kvar
	(d) 661 VA	11-21	(a) 4388 W	11-29	(a) 12.4 A
	(e) 529 W		(b) 45.7 A		(b) 40.3 percent
				11-31	7.12 Hz

CHAPTER 12

12-1	208 V	12-9	86.5 A		(b) 12 A
12-3	311 V	12-11	1329 V; 597 kVA		(c) 4320 W
12-5	439 V; 6096 W;	12-13	12.96 kW	12-21	(a) 220 V
	18 288 W	12-15	240 V; 92.6 percent		(b) 38.1 A
12-7	7977 V; 3333 kVA;	12-17	57.36 A		(c) 14 520 W
	419 A	12-19	(a) 120 V	12-23	6 Ω; 4.5 Ω

CHAPTER 13

13-1	100 turns	13-11	91 A	13-25	V_{AB} = 250 V
13-3	480 V	13-13	(a) 10 kVA		V_{BC} = 250 V
13-5	41.7 A; 833.3 A		(b) 10 kVA		V_{CA} = 250 V
13-7	4167 cmil or No. 14	13-15	5.78 A		V_{CN} = 125 V
	AWG; 41 667 cmil or	13-17	346 A		V_{NA} = 125 V
	No. 4 AWG	13-19	100 A; 2080 kVA		V_{BN} = 216.5 V
13-9	2200 V; 20 A;	13-21	Additive polarity		
	44 000 VA; 81.8	13-23	0 V; 0 V or 880 V		
	percent; 36 000 W				

CHAPTER 14

14-1	36 poles	14-5	1387 V; 250 A;	14-7	(a) 875 kW
14-3	1500 r/min		600 kVA		(b) 700 kW
					(c) 438 kW; 211 A

CHAPTER 15

15-1	900 r/min	15-5	3.33 Hz	15-9	9.73 A
15-3	1140 r/min	15-7	354.4 r/min	15-11	42.3 percent
			54.5 r/min		

CHAPTER 16

16-1	240 r/min; slow speed	16-5	54 poles; 139 r/min;	16-7	5356 kVA
16-3	60 Hz		35.6 r/min; 1247 A		

CHAPTER 17

17-1 $8.42 \; \underline{/-31.3°} \; A$

17-3 $6.8 \; \underline{/-14.22°} \; A$

CHAPTER 19

19-1	0.008 A; 0.01 A	19-5	2	19-9	165 000 Ω
19-3	0.001 A	19-7	11 998 Ω		

CHAPTER 21

21-3

21-5

Index

STUDENT REPLY CARD

In order to improve future editions, we are seeking your comments on
Electric Circuits and Machines, Second Canadian Edition
by Eugene C. Lister and Michael R. Golding. After you have read this text,
please answer the following questions and return this form via Business Reply
Mail. *Your opinions matter! Thank you in advance for your feedback!*

Name of your college or university: _____

Major program of study: _____

Course title: _____

Were you required to buy this book?   ——— yes ——— no

Did you buy this book new or used?   ——— new ——— used ($ ———)

Do you plan to keep or sell this book?   ——— keep ——— sell

Is the order of topic coverage consistent with what was taught in your course?

Are there chapters or sections of this text that were not assigned for your course?
Please specify:

Were there topics covered in your course that are not included in this text?
Please specify:

What did you like most about this text?

What did you like least?

If you would like to say more, we'd love to hear from you. Please write to us at the
address shown on the reverse of this card.

Postage will be paid by

MAIL ➤ **POSTE**

Canada Post Corporation / Société canadienne des postes

Postage paid	Port payé
If mailed in Canada	si posté au Canada
Business	**Réponse**
Reply	**d'affaires**
0183560299	01

0183560299-L1N9B6-BR01

Attn.: Sponsoring Editor
College Division

MCGRAW-HILL RYERSON LIMITED
300 WATER ST
WHITBY ON   L1N 9Z9